BROOKS MEMORIAL

CHARLES A. BROOKS

ANNA CLOYDE BROOKS

Classics in Management

Classics
in Management

Revised Edition

Edited by Harwood F. Merrill

American Management Association, Inc.

International standard book number: 0-8144-5231-0

Library of Congress catalog card number: 74-111466

Third printing revised edition

FOREWORD

THE ROOTS of the emerging profession of management go deep, just as do those of such other, older professions as theology, law, medicine, and education.

In the Bible, Jethro lectures Moses on the benefits of delegation and sound organization (Exodus 18:13–26). Socrates makes a timeless observation about the management of people when he says in his *Discourses*, ". . . those who know how to employ [men], conduct either private or public affairs judiciously, while those who do not know, will err in the management of both." The Roman Empire could not have lasted as it did without high administrative skill in government. And there are notable similarities between modern management and important segments of royal administration in the Middle Ages.

But recognition of the professional aspects of management has been delayed until comparatively recent times. Now, application of the scientific method and rebirth of the service motive have brought management within the range of Mary Parker Follett's definition of a profession: an institution based on a proved body of knowledge which is used in the service of others.

Since management is a profession, does there not then exist a "classic" body of management literature? And since it exists, should not the professional manager be familiar with it, as the theologian is familiar with the Scriptures, the lawyer with Blackstone, the physician with Osler, and the educator with Plato?

The answer to both questions would seem to be "yes." The purpose of this book is to make available to the manager selections from the works which have influenced the development of his activity toward the status of a profession. Familiarity with these classics will add meaning to the managerial task, in the same way that a knowledge of history adds perspective and richness to life. It should also broaden and deepen the sense of pride and the dedication which are the hallmarks of any true profession.

LAWRENCE A. APPLEY
Chairman of the Board
American Management Association

PREFACE

IT IS UNFORTUNATE that most of the classic writing in the field of management is inaccessible today. The manager who wishes to renew or broaden his acquaintance with the "old masters," or to explore in more depth the profound truths they expressed, finds his way to most of them blocked.

With few exceptions, the classic papers and books are out of print. Only a handful are still obtainable, and some of these only from overseas publishers. To gain access to the great majority of management classics, one must resort to the reference shelves of public libraries, principally those of large cities, and universities; to a small group of private libraries; to the collected proceedings of professional societies; and to the bound volumes of periodicals, many of which are difficult to trace because they long ago lost their identity through mergers and consolidations.

Yet, as Lawrence A. Appley points out in the Foreword to this book, it is important that those who are involved in the developing profession of management have ready access to the historic literature of the activity to which they have dedicated themselves.

In these circumstances, the need for assembling representative management classics in one volume is obvious. This book aims to fill the need. While it is not, of course, an attempt at a complete collection, it goes beyond the function of a mere sampler. It offers a generous cross section that not only indicates the rewards in store for anyone able to return to the original sources but also provides an acceptable alternative for the reader to whom they are unavailable.

The flavor of the original has been fully retained. Editing has been avoided, and each selection has been presented exactly as it first appeared—topical references, footnotes, spelling, and all.*

These selections do not necessarily include all the classics, nor are they presented as necessarily *the* classics. They are, however, *among* the classics, and a large proportion of the same papers would appear in any collection of the kind.

A number of standards have been applied in choosing them. Vitality is one; and the reader will surely agree that these selections—none of whose authors is living—hold much more than just a breath of life. Most if not all of what the authors say is as true and applicable today as when they wrote it 20, 50, or 100 years ago.

Another standard is the historic significance of the paper—the influence it exerted, the paths into the future it pointed out, the extent of vision shown. Then there is the frequency with which a paper is referred to in more recent management literature and, finally, the degree of interest the selection has for the management "generalist" as distinguished from the technician. This last standard ruled out certain highly technical works, such as Barth's treatises on slide rules. In addition, one or two books that have become management classics defy excerpting; Wallace Clark's *The Gantt Chart* is an example.

Some of the management classics presented here meet all these standards, some fewer. Obviously, an element of personal judgment entered into the selection process. This could not be avoided, but it was tempered by suggestions from a large number of people on intimate terms with the historic literature of management. In the end, though, the choices were those of the editor, and he takes full responsibility for them.

In preparing this revised edition of *Classics in Management*, the

---

* Throughout the book, numerical references indicate the authors' original footnotes. Conventional symbols—asterisk (*), dagger (†), and the like—identify the comments and explanatory notes supplied by the editor.

editor made a thorough review of the original selections, both of authors and of examples of what they wrote. In addition, he restudied the work of many who did not appear in the first edition, published in 1960, and opened for consideration material that has come into prominence since then.

The principal result of this second look has been the addition of Chester Irving Barnard and Douglas Murray McGregor to the management classicists represented in the volume. Extensive revisions have been made in the Introduction, and changes have been made in the material that introduces several of the writers. On the whole, however, the original selections stood up well under this second scrutiny.

There is one note of deep regret that the editor would like to express: Not all the great leaders in management thought who flourished during the period covered by this book appear in it. The influence exerted on the advancement of management by such men as B. Seebohm Rowntree, Henry Dennison, Alvin Dodd, Alfred P. Sloan, Jr., and Erwin Haskell Schell was very great. And while they may not have been representative management classicists in what they wrote, what they accomplished makes them classicists of a very high order in the field of management action.

H. F. M.

ACKNOWLEDGMENTS

IT IS of course impossible to name all the people who in one way or another contribute to a project of this magnitude. A number of individuals, however, certainly should be cited for their generosity in making suggestions and providing welcome encouragement. They are Lawrence A. Appley, Chairman of the Board, American Management Association; Dr. Lillian M. Gilbreth; Dr. Alex W. Rathe of New York University; Col. Lyndall F. Urwick of Urwick, Orr & Partners, Ltd.; and William Jerome Arnold, former Management Editor of *Business Week*.

The selections proposed for inclusion were reviewed, with the introductory notes, by this group of five, as well as by Col. Clarence E. Davies, Secretary Emeritus of The American Society of Mechanical Engineers; John W. Enell of the American Management Association staff; Rita H. Hopf (who also provided the translations of Dr. Hopf's quotations in French and German); Dr. William J. Jaffe of the Newark College of Engineering; and Thomas L. Norton, Dean Emeritus, and Dr. John R. Beishline of the New York University School of Commerce. The editor, however, takes full responsibility for the book in its final form.

The Department of Industrial Engineering at Purdue University was generous in making available the resources of its Gilbreth Collection, as were the General Electric Company in allowing the use of its Harry A. Hopf Memorial Library at Crotonville, New York, and the Wallace Clark Center of International Management at New York University in giving access to its files. Appreciation is also due to the New York Public Library and the Engineering Societies Library; both of them time and again came up with obscure reference material that there was little reason to expect could be located so readily.

Many other organizations were outstandingly cooperative, notably three that are rich sources of "classic" material: Sir Isaac Pitman & Sons, Ltd., the McGraw-Hill Book Company, and The American Society of Mechanical Engineers.

Two books were exceptionally helpful as guides in the various stages of the work: *The Golden Book of Management*, edited for the International Committee of Scientific Management by L. Urwick and published by Newman Neame Limited, London; and Volume I of *The Making of Scientific Management*, by L. Urwick and E. F. L. Brech, published by Management Publications Trust, London.

Finally, these acknowledgments would not be complete without mention of the AMA publications staff—in particular, Elizabeth Marting, who went well beyond the requirements of duty in offering encouragement and constructive criticism.

H. F. M.

CONTENTS

Contents

INTRODUCTION

THE CLASSIC literature of management extends over a surprisingly short span of time when it is compared with that of theology, education, medicine, and law.

While this is to be expected of a new and emerging profession, the development of management thought has been correspondingly swift. In little more than a century, it has progressed from the naïveté of Robert Owen to the subtlety and sophistication of Chester I. Barnard, and it has required only half that time to effectuate the sweeping change from Taylor's simple view of what best motivates employees to the vastly more complicated conclusions of Mayo and McGregor.

In particular, the 35 years between Taylor's presentation on shop management in 1903 and the publication of Barnard's *The Functions of the Executive* in 1938 were a period of revolutionary development in management thinking. Taylor's matter-of-fact concentration on methods (and methods largely confined, at that, to the management of shops) evolved with astonishing speed into Church's and Alford's, then Gantt's, first attempts at broadening the subject. Almost simultaneously, Fayol extended management thinking into the area of top administration, and a few years later Sheldon presented his ideas for a professional creed of management. In less than two decades from then we reach Barnard's philosophical and sociological approach, which commands the respect equally of scholars and of "practical" managers. Now comes McGregor to take matters well beyond Barnard, with the insistence that the "assumptions" on which managers have been so used to acting be replaced by conclusions more soundly based on behavioral science and reached through research, experiment, and study.

Thus what McGregor meant by a "scientific" approach to management makes a sharp contrast with Taylor's "scientific management." In the half century between the two men, the meaning of the word "scientific" as applied to management broadened and deepened immensely. So, for that matter, did the meaning of management itself: from running a shop or factory at one extreme to, at the other extreme, guiding the entire range of activities involved in the operation of any type of organization within any kind of social structure.

Nevertheless, the development of management philosophy as seen in the selections in this book offers a cohesive picture. Though the changes have been profound, there are many relationships even between the earliest and the latest presentations.

In Robert Owen, for example, the reader will find strong suggestions of the conclusions Elton Mayo was to reach, after extensive research, a century later. Babbage's observations on the division of labor were a result of the years he spent in working on a "Difference-Engine"; this device was a forerunner of the modern computer, which now makes practical Hopf's theory of the optimum in business operations, proposed in 1935 after a "tremendous amount of labor" had been exerted in processing the necessary data for examples in a single field. Towne's 1886 paper recommending that The American Society of Mechanical Engineers (ASME) provide for an exchange of experience among those concerned with the "management of industrial works" set the stage from which Taylor, Gantt, Gilbreth, and many other management pioneers offered their points of view.

In fact, with one notable exception, the sequence of the selections (which appear in order of their original publication) shows practically a straight-line progression in the development of management thought. The exception is Owen; he was so far ahead of his time in urging that at least as much attention be paid to the welfare of "vital machines" as "inanimate machines" that not until Gantt arrives on the scene almost a hundred years later does the theme recur in a dominant way.

The straight-line progression, then, really begins with Babbage's analytical approach to factory methods and costs, as exemplified in his essay on the division of labor. (Babbage, in the same book from which the selection is taken, prophetically mentions the need for specialization in *mental* labor as well.) Metcalfe brings the word "science" into the world of management when he makes the statement, a striking one as we look back to 1885, that "the administration of arsenals and other workshops is in great measure an art, and depends upon the application to a great variety of cases of certain principles, which, taken together, make up what may be called the science of administration." From this, it was only a short step to Towne's pivotal paper suggesting a forum from which such principles could be developed.

After Towne comes Taylor, and what would today be called a breakthrough in gaining wide recognition of the rational, analytical element in management—but a breakthrough that was achieved only after a decade during which Towne's proposals for an organized exchange of management experience were ignored.

The advent of Taylor opened a new era, that of "scientific management." Taylor probably did not invent the term—it is said to have been coined in 1910 by a small group which included Gantt, Gilbreth, and Louis Dembitz Brandeis (later to become the eminent Supreme Court justice), but it may have been used earlier. Nor did Taylor originate the approach, which goes back to Babbage and beyond. Taylor's enormous contribution lay in large-scale application of the "scientific" method to improving production methods in the shop and in his ability to dramatize and publicize his convictions. His studies of the use of shovels, of how to handle pig iron, and of the most efficient ways to cut metals were typical.

But Taylor went further. While he did not feel that management could ever become an exact science in the same sense as physics and chemistry, he was strong in the belief that there could be an organized body of knowledge in management and that it could be taught and learned.

As he stated in *Shop Management:*

> The writer feels that management is also destined to become more of an art, and that many of the elements which are now believed to be outside the field of exact knowledge will soon be standardized, tabulated, accepted, and used, as are now many of the elements of engineering. Management will be studied as an art and will rest upon well recognized, clearly defined, and fixed principles instead of depending upon more or less hazy ideas received from a limited observation of the few organizations with which the individual may come in contact.

The degree to which Taylor was interested in people as compared with methods and things is still a subject of lively controversy. It seems to be true, however, that a change in the development of management philosophy began to be apparent as Taylor moved off the scene in the second decade of this century and others (including some of his associates and disciples) came to the front. Now a new line of thought becomes clearly visible—the concept of the importance of the human element in management that was anticipated by Robert Owen.

Gantt is usually associated with this change. As early as 1903, he had presented an ASME paper stressing the need for winning the workman's cooperation and insisting that good management means leading rather than driving. As a result, he became known as the leader in a new phase of management thinking, a school of thought that also included Emerson and Gilbreth.

Until this shift, management was usually conceived of as an activity having to do with the direction of methods and things. Now it begins to be viewed as an activity that has to do largely, if not principally, with people—with their guidance, their motivation, their development. And management philosophy has continued to move steadily in that direction, to the point where a group of managers and management educators could agree not long ago on a definition so dominated by the human element as this:

Management is guiding human and physical resources into a hard-hitting and dynamic organization unit which attains its objectives to the satisfaction of those served, and with a high degree of morale and sense of attainment on the part of those rendering the service.

While Taylor was crystallizing management thought in the United States, in France Henri Fayol was independently reaching his own conclusions on the subject. They constitute, in the opinion of many students of management, a milestone as important as Taylor's. Both men agreed that certain principles of management exist and that they can be taught and learned. Fayol, however, concerned himself with determining and applying them in top management and administration, while Taylor confined his efforts largely to production and the shop. Fayol thus explored an area of management that is less obviously susceptible of scientific analysis than that chosen by Taylor, but he did it so thoroughly and convincingly that his *General and Industrial Management* remains an important reference work to this day. It is a major loss to the profession of management that he completed, before his death, only two of the four sections of the study he planned on the part management plays "in the government . . . of all undertakings, large or small, industrial, commercial, political, religious or any other."

Fayol's influence is evident in the papers of Mary Parker Follett; so is that of Taylor and Gantt. She is, in fact, the point of convergence of the three broad channels of management philosophy that have been described here. Her work shows the effect of the analytical, "scientific" approach Taylor made to production methods and problems; Gantt's emphasis on the importance of the human element; and Fayol's application of analysis to the field of administration. This is a measure of the great rewards open to the manager who studies her writings.

Many other rewards are to be found among these classic essays in management. Some lie in what the papers reveal about the management pioneers themselves. Any evolving science or profession stirs controversy, and management is no exception. We can feel the power of Taylor's evangelistic fervor in his fiery outburst before a congressional committee investigating systems of shop management.

Church and Alford, in turn, brand Taylor's scientific management as nothing but "a collection of axioms," and they airily dismiss Emerson's principles of efficiency by saying that discussion of them "will not detain us long." Follett feels sorry for Sheldon and his inability to see that knowledge of human relations can be systematized. While Gilbreth is frankly proud of having played a part in creating the term "scientific management," Hopf describes it as "singularly unfortunate." And to complete the circle there is McGregor's observation, made in 1957, that "if the practices of scientific management were deliberately calculated to thwart" the egoistic needs of people in the lower levels of industrial organizations, "they could hardly accomplish this purpose better than they do." So much for Taylor and his "complete mental revolution" as the key to good management and sound motivation!

But, if what the classic writers say is often revealing and sometimes amusing, it is also vastly prophetic. This gift of being able to look ahead is one of the factors that make their work live today. Russell Robb, in 1910, saw clearly that management is a horizontal activity—"There is much that is common to all effective endeavor"—at a time when few thought of it as applying to anything beyond manufacturing. Robb also anticipated management by results or objectives, with his point that the "aims" of a group should determine how it should be organized. Two years later, Emerson came even closer when he defined his first principle of efficiency as "a clearly defined ideal"—a statement of the organization's purposes and goals, and a point whose significance Church and Alford missed completely in their downgrading of his 12 principles.

Running through the selections are many other foretastes of what was to come in management. Gilbreth, in 1922, saw the future role the industrial psychologist would play in management and stressed the importance of what we now know as long-range planning. In 1925 Follett suggested that there was a need for the function now called management auditing. Hopf, in 1935, saw the necessity for the kind of analysis that 20 years later was being performed by the operations research staff. These are only a few of many examples of similarly prophetic statements that could be cited. And it is not unlikely that, a quarter century hence, one will detect the same elements of fore-sight in the final selection, by McGregor.

As much as anything else, however, these classic writings offer material of practical and immediate value to the manager; many of the authors were managers or consultants of extraordinary ability. Robb, for example, provides counsel on how to build an effective organization. Fayol has much to say on improving and maintaining discipline, an intensifying problem currently; for that matter, most of his "General Principles of Management" can be directly useful in administering an organization under today's conditions. Follett and Barnard analyze the elements of leadership, distilling out of them sound advice for the actual or would-be leader; Mayo indicates ways in which employee cooperation can be won; and Barnard, again, suggests what is involved in the acceptance of authority—in other words, what it is that induces subordinates to honor and carry out instructions.

This volume concludes, however, with papers by a social scientist rather than with the works of an active manager—though the scientist in question, Douglas McGregor, did have managerial experience. This sequence, while a coincidence resulting from the in-order-of-publication arrangement of selections, is an appropriate one because of the increasing influence of the behavioral scientist in management and the greater weight that managers are giving to his findings and conclusions.

The final paper is appropriate also because it recognizes what appear to be basic changes in management problems in the years ahead. Some of them are already upon us. The weakening of purely economic motives; the upward trend in employment of "professional" people; the computer and other technical tools, with their great possibilities for abuse as well as constructive use—these and many other factors in the turbulent world of the late twentieth century make convincing evidence that the manager of tomorrow will face problems and be required to find answers that will be very different from those of the past.

Under these conditions, it is certain that management methods and philosophy will continue to evolve, just as management itself will continue its steady development along the lines of a profession. New classics will be written as new experience and new research bring new principles to light and new points of view to the fore. There is reason to believe, however, that the principal directions in which management thought will develop in the foreseeable future have already been pointed out by the pioneer thinkers who provide the substance of this book. In more than a few cases, the reader will observe, they are still ahead of conventional management thought and practice even as it stands today.

In a very real sense, these papers constitute a history of management written by those who made the history. They present it with vision, with vitality, and with an authority that is beyond challenge.

HARWOOD F. MERRILL

ROBERT OWEN

(1771–1858)

SINCE few factory operators of a hundred and fifty years ago had any interest in their employees' working and living conditions, Robert Owen's *Address to the Superintendants of Manufactories,* published in 1813, contained ideas that were revolutionary. But they could not be dismissed lightly. Owen was a notably successful textile manufacturer in Scotland who could demonstrate in his own factories that it paid to devote as much attention to "vital machines" as to "inanimate machines." His methods entitle him to be called the father of personnel management.

As a manufacturer, Owen believed that the volume and quality of a worker's output were influenced by conditions both on and off the job— the total environment. In this respect he reached the threshold of much modern thinking, though many of his practices were what would now be called paternalistic. There is thus a direct relationship between this, the first "management classic" in the present volume, and the final one by Mayo (pp. 377–408), written 130 years later.

Owen went to work as a child and from 1800 to 1828 managed a group of textile mills in New Lanark, Scotland, where the success of his labor policies attracted wide attention but little imitation. From 1828 until his death 30 years later, he gave full time to working for social reform. He was a co-founder of the consumer cooperative movement, while another of his ventures was an unsuccessful experiment in communal living at New Harmony, Indiana, in 1824.

AN ADDRESS

To the Superintendants of Manufactories, and to those Individuals generally, who, by giving Employment to an aggregated Population, may easily adopt the Means to form the Sentiments and Manners of such a Population.

BY ROBERT OWEN

LIKE YOU, I am a manufacturer for pecuniary profit. But having for many years acted on principles the reverse in many respects of those in which you have been instructed, and having found my procedure beneficial to others and to myself, even in a pecuniary point of view, I am anxious to explain such valuable principles, that you and those under your influence may equally partake of their advantages.

In two Essays, already published, I have developed some of these principles, and in the following pages you will find still more of them explained, with some detail of their application to practice, under the particular local circumstances in which I undertook the direction of the New Lanark Mills and Establishment.

By those details you will find, that from the commencement of my management I viewed the population, with the mechanism and

Reprinted from the book, *A New View of Society,* by Robert Owen, pages 57–62. First American edition, from the third London edition. Published by E. Bliss & E. White, New York, 1825.

every other part of the establishment, as a system composed of many parts, and which it was my duty and interest so to combine, as that every hand, as well as every spring, lever, and wheel, should effectually cooperate to produce the greatest pecuniary gain to the proprietors.

Many of you have long experienced in your manufacturing operations the advantages of substantial, well-contrived, and well-executed machinery.

Experience has also shown you the difference of the results between mechanism which is neat, clean, well arranged, and always in a high state of repair; and that which is allowed to be dirty, in disorder, without the means of preventing unnecessary friction, and which therefore becomes, and works, much out of repair.

In the first case, the whole economy and management are good; every operation proceeds with ease, order, and success. In the last, the reverse must follow, and a scene be presented of counteraction, confusion, and dissatisfaction among all the agents and instruments interested or occupied in the general process, which cannot fail to create great loss.

If then due care as to the state of your inanimate machines can produce such beneficial results, what may not be expected if you devote equal attention to your vital machines, which are far more wonderfully constructed?

When you shall acquire a right knowledge of these, of their curious mechanism, of their self-adjusting powers; when the proper main spring shall be applied to their varied movements, you will become conscious of their real value, and you will be readily induced to turn your thoughts more frequently from your inanimate to your living machines; you will discover that the latter may be easily trained and directed to procure a large increase of pecuniary gain, while you may also derive from them high and substantial gratification.

Will you then continue to expend large sums of money to procure the best devised mechanism of wood, brass, or iron; to retain it in perfect repair; to provide the best substance for the prevention of unnecessary friction, and to save it from falling into premature decay? Will you also devote years of intense application to understand the connexion of the various parts of these lifeless machines, to improve their effective powers, and to calculate with mathematical precision all their minute and combined movements? And when in these transactions you estimate time by minutes, and the money expended for the chance of increased gain by fractions, will you not afford some of your attention to consider whether a portion of your time and capital would not be more advantageously applied to improve your living machines?

From experience which cannot deceive me, I venture to assure you, that your time and money so applied, if directed by a true knowledge of the subject, would return you not five, ten, or fifteen per cent, for your capital so expended, but often fifty and in many cases a hundred per cent.

I have expended much time and capital upon improvements of the living machinery; and it will soon appear that the time and money so expended in the manufactory at New Lanark, even while such improvements are in progress only, and but half their beneficial effects attained, are now producing a return exceeding fifty per cent, and will shortly create profits equal to cent. per cent. on the original capital expended in them.

Indeed, after experience of the beneficial effects, from due care and attention to the mechanical implements, it became easy to a reflecting mind to conclude at once, that at least equal advantages would arise from the application of similar care and attention to the living instruments. And when it was perceived that inanimate mechanism was greatly improved by being made firm and substantial; that it was the essence of economy to keep it neat, clean, regularly supplied with the best substance to prevent unnecessary friction, and, by proper provision for the purpose, to preserve it in good repair; it was natural to conclude that the more delicate, complex, living mechanism would be equally improved by being trained to strength and activity; and that it would also prove true economy to keep it neat and clean; to treat it with kindness, that its mental movements might not experience too much irritating friction; to endeavour by every means to make it more perfect; to supply it regularly with a sufficient quantity of wholesome food and other necessaries of life, that the body might be preserved from being out of repair, or falling prematurely to decay.

These anticipations are proved by experience to be just.

Since the general introduction of inanimate mechanism into British manufactories, man, with few exceptions, has been treated as a secondary and inferior machine; and far more attention has been given to perfect the raw materials of wood and metals than those of body and mind. Give but due reflection to the subject, and you will find that man, even as an instrument for the creation of wealth, may be still greatly improved.

But, my friends, a far more interesting and gratifying consideration remains. Adopt the means which ere long shall be rendered obvious to every understanding, and you may not only partially improve those living instruments, but learn how to impart to them such excellence as shall make them infinitely surpass those of the present and all former times.

Here then is an object which truly deserves your attention; and instead of devoting all your faculties to invent improved inanimate mechanism, let your thoughts be, at least in part, directed to discover how to combine the more excellent materials of body and mind, which, by a well-devised experiment, will be found capable of progressive improvement.

Thus seeing with the clearness of noon-day light, thus convinced with the certainty of conviction itself, let us not perpetuate the really unnecessary evils, which our present practices inflict on this large proportion of our fellow subjects. Should your pecuniary interests somewhat suffer by adopting the line of conduct now urged, many of you are so wealthy, that the expense of founding and continuing at your respective establishments the institutions necessary to improve your animate machines, would not be felt. But when you may have ocular demonstration that, instead of any pecuniary loss, a well-directed attention to form the character and increase the comforts of those who are so entirely at your mercy will essentially add to your gains, prosperity, and happiness; no reasons except those founded on ignorance of your self-interest, can in future prevent you from bestowing your chief care on the living machines which you employ; and by so doing you will prevent an accumulation of human misery, of which it is now difficult to form an adequate conception.

That you may be convinced of this most valuable truth, which due reflection will show you is founded on the evidence of unerring facts, is the sincere wish of

THE AUTHOR

CHARLES BABBAGE

(1792–1871)

CHARLES BABBAGE was a British mathematical scientist whose interests involved him in two surprising anticipations of modern management. In order to speed up mathematical calculations, he invented a 'Difference-Engine" which was a forerunner of today's electronic computer. And, during a study of many factories' methods while unsuccessfully trying to build a prototype, he perceived "principles which seemed to pervade many establishments." He thus stated a premise which led eventually to the propositions upon which Frederick W. Taylor (pp. 55–103) and those who came after him were to build the edifice of scientific management: that definite principles of management exist; that they can be determined by experience; and that they can be applied broadly through the interchange of this experience. Babbage even provided some of this interchange by writing *On the Economy of Machinery and Manufactures*, published in 1832.

The following selection from this book details what Babbage considered to be the most important "principle." In the process, it throws significant light on manufacturing conditions and problems of his day.

ON THE DIVISION OF LABOUR

BY CHARLES BABBAGE

PERHAPS the most important principle on which the economy of a manufacture depends, is the *division of labour* amongst the persons who perform the work. The first application of this principle must have been made in a very early stage of society; for it must soon have been apparent, that more comforts and conveniences could be acquired by one man restricting his occupation to the art of making bows, another to that of building houses, a third boats, and so on. This division of labour into trades was not, however, the result of an opinion that the general riches of the community would be increased by such an arrangement; but it must have arisen from the circumstance, of each individual so employed discovering that he himself could thus make a greater profit of his labour than by pursuing more varied occupations. Society must have made considerable advances before this principle could have been carried into the workshop; for it is only in countries which have attained a high degree of civilization, and in articles in which there is a great competition amongst the producers, that the most perfect system of the division of labour is to be observed. The principles on which the advantages of this system depend, have been much the subject of discussion amongst writers on Political Economy; but the relative importance of their influence does not appear, in all cases, to have been estimated with sufficient precision. It is my

Reprinted from the book, *On the Economy of Machinery and Manufactures*, by Charles Babbage, Chapter XVIII, pages 121–140. Published by Carey & Lea, Philadelphia, 1832.

intention, in the first instance, to state shortly those principles, and then to point out what appears to me to have been omitted by those who have previously treated the subject.

1. *Of the time required for learning.* It will readily be admitted, that the portion of time occupied in the acquisition of any art will depend on the difficulty of its execution; and that the greater the number of distinct processes, the longer will be the time which the apprentice must employ in acquiring it. Five or seven years have been adopted, in a great many trades, as the time considered requisite for a lad to acquire a sufficient knowledge of his art, and to repay by his labour, during the latter portion of his time, the expense incurred by his master at its commencement. If, however, instead of learning all the different processes for making a needle, for instance, his attention be confined to one operation, a very small portion of his time will be consumed unprofitably at the commencement, and the whole of the rest of it will be beneficial to his master: and if there be any competition amongst the masters, the apprentice will be able to make better terms, and diminish the period of his servitude. Again; the facility of acquiring skill in a single process, and the early period of life at which it can be made a source of profit, will induce a greater number of parents to bring up their children to it; and from this circumstance also, the number of workmen being increased, the wages will soon fall.

A certain quantity of material will be consumed unprofitably, or spoiled by every person who learns an art; and, as he applies himself to each new process, he will waste a certain quantity of the raw material, or of the partly manufactured commodity. But whether one man commits this waste in acquiring successively each process, or many persons separately learn the several processes, the quantity of waste will remain the same: in this view of the subject, therefore, the division of labour will neither increase nor diminish the price of production.

2. Another source of the advantage resulting from the division of labour is, that *time is always lost from changing from one occupation to another*. When the human hand, or the human head, has been for some time occupied in any kind of work, it cannot

instantly change its employment with full effect. The muscles of the limbs employed have acquired a flexibility during their exertion, and those to be put in action a stiffness during rest, which renders every change slow and unequal in the commencement. A similar result seems to take place in any change of mental exertion; the attention bestowed on the new subject is not so perfect at the first commencement as it becomes after some exercise. Long habit also produces in the muscles exercised a capacity for enduring fatigue to a much greater degree than they could support under other circumstances.

Another cause of the loss of time in changing from one operation to another, arises from the employment of different tools in the two processes. If these tools are simple in their nature, and the change is not frequently repeated, the loss of time is not considerable; but in many processes of the arts the tools are of great delicacy, requiring accurate adjustment whenever they are used. In many cases the time employed in adjusting, bears a large proportion to that employed in using the tool. The sliding-rest, the dividing and the drilling-engine, are of this kind; and hence in manufactories of sufficient extent, it is found to be good economy to keep one machine constantly employed in one kind of work: one lathe, for example, having a screw motion to its sliding-rest along the whole length of its bed, is kept constantly making cylinders; another, having a motion for rendering uniform the velocity of the work at the point at which it passes the tool, is kept for facing surfaces; whilst a third is constantly employed in cutting wheels.

3. *Skill acquired by frequent repetition of the same processes.* The constant repetition of the same process necessarily produces in the workman a degree of excellence and rapidity in his particular department, which is never possessed by one person who is obliged to execute many different processes. This rapidity is still farther increased from the circumstance that most of the operations in factories, where the division of labour is carried to a considerable extent, are paid for as piece work. It is difficult to estimate in numbers the effect of this cause upon production. In nail-making, Adam Smith has stated, that it is almost three to one; for, he ob-

serves, that a smith accustomed to make nails, but whose whole business has not been that of a nailer, can make only from eight hundred to a thousand per day; whilst a lad who had never exercised any other trade, can make upwards of two thousand three hundred a day.

Upon an occasion when a large issue of bank-notes was required, a clerk at the Bank of England signed his name, consisting of seven letters, including the initial of his Christian name, five thousand three hundred times during eleven working hours; and he also arranged the notes he had signed in parcels of fifty each. In different trades the economy of production arising from this cause, will necessarily be different. The case of nail-making is perhaps, rather an extreme one. It must, however, be observed that, in one sense, this is not a permanent source of advantage; for, although it acts at the commencement of an establishment, yet every month adds to the skill of the workmen; and at the end of three or four years they will not be very far behind those who have practised only the particular branch of their art.

4. *The division of labour suggests the contrivance of tools and machinery to execute its processes.* When each process, by which any article is produced, is the sole occupation of one individual, his whole attention being devoted to a very limited and simple operation, any improvement in the form of his tools, or in the mode of using them, is much more likely to occur to his mind, than if it were distracted by a greater variety of circumstances. Such an improvement in the tool is generally the first step towards a machine. If a piece of metal is to be cut in a lathe, for example, there is one angle at which the cutting-tool must be held to ensure the cleanest cut; and it is quite natural that the idea of fixing the tool at that angle should present itself to an intelligent workman. The necessity of moving the tool slowly, and in a direction parallel to itself, would suggest the use of a screw, and thus arises the sliding-rest. It was probably the idea of mounting a chisel in a frame, to prevent its cutting too deeply, which gave rise to the common carpenter's plane. In cases where a blow from a hammer is employed, experience teaches the proper force required. The transition from the hammer

held in the hand to one mounted upon an axis, and lifted regularly to a certain height by some mechanical contrivance, requires perhaps a greater degree of invention. Yet it is not difficult to perceive, that, if the hammer always falls from the same height, its effect must be always the same.

When each process has been reduced to the use of some simple tool, the union of all these tools, actuated by one moving power, constitutes a machine. In contriving tools and simplifying processes, the operative workmen are, perhaps, most successful; but it requires far other habits to combine into one machine these scattered arts. A previous education as a workman in the peculiar trade, is undoubtedly a valuable preliminary; but in order to make such combinations with any reasonable expectation of success, an extensive knowledge of machinery, and the power of making mechanical drawings, are essentially requisite. These accomplishments are now much more common than they were formerly; and their absence was, perhaps, one of the causes of the multitude of failures in the early history of many of our manufactures.

Such are the principles usually assigned as the causes of the advantage resulting from the division of labour. As in the view I have taken of the question, the most important and influential cause has been altogether unnoticed, I shall re-state those principles in the words of Adam Smith: "The great increase in the quantity of work, which, in consequence of the division of labour, the same number of people are capable of performing, is owing to three different circumstances: first, to the increase of dexterity in every particular workman; secondly, to the saving of time, which is commonly lost in passing from one species of work to another; and, lastly, to the invention of a great number of machines which facilitate and abridge labour, and enable one man to do the work of many." Now, although all these are important causes, and each has its influence on the result; yet it appears to me, that any explanation of the cheapness of manufactured articles, as consequent upon the division of labour, would be incomplete if the following principle were omitted to be stated.

That the master manufacturer, by dividing the work to be ex-

ecuted into different processes, each requiring different degrees of
skill and force, can purchase exactly that precise quantity of both
which is necessary for each process; whereas, if the whole work were
executed by one workman, that person must possess sufficient skill
to perform the most difficult, and sufficient strength to execute the
most laborious, of the operations into which the art is divided.[1]

As the clear apprehension of this principle, upon which so much
of the economy arising from the division of labour depends, is of
considerable importance, it may be desirable to illustrate it, by
pointing out its precise and numerical application in some specific
manufacture. The art of making needles is, perhaps, that which I
should have selected as comprehending a very large number of
processes remarkably different in their nature; but the less difficult
art of pin-making, has some claim to attention, from its having
been used by Adam Smith, in his illustration of the subject; and I
am confirmed in the choice, by the circumstance of our possessing
a very accurate and minute description of that art, as practised in
France above half a century ago.

Pin-making. In the manufacture of pins in England the following processes are employed:—

1. *Wire-drawing.* The brass wire used for making pins is purchased by the manufacturer in coils of about twenty-two inches in
diameter, each weighing about thirty-six pounds. The coils are
wound off into smaller ones of about six inches' diameter, and between one and two pounds' weight. The diameter of this wire is
now reduced by drawing it repeatedly through holes in steel plates,
until it becomes of the size required for the sort of pins intended
to be made. During the process of drawing the wire through these
holes it becomes hardened, and it is necessary to anneal it in order
to prevent its breaking; and, to enable it to be still farther reduced,
it is annealed two or three times, according to the diminution of
diameter required. The coils are then soaked in sulphuric acid,

---

[1] I have already stated, that this principle presented itself to me after a personal
examination of a number of manufactories and workshops devoted to different purposes; but I have since found that it has been distinctly stated, in the work of Gioja,
Nuovo Prospetto delle Scienze Economiche, 6 tom. 4to. Milano, 1815, tom. i. capo iv.

largely diluted with water, in order to clean them, and are then
beaten on stone for the purpose of removing any oxidated coating
which may adhere to them. This process is usually performed by
men, who draw and clean from thirty to thirty-six pounds of wire
a day. They are paid at the rate of five farthings per pound, and
generally earn about 3s. 6d. per day.

M. Perronet* made some experiments on the extension the wire
undergoes by this process at each hole: he took a piece of thick
Swedish brass wire, and found

	Feet.	Inch.
Its length to be before drawing	3	8
After passing the first hole	5	5
——————— second hole	7	2
——————— third hole	7	8

It was now annealed, and the length became

	Feet.	Inch.
After passing the fourth hole	10	8
——————— fifth hole	13	1
——————— sixth hole	16	8
And finally, after passing through six other holes	144	0

The holes through which the wire was drawn were not, in this
experiment, of regularly decreasing diameter; and it is extremely difficult to make such holes, and still more to preserve them in their
original dimensions.

2. *Straightening the Wire.* The coil of wire now passes into the
hands of a woman, assisted by a boy or girl. A few nails, or iron
pins, not quite in a line, are fixed into one end of a wooden table
about twenty feet in length; the end of the wire is passed alternately
between these nails, and is then pulled to the other end of the
table. The object of this process is to straighten the wire, which had
acquired a uniform curvature in the small coils into which it had
been wound. The length thus straightened is cut off, and the remainder of the coil is drawn into similar lengths. About seven

---

* The author may refer to Jean Rodolphe Perronet, 1708–1794, French construction
engineer who built roads and bridges.—EDITOR

nails or pins are employed in straightening the wire, and their adjustment is a matter of some nicety. It seems, that by passing the wire between the first three nails or pins, a bend is produced in an opposite direction to that which the wire had in the coil; this bend, by passing the next two nails, is reduced to another of larger curvature in the first direction, and so on till the curvature is at last so large that it may be confounded with a straight line.

3. *Pointing.* A man next takes about three hundred of these straightened pieces in a parcel, and putting them into a gauge, cuts off from one end, by means of a pair of shears, moved by his foot, a portion equal in length to rather more than six pins. He continues this operation until the entire parcel is reduced into similar pieces. The next step is to sharpen the ends: for this purpose the operator sits before a steel mill, which is kept rapidly revolving; and taking up a parcel between the finger and the thumb of each hand, he passes the ends before the mill, taking care with his fingers and thumbs to make each wire slowly revolve upon its axis. The mill consists of a cylinder about six inches in diameter, and two and a half inches broad, faced with steel, which is cut in the manner of a file. Another cylinder is fixed on the same axis at a few inches distant; the file on the edge of which is of a finer kind, and is used for finishing off the points. Having thus pointed all the pieces at one end, he reverses them, and performs the same process on the other. This process requires considerable skill, but it is not unhealthy whilst the similar process in needle-making is remarkably destructive of health. The pieces, now pointed at both ends, are next placed in gauges, and the pointed ends are cut off, by means of shears, to the proper length of which the pins are to be made. The remaining portions of the wire are now equal to about four pins in length, and are again pointed at each end, and their ends again cut off. This process is repeated a third time, and the small portion of wire left in the middle is thrown amongst the waste, to be melted along with the dust arising from the sharpening. It is usual for a man, his wife, and a child, to join in performing these processes; and they are paid at the rate of five farthings per pound. They can point from thirty-four to thirty-six and a half pounds per day, and

gain from 6s. 6d. to 7s., which may be apportioned thus: 5s. 6d. to the man, 1s. to the woman, 6d. to the boy or girl.

4. *Twisting and Cutting the Heads.*   The next process is making the heads. For this purpose a boy takes a piece of wire, of the same diameter as the pin to be headed, which he fixes on an axis that can be made to revolve rapidly by means of a wheel and strap connected with it. This wire is called the mould. He then takes a smaller wire, which having passed through an eye in a small tool held in his left hand, he fixes close to the bottom of the mould. The mould is now made to revolve rapidly by means of the right hand, and the smaller wire coils round it until it has covered the whole length of the mould. The boy now cuts the end of the spiral connected with the foot of the mould, and draws it off. When a sufficient quantity of heading is thus made, a man takes from thirteen to twenty of these spirals in his left hand, between his thumb and three outer fingers; these he places in such a manner that two turns of the spiral shall be beyond the upper edge of a pair of shears, and with the forefinger of the same hand he feels these two projecting turns. With his right hand he closes the shears; and the two turns of the spiral being cut off, drop into a basin. The position of the forefinger prevents the heads from flying about when cut off. The workmen who cut the heads are usually paid at the rate of 2½d. to 3d. per pound for large, but a higher price is given for the smaller heading. Out of this they pay the boy who spins the spiral; he receives from 4d. to 6d. per day. A good workman can cut from six to about thirty pounds of heading per day, according to its size.

5. *Heading.*   The process of fixing the head on the body of the pin is usually executed by women and children. Each operator sits before a small steel stake, having a cavity, into which one half of the intended head will fit; immediately above is a steel die, having a corresponding cavity for the other half of the head: this latter die can be raised by a pedal moved by the foot. The cavities in the centre of these dies are connected with the edge by a small groove, to admit of the body of the pin, which is thus prevented from being flattened by the blow of the die. The operator with his left hand dips the pointed end of the body of a pin into a tray of heads;

having passed the point through one of them, he carries it along to the other end with the forefinger. He now takes the pin in the right hand, and places the head in the cavity of the stake, and, lifting the die with his foot, allows it to fall on the head. This blow tightens the head on the shank, which is then turned round, and the head receives three or four blows on different parts of its circumference. The women and children who fix the heads are paid at the rate of 1*s*. 6*d*. for every twenty thousand. A skilful operator can with great exertion do twenty thousand per day; but from ten to fifteen thousand is the usual quantity: children head a much smaller number; varying, of course, with the degree of their skill. The weight of the hammer is from seven to ten pounds, and it falls through a very small space, perhaps from one to two inches. About one per cent. are spoiled in the process; these are picked out afterwards by women, and are reserved with the waste from other processes for the melting-pot. The form of the dies in which the heads are struck is varied according to the fashion of the time; but the repeated blows to which it is subject renders it necessary that it should be repaired after it has been used for about thirty pounds of pins.

6. *Tinning.* The pins are now fit to be tinned, a process which is usually executed, by a man, assisted by his wife, or by a lad. The quantity of pins operated upon at this stage is usually fifty-six pounds. They are first placed in a pickle, in order to remove any grease or dirt from their surface, and also to render that surface rough, which facilitates the adherence of the tin with which they are to be covered. They are then placed in a boiler full of a solution of tartar in water, in which they are mixed with a quantity of tin in small grains. They are generally kept boiling for about two hours and a half, and are then removed into a tub of water into which some bran has been thrown; this is for the purpose of washing them. They are then taken out, and, being placed in wooden trays, are well shaken in dry bran: this removes any water adhering to them; and by giving the wooden tray a peculiar kind of motion, the pins are thrown up, and the bran gradually flies off, and leaves them behind in the tray. The man who pickles and tins the pins usually

gets one penny per pound for the work, and employs himself, during the boiling of one batch of pins, with drying those previously tinned. He can earn about 9*s.* per day; but out of this he pays about 3*s.* for his assistant.

7. *Papering.* The arranging of pins side by side in paper is generally performed by women. The pins come from the last process in wooden bowls, with the points projecting in all directions. A woman takes up some, and places them on the teeth of a comb, whilst, by a few shakes, some of the pins fall back into the bowl, and the rest, being caught by their heads, are detained between the teeth of the comb. Having thus arranged them in a parallel direction, she fixes the requisite number between two pieces of iron, having twenty-five small grooves, at equal distances; and having previously doubled the paper, she presses it against the points of the pins until they have passed through the two folds which are to retain them. The pins are then relieved from the grasp of the tool, and the process repeated with others. A woman gains about 1*s.* 6*d.* per day by papering; but children are sometimes employed, who earn from 6*d.* per day, and upwards.

Having thus described the various processes of pin-making, without entering into the minuter details, and having stated the usual cost of each, it will be convenient to present a tabular view [page 30] of the time occupied by each process, and its cost, as well as of the sums which can be earned by the persons who confine themselves solely to each process. As the rate of wages is itself fluctuating, and as the prices paid and quantities executed have been given between certain limits, it is not to be expected that this table can represent with the minutest accuracy the cost of each part of the work, nor even that it shall accord perfectly with the prices above given: but it has been drawn up with some care, and will be quite sufficient for that general view, and for those reasonings, which it is meant to illustrate. A table nearly similar will be subjoined [page 31], which has been deduced from a statement of M. Perronet, respecting the art of pin-making in France, about seventy years ago.

English Manufacture. Pins, "*Elevens,*" 5,546 weigh one pound;

"one dozen" = 6,932 pins weigh twenty ounces, and require six ounces of paper.

NAME OF THE PROCESS	Work-men.	Time of making 1 lb. of Pins.	Cost of making 1 lb. of Pins.	Work-man earns per Day		Price of making each Part of a single Pin, in Millionths of a Penny.
		Hours.	*Pence.*	*s.*	*d.*	
1. Drawing Wire .	Man ..	.3636	1.2500	3	3	225
2. Straightening ⎰	Woman	.3000	.2840	1	0	51
the Wire . . . ⎱	Girl ..	.3000	.1420	0	6	26
3. Pointing	Man ..	.3000	1.7750	5	3	319
4. Twisting and ⎰	Boy ..	.0400	.0147	0	4½	3
Cutting the ⎱	Man ..	.0400	.2103	5	4½	38
Heads						
5. Heading	Woman	4.0000	5.0000	1	3	901
6. Tinning, or ⎰	Man ..	.1071	.6666	6	0	121
Whitening ..⎱	Woman	.1071	.3333	3	0	60
7. Papering	Woman	2.1314	3.1973	1	6	576
		7.6892	12.8732			2320

Number of Persons employed:—Men, 4; Women, 4; Children, 2. Total, 10.

French Manufacture. Cost of 12,000 pins, N. 6, each being eight-tenths of an English inch in length; with the cost of each operation:—deduced from the observations and statement of M. Perronet:—as they were manufactured in France about 1760.

It appears from the analysis we have given of the art of pin-making, that it occupies rather more than seven hours and a half of time, for ten different individuals working in succession on the same material, to convert it into a pound of pins; and that the total expense of their labour, each being paid in the joint ratio of his skill and of the time he is employed, amounts very nearly to 1s. 1d. But from an examination of the first of these tables, it appears that the wages earned by the persons employed vary from 4½d. per day up to 6s., and consequently the skill which is required for their respective employments may be measured by those sums. Now it is evident, that if one person be required to make the whole pound of pins, he must have skill enough to earn about 5s. 3d. per day whilst he is pointing the wires or cutting off the heads from the spiral coil,—and 6s. when he is whitening the pins; which three operations together would occupy little more than the seventeenth part of his time. It is also apparent, that during more than one half of his time he must be earning only 1s. 3d. per day in putting on the heads, although his skill, if properly employed, would, in the same time, produce nearly five times as much. If therefore we were to employ, for each of the processes, the man who whitens the pins, and who earns 6s. per day, even supposing that he could make the pounds of pins in an equally short time, yet we must pay him for his time 46.14 pence, or about 3s. 10d. *The pins would*

NAME OF THE PROCESS	Time of making Twelve Thousand Pins.	Cost of making Twelve Thousand Pins.	Workman usually earns per Day.	Expense of Tools and Materials.
	Hours.	*Pence.*	*Pence.*	*Pence.*
1. Wire	...	...	...	24.75
2. Straightening and Cutting	1.2	.5	4.5	...
Coarse Pointing	1.2	.625	10.0	...
Turning Wheel [2]	1.2	.875	7.0	...
3. Fine Pointing	.8	.5	9.375	...
Turning Wheel	1.2	.5	4.75	...
Cutting off Pointed Ends	.6	.375	7.5	...
Turning Spiral	.5	.152	3.0	...
4. Cutting off Heads	.8	.375	5.625	...
Fuel to Anneal Ditto	...	...	...	.125
5. Heading	12.0	.333	4.25	...
6. Tartar for Cleaning	...	...	...	.5
Tartar for Whitening ...	...	...	...	.5
7. Papering	4.8	.5	2.0	...
Paper	...	...	...	1.0
Wear of Tools	...	...	...	2.0
	24.3	4.708		

therefore cost in making, three times and three quarters as much as they now do by the application of the division of labour. The higher the skill required of the workman in any one process of a manufacture, and the smaller the time during which it is employed, so much the greater will be the advantage of separating that process from the rest, and devoting one person's attention en-

---

[2] The expense of turning the wheel appears to have arisen from the person so occupied being unemployed during half his time, whilst the pointer went to another manufactory.

tirely to it. Had we selected the art of needle-making as our illustration, the economy arising from the division of labour would
have been still larger; for the process of tempering the needles requires great skill, attention, and experience; and although from
three to four thousand are tempered at once, the workman is paid
a very high rate of wages. In another process of the same art, dry-
pointing, which is also executed with great rapidity, the wages
earned by the workman reach from 7s. to 12s., 15s., and even, in
some instances, to 20s. per day; whilst other processes in the same
art are carried on by children paid at the rate of 6d. per day.

Some farther reflections are suggested by the preceding analysis;
but it may be convenient, previously, to place before the reader a
brief description of a machine for making pins, invented by an
American. It is highly ingenious in point of contrivance, and, in
respect to its economical principles, will furnish a strong and interesting contrast with the manufacture of pins by the human hand.
In this machine a coil of brass wire is placed on an axis; one end of
this wire is drawn by a pair of rollers through a small hole in a plate
of steel, and is held there by a forceps. As soon as the machine is
put in action—

1. The forceps draws the wire on to a distance equal in length
to one pin: a cutting edge of steel then descends close to the hole
through which the wire entered, and severs a piece equal in length
to one pin.

2. The forceps holding this wire moves on until it brings the
wire into the centre of the *chuck* of a small lathe, which opens
to receive it. Whilst the forceps returns to fetch another piece of
wire, the lathe revolves rapidly, and grinds the projecting end of
the wire upon a steel mill, which advances towards it.

3. After this first or coarse pointing, the lathe stops, and another
forceps takes hold of the half-pointed pin, (which is instantly re-
leased by the opening of the *chuck*,) and conveys it to a similar
chuck of another lathe, which receives it, and finishes the pointing
on a finer steel mill.

4. This mill again stops, and another forceps removes the pointed
pin into a pair of strong steel clams, having a small groove in them

by which they hold the pin very firmly. A part of this groove, which terminates at that edge of the steel clams which is intended to form the head of the pin, is made conical. A small round steel punch is now driven forcibly against the end of the wire thus clamped, and the head of a pin is partially formed by compressing the wire into the conical cavity.

5. Another pair of forceps now removes the pin to another pair of clams, and the head of the pin is completed by a blow from a second punch, the end of which is slightly concave. Each pair of forceps returns as soon as it has delivered its burden; and thus there are always five pieces of wire at the same moment in different stages of advance towards a finished pin. The pins so formed are received in a tray, and whitened and papered in the usual manner. About sixty pins can thus be made by this machine in one minute; but each process occupies exactly the same time in performing.

In order to judge of the value of such a machine, compared with hand labour, it would be necessary to inquire:—1. To what defects pins so made are liable? 2. What advantages they possess over those made in the usual way? 3. What is the prime cost of a machine for making them? 4. What is the expense of keeping it in repair? 5. What is the expense of moving it and attending to it?

1. Pins made by the machine are more likely to bend, because as the head is punched up out of the solid wire, it ought to be in a soft state to admit of this process. 2. Pins made by the machine are better than common ones, because they are not subject to losing their heads. 3. With respect to the prime cost of a machine, it would be very much reduced if numbers should be required. 4. With regard to its wear and tear, experience only can decide the question: but it may be remarked, that the steel clams or dies in which the heads are punched up, will wear quickly unless the wire has been softened by annealing; and that if it has been softened, the bodies of the pins will bend too readily. Such an inconvenience might be remedied, either by making the machine spin the heads and fix them on, or by annealing only that end of the wire which is to become the head of the pin: but this would cause a delay between the operations, since the brass is too brittle while heated

to bear a blow without crumbling. 5. On comparing the time occupied by the machine with that stated in the analysis, we find, except in the process of heading, if time alone is considered, that the human hand is more rapid. Three thousand six hundred pins are pointed by the machine in one hour, whilst a man can point fifteen thousand six hundred in the same time. But in the process of heading, the rapidity of the machine is two and a half times that of the human hand. It must, however, be observed, that the process of grinding does not require the application of force to the machine equal to that of one man; for all the processes we have described are executed at once by the machine, and one labourer can easily work it.

CAPTAIN HENRY METCALFE

(1847–1917)

IN THE YEAR 1885 the manager of an army arsenal published a book called *The Cost of Manufactures and the Administration of Workshops, Public and Private*. It stated the proposition that there is a "science of administration" based on principles which can be applied to a great variety of cases. It further suggested that these principles can be found by recording observations and experiences and comparing them. Finally, the book described a pioneering system for cost and materials control which makes sense even today: It was simple, it gave a continuous flow of information, and it assigned responsibility precisely.

One of the interesting facts about this author, with his prophetic vision of management as we know it today, was that he was a career army officer. Captain Henry Metcalfe graduated from West Point in 1868, was assigned to the Ordnance Department, and as superintendent of several arsenals developed and applied the methods he described in his book. He retired from the army in 1893, ten years before Frederick W. Taylor presented his important paper, *Shop Management* (pp. 57–66).

The introduction to Metcalfe's book, which follows, outlines his approach. It remains worthwhile on its merits alone; considering that it was written more than 75 years ago, it is an unusual achievement indeed.

THE SCIENCE OF ADMINISTRATION

BY CAPT. HENRY METCALFE

IT MAY BE stated as a general principle that while Art seeks to produce certain effects, Science is principally concerned with investigating the causes of these effects.

Thus, independently of the intrinsic importance of the art selected for illustration, there always seems room for a corresponding science, collecting and classifying the records of the past so that the future operations of the art may be more effective.

The administration of arsenals and other workshops is in great measure an art, and depends upon the application to a great variety of cases of certain principles, which, taken together, make up what may be called the science of administration.

These principles need not be formulated, nor even recognized as such, and they vary with the conditions which call them forth; so that while their essence may be the same, the special rules of conduct derived from them may, in various circumstances, be widely different. Yet, for each set of conditions their character is the same, and in all they constitute what is known as our experience.

Some men have the gift of so arranging their experience that it is always ready with an answer to whatever question new conditions may propose. But such men are rare and are seldom found

Reprinted from the book, *The Cost of Manufactures and the Administration of Workshops, Public and Private,* by Capt. Henry Metcalfe, Chapter II, pages 15–24. Published by John Wiley & Sons, New York, 1885. Used by permission of the publisher.

in subordinate positions. In any case their knowledge goes with them when they depart, instead of remaining, as it should, and in great measure might do, as one of the most valuable earnings of the business in which it was acquired.

For this purpose it should be formulated, if a way were found, so that its record might be plain to whoever had the right to read it.

Now, since the operations of good administration are in their nature gradual, and for their successful issue depend rather upon uniform attention to their progress than upon occasional violent efforts to adjust them to the current of affairs, it will be seen that the most useful teachings are those gained from a continuous record of events; for these may be expected to recur with time, while great catastrophes can seldom be provided for, or, in fact, prevented, better than by the daily discharge of the duties pertaining to direction.

If there be a science correlative to the art of administration, it must, like every other physical science, be founded on the comparison of acumulated observations.

Since the accuracy of the knowledge sought can be no greater than the exactness of the data from which it is derived, in order to make a proper comparison it is important that the observations be as free from error as possible, and that they be measured by a common standard.

Errors of observation may be divided into two general classes; the instrumental, and those due to the personal bias of the observer; the former referring to the standard itself, and the latter to the application of the standard and the record of the measurement.

Whatever be the standard of measurement, it suffices for comparison if it be generally accepted, if it be impartially applied and if the results be fairly recorded.

In regard to personal errors of observation it is generally admitted that truth is most nearly approached when, having observers of equal goodness they are most numerous, and when they individually know least of the immediate consequences of what they report.

Hence the most truthful records will be had when each observer's share of the work is reduced to a minimum; for the number of observers being the greatest possible, each one will have so much the less to do, and being, therefore, better able to do his share, each will feel more responsible for the accuracy of the aggregate result and will besides be most likely to have his bias neutralized by the opposing tendencies of the other observers.

Now, efficiency being admitted, the excellence of an administration is universally measured by its cost.

This cost is composed of the sum of the costs of each of its actions; so that to properly value an administration we require to know both what it has done and the cost of doing it.

The greater the detail of this knowledge the greater its value; for the more exactly then can causes of past expenditure be traced back from their effects, and the more certainly may estimates of future cost be based on what is already known and established.

Success in manufacturing depends almost entirely upon accuracy of estimate.

The extent to which the analysis of cost and product may be carried need only be limited by the expense of making it or by the power of comprehending and comparing the results which it affords.

To utilize such an examination two processes are necessary, one inductive and the other deductive; for the product and its cost having been analyzed as far as convenience will permit, the resulting items must be recombined into forms admitting of a comparison from which may be deduced certain general rules for the future conduct of affairs.

Then will Experience take definite form and become indeed a teacher; thus Science be the handmaid of the art.

It is the object of this book to show how the cost of administration may be determined, both in gross and the remotest details, by such impersonal, invariable means that their record may be looked upon as being as nearly absolutely true as that of any other similarly extended series of observations.

Together with this comes a method of administration which reduces its labors to a minimum and yet immensely increases its scope, by recording, in whatever minuteness of detail may ever be required, full information as to services performed and as to material in all stages of manufacture, received, expended and remaining on hand.

Furthermore, its records will be made continuously from day to day, it may be from hour to hour, so that, being disposed of in detail, the turmoil and anxiety of periodical accounting will be unknown.

Few will deny the advantages of such a scheme; many will consider it utopian. To such I offer the following account of what it has done.

While in charge of the workshops of Frankford Arsenal [Philadelphia], in order to keep track of the list of shop, or work orders, of which 80 to 100 were always in hand, I began a book in which they were entered as received from the Commanding Officer and crossed off when completed. This worked for but a short time, when it became so inconvenient that I was led to give to each order a serial number as a symbol by which it was to be known.

To communicate these orders to the foremen came the order tickets, correspondingly numbered and distinguished as described in the text. The analysis of the character of the work, and of the objects and operations came later, and led to the Time Card now in use at Frankford Arsenal, the idea of which was remotely derived from that in use at the National Armory during my service there. This carried the labor question as far as it was considered at Frankford Arsenal, and completed by far the easier portion of the task.

For the reasons stated in the text, the question of material gave much more trouble. One form of card after another was tried, each one more simple and comprehensive than the last, until the form of Material Card now used at the arsenal was devised.

The plan was unfolded to the foremen by a lecture on the 18th of June, 1881. Seven working days afterwards I was detailed to other duty and have never since had anything to do with the working of the system at the Arsenal. Yet, as official reports lately made declare, it continues to give satisfaction and is followed substantially as it left my hands.

I have much for which to thank Colonel Lyford and Captain Michaelis, the former for the support given as Commanding Officer to the operation of a scheme, the development of which he did so much to encourage; and the latter, my successor in charge, both for his interest in its continuance and for improvements from which I have borrowed the suggestions noted in the text.

Still, I think it will be acknowledged that it must have had considerable intrinsic vitality to have endured so well my early removal from its charge. I am fain to believe that it was because it met a real want, not only that it furnished the Commanding Officer with superior information without abridging in any way his prerogatives, or that it relieved the foremen of all their clerical labors; but that besides these and above all other advantages it gave the foremen an assurance that good work done cheaply would be known as such and that a method was provided by the certain and automatic action of which their work would be surely gauged.

Foremen, as a class, are necessarily among the most intelligent of men and are as quick as any to appreciate the advantages of a good tool. Direct methods suit them best; they like to work as a dog digs a hole, disposing immediately of present necessities and throwing what they have accomplished behind them, out of sight and mind. They do better and more trustworthy work when not required to record their own performances, and are all the better able to appreciate the efforts of others who can classify and arrange their results for future reference.

Then, besides, clerks and storekeepers were relieved from the keeping of many books, books which for evident reasons were very imperfectly kept by foremen and storekeepers, and which if correctly prepared by clerks were of necessity based upon the incorrect data given by the others. For example, how expect books to be accurately kept in winter time in storehouses in which fire is not allowed?

The adoption of the last model of cards did away with the following books and papers kept by foremen:

1. Reports of fabrication.
2. Reports of material returned to store.
3. Stock books of all kinds.

4. Requisition books for materials to be purchased or to be drawn from store.
5. All time books.
6. All statements of costs.

And the following by storekeepers:

7. "Stock" day-books.
8. "Material" day-books.
9. Stock ledgers.
10. Memorandum orders.
11. Teamsters' receipts.

And the following by clerks:

12. Register of orders of supply.
13. Invoice book.

(As an illustration of what this amounted to, I have in mind an establishment employing not many more than 100 men, where the books required to transact the morning's business number 18 and weigh about 60 lbs. This includes only those carried to and from the office more or less every day, and does not include those kept permanently at either end of the route.)

A few books on the ordinary plan of Day-book, Journal and Ledger were added, but these were afterwards abolished by Captain Michaelis, who wisely extended the principles of the card system, so as to make the book form of record unnecessary. These were kept by the Cost Clerk, a new creation.

I do not remember that any new books were added to those kept by the other clerks; but, on the contrary, by the use of the ledger form, devised by Mr. Fries, the Stock Clerk, he was enabled to deal single-handed with the enormous variety of material on hand at the Arsenal, embracing thousands of different names. This had previously required the attention, for prolonged periods, of about two-thirds of the clerical force.

The Cost Clerk knew nothing of the shops when appointed to

them. He was employed at $2.00 per day, and had two boys, of about fourteen, to assist him in keeping the accounts and taking care of the shop store-room, also new. This force was certainly insignificant, compared with the results achieved, particularly so, when it is remembered how many new items were dealt with, and how much more information was available than ever before.

Owing to the kindness of Colonel J. McAllister, commanding Benicia Arsenal, I have been allowed to apply the system here. In beginning, where everything was new, I was forced to simplify and reduce the work as much as possible, for I had most of it to do myself; in consequence, when I got a helper, I was able to teach him his duties in about a week's time.

The comparatively crude means adopted, forming the basis of the improvements hereafter described, have worked as great a change as at Frankford. The foreman has no books to keep, and all the clerical work, much more than formerly, is done by a soldier who is employed for the greater part of his time as a copyist in the Ordnance Storekeeper's office.

Thus it will be seen that the results claimed have not been achieved at a sacrifice, but that each advance in expansion and efficiency has been accompanied by a gain in simplicity and directness.

While doing this work, I had been educating myself to a fuller comprehension of the possibilities of the system, so that, starting to explain the Frankford system as I had left it, I found my subject unsatisfactory, and discovered creeping in exceptions and inconsistencies which I knew would be confusing to those who might have to undertake the work afresh. I soon determined that such special rules were but a sign of incomplete investigation and that the necessity for them must be removed.

In consequence, both Time and Material cards were revised. The former was adapted to piece work as well as to time work by the day or by any of its subdivisions, and also to rendering an account of services by whomsoever performed; and the new Material Card was placed in such accord with the Ordnance Property Regulations that it sometimes seems their latent spirit. The most radical change lay in limiting the cards to a single entry each; this simple matter led to most important consequences.

Every transaction with material that could be imagined has been traced to its conclusion by certain uniform rules, every anomaly being considered due to some intrinsic defect in the rules, which being eliminated, they were re-applied until further exceptions seemed impossible.

These rules were:

1. To reduce all writing to a minimum by the use for all purposes of the same general kind of one comprehensive tabular form, completed by a simple symbolic notation and certified by characteristic punch marks.

2. To make each card a representative unit, capable of combination with others, according to any one or more of their common features; thereby attaining by the mechanical operation of sorting, the results otherwise achieved only by the tardy and laborious processes of book-keeping.

3. To avoid transcription by providing that the same card shall be dealt with by as many consecutive agents as require it, thereby saving time and preventing errors in copying.

4. For the preservation of the cards and their record to trust rather to their equivalency with the units they represent, and with which they are convertible, than to mere rules of conduct concerning their employment; and so, by depending upon the cards for all the temporary purposes for which books are now employed, to make books unnecessary except for final records.

5. To disregard the number of cards consumed by using them singly as an immediate record of all transactions deemed worthy of note, in view of the ultimate saving in labor and the absolute avoidance of confusion due to their unrestricted employment for such purposes.

6. To render entirely unnecessary the removal to the workshops or storehouses of any records or correspondence pertaining to the external relations of the arsenal.

7. To make the cards so full of meaning that no one under-

standing the principles on which they were based could ever go amiss in using them; that no special rules should be required for special cases, but that the part of each user should be fixed by evident principles of general application: in a word, to make the cards suffice for all purposes to all who had to use them.

The departures from the letter of the Regulations are so slight that in view of the concluding portion of par. 48, Property Regulations, 1877, p. 14, it seems not unreasonable to hope that they may be condoned.

The principles on which the system is founded are so broad that though it may fully comply with every precaution required of trustees of public property, it seems none the less applicable to the smallest shop in the land. But it would not be necessary, nor even advisable, to follow their application in every case to the extent required by the uses of the Ordnance Department. However far this may be done, it seems plain to me that the results which those who have charge of workshops seem universally to desire can be attained in no other way so economically as by this Mechanical Book-keeping.

It seems as proper for a reformer to show that a change is needed as to explain the changes he proposes to make: so wholesome is conservatism, that a new thing should not only be shown to be good, but that which it proposes to replace should be proved to be relatively bad. I have been forced, therefore, not only to criticize much in our present methods that seemed bad; but I have also, for want of other sources of general information, been obliged to explain that which I criticized. I need hardly say that my only object has been to make evident the evils from which not only we of the Ordnance Department have been suffering, but which, in some form, few of the private workshops of my acquaintance have escaped.

Having been compelled to do the greater part of this work thousands of miles away from, and years after leaving the scenes and circumstances most in mind, it is to be expected that many inaccuracies will be found in my statements of details. Still I believe that it is all true in spirit, if not of all of the places considered, at least of some of them. It is hard to select examples which shall be typical and not appear invidious or exaggerated; but I have done my best to make sure that all the examples shall be at least possible and as true to the facts as my own memory and the concurrent testimony at my command would permit.

The use of cards in workshops as well as in libraries, is no new thing; others besides the men with whom I have worked have been driven to appreciate their advantages and have turned them to more or less account. But the administration of private workshops is in general limited by responsibilities so immediate and self-contained, that I doubt whether there are any where as strict an accounting has been made as is required by our trusteeship of public property. Indeed, had it not been for the rigorous exactions of the Ordnance Regulations, I doubt whether I would have been led to formulate a scheme as comprehensive as I hope that this will be found. It is their spirit which has led me through this self-imposed task, and it is in extending its influence that I find my reward.

I have to thank William Sellers & Co. of Philadelphia for suggesting the manner of distributing miscellaneous expenses and the use of the ticket punch for signatures; also for much information and encouragement, the details of which have escaped me. Besides those whose names appear in the body of the report I wish particularly to thank Lieut. A. H. Russell, of the Ordnance Department, for his assistance, and Mr. H. T. Fries, Stock Clerk at Frankford Arsenal, to whose familiarity with existing requirements and to whose zeal in meeting them I am under obligations which it is difficult to express and impossible to repay.

HENRY METCALFE

BENICIA ARSENAL, CALIFORNIA, *May*, 1884.

POSTSCRIPT.—A change of station to Watervliet Arsenal has enabled me to revise the MS. prepared in California by the light of a wider experience.

HENRY ROBINSON TOWNE

(1844–1924)

IN THE preceding selection, Captain Henry Metcalfe called for the recording of experience in a particular business so that its managers might use it as a guide. In the following proposal, made to The American Society of Mechanical Engineers just a year after Metcalfe published his book in 1885, Henry Robinson Towne went a step further. He urged an exchange of experience among the works managers of different companies, with the ASME taking the lead in thus developing data on which a science of management could be based. A number of years passed before Towne's recommendation was formally adopted. But in his inspired proposal for an organized exchange of experience among managers lay the seeds of the tremendous development of management knowledge that has taken place since Taylor appeared on the scene.

A co-founder and the president of Yale & Towne Manufacturing Company for 48 years, Towne was instrumental in gaining recognition for Taylor and his methods. He was also an innovator in his own right, notably in attempts to improve on piece-rate wage systems.

THE ENGINEER AS AN ECONOMIST

BY HENRY R. TOWNE, *Stamford, Conn.*

THE MONOGRAM of our national initials, which is the symbol of our monetary unit, the dollar, is almost as frequently con-
joined to the figures of an engineer's calculations as are the symbols
indicating feet, minutes, pounds, or gallons. The final issue of his
work, in probably a majority of cases, resolves itself into a question
of dollars and cents, of relative or absolute values. This statement,
while true in regard to the work of all engineers, applies particularly
to that of the mechanical engineer, for the reason that his functions,
more frequently than in the case of others, include the executive
duties of organizing and superintending the operations of industrial establishments, and of directing the labor of the artisans whose
organized efforts yield the fruition of his work.

To insure the best results, the organization of productive labor
must be directed and controlled by persons having not only good
executive ability, and possessing the practical familiarity of a
mechanic or engineer with the goods produced and the processes
employed, but having also, and equally, a practical knowledge of
how to observe, record, analyze and compare essential facts in
relation to wages, supplies, expense accounts, and all else that enters
into or affects the economy of production and the cost of the product. There are many good mechanical engineers; — there are also

Reprinted from *Transactions of The American Society of Mechanical Engineers,*
Volume 7, pages 428–432. Paper presented at May 1886 meeting of the Society,
Chicago. Used by permission of the Society.

many good "business men";—but the two are rarely combined in one person. But this combination of qualities, together with at least some skill as an accountant, either in one person or more, is essential to the successful management of industrial works, and has its highest effectiveness if united in one person, who is thus qualified to supervise, either personally or through assistants, the operations of all departments of a business, and to subordinate each to the harmonious development of the whole.

Engineering has long been conceded a place as one of the modern arts, and has become a well-defined science, with a large and growing literature of its own, and of late years has subdivided itself into numerous and distinct divisions, one of which is that of mechanical engineering. It will probably not be disputed that the matter of shop management is of equal importance with that of engineering, as affecting the successful conduct of most, if not all, of our great industrial establishments, and that the *management of works* has become a matter of such great and far-reaching importance as perhaps to justify its classification also as one of the modern arts. The one is a well-defined science, with a distinct literature, with numerous journals and with many associations for the interchange of experience; the other is unorganized, is almost without literature, has no organ or medium for the interchange of experience, and is without association or organization of any kind. A vast amount of accumulated experience in the art of workshop management already exists, but there is no record of it available to the world in general, and each old enterprise is managed more or less in its own way, receiving little benefit from the parallel experience of other similar enterprises, and imparting as little of its own to them; while each new enterprise, starting *de novo* and with much labor, and usually at much cost for experience, gradually develops a more or less perfect system of its own, according to the ability of its managers, receiving little benefit or aid from all that may have been done previously by others in precisely the same field of work.

Surely this condition of things is wrong and should be remedied. But the remedy must not be looked for from those who are "business men" or clerks and accountants only; it should come from those whose training and experience has given them an understanding of both sides (viz.: the mechanical and the clerical) of the important questions involved. It should originate, therefore, from those who are also engineers, and, for the reasons above indicated, particularly from mechanical engineers. Granting this, why should it not originate from, and be promoted by The American Society of Mechanical Engineers?

To consider this proposition more definitely, let us state the work which requires to be done. The questions to be considered, and which need recording and publication as conducing to discussion and the dissemination of useful knowledge in this specialty, group themselves under two principal heads, namely: Shop Management, and Shop Accounting. A third head may be named which is subordinate to, and partly included in each of these, namely: Shop Forms and Blanks. Under the head of Shop Management fall the questions of organization, responsibility, reports, systems of contract and piece work, and all that relates to the executive management of works, mills and factories. Under the head of Shop Accounting fall the questions of time and wages systems, determination of costs, whether by piece or day-work, the distribution of the various expense accounts, the ascertainment of profits, methods of book-keeping, and all that enters into the system of accounts which relates to the manufacturing departments of a business, and to the determination and record of its results.

There already exists an enormous fund of information relating to such matters, based upon actual and most extensive experience. What is now needed is a medium for the interchange of this experience among those whom it interests and concerns. Probably no better way for this exists than that obtaining in other instances, namely, by the publication of papers and reports, and by meetings for the discussion of papers and interchange of opinions.

The subject thus outlined, however distinct and apart from the primary functions of this society, is, nevertheless, germane to the interests of most, if not all, of its members. Conceding this, why should not the functions of the society be so enlarged as to embrace this new field of usefulness? This work, if undertaken, may be kept separate and distinct from the present work of the society by organizing a new "section" (which might be designated the "Economic Section"), the scope of which would embrace all papers and discussions relating to the topics herein referred to. The meetings of this section could be held either separately from, or immediately following the regular meetings of the society, and its papers could appear as a supplement to the regular transactions. In this way all interference would be avoided with the primary and chief business of the society, and the attendance at the meetings of the new section would naturally resolve itself into such portion of the membership as is interested in the objects for which it would be organized.

As a single illustration of the class of subjects to be covered by the discussions and papers of the proposed new section, and of the benefit to be derived therefrom, there may be cited the case of a manufacturing establishment in which there are now in use, in connection with the manufacturing accounts and exclusive of the ordinary commercial accounts, some twenty various forms of special record and account books, and more than one hundred printed forms and blanks. The primary object to which all of these contribute is the systematic recording of the operations of the different departments of the works, and the computation therefrom of such statistical information as is essential to the efficient management of the business, and especially to increased economy of production. All of these special books and forms have been the outgrowth of experience extending over many years, and represent a large amount of thoughtful planning and intelligent effort at constant development and improvement. The methods thus arrived at would undoubtedly be of great value to others engaged in similar operations, and particularly to persons engaged in organizing and starting new enterprises. It is probable that much, if not all, of the information and experience referred to would be willingly made public through such a channel as is herein suggested, particularly if such action on the part of one firm or corporation would be responded to in like manner by others, so that each member could reasonably

expect to receive some equivalent for his contributions by the benefit which he would derive from the experience of others.

In the case of the establishment above referred to, a special system
of contract and piece-work has been in operation for some fifteen
years, the results from which, in reducing the labor cost on certain
products without encroaching upon the earnings of the men
engaged, have been quite striking. A few of these results, selected
at random, are indicated by the accompanying diagram, the diagonal
lines on which represent the fluctuations in the labor cost of certain
special products during the time covered by the table, the vertical
scale representing values.

Undoubtedly a portion of the reductions thus indicated resulted
from improved appliances, larger product, and increased experience, but after making due allowance for all of these, there remains
a large portion of the reduction which, to the writer's knowledge,
is fairly attributable to the operation of the peculiar piece-work

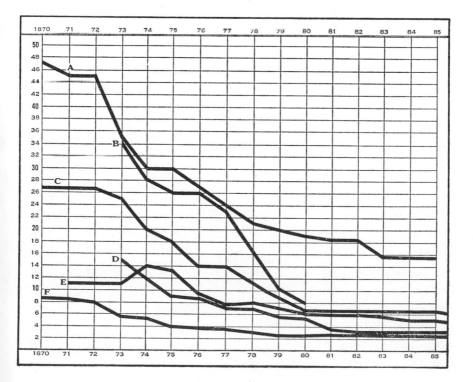

system adopted. The details and operations of this system would probably be placed before the society, in due time, through the channel of the proposed new section, should the latter take definite form. Other, and probably much more valuable, information and experience relating to systems of contract and piece-work would doubtless be contributed by other members, and in the aggregate a great amount of information of a most valuable character would thus be made available to the whole membership of the society.

In conclusion, it is suggested that if the plan herein proposed commends itself favorably to the members present at the meeting at which it is presented, the subject had best be referred to a special committee, by whom it can be carefully considered, and by whom, if it seems expedient to proceed further, the whole matter can be matured and formulated in an orderly manner, and thus be so presented at a future meeting as to enable the society then intelligently to act upon the question, and to decide whether or not to adopt the recommendations made by such committee.

FREDERICK WINSLOW TAYLOR

(1856–1915)

FREDERICK WINSLOW TAYLOR, production man, executive, and consultant, was the most influential of the management pioneers. He applied the scientific method to the solution of factory problems and from these analyses built up orderly sets of principles which could be substituted for the trial-and-error methods then in use. A detailed example of how he applied the methods which came to be called scientific management is contained in the selection (pp. 57–66) from the famous paper, *Shop Management*, which he presented at a meeting of The American Society of Mechanical Engineers in 1903.

Today, Taylor's general approach is widely accepted. But 50 years ago its challenge to the established way of doing things made it a controversial subject—so much so that the House of Representatives in 1911 appointed a special committee to investigate it and other "systems of shop management." In January 1912, after many hearings during which Taylor believed scientific management had been distorted and misrepresented, he took the stand and delivered the testimony from which the section beginning on page 67 was taken. His fiery words reveal the crusader behind the analyst. At the same time they provide a definitive statement of exactly what he meant by scientific management which will clear up misconceptions that continue even today.

Taylor's philosophy is described more specifically in *The Principles of Scientific Management* (pp. 72–103), a speech he delivered at a conference on the subject held at the Amos Tuck School, Dartmouth College, in October 1911. Here, Taylor also tells the stories behind two milestones in management history: his study of the "science" of shoveling at the Bethlehem Steel Company and his experiments in the technique of metal cutting at the Midvale Steel Works.

TIME STUDY, PIECE WORK, AND THE FIRST-CLASS MAN

BY FREDERICK W. TAYLOR

THE WRITER has found, through an experience of twenty years, covering a large variety in manufactures, as well as in the building trades, structural and engineering work, that it is not only practicable but comparatively easy to obtain through a systematic and scientific TIME STUDY, exact information as to how much of any given kind of work either a first-class or an average man can do in a day, and with this information as a foundation, he has over and over again seen the fact demonstrated that workmen of all classes are not only willing, but glad to give up all idea of soldiering, and devote all of their energies to turning out the maximum work possible, providing they are sure of a suitable permanent reward.

With accurate time knowledge as a basis, surprisingly large results can be obtained under any scheme of management from day work up; there is no question that even ordinary day work resting upon this foundation will give greater satisfaction than any of the systems in common use, standing as they do upon soldiering as a basis.

To many of the readers of this paper both the fundamental

Reprinted from *Transactions of The American Society of Mechanical Engineers,* Volume 24, pages 1356–1364. Excerpt from *Shop Management,* paper presented at June 1903 meeting of the Society, Saratoga, New York. Used by permission of the Society.

objects to be aimed at, namely, HIGH WAGES WITH LOW LABOR COST, and the means advocated by the writer for attaining this end; namely, ACCURATE TIME STUDY, will appear so theoretical and so far outside of the range of their personal observation and experience that it would seem desirable, before proceeding farther, to give a brief illustration of what has been accomplished in this line.

The writer chooses from among a large variety of trades to which these principles have been applied, the yard labor handling raw materials in the works of the Bethlehem Steel Company at South Bethlehem, Pa., not because the results attained there have been greater than in many other instances, but because the case is so elementary that the results are evidently due to no other cause than thorough time study as a basis, followed by the application of a few simple principles with which all of us are familiar.

In almost all of the other more complicated cases the large increase in output is due partly to the actual physical changes, either in the machines or small tools and appliances, which a preliminary time study almost always shows to be necessary, so that for purposes of illustration the simple case chosen is the better, although the gain made in the more complicated cases is none the less legitimately due to the system.

Up to the spring of the year 1899, all of the materials in the yard of the Bethlehem Steel Company had been handled by gangs of men working by the day, and under the foremanship of men who had themselves formerly worked at similar work as laborers. Their management was about as good as the average of similar work, although it was bad, all of the men being paid the ruling wages of laborers in this section of the country, namely, $1.15 per day, the only means of encouraging or disciplining them being either talking to them or discharging them; occasionally, however, a man was selected from among these men and given a better class of work with slightly higher wages in some of the company's shops, and this had the effect of slightly stimulating them. From four to six hundred men were employed on this class of work throughout the year.

The work of these men consisted mainly of unloading from railway cars and shovelling on to piles, and from these piles again loading as required, the raw materials used in .running three blast furnaces and seven large open-hearth furnaces, such as ore of various kinds, varying from fine, gravelly ore to that which comes in large lumps, coke, limestone, special pig, sand, etc., unloading hard and soft coal for boilers, gas-producers, etc., and also for storage and again loading the stored coal as required for use, loading the pig iron produced at the furnaces for shipment, for storage, and for local use, and handling billets, etc., produced by the rolling mills. The work covered a large variety as laboring work goes, and it was not usual that a man was kept continuously at the same class of work.

Before undertaking the management of these men, the writer was informed that they were steady workers, but slow and phlegmatic, and that nothing would induce them to work fast.

His first step was to place an intelligent, college-educated man in charge of progress in this line. This man had not before handled this class of labor, although he understood managing workmen. He was not familiar with the methods pursued by the writer, but was soon taught the art of determining how much work a first-class man can do in a day. This was done by timing with a stop watch a first-class man while he was working fast. The best way to do this, in fact almost the only way in which the timing can be done with certainty, is to divide the man's work into its elements and time each element separately. For example, in the case of a man loading pig iron on to a car, the elements should be: Picking up the pig from the ground or pile (time in hundredths of a minute). Walking with it on a level (time per foot walked). Walking with it up an incline to car (time per foot walked). Throwing the pig down (time in hundredths of a minute). Walking back empty to get a load (time per foot walked).

In case of important elements which were to enter into a number of rates, a large number of observations were taken when practicable on different first-class men, and at different times, and they were averaged.

The most difficult elements to time and decide upon in this, as in most cases, are the percentage of the day required for rest, and the time to allow for accidental or unavoidable delays.

In the case of the yard labor at Bethlehem, each class of work was studied as above, each element being timed separately, and in addition, a record was kept in many cases of the total amount of work done by the man in a day. The record of the gross work of the man (who is being timed) is, in most cases, not necessary after the observer is skilled in his work. As the Bethlehem time observer was new to this work, the gross time was useful in checking his detailed observations and so gradually educating him and giving him confidence in the new methods.

The writer had so many other duties that his personal help was confined to teaching the proper methods and approving the details of the various changes which were in all cases outlined in written reports before being carried out.

As soon as a careful study had been made of the time elements entering into one class of work, a single first-class workman was picked out and started on ordinary piece work on this job. His task required him to do between *three and one-half* and *four times* as much work in a day as had been done in the past on an average.

Between twelve and thirteen tons of pig iron per man had been carried from a pile on the ground, up an inclined plank, and loaded on to a gondola car by the average pig iron handler while working by the day. The men in doing this work had worked in gangs of from five to twenty men.

The man selected from one of these gangs to make the first start under the writer's system was called upon to load on piece work from forty-five to forty-eight tons (2,240 lbs. each) per day.

He regarded this task as an entirely fair one, and earned on an average, from the start, $1.85 per day, which was 60 per cent. more than he had been paid by the day. This man happened to be considerably lighter than the average good workman at this class of work. He weighed about 130 pounds. He proved, however, to be especially well suited to this job, and was kept at it steadily throughout the time that the writer was in Bethlehem, and I believe is still at the same work.

Being the first piece work started in the works, it excited considerable opposition, both on the part of the workmen and of several of the leading men in the town, their opposition being based mainly on the old fallacy that if piece work proved successful a great many men would be thrown out of work, and that thereby not only the workmen but the whole town would suffer.

One after another of the new men who were started singly on this job were either persuaded or intimidated into giving it up. In many cases they were given other work by those interested in preventing piece work, at wages higher than the ruling wages. In the meantime, however, the first man who started on the work earned steadily $1.85 per day, and this object lesson gradually wore out the concerted opposition, which ceased rather suddenly after about two and one-half months. From this time on there was no difficulty in getting plenty of good men who were anxious to start on piece work, and the difficulty lay in making with sufficient rapidity the accurate time study of the elements or "unit times" which forms the foundation of this kind of piece work.

Throughout the introduction of piece work, when after a thorough time study a new section of the work was started, one man only was put on each new job, and not more than one man was allowed to work at it until he had demonstrated that the task set was a fair one by earning an average of $1.85 per day. After a few sections of the work had been started in this way, the complaint on the part of the better workmen was that they were not allowed to go on to piece work fast enough.

It required about two years to transfer practically all of the yard labor from day to piece work. And the larger part of the transfer was made during the last six months of this time.

As stated above, the greater part of the time was taken up in studying "unit times," and this time study was greatly delayed by having successively the two leading men who had been trained to the work leave because they were offered much larger salaries elsewhere. The study of "unit times" for the yard labor took practically the time of two trained men for two years. Throughout this time the day and piece workers were under entirely separate and distinct management. The original foremen continued to manage the day work, and day and piece workers were never allowed to work together. Gradually the day work gang was diminished and the piece workers were increased as one section of work after another was transformed from the former to the latter.

Two elements which were important to the success of this work should be noted:

First, on the morning following each day's work, each workman was given a slip of paper informing him in detail just how much work he had done the day before, and the amount he had earned. Thus enabling him to measure his performance against his earnings while the details were fresh in his mind.

Without this there would have been great dissatisfaction among those who failed to climb up to the task asked of them, and many would have gradually fallen off in their performance.

Second, whenever it was practicable, each man's work was measured by itself. Only when absolutely necessary was the work of two men measured up together and the price divided between them, and then care was taken to select two men of as nearly as possible the same capacity.

Only on few occasions, and then upon special permission signed by the writer, were more than two men allowed to work on gang work, dividing their earnings between them.

Gang work almost invariably results in a falling off in earnings and consequent dissatisfaction.

An interesting illustration of the desirability of individual piece work instead of gang work came to our attention at Bethlehem. Several of the best piece workers among the Bethlehem yard laborers were informed by their friends that a much higher price per ton was paid for shovelling ore in another works than the rate given at Bethlehem. After talking the matter over with the writer he advised them to go to the other works, which they accordingly did.

In about a month they were all back at work in Bethlehem again, having found that at the other works they were obliged to work with a gang of men instead of on individual piece work, and that the rest of the gang worked so slowly that in spite of the high price paid per ton they earned much less than at Bethlehem.

The table below gives a summary of the work done by the piece work laborers in handling raw materials, such as ores, anthracite and bituminous coal, coke, pig iron, sand, limestone, cinder, scale, ashes, etc., in the works of the Bethlehem Steel Company, during the year ending April 30, 1901. This work consisted mainly in loading and unloading cars on arrival or departure from the works, and for local transportation, and was done entirely by hand, *i. e.*, without the use of cranes or other machinery.

	Piece Work.	Day Work.
Number of tons (2,240 lbs. per ton) handled on piece work during the year ending April 30, 1901........................	$924,040 \frac{13}{100}$	
Total cost of handling $924,040 \frac{13}{100}$ tons including the piece work wages paid the men, and in addition all incidental day labor used	$30,797.78	
Former cost of handling the same number of tons of similar materials on day work......	....	$67,215.47
Net saving in handling $924,040 \frac{13}{100}$ tons of materials, effected in one year through substituting piece work for day work........	$36,417.69	
Average cost for handling a ton (2,240 lbs.) on piece and day work.................	$0.033	$0.072
Average earnings per day, per man..........	*$1.88	$1.15
Average number of tons handled per day per man	57	16
The piece workers handled on an average $3 \frac{56}{100}$ times as many tons per man per day as the day workers.		

*It was our intention to fix piece work rates which should enable first-class workmen to average about 60 per cent more than they had been earning on day work, namely $1.85 per day. A year's average shows them to have earned $1.88 per day, or three cents per man per day more than we expected. An error of $1 \frac{6}{10}$ per cent.

The greater part of the credit for making the accurate time study and actually managing the men on this work, should be given to Mr. A. B. Wadleigh, the writer's assistant in this section at that time.

When the writer left the steel works, the Bethlehem piece workers were the finest body of picked laborers that he has ever seen together. They were practically all first-class men because in each case the task which they were called upon to perform was such that only a first-class man could do it. The tasks were all purposely made so severe that not more than one out of five laborers (perhaps even a smaller percentage than this) could keep up.

It was clearly understood by each newcomer as he went to work that unless he was able to average at least $1.85 per day he would have to make way for another man who could do so. As a result, first-class men from all over that part of the country, who were in most cases earning from $1.05 to $1.15 per day, were anxious to try their hands at earning $1.85 per day. If they succeeded they were naturally contented, and if they failed they left, sorry that they were unable to maintain the proper pace, but with no hard feelings either toward the system or the management. Throughout the time that the writer was there, labor was as scarce and as difficult to get as it ever has been in the history of this country, and yet there was always a surplus of first-class men ready to leave other jobs and try their hand at Bethlehem piece work.

Perhaps the most notable difference between these men and ordinary piece workers lay in their changed mental attitude toward their employers and their work, and in the total absence of soldiering on their part. The ordinary piece worker would have spent a considerable part of his time in deciding just how much his employer would allow him to earn without cutting prices and in then trying to come as close as possible to this figure, while carefully guarding each job so as to keep the management from finding out how fast it really could be done. These men, however, were faced with a new but very simple and straightforward proposition, namely, am I a first-class laborer or not? Each man felt that if he belonged in the first class all he had to do was work at his best and he would be paid sixty per cent more than he had been paid in the past. Each new piece work price was accepted by the men without question. They never bargained over nor complained about rates, and there was no occasion to do so, since they were all equally fair, and called for almost exactly the same amount of work and fatigue per dollar of wages.

A careful inquiry into the condition of these men when away from work developed the fact that out of the whole gang, only two were said to be drinking men. This does not, of course, imply that many of them did not take an occasional drink. The fact is that a steady drinker would find it almost impossible to keep up with the pace which was set, so that they were practically all sober. Many if not most of them were saving money, and they all lived better than they had before. The results attained under this system were most satisfactory both to employer and workmen, and show in a convincing way the possibility of uniting high wages with a low labor cost.

This is virtually a labor union of first-class men, who are united together to secure the extra high wages, which belong to them by right and which in this case are begrudged them by none, and which will be theirs through dull times as well as periods of activity. Such a union commands the unqualified admiration and respect of all classes of the community; the respect equally of workmen, employers, political economists, and philanthropists. There are no dues for membership, since all of the expenses are paid by the company. The employers act as the officers of the Union, to enforce its rules and keep its records, since the interests of the company are identical and bound up with those of the men. It is never necessary to plead with, or persuade men to join this Union, since the employers themselves organize it free of cost; the best workmen in the community are always anxious to belong to it. The feature most to be regretted about it is that the membership is limited.

The words "labor union" are, however, unfortunately so closely associated in the minds of most people with the idea of disagreement and strife between the employers and men, that it seems almost incongruous to apply them to this case.

Is not this, however, the ideal "labor union," with character and special ability of a high order as the only qualifications for membership?

It is a curious fact that with the people to whom the writer has described this system, the first feeling, particularly among those more philanthropically inclined, is one of pity for the inferior workmen who lost their jobs in order to make way for the first-class men. This sympathy is entirely misplaced. There was such a demand for labor at the time, that no workman was obliged to be out of work for more than a day or two, and so the poor workmen were practically as well off as ever. The feeling, instead of being one of pity for the inferior workmen, should be one of congratulation and rejoicing that many first-class men—who through unfortunate circumstances had never had the opportunity of proving their worth —at last were given the chance to earn high wages and become prosperous.

What the writer wishes particularly to emphasize is that this whole system rests upon an accurate and scientific study of "unit times," which is by far the most important element in modern management. With it, greater and more permanent results can be attained even under ordinary day work or piece work than can be reached under any of the more elaborate systems without it.

WHAT IS SCIENTIFIC MANAGEMENT?

BY FREDERICK W. TAYLOR

SCIENTIFIC MANAGEMENT is not any efficiency device, not a device of any kind for securing efficiency; nor is it any bunch or group of efficiency devices. It is not a new system of figuring costs; it is not a new scheme of paying men; it is not a piecework system; it is not a bonus system; it is not a premium system; it is no scheme for paying men; it is not holding a stop watch on a man and writing things down about him; it is not time study; it is not motion study nor an analysis of the movements of men; it is not the printing and ruling and unloading of a ton or two of blanks on a set of men and saying, "Here's your system; go use it." It is not divided foremanship or functional foremanship; it is not any of the devices which the average man calls to mind when scientific management is spoken of. The average man thinks of one or more of these things when he hears the words "scientific management" mentioned, but scientific management is not any of these devices. I am not sneering at cost-keeping systems, at time study, at functional foremanship, nor at any new and improved scheme of paying men, nor at any efficiency devices, if they are really devices that make for efficiency. I believe in them; but what I am emphasizing is that these devices in whole or in part are not scientific management; they are useful adjuncts to scientific management, so are they also useful adjuncts of other systems of management.

Excerpt from testimony of Frederick W. Taylor at hearings before the Special Committee of the House of Representatives to Investigate the Taylor and Other Systems of Shop Management, January 25, 1912, pages 1387–1389.

Now, in its essence, scientific management involves a complete mental revolution on the part of the workingman engaged in any particular establishment or industry—a complete mental revolution on the part of these men as to their duties toward their work, toward their fellow men, and toward their employees. And it involves the equally complete mental revolution on the part of those on the management's side—the foreman, the superintendent, the owner of the business, the board of directors—a complete mental revolution on their part as to their duties toward their fellow workers in the management, toward their workmen, and toward all of their daily problems. And without this complete mental revolution on both sides scientific management does not exist.

That is the essence of scientific management, this great mental revolution. Now, later on, I want to show you more clearly what I mean by this great mental revolution. I know that it perhaps sounds to you like nothing but bluff—like buncombe—but I am going to try and make clear to you just what this great mental revolution involves, for it does involve an immense change in the minds and attitude of both sides, and the greater part of what I shall say today has relation to the bringing about of this great mental revolution. So that whether the details may be interesting or uninteresting, what I hope you will see is that this great change in attitude and viewpoint must produce results which are magnificent for both sides, just as fine for one as for the other. Now, perhaps I can make clear to you at once one of the very great changes in outlook which come to the workmen, on the one hand, and to those in the management on the other hand.

I think it is safe to say that in the past a great part of the thought and interest both of the men, on the side of the management, and of those on the side of the workmen in manufacturing establishments has been centered upon what may be called the proper division of the surplus resulting from their joint efforts, between the management on the one hand, and the workmen on the other hand. The management have been looking for as large a profit as possible for themselves, and the workmen have been looking for as large wages as possible for themselves, and that is what I mean by the division of the surplus. Now, this question of the division of the surplus is a very plain and simple one (for I am announcing no great fact in political economy or anything of that sort). Each article produced in the establishment has its definite selling price. Into the manufacture of this article have gone certain expenses, namely, the cost of materials, the expenses connected with selling it, and certain indirect expenses, such as the rent of the building, taxes, insurance, light and power, maintenance of machinery, interest on the plant, etc. Now, if we deduct these several expenses from the selling price, what is left over may be called the surplus. And out of this surplus comes the profit to the manufacturer on the one hand, and the wages of the workmen on the other hand. And it is largely upon the division of this surplus that the attention of the workmen and of the management has been centered in the past. Each side has had its eye upon this surplus, the working man wanting as large a share in the form of wages as he could get, and the management wanting as large a share in the form of profits as it could get; I think I am safe in saying that in the past it has been in the division of this surplus that the great labor troubles have come between employers and employees.

Frequently, when the management have found the selling price going down they have turned toward a cut in the wages—toward reducing the workman's share of the surplus—as their way of getting out whole, of preserving their profits intact. While the workman (and you can hardly blame him) rarely feels willing to relinquish a dollar of his wages, even in dull times, he wants to keep all that he has had in the past, and when busy times come again very naturally he wants to get more. Thus it is over this division of the surplus that most of the troubles have arisen; in the extreme cases this has been the cause of serious disagreements and strikes. Gradually the two sides have come to look upon one another as antagonists, and at times even as enemies—pulling apart and matching the strength of the one against the strength of the other.

The great revolution that takes place in the mental attitude of the two parties under scientific management is that both sides take their eyes off of the division of the surplus as the all-important matter, and together turn their attention toward increasing the size of the surplus until this surplus becomes so large that it is unnecessary to quarrel over how it shall be divided. They come to see that when they stop pulling against one another, and instead both turn and push shoulder to shoulder in the same direction, the size of the surplus created by their joint efforts is truly astounding. They both realize that when they substitute friendly cooperation and mutual helpfulness for antagonism and strife they are together able to make this surplus so enormously greater than it was in the past that there is ample room for a large increase in wages for the workmen and an equally great increase in profits for the manufacturer. This, gentlemen, is the beginning of the great mental revolution which constitutes the first step toward scientific management. It is along this line of complete change in the mental attitude of both sides; of the substitution of peace for war; the substitution of hearty brotherly cooperation for contention and strife; of both pulling hard in the same direction instead of pulling apart; of replacing suspicious watchfulness with mutual confidence; of becoming friends instead of enemies; it is along this line, I say, that scientific management must be developed.

The substitution of this new outlook—this new viewpoint—is of the very essence of scientific management, and scientific management exists nowhere until after this has become the central idea of both sides; until this new idea of cooperation and peace has been substituted for the old idea of discord and war.

This change in the mental attitude of both sides toward the "surplus" is only a part of the great mental revolution which occurs under scientific management. I will later point out other elements of this mental revolution. There is, however, one more change in viewpoint which is absolutely essential to the existence of scientific management. Both sides must recognize as essential the substitution of exact scientific investigation and knowledge for the old individual judgment or opinion, either of the workman or the boss, in all matters relating to the work done in the establishment. And this applies both as to the methods to be employed in doing the work and the time in which each job should be done.

Scientific management cannot be said to exist, then, in any establishment until after this change has taken place in the mental attitude of both the management and the men, both as to their duty to cooperate in producing the largest possible surplus and as to the necessity for substituting exact scientific knowledge for opinions or the old rule of thumb or individual knowledge.

These are the two absolutely essential elements of scientific management.

THE PRINCIPLES OF
SCIENTIFIC MANAGEMENT

BY FREDERICK W. TAYLOR
Consulting Engineer, Philadelphia

MR. CHAIRMAN, LADIES AND GENTLEMEN:

ON BEHALF of several of my colleagues who are here tonight, and more particularly on my own behalf, I wish to express the appreciation which we feel for the honor which is being conferred on us by the presence of this platform of the present governor of this state and of one of its most distinguished past governors. I think that I can say that it is the most distinguished honor which has yet been conferred on any meeting at which Scientific Management has been discussed, and we are deeply grateful that these gentlemen, busy as they are, should have taken the time and the trouble to come here.

There is one fact which has been impressed on me more than any other during the past six months. I knew it to be a fact before, but it had never been brought home to me in the same way as during the past six months. It is the fundamental and the very sad fact that almost every workman who is engaged in the mechanic arts, who is engaged in anything like cooperative work, looks upon it as his duty to go slow instead of to go fast. This is the most unfortunate fact in any way connected with Scientific Management,

Reprinted from the book, *Scientific Management*, pages 22–55. Published by Dartmouth College, Hanover, N. H., 1912. Paper presented at First Conference on Scientific Management, The Amos Tuck School, Dartmouth College, October 1911. Used by permission of The Amos Tuck School.

and the causes which lead to it should therefore be very carefully considered.

I may say at the start, that if any one is to blame for this attitude, we are, and not the laborers. It is our fault more than the laborers', that almost every workman looks upon it as his duty to do as small a day's work as he can instead of as large a day's work as he can. Now do not misunderstand me on this point; I am referring only to those workmen who are engaged in what may be called organized industry. I am not referring to the isolated men who work perhaps for themselves, perhaps for an employer with one or two employees, but I am speaking chiefly of the great mass of men who are doing the industrial work of this country. This going slow, instead of going fast, to my mind is the most serious fact that we have to face in this country. It is certainly the most serious fact that is being faced by the English people at this time.

If any of you will get close to the average workman in this country—close enough to him so that he will talk to you as an intimate friend—he will tell you that in his particular trade if, we will say, each man were to turn out twice as much work he is now doing, there could but one result follow: namely, that one-half the men in his trade would be thrown out of work. Now this fallacy is firmly believed by nineteen men out of twenty of all the workmen throughout the country, and, strange to say, I have found that perhaps three-quarters of the people in this country who have spent the larger proportion of their life in getting an education doubt very much if it would be of any great advantage to the working people to turn out more work than they are doing. The average man then, in all classes in this country, doubts if it would really be of any great benefit to the working people to turn out a larger output than they are now doing. Every labor union in this country, so far as I know, has taken steps, or is taking steps, to restrict output.

In this these men are strictly honest; they are doing just what you and I would do if we were in their position and held their views. If any of us thought that by increasing our work we should throw one-half of our friends out of employment, we should take the same view that they do.

This doctrine is preached by almost every labor leader in the country, and is taught by every workman to his children as they are growing up; and I repeat, as I said in the beginning, that it is our fault more than theirs that this fallacy prevails.

What men here—not more than two or three—have ever spoken to an audience of workmen and attempted to counteract that fallacy? Not more than two or three in this audience have ever gone before an audience of workingmen and tried to point out the truth, that the greatest blessing that working-men can confer on their brothers and themselves is to increase their output.

While the labor leaders and the workmen themselves in season and out of season are pointing out the necessity of restriction of output, not one step are we taking to counteract that fallacy; therefore, I say, the fault is ours and not theirs.

All that it is necessary to do, for any one who questions the fact whether it is a good thing for working people to increase their output or not, is to look into the history of any trade in this country. Look into the history of any trade in this country, and you will see that directly the opposite is true; that an increased output invariably gives more work to more men, and never in the history of the world has it more than temporarily, and then for only a very short time, diminished the number of men at work in any trade. That is the truth! Just look into any trade and you will see it.

I shall take the time to give one illustration only. Take the great cotton industry, one of the greatest industries of your state; one of the greatest, if not the greatest industry of New England. In Manchester, England, in 1840 or thereabouts, there were 5,000 cotton operatives. Power machinery began to be introduced in the cotton mills about that time, and the moment those 5,000 men saw the new machinery coming they *knew* that there would not be work for more than 1,000 out of the 5,000 in their trade. There was no question about it whatever. So what did they do? They did just what you or I would have done under similar circumstances. They broke into the mills where the machinery was being installed and smashed it up; they burned down the mills and beat up the "scabs" who were employed to run the new machinery; and they did it for self-protection, just as you or I would have done it, believing what they did as firmly as they did.

Now power machinery came in the cotton industry, just as all labor-saving machinery is sure to come in any industry, in spite of any opposition from any source. It always has come, and it always will come. And what was the result? I am told that the average yardage of cloth now turned out per man in the cotton industry is about eight or ten times the yardage turned out under the old hand conditions.

In 1840, in Manchester, England, there were 5,000 cotton operatives; in Manchester, England, now there are 265,000 cotton operatives. Multiply that ratio by eight to ten and you will see that between 400 and 500 times the yardage of cloth is now being turned out from Manchester, England, that was turned out in 1840. Has the increase in production thrown people out of work? No. It is merely typical of what has taken place and is taking place in every trade. The increase of output merely means bringing more wealth into this world. That is the meaning of it; that now 450 times as much wealth in cotton goods is brought into this world as was brought in 1840, and that is the real wealth of the world. And the workmen, the trades union, the philanthropist or the mill owner who restrict output as a permanent policy (I do not mean to say it is not necessary both for workmen and manufacturers at times to temporarily restrict output) are about the worst enemies to their fellow-men there are. There is hardly any worse crime to my mind than that of deliberately restricting output; of failing to bring the only things into the world which are of real use to the world, the products of men and the soil. The world's history shows that just as fast as you bring the good things that are needed by man into the world, man takes and uses them. That one fact, the immense increase in the productivity of man, marks the difference between civilized and uncivilized countries, marks the one great advance we have made on 100 to 200 years ago; it is due to that increase of productivity that the working people of today, with all the talk about their misery and their horrible treatment, live almost as well as kings did 250 years ago. They have better food, better clothing, and on the whole more comforts than kings had 250 years ago. And that is due to just one thing, *increase of output.*

Take this matter of cotton goods. Tell the average workman of today that when he has a cotton shirt on he has a luxury. Will he not laugh at you? In 1840 a cotton shirt worn by a workman was a luxury; now every man, woman and child in every work-man's family wears cotton goods as an absolute necessity. Just so with a hundred other things that we have come to look upon as necessities, which a hundred years ago were luxuries. And to what is that due? To the increased productivity of man.

I am talking so long on this subject because it lies at the very root of Scientific Management, for Scientific Management has for its object just what labor-saving machinery has for its object, *increased output per unit of human effort.*

The second cause for going slow is *entirely* due to us. I think we are more to blame than they for the first cause, the fallacy that the increase of output will throw men out of work, but we are entirely to blame for the second cause. *It lies in our own inefficient systems of management.*

The piece-work system has been introduced in the industries of this country to such an extent that hardly a workman can be found in any industry who does not know something about its working. All of you gentlemen doubtless understand all about the piece-work system. If you do, then I will remind you that when you put a workman on piece-work and ask him to make, we will say, ten implements like this slide-rule in a day, and offer to pay him twenty-five cents for making each of them, you count on his using his ingenuity and on his making a careful study of the methods by which he is going to make them, and so increase his daily output. You hope that later instead of making ten pieces per day, he will make twelve, fourteen, fifteen or even twenty pieces a day. This is the hope of the manufacturer.

We will assume that that workman knows nothing about the piece-work system. With the opportunity before him to have his ingenuity and his harder work rewarded by getting more pay per day, he would very likely, after six months or a year, learn how to make fifteen of these instead of ten, or, let us say, twenty instead of ten. If he made twenty he would be earning $5 per day in place of $2.50 which he earned before he was put on piece-work.

The foreman over those men, we will say, is a straight, square man, and in all honesty he encourages them to turn out more than ten pieces; we will say he encourages them to get out twenty pieces. Now in almost all boards of directors of our companies there are a number of very wise gentlemen who are perhaps members of other boards of directors, and at certain intervals these wise and philanthropic men are very apt to ask for an analysis of the pay-roll of their company. And when they see that a certain workman in their employ is earning $5 a day, they are naturally horror-stricken. "Why," they say, "our orders to that superintendent were that he was to pay the ruling wages which prevail around here; $2.50 a day is all any machinist ought to earn; it is horrible to think of a mere machinist with no education earning $5 a day; Mr. President, I move that our superintendent be instructed to see that the men in this establishment are paid no more than other machinists in other establishments. Why should we be spoiling the labor of this part of the country?" So Mr. Foreman, although he may be an honest man, and although he has encouraged those men to turn out that work, in many cases perhaps has actually made promises to them that if they increased their output their wages would not be cut, that man is forced by the board of directors to go back on his word, to cut down the piece-work price; he has to force those men to make twenty pieces for $2.50 a day where before they made ten pieces for $2.50 a day. Now the working people of this country are not fools; generally one cut of that sort is enough; two always are enough; and from that time forward a workman is nothing but a fool if he does not soldier to "beat the band," if he does not deliberately try to make the people around him believe that he is working as fast as he can, while he is really doing a very ordinary day's work. And, gentlemen, that is our fault, not his, and not a thing are we doing as a whole to remedy that state of affairs.

It was precisely this condition which forced us to take the first step which led towards Scientific Management. I had had a war lasting some two or three years with the workmen who were my friends, over whom I was finally placed, a constant running fight for two or three years, in which I was trying to drive them in spite of their resistance to do a larger amount of work. Having worked with them, I knew they were soldiering to the extent of about two-thirds, and I hoped to be able to get them to at least double their work, and finally I did, and then they were one-third short of what they could have done. After three years of that fight, three years of never looking a man in the face from morning till night except as a tactical enemy, three years of wondering what that fellow was going to do to me next and wondering what I could do to him next, I made up my mind that some remedy would have to be devised for that state of things or I would cease to be a foreman and go into some other business. It was in an endeavor to remedy such a state of things that the first step was taken leading towards Scientific Management.

In taking account of stock, after I had definitely made up my mind either to try to remedy that state of things or get out of industrial management, I found that the chief lack was the lack of knowledge. I had no illusions as to my own knowledge; I knew that these workmen knew ten times as much collectively as I knew. And we started to take measures which should enable the foreman of that shop to know approximately what his men knew. We started then along various lines of study with the purpose of educating the owners and managers of the shops of the Midvale Steel Works so that they also should know approximately what their men knew. That was the first step leading towards Scientific Management.

I want to tell you as briefly as I can what Scientific Management is. It certainly is not what most people think it to be. It is not a lot of efficiency expedients. It is not the printing and ruling of a lot of pieces of blank paper and spreading them by the ton about the country. It is not any particular system of paying men. It is not a system of figuring costs of manufacture. It is none of the ordinary devices which unfortunately are going by the name of Scientific Management. It may in its essence be said in the present state of industry to involve a complete mental revolution, both on the part of the management and of the men. It is a complete change in the mental attitude of both sides towards their respective duties and towards their opponents. That is what constitutes Scientific Management.

There are now, I don't know exactly how many, but at a fair estimate I should say 50,000 men working under Scientific Management. These men are on the average turning out twice as much work per day as they formerly did.

As a result of this increase in output, their employers are profiting by a very material reduction of the cost of whatever they are making. This diminution of cost has enabled them, on the one hand, to earn a larger profit and, on the other hand, in most cases to somewhat reduce the selling price of the goods which they make. And let me tell you, gentlemen, that in all cases of Scientific Management, in all cases of increase in efficiency, the general public takes almost the whole of the increase in the end. We consumers are the beneficiaries of the increase in output. The history of the matter shows that neither the manufacturer nor the workman through any long period gets very much benefit from increased output except as the whole world takes it. The world takes that benefit and is perfectly entitled to it. Now the workman: what have these 50,000 men who are working under Scientific Management got out of it? On an average those men are earning from 30 per cent to 100 per cent higher wages than they did, and I look upon that as perhaps the smallest part of their gain. Those workmen, to my mind, have gained something far greater than that; in place of looking at their employers with suspicion, in place of looking upon them as at least tactical enemies, although they may be personal friends, they look upon their employers as the very best friends they have in the world. I look at that as the greatest gain that can come under Scientific Management, far greater than any increase in wages. The harmony that exists between employer and employee under Scientific Management is the greatest gain that can come to both.

That is mere assertion, but in proof of the fact that this harmony does exist between the workman and the employers under Scientific Management, I wish to make the statement that until perhaps three months ago there never had been a single strike of men employed under Scientific Management. Even during the difficult period of changing from the old management to the new, that difficult and dangerous period when a mental revolution was taking place and causing readjustment of attitude towards their own duties and towards the duties of the management, there had never been a strike until this year. This system has been applied to a great number and variety of industries, and the fact that until recently there had never been a single strike is ample proof that these friendly relations actually exist between both sides. That, perhaps, is the most important characteristic of Scientific Management.

In order to explain what Scientific Management is, I want to present first what I believe all of you gentlemen will recognize as the best of the older types of management and to contrast with that type the principles of Scientific Management. If you have an establishment with 500 or 1,000 men, there will be, perhaps, twenty different trades represented. Each of the workmen in those trades has learned practically all he knows from watching other workmen. When he was a young apprentice he would watch a journeyman, imitate his motions, and finally perhaps the journeyman would get interested and turn around and give the boy a little friendly advice; and thus the boy, merely by personal observation and a very small amount of incidental teaching, learned the trade. In just this way every operative in every one of those twenty different trades in your establishment has learned his trade; it has come to him just as it did in the Middle Ages, from mouth to mouth, or rather from hand to eye, not through teaching. Nevertheless, in spite of the old traditional way of learning a trade, this knowledge is the greatest asset that a workman possesses. It is his capital.

The manufacturer who has any intelligence must realize that his first duty should be to obtain the initiative of all these tradesmen who are working under him, to obtain their hard work, their good-will, their ingenuity, their determination to treat their employer's business as if it were their own. And in this connection I wish to strain the meaning of the word "initiative" to indicate all of those good qualities. It should be the first object of a good employer to obtain the real initiative of his workmen.

There is an occasional employer, possibly one in a hundred, who deliberately sets out to give his employees something better in the way of wages and opportunities than his competitors give their men. These very few rare employers who are farther sighted than the average, deliberately set out to give their men a special incentive, and in return they expect, and they frequently get, from their men an initiative which other employers do not dream of getting. However, this initiative is generally spasmodic. Workmen come to have confidence in their superintendent, or in their foreman, and in the honor of their company; and when the superintendent tells them that he intends to have them earn more money than other employers are paying their workmen, they believe it and respond in a generous way. But I want to tell what happens almost always, even in such a case: some new workman comes in for whom they have respect; he tells the men the usual story; that the same promise had been made to him or to friends of his in some other shop by a foreman, a square man, but it happened that that foreman died, or was replaced, or the board of directors did just what I outlined at the beginning, and then those promises went to the winds, and the men found themselves working harder than before at the old wages. When a man comes in among them and tells them that story the men think, "Perhaps that is so—it is likely to happen in our shop; I guess we had better not work too hard," and they slow down. Finally, as they think it over and realize that their foreman can be relied on, they say, "This fellow is all right, he can't treat us like that, we have got to be square," and eventually they will work hard again. But under the old system the initiative of the workmen is obained spasmodically at best; it is rarely obtained to the fullest extent.

The first advantage which Scientific Management has over the older type is that under Scientific Management the initiative of the workmen is obtained with absolute regularity; their hard work, good-will and ingenuity are obtained with absolute regularity. I refer of course only to those cases in which Scientific Management is actually introduced and in operation, not where it has just been started; but in practically all cases where Scientific Management has been once established the initiative of the workmen is obtained with absolute regularity. That alone is a marked advantage of Scientific Management over the best of the other types.

This is not, however, the greatest advantage of Scientific Management. This is the lesser of two advantages. The greater advantage comes from the new and unheard-of burdens and duties which are assumed by the men in the management, duties which have never been performed before by the men on the management side. These new duties are divided into four large classes which have been, properly or improperly, called "The Four Principles of Scientific Management."

The first of these four great duties which are undertaken by the management is to deliberately gather in all of the rule-of-thumb knowledge which is possessed by all the twenty different kinds of tradesmen who are at work in the establishment—knowledge which has never been recorded, which is in the heads, hands, and bodies, in the knack, skill, dexterity which these men possess—to gather that knowledge, classify it, tabulate it, and in most cases reduce it to laws and rules; in many cases, work out mathematical formulæ which, when applied with the cooperation of the management to the work of the men, will lead to an enormous increase of the output of the workmen. That is the first of the four great principles of Scientific Management, the development of a science to replace the old rule-of-thumb knowledge of the workmen.

The second of the new duties assumed by the management is the scientific selection and then the progressive development of the workmen. The workmen are studied; it may seem preposterous, but they are studied just as machines have been studied in the past and are being more than ever studied. In the past we have given a great deal of study to machines and little to workmen, but under Scientific Management the workman becomes the subject of far more careful and accurate study than was ever given to machines.

After we have studied the workman, so that we know his possibilities, we then proceed, as one friend to another, to try to develop every workman in our employ, so as to bring out his best faculties and to train him to do a higher, more interesting and more profitable class of work than he has done in the past. This is the second of the principles of Scientific Management.

The third duty is to bring the scientifically selected workman and the science together. They must be *brought* together; they will not come together without it. I do not wish for an instant to have any one think I have a poor opinion of a workman; far from it. I am merely stating a fact when I say that you may put your scientific methods before a workman all you are of a mind to, and nine times out of ten he will do the same old way. Unless some one brings the science and the workman together, the workman will slip back as sure as fate into the same old ways, and will not practice the better, the scientific, method. When I say, make the workman do his work in accordance with the laws of science, I do not say *make* in an arbitrary sense. If I did it would apply far more to the employing than to the working class, because in the work of changing from the old to the new system, nine-tenths of our troubles are concerned with those on the management side, and only one-tenth with the workmen. Those in the management are infinitely more stubborn, infinitely harder to make change their ways than are the workmen. So I want to qualify the word *make;* it has rather a hard sound. Some one must *inspire* the men to make the change, for it will not occur naturally. If you allow things to wait, it will not occur in ten years when it should occur in two months. Some one must take it in hand.

The fourth principle of Scientific Management is a little more difficult than the others to make clear. It is almost impossible to explain to the average man what I mean by it, until he sees one of our companies organized under Scientific Management.

The fourth principle is a deliberate division of the work which was formerly done by the workmen into two sections, one of which is handed over to the management. An immense mass of new duties is thrown on the management which formerly belonged to the workmen. And it is this handing of duties which they never dreamed of assuming before over to those on the management side, requiring cooperation between the management and the workmen, which accounts more than anything else for the fact that there has never been a strike under Scientific Management. If you and I are doing a piece of work together, and realize that we are mutually dependent upon one another, it is impossible for us to quarrel. We may quarrel, perhaps, during the first few days. Some men find it difficult to cooperate. But when they once get to going and see that the prosperity of both sides depends on each man doing his share of the work, what is there to strike about? They realize they cannot strike against the friend who is helping them. That is what it is, a case of helpfulness. I think I can say truthfully that under Scientific Management the managers are more the servants of the men than the men are the servants of the managers. I think I can say that the sense of obligation is greater on the part of the management than on the part of the men. They have to do their share and be always ready. That is the feeling of those on the management side under Scientific Management.

In order to make that equal division a little clearer, I will say that in one of our machine shops, for instance where we do miscellaneous work, not work that is repeated over and over again, there will be at least one man on the management side for every three workmen throughout the whole establishment. That indicates a real division of work between the two sides. And those men on the management side are busy, just as busy as the workmen, and far more profitably busy than they were before.

Let me repeat briefly these four principles of Scientific Management. I want you to see these four principles plainly as the essence of the illustration I am going to give you of Scientific Management. They are the development of a science to replace the old rule-of-thumb methods; the scientific selection and then the progressive teaching and development of the workmen; the bringing of the scientifically selected workmen and the science together; and then this almost equal division of the work between the management and the men.

I wish to convince you of the importance of these principles. So far what I have said has been mere assertion. The only means that I have of convincing you of the value of these principles is to give illustrations of their application. But I fear my time is too short to give more than two or three.

I usually begin with the most elementary kind of labor that I know, and try to show the immense power of those four principles when applied even to that extraordinarily elementary form of labor. The simplest kind of work that I know is handling pig iron. A man stoops down to the ground or a pile, picks up with his hands a piece of pig iron weighing usually about ninety pounds, walks a certain number of steps and drops it on a pile or on the ground. I dare say that it seems preposterous to you to say that there is any such thing as the science of handling pig iron, that there is any such thing as the training of a workman and the cooperation and the equal division of the work between the two sides in handling pig iron. It seems absolutely preposterous. But I assure you that had I time I could convince every one of you that there is a great science in handling pig iron. It takes a little too long to give that particular illustration,* and I very much regret that I must begin with a form of labor which is far more scientific than handling pig iron, namely, shoveling dirt.

I dare say that you think there is no science in shoveling dirt, that any one can shovel dirt. "Why," you say, "to shovel it you just shovel, that is all there is to it." Those who have had anything to do with Scientific Management realize, however, that *there is a best way in doing everything*, and that that best way can always be formulated into certain rules; that you can get your knowledge away from the old chaotic rule-of-thumb knowledge into organized knowledge. And if any one of you should start to find the most important element in the science of shoveling, every one of you with a day's or two days' thought would be on the track of finding it. You would not find it in a day, but you would know what to look for. We found it after we started to think on the subject

---

* It is given on pages 58–65.—EDITOR

of shoveling. And what is it? There are very many elements, but I want to call your attention to this important one. At what shovel-load will a man do his biggest day's work? There must be some best shovel-load; what is it?

The workers of the Bethlehem Steel Company, for instance, almost all owned their own shovels, and I have seen them go day after day to the same shovel for every kind of work, from shoveling rice coal, three and a half pounds to a shovel-load, to shoveling heavy wet ore, about thirty-eight pounds to the shovel-load. Is three and a half pounds right or is thirty-eight pounds right? Now the moment the question "What is the proper shovel-load?" is asked under Scientific Management, it does not become the duty of the manager to ask some one, to ask any shoveler, what is the best. The old style was, "John, how much ought you to take on your shovel?" Under Scientific Management it is the duty of the management to *know* what is the best, not to take what some one thinks. We selected two first-class shovelers. Never examine any one but a first-class man. By first-class I do not mean something impossible to get, or even difficult to get. Very few people know what you mean when you say first-class. I think I can explain it to you better by talking about something with which we are all familiar. We know mighty little about men, but there is hardly one of us here who does not know a good deal about horses, because we are in the habit of studying horses. Now if you have a stable full of horses containing large dray horses, carriage horses, saddle horses and so on, and want to pick a first-class horse for hauling a coal wagon, I know every one of you here would take the dray horse. I do not believe any of you would take the trotting horse and call him first-class at all. That is what I mean when I say *first-class man*. If you have a very small stable, when you have a good deal of coal to haul you may have to hitch your trotting horse to a light grocery wagon or even to your buggy to haul coal. But that is not a first-class horse for the purpose, and no one would think of studying a trotting horse hauling a buggy of coal to find what a first-class horse should do in hauling coal. There are many people who say, "You are looking for impossible people; you are setting a pace that nobody can live up to." Not at all. We are taking the man adapted to the work we wish done.

So when we wanted to study the science of shoveling we took two men and said, "You are good shovelers; we want you to work squarely. We are going to ask you to do a lot of fool things, and we are going to pay you double wages while this investigation is going on. It will probably last two or three months. This man will be over you all day long with a stop-watch. He will time you; he will count the shovel-loads and tell you what to do. He does not want you to hurry; just go at your ordinary fair pace. But if either of you fellows tries to soldier on us, that will be the end of it; we will find you out as sure as you are born, and we will fire you out of this place. All we want is a square day's work; no soldiering. If you don't want to take that job, don't, but if you do we are very glad to pay you double wages while you are doing it." These men said they would be very glad to do it, and they were perfectly square; they were ready to do a fair day's work. That was all we asked of them, not something that would tire them out or exhaust them, but something they could live under forty years and be all right.

We began by taking the maximum load on the shovel and counting the shovelfuls all day long and weighing the tonnage at the end of the day. I think it was about thirty-eight pounds to the shovel. We found how much those men could do when they were shoveling at thirty-eight pounds to the shovel on an average. And then we got shorter shovels holding about thirty-four pounds, and measured the tonnage per day, and it was greater than when they were using the thirty-eight pound shovel. They shoveled more with the thirty-four pound shovel-loads than with the thirty-eight pound shovel-loads. Again we reduced the load to thirty pounds and they did a still greater tonnage; again to twenty-eight pounds, and another increase; and the load kept on increasing as we diminished the shovel-load until we reached about twenty-one pounds; at twenty-one pounds the man did his biggest day's work. With twenty pounds, with eighteen pounds, with seventeen, and with fourteen, they did again a smaller day's work. Starting with a thirty-eight pound shovel, they went higher and higher until the biggest day's work was done with a twenty-one pound shovel; but when they got the lighter shovel the load went down as the shovel-load diminished.

The foundation of that part of the science of shoveling, then, lies in always giving a shoveler a shovel which will hold twenty-one pounds, whatever the material he is using.

What were the consequences of that? In the Bethlehem Steel Works we had to build a shovel-room for our common laborers. Up to that time the men had owned their own shovels. We had to equip this room with eight or ten different kinds of shovels, so that whatever the man went at, whether rice coal on the one hand, or very heavy ore on the other, he would have just a twenty-one pound load. That meant organization in place of no organization.

It meant also arranging that each one of the laborers in that yard had the right shovel every day for the kind of material he was going to work on. That required more organization. In place of the old-fashioned foreman who walked around with his men to work with them, telling them what to do, it meant the building of a large, elaborate labor office where three college men worked, besides their clerks and assistants, planning the work for each of these workmen at least one day in advance. That yard was about two miles long and half a mile wide; you cannot scatter 500 to 600 men over a space of that size, doing all kinds of miscellaneous work, and get the man, the shovel and the other implements, and the work together at the right time unless you have an organization. It meant, then, building a big labor office and playing a game of chess one day in advance with these 500 men, locating them just as you would locate chessmen on your board. It required a time-table and a knowledge of how long it took them to do each kind of work.

It meant also informing the men each day just what they had done the day before and just what they were to do that day. In order to do that, as each man came in the morning he had to reach his hand up to a pigeonhole (most of them could not read and write, but they could all find their pigeonholes) and take out two slips of paper. One was a yellow slip and one was a white slip. If they found the yellow slip, those men who could not read and write knew perfectly well what it meant; it was just the general information: "Yesterday you did not earn the money that a first-class man ought to earn. We want you to earn at least 60 per cent beyond what other laborers are paid around Bethlehem. You failed to earn that much yesterday; there is something wrong." It is merely a notice to the man that there is something wrong. The other piece of paper told him what implement to use. He went to the tool-room, presented it, received the proper implement, and took it down to the part of the yard in which he was to work.

When any of these workmen fell down for three or four days in succession, the old way would be to call him up and say, "Here, John, you are no good; get out of this; you are not doing a day's work. I don't have any man here who is not doing a day's work. Now get out of this." But that is not the way with Scientific Management. The moment the management sees that this man has fallen down, that it is something more than an accident, then a teacher—not a bulldozer, but a *teacher*—is sent out to him to find out what is the matter, and to study the man for the purpose of correcting his fault. In nine cases out of ten that teacher would perhaps find that the man had simply forgotten something about the art of shoveling. I suppose you are skeptical about this "art of shoveling," but let me tell you there is a great deal to it. We have found that the most efficient method of shoveling is to put your right arm down on your right hip, hold your shovel on your left leg, and when you shovel into the pile throw the weight of your body upon the shovel. It does not take any muscle to do that; the weight of your body throws it if you get your arm braced. But if you attempt to do as most shovelers do, take it with your arms and shove into a stubborn pile, you are wasting a great deal of effort. Time and again we found that a man had forgotten his instructions and was throwing the weight of his arms instead of the weight of his body. The teacher would go to him and say, "You have forgotten what I told you about shoveling; I don't wonder you are not getting your premium; you ought to be getting 60 per cent more money. You are falling out of the first class. Now I want to show you again. Just watch the way this thing is done." The teacher would stand by him *as a friend* and show him how to earn his premium. Or perhaps if he found that the man was really not suited to that work, for instance that he was too light for it, the man would then be transferred to a lighter kind of work for which he was suited. It is in that way, by kindly and intimate personal study of them, that we find to what workmen are adapted.

All of that takes money, and it is an important and very fair question whether it pays. Can you pay for all these time-study men who are developing the art of shoveling? Can you pay for your shovel tool-room, for the telephone system and all the clerks and teachers? The only answer to that is these facts. At the end of about three years we had practically the whole of the yard labor of the Bethlehem Steel Works transferred from the old piece-work and day-work plan to the new scientific plan. Those workmen under the old plan had earned $1.15 a day. Under the new plan they earned $1.85 a day, an increase of more than 60 per cent in wages. We had them studied and a report made. We found that they were practically all sober, that most of them were saving some little money, that they lived better than they ever had before, and that they were as contented a set of men as could be found together anywhere, a magnificent body of carefully selected men. That is what the men got out of it.

What did the company get out of it? The old cost for handling a ton of materials in the yard of the Bethlehem Steel Company was between seven and eight cents a ton. The new cost, after all the costs of the clerical work in the office and the tool-room, of the teaching, the telephone system, the new implements and the higher wages, were taken into consideration, was between three and four cents a ton. And the actual cash saving to the Bethlehem Steel Company during the last year was between $70,000 and $80,000. That is what the company got out of it, and therefore the system is justified from the points of view both of the men and of the management.

I am very sure that I could convince you that the ratio of gain of Scientific Management when applied to a trade that requires a high-class mechanic, is far greater than when applied to work like shoveling. The difficulty which I find is to convince men of the universality of these principles, that *they are applicable to all kinds of human effort.* I should like to convince you, I am sure that I could convince you, that with *any* of the more intricate kinds of work, the gain must be enormously greater than with the simple work; that no high-class mechanic can possibly do what he should for his own sake and for the employer's sake, without the friendly cooperation of a man on the management side. That is what I should like to prove to you, prove beyond the shadow of a doubt.

Take the case of a machinist who is doing work that is repeated, we will say, over and over again. He is not the highest class mechanic, but he is fairly well up. It may be questioned whether it is possible for any scientific knowledge to help an intelligent mechanic, a man, for instance, who has had a high school education and who has worked for his whole life as a machinist. I want to show you that that man needs the help of—not a higher order of man, nothing of that sort, but of a man with a different type of education from his own; that the skilled workman needs it far more even than the cheap laborer needs it in order to do his work right.

I take an actual case, that of a shop manufacturing small machines. This was a department of a large company which had been running under the old system many years. The article was a patented device that had been manufactured in this department about twelve years, perhaps more, by some 300 workmen. These articles varied somewhat in size but they were made by the thousands. The men would naturally become highly skilled. Each man had his own machine, ran it from year end to year end, made comparatively few parts, and therefore became skilled in his work.

Now the owner of this establishment was a very progressive man, and he came to the conclusion that he wanted to investigate Scientific Management. So he sent for my friend, Mr. Barth† to see what

---

† Carl George Lange Barth, 1860–1939, mechanical engineer and instructor in manual work and mathematics. He introduced the Taylor System in machine shops. —EDITOR

Mr. Barth could do for him. After they had had a little sparring on the subject, Mr. Barth rather mortified the owner by telling him that he could come pretty close to doubling the output of his shop. After they had sparred a little over that, Mr. Barth suggested that he make a test to show the men in the shop what he could do. So a typical machine was selected, a machine which they both agreed was fairly representative of the machines in the shop, and the work which was then being done noted; the kind of work, the character of it and the time which it should take to do it was written down. Then Mr. Barth proceeded to study the machine, in just the way under Scientific Management all machines are analyzed in all shops that we go to. We do not go to some foreman or superintendent, or to the maker of the machine, and ask, "How fast do you think we should run this machine?" Not at all. A careful, thorough analysis was made of the possibilities of that machine, and to do that Mr. Barth used four slide-rules. One slide-rule will solve any problem in gearing in almost no time. It is a gear slide-rule. Another solves any problem about belts in a fraction of a minute. Another tells you how many pounds pressure a chip of any shape or kind will exert on the cutting tool, and therefore shows you how much resistance you have to overcome with your machine. The fourth slide-rule tells you what cutting-speed you can use with any kind of metal, with any depth of cut, with any feed and with any shape tool.

Now with these four rules it is possible scientifically to analyze the machine, to know how it should be speeded for the particular kind of work that is in hand. And let me tell you—this may seem an extraordinary statement—let me tell you that there is not one machine in fifty in the average machine shop in this country that is speeded right. I say that with all confidence. I say it with perfect confidence, because last spring I was invited by the tool builders, the makers of these machines, to address them at their annual meeting, and I challenged them to contradict that fact. They were there, representatives of the tool builders of this country, and not one man took up my challenge. They knew, just as well as I know, that their speeds are nine-tenths guess and one-tenth knowledge, that they do not take into consideration the peculiarities of the shop their machines go into, in one case in fifty. They have no means of knowing the kind of material the machines are to cut, and the machines are speeded practically the same for every shop they go to, whereas each machine should be speeded to suit the average of the work that is to be done in a particular shop.

After Mr. Barth had inspected that machine by means of these slide-rules, in two or three hours he was able to write the prescription for it, showing what should be done to have it right. And then, after he had given directions to have the machine speeded right, he went home and made a slide-rule by means of which, when he returned to the shop, he was able to show the workmen, the foreman, and the owner of that shop just how the machine should be run in various cases. Pieces of metal were put into the machine, similar to those which were ordinarily run in it, and his smallest gain was two and a half times as much, and his largest gain nine times as much work as had been done before. That is typical of what can be done in the average machine shop in this country.

Why? Because the science of cutting metals is a true science, and because the machine shops of this country are run, we can almost say, without the slightest reference to that science. They are run by the old rule-of-thumb method just as they were fifty years ago. The science is almost neglected, and yet it is true science.

I want to show you in a general way what that science is, so that you will understand why it is that a man who had never seen that particular machine, who had never seen that work, was able to compete with the workman who had been working for ten or twelve years on the same machine, who had the help of the foreman and of his superintendent,—for it was a well-run establishment; how a man who had never seen that work, but who was equipped with a knowledge of the science, was able to make it do from two and a half to nine times as much work as had been done before. I want to show you what it is, because that is the essence of Scientific Management, the development of a science which is of real use when applied with the cooperation of the management to help the workmen.

I spoke at the beginning about an ordinary piece-work fight which went on between a foreman who tried to do his duty and his men. At the end of that bitter fight of two or three years, I obtained permission from William Sellers, who was then the president of the Midvale Steel Works, to spend some money in educating the foreman of the Midvale Steel Works so that he should have at least a fraction of the knowledge of his men. And one of the subjects which we took up at that time, one in which the foreman needed most education, was the science of cutting metals, for metal-cutting was the whole work of the shop. And I believed, just as Mr. Sellers believed, just as almost every mechanic at that time believed, that the science of cutting metals consisted mainly if not entirely in finding the proper cutting angles of the tool.

As you all know, each metal-cutting tool has, properly speaking, three cutting angles. It has the clearance angle, the side slope and the back slope. And it was my opinion, just as it was the opinion of almost every machinist that I knew, that if you could get the right combination of cutting angles you could cut steel and iron a great deal faster than we were then doing. So we started out to make a careful investigation as to what those cutting angles should be.

We were exceedingly fortunate in having what hardly any shop in the United States had at that time, a very large boring room. We were then making locomotive tires. That was a considerable part of the business of the Midvale Steel Works at that time. We had a very large boring mill available, sixty-six inches in diameter, and a very large uniform body of metal and tires weighing 2,000 pounds to put on it. So we had an opportunity to do what very few people had the opportunity to do. A sixty-six-inch diameter mill was at that time an unusually large one, so we put our tire on that mill and, having enough metal in that one piece to run three or four months, we could eliminate possible errors resulting from variability of the metal. At the end of six months we found that these angles which we supposed were of the greatest consequence counted for but little in the art of cutting metals. The two things which every machinist must know every time he puts a piece of work into his lathe, if he wishes to do it right, are the speed he should run his machine and the feed he should use in order to do his fastest work. Those two things sound very simple indeed. But to know them is to know the science of cutting metals. At the end of six months we found that the thing we were hunting for, the question of angles, had very little bearing on the problem, but we had unearthed a gold mine of possible information. And when I was able to show Mr. Sellers the possibilities of knowledge ahead, he said at once, "Go right ahead, go on spending the money." And for practically twenty-six years, with here and there a year or two of intermission, went on that series of experiments to determine the laws of the science of cutting metals. It was found that there were twelve great variable elements which enter into metal-cutting operations. All that was done in twenty-six years was to investigate these twelve elements, to find out the facts connected with them, to record and tabulate these facts, to reduce them to mathematical formulae, and finally to make those mathematical formulae applicable in everyday work.

I know that it will seem almost inconceivable that such a time should be taken, and I want to show you how it is possible that it took that length of time. At various times in this investigation ten different machines were built and equipped and run for the purpose of determining the various elements of this science. While we were at the Midvale Steel Works we had no trouble at all, because they knew the value of the elements which we were studying; they knew the commercial value of them; but after we left there our only means of continuing these experiments was to give the information which we had up to date in payment to any one who would build us a machine and furnish the labor and materials to continue the investigation. So most of these ten different machines were built in that way by men who were willing and anxious to trade their money, in the shape of new equipment, new forgings, new castings, and new labor, for the knowledge that had been obtained from previous experiments.

Let me briefly call your attention to some of the variable elements. I will not bother you with all the twelve, but I want to let you see enough of them to appreciate what I mean by this science of cutting metals. Investigations similar to this are bound to be made in every industry in this country, scientific investigations of those elements which go to make up the science, whatever that science is; that is the reason why I am dwelling on it. It is not an isolated case. It is perhaps the longest-drawn-out investigation that has been made, but it is simply typical of what is bound to take place in every industry.

One of the first discoveries which we made—and it seems an exceedingly simple one—was that if you throw a stream of water on the chip and tool at the point at which the shaving of iron is being cut off from the forging, you can increase your cutting speed 40 per cent. You have a 40 per cent gain just by doing that little thing alone. That we found out within the first six months. Mr. Sellers had the courage of his convictions; he did not believe it at first, but when we proved to him that it was true, he tore down the old shop and replaced it with another so as to get that 40 per cent increase in the cutting speed. He built a shop with water drains extending under the floor to carry off the water with which the tools were cooled to a central settling tank; from there it was pumped up again to a tank in the roof and carried from there through proper piping to every tool, so that the workman did not need to spend much time in adjusting a stream which would flow on to any tool in any position. He was a broad enough man to see that it paid him to build a new shop to get that 40 per cent.

Now our competitors came right to the Midvale Steel Works without any hesitation. They were invited to come there, and in twenty years just one competitor used that knowledge and built a shop in which it was possible to throw a heavy stream of water on the tools, and that was a shop started by men who had left the Midvale Steel Works and who knew enough to do this. That shows the slowness of men, in that trade at least, to take advantage of a 40 per cent gain in cutting.

That is one of the twelve elements, a very simple one, the simplest of all. Let me show you one or two more.

There is the old diamond-point tool, used when I was a boy in practically all shops throughout the country. One of the first suggestions that I had for an experiment was from Mr. John Bancroft,‡ now one of the ablest engineers in the country. He suggested that I try the effect of using a round-nose tool, with a round cutting-edge. Hardly a single piece of original work was done by us in Scientific Management. Everything that we have has come from the suggestion of some one else. There is no originality about Scientific Management. And, gentlemen, I am proud of it; I am not ashamed of it, because the man who thinks he can place his originality against the world's evolution, against the combined knowledge of the world, is pretty poor stuff.

Now, that diamond-point tool was almost universally used at that time, and I do not believe there is one mechanic in fifty now who knows why it was used. It was used because in the primitive shops, such as the one in which I served my apprenticeship, we all had to make and dress our own tools. There was no tool dresser. We would heat the metal, lay it on the edge of the anvil one way and ask a friend to hit it a crack, and then turn it around and repeat the process, and simply turning it and hitting it with the sledge would give it the diamond point. That is the only reason why a tool of that shape was in use. It was a tradition. It had no scientific basis.

After a sufficient number of experiments, we found that a round-nose tool was far superior to a diamond-point tool, but it took a long time after we made that discovery before we found what kind of a round-nose tool. It took years before we were through with the experiment to determine what curve was the best when all things were considered, because there are many considerations which come in. There is the speed, the convenience of handling, the kind of work to be done, and so on.

Having, then, decided that a round-nose tool was the best, we had to make another investigation. If you have a light cut taken on your tool in one case, a heavy cut in another, and a still heavier one in another, it is a matter of plain common sense that you could

‡ John Sellers Bancroft, 1843–1919, mechanical engineer and inventor. Member ASME.—EDITOR

of course in one case run a very much higher cutting-speed than in another. How fast can you run? That is a question for accurate scientific investigation. The investigation, simply to determine that fact, took altogether, I think, as much as two years. And even after we had determined the facts, it was many years before we finally got the proper mathematical expression of those facts. That is a totally different matter. Before we had reduced our knowledge to a true mathematical formula which could be worked with, it was a question of years.

The next investigation, perhaps the most spectacular of all, was to answer the question, what is the effect of the chemical composition of the tool and its best treatment? The old-fashioned tools when I served my apprenticeship were all made of carbon steel. But it has been found that by putting tungsten in those tools one can make them withstand a higher amount of heat and still not lose their cutting-edge. A part, then, of the study of the art or science of cutting metals was to make a thorough, scientific investigation of the possibilities of alloy steel, not only with the new metal tungsten, but with other alloys which presented possibilities; so we varied the quantities of tungsten, chromium, molybdenum and one or two other elements, until at the end of three years of continuous experimenting the modern high-speed steel was developed; that is, a certain kind of steel which when heated in a certain revolutionary way would enable you to run, to be accurate, just seven times as fast as with the carbon steel. The discovery of high-speed steel and its treatment was the result of investigations. Most people think it was a mere accident, that some fools were fooling around and by accident discovered this thing; but I assure you three or four years of hard study and investigation by chemists and metallurgists working according to the most scientific methods were required. In these various experiments $200,000 were spent and from 800,000 to 1,000,000 pounds of metal were cut up into chips.

Perhaps the most difficult phase of the experiments was getting steel of uniform hardness for experimental purposes. To carry on our elaborate experiments when high-speed steel came in, we had to have at least 20,000 pounds of metal to experiment on, and it is almost impossible to get 20,000 pounds which are uniform. We finally solved it and obtained metal which was sufficiently uniform by using exactly the same processes which are used in making the great high-power cannon for the army and navy. That is, we forged metal under a forging-press, and then oil-tempered and annealed it until we got a uniform body of metal. The tempering and annealing resulted in making the steel finer and finer and making all the crystallized structure uniform.

I want to explain why twenty-six years were necessary to carry out these experiments. Time after time we would have to throw away six months' work because eleven of these elements had slipped up while we were experimenting with the twelfth. If hard spots appeared in the steel, a whole line of experiments was thrown out and we would have to get a new forging and start all over again. It was the difficulty of that sort of thing, holding eleven elements constant while we were getting the twelfth, which made that problem as difficult as it was. When those experiments had first been reduced to facts, and then the facts to diagrams, and then curves drawn through the diagrams and finally mathematical formulae made to fit those diagrams, then we were on the road towards the development of a science. We finally developed twelve formulae to represent the twelve variables, of which this is a specimen:

$$V = \frac{11.9}{F^{0.665}\left(\dfrac{48}{3}D\right)^{0.2373} + \frac{2.4}{18 + 48D}}$$

When one has a lot of mathematical formulae of that sort, it seems at first the idea of a lunatic to imagine that any one could get any use out of them. That is, all of our friends, when they found that our experiments were resulting in such formulae as these, said, "Why, you are nothing but rank crazy; you will never be able to use these things." And a great work, greater than the experiments which gave us these formulae, was the work of giving these formulae a form which would make them usable for the ordinary machinist. We kept mathematicians working on that problem for about eighteen years.

Now you must realize that a mathematical problem with twelve variables is a big thing. During that time we went to the great mathematicians in the country, the professors in our universities, and offered them any price to solve that problem for us. Not one of them would touch it; they all said, "You can solve a problem with four variables if you have your four equations, possibly; beyond that it is an indeterminate problem, and it is all nonsense thinking of getting a mathematical solution for it." I dare say you people think I am trying to prove that Mr. Barth and Mr. Gantt§ and these other gentlemen are very remarkable men. Nothing of the kind. This is the point I want to make: that it is a long, tedious operation to solve a problem of that sort, or to solve any of the intricate problems connected with the mechanic arts, or those that are going to arise in any art. It is a difficult thing to do. But very ordinary men with ordinary equipment can solve and make useful any problem, I do not care how difficult it is, if they will only give the time and the money and the patience; they will solve it.

At the end of eighteen years these men had devised a little machine, a slide-rule, which solves the problem with twelve independent variables in about twenty seconds. That is put into the hands of an ordinary lathe man who knows nothing about mathematics, and by means of it that man determines under which one of 800 or 900 conditions pertaining to the particular job he will do his fastest work. It was for that reason that Mr. Barth, with his slide-rule, was able to more than compete with the mechanic who had spent twelve years in the old-fashioned rule-of-thumb way of cutting a particular kind of metal on his particular kind of machine; just for that reason, because the amount of knowledge which that machinist needed to have in order to solve that problem was utterly impossible for any one to have.

What I am trying to show you is, that the more intelligent the high-class mechanic the more he needs the help of the man with

---

§ See pages 105–129.—EDITOR

the theoretical knowledge; he must have it even more than the ordinary laborer must have it. And that is why this cooperation, in which the management does one part of the work and the workman another, must accomplish overwhelmingly more work in all cases than the old method of leaving to the workman both the determining how and the performance.

There is just one thing more that I want to say; something that I am sure you are all thinking of. I find this question in the mind of every one who is considering Scientific Management. It may be that this combination of the science and the workman turns out more work than before, but doesn't it make a wooden man out of the workman? Doesn't it make him a machine? Doesn't it reduce him to the level of an implement?

I want to give one or two answers to that. The first is this: that under the new system every single workingman is raised up, is developed, is taught, so that he can do a higher, a better, and a more interesting class of work than he could before. The ordinary laborer is taught to run the drill-press in the machine shop; the drill-press hand becomes a lathe hand; the lathe hand becomes a tool maker; the tool maker—now I am speaking of types of men, you understand, not literally—the tool maker becomes one of the teachers. He is the man in the planning room. He is the man who makes up this one out of three who is transferred to the management side, so that the best workmen, who before would have remained workmen, are on the management side and become teachers and helpers of the other workmen. I want to emphasize the brotherly feeling which exists under Scientific Management. It is no longer a case of master and men, as under the old system, but it is a case of one friend helping another and each fellow doing the kind of work that he is best fitted for. You boys have here in the college one pretty good piece of Scientific Management, and that is football,—a good case of cooperation, training and teaching, and that is the fine feature about football, that it does enforce a fine method of friendly cooperation.

Does this make workmen into wooden men? Let us answer the second question. I have said, and I repeat, that no one claims any originality for Scientific Management; it was all done before. I do not know of a person who claims any originality for it whatever. It has simply taken what other people were doing before. Long before we had any development of Scientific Management, there was in existence a far finer case of Scientific Management than we have ever succeeded in developing. The finest mechanic in the world had developed Scientific Management long before we touched it or ever dreamed of it. You all know him, every one of you; he is the modern surgeon. In his operations five or six men cooperate, each one doing in turn just what he should do. How does that finest mechanic teach his apprentices? Do you suppose that when the young surgeons come to their teachers, the skilled surgeons, they are told first of all: "Now, boys, what we want first is your initiative; we want you to use your brains and originality to develop the best methods of doing surgical work. Of course you know we do have our own ways of performing these operations, but don't let that hamper you for one instant in your work. What we want is your originality and your initiative. Of course you know, for example, when we are amputating a leg and come to the bone, we take a saw and cut the bone off. Don't let that disturb you for a minute; if you like it better, take an axe, take a hatchet, anything you please; what we want is originality. What we want of all things is originality on your part."

Now that surgeon says to his apprentices just what we say to our apprentices under Scientific Management. He says: "Not on your life. We want your originality, but we want you to invent upward and not downward. We do not want any of your originality until you know the best method of doing work that we know, the best method that is now known to modern surgery. So you just get busy and learn the best method that is known to date under modern surgery; then, when you have got to the top by the present method, invent upward; then use your originality."

That is exactly what we say to our men. We say, "We do not know the best; we are sure that within two or three years a better method will be developed than we know of; but what we know is the result of a long series of experiments and careful study of every element connected with shop practice; these standards that lie before you are the results of these studies. We ask you to learn how to use these standards as they are, and after that, the moment any man sees an improved standard, a better way of doing anything than we are doing, come to us with it; your suggestion will not only be welcome but we will join you in making a carefully tried experiment, which will satisfy both you and us and any other man that your improvement is or is not better than anything before. If that experiment shows that your method is better than ours, your method will become our method and every one of us will adopt that method until somebody gets a better one."

In that way you are able to apply a true science to mechanical work, and only in that way. If you allow each man to do his own way, just exactly as he pleases, without any regard to science, science melts right away. You must have standards. We get some of our greatest improvements from the workmen in that way. The workmen, instead of holding back, are eager to make suggestions. When one is adopted it is named after the man who suggested it, and he is given a premium for having developed a new standard. So in that way we get the finest kind of team work, we have true cooperation, and our method, instead of inventing things that were out of date forty years ago, leads on always to something better than has been known before.

HENRY LAURENCE GANTT

(1861–1919)

HENRY LAURENCE GANTT was for many years a close associate of Frederick W. Taylor (pp. 55–103), later branching out as a consultant on his own. Their viewpoints on management were in many respects the same. But where Taylor's somewhat austere attitude emphasized analysis and organization of the work in solving problems, Gantt gave major attention to the man who was doing it. He insisted that willingness to use correct methods and skills in performing a task is as important as knowing the methods and having the skills in the first place. Thus he perceived the weight of the human element in productivity and approached the concept of motivation as we understand it today.

In one presentation that he made to The American Society of Mechanical Engineers, Gantt described a task and bonus system of wage payments that exemplified this point of view and had a far-reaching effect on compensation methods; the emphasis on the common interests of employer and employee is characteristic. In another paper (pp. 107–121) he stressed his philosophy that "to teach and to lead" will be the management technique of the future, as compared with the then-prevailing "to drive."

As time went on, Gantt became increasingly interested in management's broad obligations to society. In "The Parting of the Ways," published in 1919, he called for a return to the public service philosophy of business, from which he felt management had departed (pp. 107–121)—a return that gained momentum in the 1930's and has been strongly influential ever since.

TRAINING WORKMEN IN HABITS OF INDUSTRY AND COOPERATION

BY H. L. GANTT, *Pawtucket, R.I.*
(*Member of the Society*).

THE WIDESPREAD INTEREST in the training of work-
men which has been so marked for several years is due to the evident
need for better methods of training than those now generally in
vogue.

The one point in which these methods as a class seem to be
lacking is that they do not lay enough stress on the fact that workmen must have industry as well as knowledge and skill.

Habits of industry are far more valuable than any kind of knowledge or skill, for with such habits as a basis, the problem of acquiring knowledge and skill is much simplified. Without industry,
knowledge and skill are of little value, and sometimes a great
detriment.

If workmen are systematically trained in habits of industry, it
has been found possible, not only to train many of them to be
efficient in whatever capacity they are needed, but to develop an
effective system of cooperation between workmen and foreman.

This is not a theory, but the record of a fact.

It is too much to hope, however, that the methods about to be
described will be adopted extensively in the near future, for the

Reprinted from *Transactions of The American Society of Mechanical Engineers*, Volume 30, pages 1037–1048. Paper presented at December 1908 meeting of the Society,
New York. Used by permission of the Society.

great majority of managers, whose success is based mainly on their personal ability, will hesitate before adopting what seems to them the slower and less forceful policy of studying problems and training workmen; but should they do so they will have absolutely no desire to return to their former methods.

The general policy of the past has been to drive, but the era of force must give way to that of knowledge, and the policy of the future will be to teach and to lead, to the advantage of all concerned. The vision of workmen in general eager to cooperate in carrying out the results of scientific investigations must be dismissed as a dream of the millennium, but results so far accomplished indicate that nothing will do more to bring about that millennium than training workmen in habits of industry and cooperation. A study of the principles on which such training has been successfully established will convince the most skeptical that if they are carried out good results must follow. An outline of these principles has already been submitted to the Society in a paper entitled "A Bonus System of Rewarding Labor."[1]

Under this system each man has his work assigned to him in the form of a task to be done by a prescribed method with definite appliances and to be completed within a certain time. The task is based on a detailed investigation by a trained expert of the best methods of doing the work; and the task setter, or his assistant, acts as an instructor to teach the workmen to do the work in the manner and time specified. If the work is done within the time allowed by the expert, and is up to the standard for quality, the workman receives extra compensation in addition to his day's pay. If it is not done in the time set, or is not up to the standard for quality, the workman receives his day's pay only.

This system, in connection with the other work of Mr. F. W. Taylor, so greatly increased the output and reduced the cost of the work in the large machine shop of the Bethlehem Steel Company

---

[1] A Bonus System of Rewarding Labor, December 1901, a system of task work with a bonus which had recently been introduced by the writer into the large machine shop of the Bethlehem Steel Company, as a part of the system of management being introduced into their works by Mr. F. W. Taylor.

that for the past seven years the writer has given a large portion of his time to the development of its possibilities. The results have far exceeded his expectations.

In his closing remarks on the above paper, the writer emphasized the value of the system as a means of training workmen, and the late Dr. Robert H. Thurston* in his discussion of it was so optimistic as to the results it would produce on "workmen and foremen and employer alike" that the writer felt that his enthusiasm over a new and promising method had carried him, perhaps, a little too far. Results have fully justified Dr. Thurston's predictions, however, for today the method has been developed as a practical system of education and training for all, from the highest to the lowest. The fact, so repeatedly emphasized by Mr. Taylor, *that tasks should be set only as the result of a scientific investigation,* has proved of an educational value hardly to be over-estimated, for the scientific investigation of a process that has been developed without the assistance of science almost always reveals inconsistencies which it is possible to eliminate, thus perfecting the process and at the same time reducing its cost.

It is this scientific investigation that points to improvement in methods and educates owners and managers; but the average work-man is interested only in his daily wage and has no special desire to learn improved methods. The results of our investigations are of little practical value, therefore, unless we can first teach our work-men how to use them, and then can induce them to do as they are taught.

Practical Application

For this purpose *an instructor, a task and a bonus* have been found most useful. People as a rule prefer to work at the speed and in the manner to which they have been accustomed, but are usually willing to work at any reasonable speed and in any reason-able manner, if sufficient inducement is offered for so doing, and

---

* Robert Henry Thurston, 1839–1903. American engineer and educator. Founder and first president of ASME.—EDITOR

if they are so trained as to be able to earn the reward. In carrying out this plan we try to find men who are already skilled and able to perform the task set. It frequently happens, however, that the number of such men is insufficient and it takes time to train the unskilled to a proper degree of efficiency; but with a bonus as an incentive, and a proper instructor, a very fair proportion of the unskilled finally succeed in performing a task that was at first entirely beyond them.

Unskilled workmen, who under these conditions have become skilled in one kind of work, readily learn another, and soon begin to realize that they can, in a measure at least, make up for their loss in not having learned a trade.

As they become more skilled, they form better habits of work, lose less time and become more reliable. Their health improves, and the improvement in their general appearance is very marked. This improvement in health seems to be due to a more regular and active life, combined with a greater interest in their work, for it is a well known fact that *work in which we are interested and which holds our attention without any effort on our part, tires us much less than that we have to force ourselves to do.* The task with a reward for its accomplishment produces this interest and holds the attention, with the invariable results of more work, better work and better satisfied workers.

The Task and Bonus method of training not only furnishes the workman with the required knowledge, but by offering an inducement to utilize that knowledge properly, trains him in proper habits of work.

Habits of Work

In all work both *quantity* and *quality* must be considered, and our task method demands a maximum quantity, all of which must be up to the standard for quality. Workmen trained under this method acquire the habit of doing a large amount of work well, and disprove the oft-repeated fallacy that good work must be done slowly. As a matter of fact, our quickest workers almost always do the best work when following instructions. We set great store by the habit of working quickly, for no matter how much skill a workman may have, he will not attain the best success without quickness as well.

Habits of work in a mechanic are comparable with *habits of thought* in an engineer, and our industrial schools should make proper habits of work the basis on which to build their training in manual dexterity. The engineering school does not make engineers, but tries to furnish its graduates with an equipment that will enable them to utilize readily and rapidly their own experience and that of others. In the same manner, industrial training schools should equip their graduates with habits of industry that will make them as mechanics capable, and willing to do a large amount of good work.

As the writer sees it, one of the most valuable assets that the graduate of a technical college or an industrial school can have *is the habit of doing promptly and to the best of his ability the work set before him*. With this habit and reasonable intelligence he can make good progress. This habit is one of the first results of the Task and Bonus system, for it is a noticeable fact that task workers form habits of industry which they maintain when on day's work with no bonus in sight.

In all schemes for technical or industrial education or training that the writer has seen, emphasis has been laid on the importance of knowing how. The writer wishes to add that ability and willingness to do are of at least equal importance. Many skilled workmen make their skill an excuse for slow work. Those that have not been trained to utilize efficiently what they have learned never attain the success that should be theirs.

Under our task system the workman is *taught how* and *trained to do* at the same time. *Knowing* and *doing* are thus closely associated in his mind, and it is our experience that the habit of doing efficiently what is laid out for him becomes so fixed that he performs without hesitation tasks at which a man not trained to follow instructions would absolutely fail. This is exactly what should be expected and means nothing more than that in our industrial army the workman who has gained confidence in his superior follows his orders without hesitation, just as the private soldier follows the orders of his officer even though he does not see where they lead.

This is not a fanciful comparison, for I have known more than one case in which a workman expressed his doubts as to the possibility of doing a task, and on getting the reply that the task was all right, said, "If you say it can be done, I will do it."

Workers who have been unable to perform their tasks in the time set have frequently asked to have an instructor stand by them with a stop-watch to time the detail operations and show them just wherein they failed, with the result that they soon learned to earn their bonus regularly.

The first essential for a workman to become successful under our task system is to obey *orders,* and having acquired this habit he soon finds out that a skilled investigator can learn more about doing a piece of work than he knows "off hand." Having satisfied himself on this point, he goes to work at the tasks set him with the determination to earn his bonus, with the result, if he has the natural ability, that he soon becomes a rapid and skillful workman.

Learning to obey orders is often the hardest part of the workman's task, for a large percentage of men seem so constituted as to be apparently unable to do as they are told. As a rule, however, this is a feature of a certain stage of their development only, which under proper conditions they overcome at a later date. For instance, many very capable men who were impatient of restraint when they should have learned a trade, find themselves at the age of twenty-five or less in the class of unskilled workmen, although their ability would have enabled them to do well at almost any trade. It is this class of men, when they have come to realize the difference between a skilled workman and one not skilled, that furnishes us with many of our best task workers. Such men often see in our *instructor, task,* and *bonus* a chance to redeem some of their earlier errors, and by learning thoroughly how to do, and doing one thing after another, in the best way that can be devised, get a training, in a short time, that does much to make up for the previous neglect of their opportunities.

Bosses as Servants and Teachers

In a shop operated on this system, where each workman has his task, one man whom we term a *gang boss* usually tends a group of workmen, supplying them with work and appliances and removing the work when finished. Such a man is paid a bonus for each workman who earns a bonus, and an extra bonus if all of his group earn their bonuses. The result is that so long as the workmen perform their tasks, though nominally their boss, he is really their servant, and becomes the boss only when a workman fails to perform his task. The loss of money to the gang boss in case a workman fails to earn his bonus is such that he constantly has his eye on the poor workman and helps him all he can. If, however, he finds the workman is incapable of being taught, he uses his influence to have a better man put in his place.

In starting a shop on task work, an instructor who is capable of teaching each workman how to perform his task must be constantly on hand, and must as a rule teach one workman at a time. This instructor may be the man who has investigated the work and set the task, or he may simply be an instructor capable of following out the work of such an investigator, but he must be readily available as long as any of the workmen need his services, for we make it a rule not to ask a man to do anything in a certain manner and time unless we are prepared to show him how to do it as we specify.

Task Setting

A task must always be set for performing a definite operation in a specific manner, a minimum time being set for its accomplishment. As compensation, the workman is paid for the time set plus a percentage (usually 20 to 50) of that time, provided the work is done in the time allowed or less. If the time taken is more than the time allowed, the workman gets his day's pay only. The fact that in setting the task the manner of performing the operation is specified enables us to set another task for the same operation if we develop a better or quicker method.

If after having performed his task a workman wishes to suggest a quicker or better method for doing the same work, he is given an opportunity if possible to demonstrate his method. If the suggested method really proves to be quicker or better, it is adopted as the standard, and the workman is given a suitable reward. *No workman, however, is allowed to make suggestions until he has first done the work in the manner and time specified.*

It is the duty of the investigator to develop methods and set tasks, and unless the methods developed by him are pretty generally a great deal better than those suggested by the workmen, he is not retained in the position. Working at tasks is pretty good training for task setting, and the writer has gotten more than one task setter from the ranks of task doers.

Inasmuch as, after a satisfactory method has been established, a large proportion of the work of the task setter is the study of the time in which operations can be performed, he is popularly known as the *Time Study* man. This term has led to a misconception of his duties and has caused many honest people to claim that they were putting in our methods when they have put a stop watch in the hands of a bright clerk and told him to find out how quickly the best men were doing certain work. Unquestionably they have in many cases been able to set more accurate piece rates by this method than they had been able to set by the older methods, but they are still far from our ideal, in which the best expert available investigates the work, standardizes the appliances and methods and sets a task that involves utilizing them to their very best efficiency. While the stop watch is often used to establish a method, it is used to determine the time needed to do the work only when the standard methods and appliances are used efficiently. Stop-watch observation on work done inefficiently or with ill-adapted appliances, or by poor methods, is absurd and serves only to bring into disrepute all work in which the stop watch is used. Moreover, such use of the stop watch justly excites the contempt and opposition of the workman.

To make real and permanent progress, the expert must be able to standardize appliances and methods and write up such instructions as will enable an intelligent workman to follow them. Such standards become permanent, and if the workman is paid a proper bonus for doing the work in the manner and time set, he not only helps maintain the standards, but soon begins to exert his influence to help the progress of standardization.

Standardization

All work, and all knowledge, for that matter, may be divided into two classes: *expert* and *standard.* Expert knowledge may be described as that which has not been reduced to writing in such a manner as to be generally available, or exists only in the minds of a few. By analogy, expert work is work, the methods of doing which either are known only to a few or have not been so clearly described as to enable a man familiar with that class of work to understand them.

On the other hand, standard methods are those that are generally used, or have been so clearly described and proved that a man familiar with that class of work can understand them and safely employ them.

The largest problem of our expert is to standardize expert methods and knowledge. When a method has been standardized, a task may be set, and by means of *an instructor and a bonus* a method of maintaining that standard permanently may be established. With increasing efficiency on the part of the workman the standard always has a tendency to become higher.

We have here the workman and the foreman using their efforts to maintain standards, for both fail to obtain a bonus if the standard is not maintained. This is so different from the case in which the standard is maintained only by the man in authority with a club that there can be no comparison.

From workmen trained under these methods, we get a good supply of instructors and foremen, and occasionally an investigator. From our investigators, who standardize our methods and appliances, we get our superintendents, and our system of management thus becomes self-perpetuating.

The superintendent who believes that the sovereign cure for all troubles is to go into the shop and raise a row, has no place under our methods, for when the task and bonus has been established, errors are far more frequent in the office than in the shop, and the man who is given to bluffing soon finds that his methods produce no effect on men that are following written instructions.

Obstacles

Among the obstacles to the introduction of this system is the fact that it forces everybody to do his duty. Many people in authority want a system that will force everybody else to do his duty, but will allow them to do as they please.

The Task and Bonus system when carried out properly is no respecter of persons, and the man who wishes to force the workman to do his task properly must see that the task is properly set and that proper means are available for doing it. It is not only the workman's privilege, but his duty, to report whatever interferes with his earning his bonus, and the loss of time educates him to perform this duty no matter how disagreeable it is at first. We investigate every loss of bonus, and place the blame where it belongs. Sometimes we find it belongs pretty high up, for the man who has neglected his duty under one system of management is pretty apt to neglect it at first under another. He must either learn to perform his duty or yield his place, for the pressure from those who lose money by his neglect or incompetence is continuous and insistent.

This becomes evident as soon as the task and bonus gets fairly started, and the effect is that opposition to its extension develops on the part of all who are not sure of making good under it, or whose expert knowledge is such that they fear it will all soon be standardized. The opposition of such people, however, is bound to give way sooner or later, for the really capable man and the true expert welcome these methods as soon as they understand them.

Helps

The fact that the task and the bonus enable us to utilize our knowledge and maintain our standards, and that the setting of tasks after a scientific investigation must necessarily not only increase our knowledge but standardize it, brings to our assistance the clearest thinkers and hardest workers in any organization. Our greatest help, however, comes from the workmen themselves. The most intelligent realize that we really mean to help them advance themselves, and the ambitious ones welcome the aid of our instructor to remove obstacles that have been in their way for perhaps years. As soon as one such man has earned his bonus for several days, there is usually another man ready to try the task, and unless there is a great lack of confidence on the part of the men in the management, the sentiment rapidly grows in favor of our task work.

Day Work and Piece Work

As used by the writer, the Task and Bonus system of pay is really a combination of the best features of both day and piece work. The workman is assured his day rate while being taught to perform his task, and as the bonus for its accomplishment is a percentage of the time allowed, the compensation when the task has been performed is a fixed quantity, and is thus really the equivalent of a piece rate. Our method of payment then is piece work for the skilled, and day work for the unskilled, it being remembered that if there is only work enough for a few, it will always be given to the skilled. This acts as a powerful stimulus to the unskilled, and all who have any ambition try to get into the bonus class. This cannot be too clearly borne in mind, *for we have here all the advantages of day work combined with those of piece work without the disadvantage of either,* for the day worker who has no ambition to become a bonus worker usually of his own accord seeks work elsewhere, and our working force soon becomes composed of Bonus Workers, and day workers who are trying to become Bonus Workers.

Cooperation

When 25 per cent of the workers in a plant are Bonus Workers, they, with those who are striving to get into their class, control the sentiment, and a strong spirit of cooperation develops. This spirit of cooperation in living up to the standards set by the experts, which is the only way a bonus can be earned, benefits the employer by the production of

More work.
Better Work.
Cheaper work.

It benefits the workmen by giving them

Better wages.
Increased skill.
Better habits of work.
More pleasure and pride in their work.

Not the least important of these results is the fact that the workmen take more pride in their work, for this of itself insures good work. As an instance of this pride, the writer has known girls working under the task system to form a society, admission to which was confined to those that could earn bonus on their work; the workers themselves thus putting a premium on industry and efficiency.

The fact that we get better work as well as quicker work seems inconceivable to some. The reasons are:

a. Careful inspection, for no bonus is paid unless the work is up to the standard.

b. Work done by a prescribed method, and always in the same way.

c. Attention needed to do high-speed work, which keeps the mind of the worker on what he is doing and soon results in exceptional skill.

The development of skilled workmen by this method is sure and rapid, and wherever the method has been properly established, *the problem of securing satisfactory help has been solved.* During the past few years while there has been so much talk about the "growing inefficiency of labor," the writer has repeatedly proved the value of this method in increasing its efficiency, and the fact that the system works automatically, when once thoroughly established, puts the *possibility of training their own workmen within the reach of all manufacturers.*

Training Help a Function of Management

Any system of management that did not make provision for obtaining proper materials to work with would be thought very lax. The day is not far distant when any management that does not make provision for training the workmen it needs will not be regarded as much better, for it is by this means only that a system of management can be made permanent.

To be satisfied to draw skilled workmen from the surplus of other plants means as a rule that second rate men only are wanted, and indicates a lack of appreciation of the value of well trained, capable men. The fact that few plants only have established methods of training workmen does not necessarily mean that the managers are satisfied with that condition, but rather that they know of no training system that can be satisfactorily operated in their plants; and as questions are sure to be asked about the method of introducing this system, a few words on that subject may not be amiss, it being borne in mind that *the changing of a system of management is a very serious matter, and cannot be done by a busy superintendent in his spare time.*

Method of Introduction

In order to set tasks we must know beforehand what work is to be done and who is to do it. In order to pay a bonus, we must know after the work is done whether it was done exactly as specified. Hence our first care in starting to introduce this method is to provide means for assigning tasks to the workmen, and means for obtaining such a complete set of returns as will show just what each man has done. When this much has been introduced, the output of a plant is always increased and the cost of manufacture reduced.

The next step is to separate such of the work as is standard, or can be readily made standard, from the more miscellaneous work and set tasks for the standard work. Then we begin to standardize, and as fast as possible reduce the expert and increase the routine work. The effort to classify and standardize expert knowledge is most helpful to the experts themselves, and in a short time they begin to realize that they can use their knowledge far more efficiently than they ever dreamed.

As soon as work has been standardized, it can be intelligently planned and scheduled, each workman being given his specific task, for which he is paid a bonus when it is done in the manner and time specified. As bonus is paid only on the written statement of the inspector that the whole task has been properly done, failure to earn a bonus indicates that our plans have not been carried out.

An investigation of every case of lost bonus keeps the management closely in touch with the progress of the work, and as the workmen are ever ready to help disclose and remove the obstacles that prevent their earning their bonus, the managing problem is greatly simplified; for, as one of my co-workers has very aptly put it, *"the frictional lag due to the inertia of the workman is changed by the bonus into an acceleration."*

With increase in the number of bonus workers, this force of acceleration increases, and not only does the careless worker, who by his bad work prevents some other from earning his bonus, fall into disfavor, but the foreman or superintendent who is lax in his duty finds his short-comings constantly brought before him by the man whose duty it is to investigate all cases of lost bonus.

Moral Training

The fact that under this system, everybody, high and low, is forced by his co-workers to do his duty, for some one else always suffers when he fails, acts as a strong moral tonic to the community, and many whose ideas of truth and honesty are vague find habits of truth and honesty forced upon them. This is the case with those in high authority as well as those in humble positions, and the man highest in authority finds that he also must conform to laws, if he wishes the proper cooperation of those under him.

THE PARTING OF THE WAYS

BY H. L. GANTT

MODERN CIVILIZATION is dependent for its existence absolutely upon the proper functioning of the industrial and business system. If the industrial and business system fails to function properly in any important particular, such, for instance, as transportation, or the mining of coal, the large cities will in a short time run short of food, and industry throughout the country will be brought to a standstill for lack of power.

It is thus clearly seen that the maintenance of our modern civilization is dependent absolutely upon the service it gets from the industrial and business system.

This system as developed throughout the world had its origin in the service it could and did render the community in which it originated. With the rise of a better technology it was found that larger industrial aggregations could render better and more effective service than the original smaller ones, hence the smaller ones gradually disappeared leaving the field to those that could give the better service.

Such was the normal and natural growth of business and industry which obtained its profits because of its superior service. Toward the latter part of the nineteenth century it was discovered that a relatively small number of factories, or industrial units, had replaced the numerous mechanics with their little shops, such as the village shoemaker and the village wheelwright, who made shoes and wagons for the community, and that the community at large was dependent upon the relatively smaller number of larger establishments in each industry.

Under these conditions it was but natural that a new class of business man should arise who realized that if all the plants in any industry were combined under one control, the community would have to accept such service as it was willing to offer, and pay the price which it demanded. In other words, it was clearly realized that if such combinations could be made to cover a large enough field, they would no longer need to serve the community but could force the community to do their bidding. The Sherman Anti-Trust Law was the first attempt to curb this tendency. It was, however, successful only to a very limited extent, for the idea that the profits of a business were justified only on account of the service it rendered was rapidly giving way to one in which profits took the first place and service the second. This idea has grown so rapidly and has become so firmly imbedded in the mind of the business man of today, that it is inconceivable to many leaders of big business that it is possible to operate a business system on the lines along which our present system grew up; namely, that its first aim should be to render service.

It is this conflict of ideals which is the source of the confusion into which the world now seems to be driving headlong. *The community needs service first, regardless of who gets the profits, because its life depends upon the service it gets.* The business man says profits are more important to him than the service he renders; that the wheels of business shall not turn, whether the community needs the service or not, unless he can have his measure of profit. *He has forgotten that his business system had its foundation in service, and as far as the community is concerned has no reason for existence except the service it can render.* A clash between these two ideals will ultimately bring a deadlock between the business system and the community. The "laissez faire" process in which we all seem to have so much faith, does not promise any other result, for there is no doubt that industrial and social unrest is distinctly on the increase throughout the country.

I say, therefore, we have come to the *Parting of the Ways,* for we must not drift on indefinitely toward an economic catastrophe such as Europe exhibits to us. We probably have abundant time to revise our methods and stave off such a catastrophe if those in control of industry will recognize the seriousness of the situation and promptly present a positive program which definitely recognizes the responsibility of the industrial and business system to render such service as the community needs. The extreme radicals have always had a clear vision of the desirability of accomplishing this end, but they have always fallen short in the production of a mechanism that would enable them to materialize their vision.

American workmen will prefer to follow a definite mechanism, which they comprehend, rather than to take the chance of accomplishing the same end by the methods advocated by extremists. In Russia and throughout eastern Europe, the community through the Soviet form of government is attempting to take over the business system in its effort to secure the service it needs. Their methods seem to us crude, and to violate our ideas of justice; but in Russia they replaced a business system which was rotten beyond anything we can imagine. It would not require a very perfect system to be better than what they had, for the dealings of our manufacturers with the Russian business agents during the war indicated that graft was almost the controlling factor in all deals. The Soviet government is not necessarily Bolshevistic nor Socialistic, nor is it political in the ordinary sense, but industrial. It is the first attempt to found a government on industrialism. Whether it will be ultimately successful or not, remains to be seen. While the movement is going through its initial stages, however, it is unquestionably working great hardships, which are enormously aggravated by the fact that it has fallen under the control of the extreme radicals. Would it not be better for our business men to return to the ideals upon which their system was founded and upon which it grew to such strength; namely, that reward should be dependent solely upon the service rendered, rather than to risk any such attempt on the part of the workmen in this country, even if we could keep it clear of extreme radicals, which is not likely? *We all realize that any reward or profit that business arbitrarily takes, over and above that to which it is justly entitled for service rendered, is just as much the exercise of autocratic power and a menace to the industrial peace of the world, as the autocratic military power of the Kaiser was a menace to international peace. This applies to Bolshevists as well as to Bankers.*

I am not suggesting anything new, when I say reward must be based on service rendered, but am simply proposing that we go back to the first principles, which still exist in many rural communities where the newer idea of big business has not yet penetrated. Unquestionably many leading business men recognize this general principle and successfully operate their business accordingly. Many others would like to go back to it, if they saw how such a move could be accomplished.

Under stress of war, when it was clearly seen that a business and industrial system run primarily for profits could not produce the war gear needed, we promptly adopted a method of finance which was new to us. The Federal Government took over the financing of such corporations as were needed to furnish the munitions of war. The financing power did not except any profit from these organizations, but attempted to run them in such a manner as to deliver the greatest possible amount of goods.

The best known of these is the Emergency Fleet Corporation. It is not surprising that such a large corporation developed in such great haste should have been inefficient in its operating methods, but there are reasons to believe that it will, in the long run, prove to have handled its business better than similar undertakings that were handled directly through the Washington bureaus. It gave us a concrete example of how to build a Public Service corporation, the fundamental fact concerning which is that it must be *financed by public money.* That it has not been more successful is due, not to the methods of its financing, but to the method of its operation. The sole object of the Fleet Corporation was to produce ships, but there has never been among the higher officers of the Corporation a single person, who, during the past twenty years, has made a record in production. They have all without exception been men of the "business" type of mind who have made their success through financiering, buying, selling, etc. If the higher officers of the Fleet Corporation had been men who understood modern production methods, and had in the past been successful in getting results through their use, it is probable that the Corporation would have been highly successful, and would have given us a good example of how to build an effective Public Service corporation.

Mr. William B. Colver, Chairman of the Federal Trade Commission, in the summer of 1917, explained how we might have a Public Service corporation for the distribution of coal. In such a corporation as Mr. Colver outlined, there would be good pay for all who rendered good service, but no "profit." Of course, all those who are now making profits over and above the proper reward for service rendered in the distribution of coal, opposed Mr. Colver's plan, which was that a corporation, financed by the Federal Government, should buy at the mouth of each mine such coal as it needed, at a fair price based on the cost of operating that mine; that this corporation should distribute to the community the coal at an average price, including the cost of distribution. We see no reason why such a corporation should not have solved the coal problem, and furnished us with an example of how to solve other similar problems. We need such information badly, for we are rapidly coming to a point where we realize that *disagreements between employer and employee as to how the profits shall be shared can no longer be allowed to work hardship to the community.*

The chaotic condition into which Europe is rapidly drifting by the failure of the present industrial and financial system, emphasizes the fact that in a civilization like ours the problems of peace may be quite as serious as the problems of war, and the emergencies created by them therefore justify the same kind of action on the part of the government as was justified by war.

Before proper action can be taken in this matter it must be clearly recognized that today economic conditions have far more power for good or for evil than political theories. This is becoming so evident in Europe that it is impossible to fail much longer to recognize it here. The revolutions which have occurred in Europe and the agitation which seems about to create other revolutions, are far more economic than political, and hence can be offset only by economic methods.

The Labor Unions of Great Britain, and the Soviet System of Russia, both aim, by different methods, to render service to the community, but whether they will do it effectively or not is uncertain, for they are revolutionary, and a revolution is a dangerous experiment, the result of which cannot be foreseen. The desired result can be obtained *without a revolution* and by methods with which we are already familiar, if we will only establish real public service corporations to handle problems which are of most importance to the community, and realize that capital like labor is entitled only to the reward it earns.

Inasmuch as the profits in any corporation go to those who finance that corporation, the only guarantee that a corporation is a real public service corporation is that it is financed by public money. If it is so financed all the profits go to the community, and if service is more important than profits, it is always possible to get a maximum service by eliminating profits.

This is the basis of the Emergency Fleet Corporation, and numerous other war corporations, which rendered such public service as it was impossible to get from any private corporations. Realizing that on the return of peace many private corporations feel that they have no longer such social responsibilities as they cheerfully accepted during the war, it would seem that real public service corporations would be of the greatest possible advantage in the industrial and business reorganization that is before us.

We have in this country a little time to think, because economic conditions here are not as acute as they are in Europe, and because of the greater prosperity of our country. But we must recognize the fact that our great complicated system of modern civilization, whose very life depends upon the proper functioning of the business and industrial system, cannot be supported very much longer unless the business and industrial system devotes its energies as a primary object to rendering the service necessary to support it. We have no hesitation in saying that the workmen cannot continue to get high wages unless they do a big day's work. *Is it not an equally self-evident fact that the business man cannot continue to get big rewards unless he renders a corresponding amount of service?* Apparently the similarity of these two propositions has not clearly dawned upon the man with the financial type of mind, for the reason, perhaps, that he has never compared them.

Such a change would produce hardships only for those who are getting the rewards they are not earning. It would greatly benefit those who are actually doing the work.

In order that we may get a clear conception of what such a condition would mean, let us imagine two nations as nearly identical as we can picture them, one of which had a business system which was based upon and supported by the service it rendered to the community. Let us imagine that the other nation, having the same degree of civilization, had a business system run primarily to give profits to those who controlled that system, which rendered service when such service increased its profits, but failed to render service when such service did not make for profits. To make the comparison more exact, let us further imagine a large portion of the most capable men of the latter community engaged continually in a pull and haul, one against the other, to secure the largest possible profits. Then let us ask ourselves in what relative state of economic development these two nations would find themselves at the end of ten years? It is not necessary to answer this question.

I say again, then, we have come to the *Parting of the Ways,* for a nation whose business system is based on service will in a short time show such advancement over one whose business system is operated primarily with the object of securing the greatest possible profits for the investing class, that the latter nation will not be long in the running.

America holds a unique place in the world and by its traditions is the logical nation to continue to develop its business system on the line of service. What is happening in Europe should hasten our decision to take this step, for the business system of this country is identical with the business system of Europe, which, if we are to believe the reports, is so endangered by the crude efforts of the Soviet to make business serve the community.

The lesson is this: *the business system must accept its social responsibility and devote itself primarily to service, or the community will ultimately make the attempt to take it over in order to operate it in its own interest.*

The spectacle of the attempt to accomplish this result in eastern Europe is certainly not so attractive as to make us desire to try the same experiment here. Hence, we should act, and act quickly, on the former proposition.

RUSSELL ROBB

(1864–1927)

FROM THE TIME when the idea of management first began to be formulated, one aspect of it has been repeatedly studied and discussed: the pertinence of military organizational methods to management organization. The topic is as much alive today as it was before World War I when Russell Robb delivered a series of lectures on industrial organization (pp. 133–147) at the invitation of the newly opened Harvard Business School. The basic point he made was one that authorities on organization have been making ever since: Managers can learn much from the centuries of experience with military organization; but they must always keep in mind the principle that the kind of organization they should have depends on the kind of results they want to achieve.

Robb was an engineer who served 36 years with Stone & Webster, Inc., of Boston, managers of public service corporations. He became senior vice president and treasurer and an acknowledged leader in the management of public utilities. That he also thoroughly understood management as a horizontal technique, applicable in all kinds of activities, can be seen in the selection on the following pages.

———————

ORGANIZATION AS AFFECTED BY PURPOSE AND CONDITIONS

BY RUSSELL ROBB

AS AN INDUSTRY or business begins to involve large size, great numbers, and complexity, organization becomes necessary simply for the direction, control, and handling of affairs, quite aside from any question of direct economy. It becomes necessary to set off groups of workers, to divide responsibilities, duties, and processes, so that affairs may be kept within the scope and ability of those who are directing the undertaking. A virtue has, however, been made of this necessity for division, because it becomes possible, by dividing duties and functions, to conserve special skill, ability, and use, and to direct all effort into definite paths, to which it becomes accustomed and thus gains in efficiency.

It is of little importance how the great growth in industries has come,—whether a realization of the benefits that arise with division of labor and conserving of skill induced us to gain size so that these advantages might be brought into play, or whether size came first and the advantages were a fortuitous accompaniment. It seems, however, to be true in most cases that the need for having matters more thoroughly in hand, the need for better command of affairs by administrative officers, usually results in a division that makes plainer the lines of authority, that places responsibility more

Reprinted from the book, *Lectures on Organization*, by Russell Robb, Chapter I, pages 1–23. Privately printed, 1910. Used by permission of Mrs. Russell Robb.

definitely, and secures discipline, while in the consideration of the economies to be secured in the different parts of the organization, attention is more often given to questions of division of duties to secure specialization in skill and plant, to the limiting of duties to functions instead of parts only.

If, for instance, one were suddenly required to organize a body of thousands of men to clear the streets of a city from an abnormally heavy fall of snow, it is probable that these men would be divided into divisions, each with a chief, and that these divisions would be divided into squads, each with a foreman. The division would be divided into similar kinds of units, headed by men in absolute authority over their units and with no collateral relations to cause complications and delay. The organization would be for the purpose of control, for the purpose of intimate command and effective direction. If, however, one were to organize a great industrial establishment to manufacture machines that had very close competition both as to quality and price, the greatest care would have to be given in the organization to the different functions in the manufacture, and to the segregation of such functions as designing, purchasing, and selling, so that every advantage could be taken of special knowledge and specialization of effort.

Other activities that are not industrial, such as the church, the civil government, the army, the navy, educational organizations, charitable organizations, all involve size and numbers and complexity, and they are all organized; but good industrial organization will be likely to differ from these other organizations, and all organizations will differ somewhat from each other, because the objects, the results that are sought, and the way these results must be attained, are different; and, moreover, the material out of which the organization is made, differs in kind.

It is, of course, true that there is much that is common to all effective endeavor: the definite knowledge of what one wishes to accomplish; the principles of directing and controlling effectively large numbers of people; making the most of different kinds of skill; the securing of cooperation, so that each one helps instead of hinders another; the systematic and orderly way of doing things, so that there are no neglected steps, no false movements, no lost time—are all common to good organizations of all kinds. But, with differing purposes, the factors that make organization have varying importance. With one purpose in view, the principle of the division of labor for specialization of skill may be all-important; in another situation, this may become insignificant in comparison with the proper control and direction of large numbers. The problem in another organization may be the systematization and division of work mainly to bring order and efficiency into a situation of complexity. The significant feature in another case may be almost wholly a question of dispatch, where the question of economy even may hinge much more on the time required than on any other factor. Again, we may have success hinging upon systems of accounting, records, and statistics, where the accurate knowledge of costs and other details of the business, and the system for securing these, may be the central factor about which the organization is constructed.

It is interesting to consider some of the different forms that organizations take and some of the results that are sought, because such a consideration brings out more clearly this question of purpose and conditions and material, and helps to prevent one from assuming that organization always means the application of a perfectly definite method or system to the carrying out of any large and complicated undertaking.

In the popular mind, perfect organization usually is associated with the army. The division of the men into companies and regiments, the clearly defined duties and authority of the officers, the discipline that secures precision in all evolutions and obedience to all commands of the superiors, suggest to most people the perfection of concerted action, and furnish the type to which they feel that all organizations should conform as nearly as possible. And so, when they see that an industrial establishment is large, they speak of its members as an "industrial army" and its head as a "captain of industry." The regularity of hours in an organized industry, the definite and formal orders, and the established lines of authority, all suggest to us that very old type of organization that has had for its purpose the handling of large numbers of men in fighting. An army in modern times, with its different branches of service, its attention to commissary and sanitation, its great multiplicity of technical appliances of war, its connection with the activities of civil life, becomes very complex; but in the beginning, military organization was a necessity in order to direct and handle effectively large numbers of men, and so to prevent the hordes who went fighting from being merely a mob. The great numbers acting together could not act effectively unless there were order and system in all their evolutions, and an organization binding the order and system together. Moreover, the product came in one supreme moment: the organization was for an emergency. Its whole success or failure was shown by the action of the army at a critical time; and for this reason military organization has taken a severe line, in which everything is subordinated to obedience and definiteness of procedure and certainty of predetermined evolution and action upon command. Authority and responsibility taper down with evenness, each one knowing his exact limitations and his part. Each one in authority must be trained to assume instantly all the duties of the one next above, for the captain of one moment may be colonel in the next.

Military organization has contributed much to all other types of organization through its example of the value of discipline, the usefulness of definite procedure, and the effectiveness in administration of placing responsibility, but it has been the cause of mistakes in building up other organizations, through the forcing into prominence of the main features of a military organization when the end that is sought is much more influenced by other factors, when the necessity for control is less than for specialization of effort and for the coordination of different kinds of action. This becomes plainer when one considers, for instance, an industrial organization depending for its success very largely upon the ability with which the principles of division of labor are applied. There are many examples. Take the making of watches. Here we have great numbers working together, but they are not interchangeable units, nor are those who direct the workers interchangeable and in direct line of authority. There are numberless processes, in each of which workers are trained and practiced until their skill vastly exceeds that of a novice. There are large numbers of different machines,—processes are divided and subdivided and simplified, to attain the acme of the worker's deftness, and to sift from his duties all but the one in which he is supreme. The military virtues here are still desirable to an extent, but they are only incidental. They are not the factors that determine whether good watches are or are not to be turned out at a low cost. The success or failure of the watch-industry would not depend upon instant obedience, upon definite evolutions of men, upon predetermined movement in emergency, upon a definite line of succession in authority; it would depend upon such things as study and care and economy in purchasing materials, upon the development of processes to make the most of each worker's special skill and ability, the saving of time in the handling of the product, the working of the plant to save interest and rent, the discovery of consumers, and the prompt delivery of the product. The main purpose is different from the main military purpose, and the organization must vary accordingly.

Large and complex construction is often undertaken where, in the words of contracts, "time is of the essence." The need for the structure may be vital to the integrity of an important business already established. The saving in interest and in earning power, if the work is completed in months instead of in a year or two, may be a large amount. The organization for such an undertaking will not be the same as for deliberate construction systematized in all details for the lowest total construction-cost. It may be necessary to cut "red tape" that would be desirable in other situations, it may pay to take the chances of less thorough deliberation of plans, the lines of authority even may be changed,—all because the relative importance of factors is changed. The harmony of the organization is upset, and modifications must be made to suit the new conditions.

This was shown two years ago when the Boston Elevated Railway Company discovered that it must have very large additions to three different power stations in order to care properly for its maximum load the following Christmas. There were but twelve months in which to design and build the stations. The organization of a street railway could not economically provide for emergency construction of such magnitude, and even the engineering company that did the work found it necessary to make important modifications in its organization in order to secure dispatch, even at the risk of losing the greatest economy in all details. It was necessary to place as much responsibility down along the line as possible, so that time would not be lost in referring questions for confirmation. It was necessary that the work be segregated, so that in functional departments there would be no question of "right of way." The specialization was in the direction of "Boston Elevated work," not in the direction of "electrical engineering," or "purchasing," or "drafting." A special smaller organization was set off for this particular piece of work. The construction manager in charge had complete authority over it, except as he was responsible to the president of the engineering company. He had under him three assistant construction managers, each of whom was responsible for one of the stations. Each of these assistants had a night and day engineer in charge of the actual construction. Each station had its own inspectors and its own survey corps. The special organization for this work had its own draftsmen and its own purchasing department and its own accounting department. There was no attempt to serve it from the functional departments of the engineering company organization. Every endeavor was to secure short-cuts in time. The stations were operating in ten months from the time they were begun, and ordinarily it had taken a year and a half or two years to accomplish the same thing. This was an organization for dispatch,—to get a piece of work done in order to save the expense of delay, which would have greatly overbalanced any economy there might have been in a less military but more functional form of organization.

The construction of the great irrigating reservoirs in India, where a few years ago during the famine so many of the natives were employed, furnishes a good example of the variation in organizations according to the material one has to work with. One can imagine approximately what sort of an organization would be necessary in most other places to undertake the vast excavations necessary to form reservoirs in great irrigating works: there would be a large mechanical equipment of steam-shovels, with the minor organization of drivers, mechanicians, and superintendents, the systems of records, of fuel-supply and repairs; the placing of equipment; the orderly procedure of the work; the great number of workmen to direct and supervise; the systems of pay, shelter, commissary, sanitation,—all would have to be moulded into a great comprehensive organization. In India there were no steam-shovels, mechanicians, fuel-supply, repairs, shelters, or commissary. The excavation was done directly by hordes of natives in gangs of twenty or thirty, each with his or her basket, and one with his little "scooper" or koiti. When the basket was filled, it went on the worker's head and was carried to the dump, where the native received a small tag that entitled him to payment for one basketful of excavation. The workers consisted of gangs, over which were the foremen who furnished the laborers for the work. There was no system of housing, for there were no shelters: all slept on the ground in the open. There was no commissary organization, for the workers "found themselves," and in any case would have refused any food prepared for them, because of caste prejudice. The payment of workers required no elaborate system of pay-rolls and receipts, because each worker simply cashed in the tags he had received. No doubt those in charge of these Indian excavations had their problems of organization, but they were different from our problems, and probably the most of our approved systems would have been of about as much use as an American typewriter to a Chinese merchant.

There are all kinds of industries, and one is perhaps as good as another for the purpose of illustrating organization. If one is credibly informed, the organization of some of the patent-medicine companies differs considerably from that of other manufacturing companies, and yet they are still ably organized. There is at least one where two or three rooms in a large building are devoted to the manufacture of the medicine, a minor function in the organization. The remainder of the building is largely devoted to a printing establishment for the preparation of advertising matter, to advertising departments, correspondence-clerks, and stenographers. Here we have a manufacturing establishment, but the purpose and conditions require special attention to the office-system. The accomplishment of the purpose is not greatly affected by attention to manufacturing methods and details, but is very greatly affected by skill in advertisement and system in the departments where the real effort and most of the expense lie.

Four or five in particular of the insurance companies learned at the time of the Chelsea fire to appreciate the importance in their organizations of complete and systematic records, and will doubtless have increased respect for this factor in their organizations. As soon as it became known that the conflagration would be wide-spread and cause great loss, one of the insurance companies card-indexed all its risks in the burned district. From their records they were able to set down at once the different companies that were interested in the insurance, and what the amounts of their risks were. Four or five of the companies cooperated, all necessary information was compiled, and members of the group were able to write each policy-holder within a day or two that the companies were ready to make appointments with the insured and the adjustment-bureau, and settle claims. The satisfaction of the insured may well be imagined, for the ordinary procedure would have required about a month; thus the efficient recording systems proved their great value, not only as an adjunct in office-system, but as a very important factor in the relations between the company and those with whom it did business.

There has grown up in this country of late years a new form of business organization that is of interest in this consideration of different purposes and material. This is the organization for the selling of negotiable securities, principally bonds to investors. The larger bond houses have a very large number of salesmen,—a number large enough to suggest in a manufacturing establishment division of labor, lines of authority, systems of time-keeping, and other approved principles for the securing of good and economical work. But these particular principles of organization in a bond house sink to a very subordinate place. These salesmen are very nearly independent units; many of them have their own clients; they will have their own ways of finding, meeting, and convincing investors. Organization here takes a different line: it is in the direction of systematic buying of securities suitable to offer to purchasers, of acquainting the men with the principles of the house, the systematic presentation to them of the merits of the security they are to sell, the card-indexing of customers, records of transactions, dissemination of information, canvassing of fields; but not very much thought about the principles of division of labor or of the military virtues.

Most organizations have grown gradually, and the conditions surrounding this growth often influence greatly the form that the final organization takes. Long existence of customs and methods, and the consequent knowledge of the plan throughout the organization, may be of more importance than the features that might be secured by a theoretically better structure. It is understood, for instance, that the very successful Studebaker organization is administered by an executive committee of five members, each member of which is at the head of a functional department of the business. Committees are not ordinarily very effective as heads of undertakings. They have difficulty in reaching decisions, and one member is likely to prove dominant and carry his ideas without being responsible for the results. The Studebaker organization, however, has grown up about a family of five brothers, all able and active in the business. From small beginnings they had threshed out their problems together and had learned the art of conference. They had found how to draw from each his contribution to the general knowledge and to the particular question, and they had discovered ways of reaching conclusions without interminable discussions or unplaced responsibility. One might hestitate to form a new organization on this plan, but he would just as surely fail to discard it, when so completely established and so well proved in efficiency. In parts, at least, of many organizations, one finds variations from the theoretically best plan on account of the personality or particular ability of important officers or heads. The individual ordinarily has small influence on the general plan of very large organizations, but in the lesser ones the failure to benefit from exceptional ability in broad grasp and direction, or the failure to make the most of unusual knowledge and skill in special directions, may lose to the undertaking far more than the seemingly perfect structure could secure.

It will be unfortunate if the emphasis given here to the diversity of conditions and to the difference in the purposes of undertakings should be construed as an argument that no general principles can be applied to organization. It is intended simply to show that there is no "royal road," no formula that, once learned, may be applied in all cases with the assurance that the result will be perfect harmony, efficiency, and economy, and a sure path to the main purpose in view. This is not an imagined difficulty. We all are inclined to get a bit twisted toward some favorite panacea, and if one is to attempt to better a business organization, it helps greatly to be able to approach the problem with an open mind, and not to have a special predilection toward a factor that one has somewhere found admirable. One sees frequently men who are biased in favor of military organization—they have admired the precision, the definiteness, and the well-defined authority and responsibility, and once enamored, they would apply it indiscriminately. Another man in his experience has seen kinds of work clearly defined and important in their functions, and has been impressed with special skill. He becomes twisted toward specialization, and would apply "functional organization" everywhere, often regardless of the advantages of clearly defined responsibility for results as a whole. Now and then when a man discovers in his business some remarkable facts, through the medium of records and statistics, he begins to look upon these as embodying real organization, and this may become one of the most fatal of twists, because of possible records and statistics there is no end. It is one of the important factors in organization because it has to do with the very first principles—our knowledge of what we are accomplishing and can accomplish; but in an organization for doing things, this gathering of knowledge has its limits,—in organizations of some kinds it has narrow limits, and our enthusiast for records and statistics becomes sometimes like the perennial student, who absorbs during all his life and never produces.

There has been a tremendous advance in the last generation in "system." So great has been the improvement in the method and order with which business of all kinds is conducted, and so important is it in the prevention of waste, that we find many who look upon the systematic doing of things as organization itself. And so it is nearly the whole of organization in some cases; but it is easy here to fall into thinking that a system that saves much in one organization is a universal factor, and will be just as effectual wherever applied. An illustration of this is a detail in the letter-filing system of a certain business house. The needs of this particular business often require that letters be referred to several different departments, that notations or remarks be made by one or more department heads, and sometimes that letters be retained by a department pending investigation. It was found that notations were often so many that a special tag attached to the letter was advisable, and moreover that letters were often missing from the files when wanted, and it was necessary to search many departments to find them. There was danger of important letters being lost altogether in their wanderings. The difficulties are met by pasting on each letter as it is received a tag about four inches by five. On this tag is stamped the time when it is received, a serial number, the department to which it is referred, spaces for remarks, and spaces for noting date of answer and date of filing. In a record-book are entered by the mailing department the date and serial number of every letter as received, the department to which it is referred, and the number of the correspondent. Every letter that is referred from one department to another is taken by a mailing-department boy, and the change is noted on the record-book. In this way there is a record of every letter, who has had it, and where it is. This all, of course, is a detail in a system, but in the particular organization where it is used, it is an important detail and has saved a tremendous amount of the time of the head men directly and indirectly, as well as furnishing assurance that important letters can always be placed when wanted. Now, in certainly nine out of ten organizations this system of recording letters would be an over-elaboration. It would be a needless expense, and would often clog rather than lubricate the machinery of business; yet if one of the mail-clerks brought up in this system were called upon to systematize a mailing department in another organization, it would be perfectly natural for him to base his system on the one that he knew had proved a good one.

Yet, in spite of the wide differences in organizations, we do, to use a mathematical term, know the "dimensions" of organization. We do know the quantities which, of some magnitude or other, according to purposes and conditions, are the component parts.

We can conceive of no real organization, for instance, without a structure of some kind, without a definite plan. However work is apportioned, and by whatever means it is directed and carried out, we may be sure that the method must have definiteness. We may choose the wrong kind of men to do things, we may not plan to bring their work to them so that their time is most efficiently used, we may not use care that special skill is conserved; but if we have some plan that assigns definite duties, if we have some order by which all the necessary action is taken, we have made a beginning in organization.

We have, too, from our earlier organizations, the examples of the value of lines of authority. They add to definiteness. They provide the control and direction by subdividing for that purpose. As authority tapers down, it relieves from responsibility except in the fields for which men are fitted. It provides a definite court of appeal in case of difficulty, and thus saves endless disputes and arguments and consequent confusion. This tapering authority never leaves affairs without a head, and it assures the steady progress of the undertaking because it provides a properly trained supply of new men to fill vacated superior positions.

We know also the value of the factor of responsibility in organization, the great incentive there is to careful and energetic work when praise and blame can be accurately placed, and we know that, as this responsibility is segregated, as men are relieved from divided responsibility, initiative increases, and we get the vigor of independent action and leave ability untrammeled.

As undertakings become more complex, the factor of division of labor, of specialization, grows in importance. We use great care in choosing men for their different duties according to their fitness, and we increase this fitness and create special skill by narrowing duties so that all attention and study and practice are confined in one direction. In division of labor, advantage is taken of a natural tendency. Men do most readily what they can do best. It increases their interest and enthusiasm and efficiency.

We know that a great factor in organization is "system," the mechanism of the whole. It transmits intellectual power, physical power, and skill to the main purpose. It touches all parts of the undertaking, for it is the introduction everywhere of order and method. It relieves those who direct from the details of execution, and it relieves the man with special skill from the duties for which he is less well fitted. It brings work to men in condition for the application of their particular function. It moves all in accustomed routine so that the waste involved in initial effort is avoided. It insures that important steps will not be forgotten. It makes use of mechanical aids to save human labor and thought. It arranges the processes so that the greatest good is secured from the use of the property devoted to the undertaking, and it introduces method into the use, so that the property is not idle,—so that time, the opportunity for accomplishment, is not wasted.

With system and order, the value of discipline appears as a factor, for it holds all to the chosen system of working. It has to do with the rules and regulations necessary to carry out the system, with securing obedience to these rules, and with the training and instruction that assures full understanding. As a part of the maintaining of the system, is the provision for watchfulness and supervision to keep the movement in the right direction, and the provision for checks to insure against dishonesty, against errors in judgment, and errors from carelessness.

We have another very important factor in organization, in accounting, records, and statistics, for these furnish the chart and the compass, the sounding-lead and the log. They are to show us where we are, where we have come from, where we are tending and how fast, and where the shoals lie, and they can tell us, too, how the craft is working. They must be largely depended upon to acquaint those who are directing undertakings with the progress and with the conditions, and this becomes more marked as organizations become larger and more complex, because it becomes increasingly difficult for those at the top to gather their knowledge from their own observation. It is not only from lack of time to observe that this is so, but in the complexity of modern organizations a great amount of analysis is necessary, simply to segregate information, so that a problem may be clearly presented. One hears less in these days of the successful and shrewd old men of affairs who kept little more than memorandum-books and had all the detail of their business in their heads; that was a possibility in competing with lesser men doing the same thing, and in a time when the product of even a very rough organization was worth much more than the cost of all that went into it. Modern industrial organizations are by no means wholly a fortunate development that widens the difference between cost and value of product. They are also born of necessity to save a margin growing smaller; and when one has to do with disappearing margins he can no longer depend upon inclinations and rough judgments. He has to deal with figures, and his system of figures must represent the true state of affairs. Naturally enough, it is here that one usually finds the greatest difference between industrial organizations and other organizations, because it is the price of the life of an industry,—this knowledge of exactly what is being accomplished and what it is costing to accomplish it.

An organization is much looked upon as a machine, as a cold-blooded product of synthesis, as an artificial sort of being that recognizes such realities as order, system, discipline, skill, and ability, but has no place anywhere for the "spirit" of anything. But if we are to look upon "organization" as something more than "system," if it is to be a sort of organism, we must recognize another factor, and that is *esprit de corps*. It induces enthusiastic and unselfish working together, with regard more to the whole result than immediately to one's own personal part in the achievement. It leads one to do his part well for the advancement of the whole. It leads one to see the advancement in his part because the whole is gaining in achievement and stability. If we have the military groups, it makes those groups support one another and act together as one; if we have the functional groups, it removes the friction, it covers the borderland, it helps to coordinate. It is not easy to define this spirit exactly. It is not mechanical and is not obtainable on command, but it gives life and power to the organization. It will not exist without some understanding of the whole and without respect for the purpose and methods. It comes down from the top. It is a reflection of the feeling and the policy of those directing, a reflection of the respect of the superiors for their purpose, and of their earnestness in their work, and of their feeling toward those farther down who are joining in the work. It is a spirit of the whole, and cannot exist without consideration of the units. Organizations are not difficult to sketch out on paper. They always have there a definite and workable look, as if nothing could escape a far-reaching arm that would pull all into the hopper somewhere; but in the working organization, unless it be the most simple, there is constant call for the unscheduled cooperation, for the action that can be secured only through a genuine, lively, and loyal interest in the success of the whole undertaking. And it is interesting here to note that this sort of thing is often expressed by a simile that is the outcome of the activities of intercollegiate life, for we urge this spirit by urging "team play."

Thus, we know pretty definitely the factors that make organization. They are structure, lines of authority, responsibility, division of labor, system, discipline; accounting, records, and statistics; and *esprit de corps,* cooperation, "team play"; but when we attempt to determine the parts played by these factors, we find that their relative importance changes with purpose, conditions, and material. We begin to realize that there is an art of organizing that requires knowledge of aims, processes, men, and conditions, as well as of the principles of organization.

HARRINGTON EMERSON

(1853–1931)

RECENT studies by social scientists, and much practical experience by managers themselves, have indicated that people work most fruitfully when they know the goals toward which they should be striving. This simple truth has created considerable interest in company statements of management creeds and philosophies, and it has given acceptance to the technique of "management by objective."

None of this would have been news to Taylor, Gantt, and Harrington Emerson. They knew it intuitively; and in the early years of this century Emerson presented the idea with evangelistic fervor as the first of his *Twelve Principles of Efficiency*. He called them "ideals" rather than "goals" or "objectives"; but they were all the same, as is apparent in *The First Principle: Clearly Defined Ideals*, which follows.

Emerson was active in teaching, banking, real estate, and industrial production before he became a consulting management engineer in 1901. A born salesman with the mind of an intellectual, he did a great deal to promote the principles and practices of scientific management in the business world.

THE FIRST PRINCIPLE:
CLEARLY DEFINED IDEALS

BY HARRINGTON EMERSON

ASSUMING an organization adapted to their application, it will be found that efficiency principles, although all interrelated, all necessary to each other for highest results, nevertheless stand in a logical sequence.

The first principle is *a clearly defined ideal.*

In the earlier days of American manufacturing and transportation, a century ago, a bright young journeyman who started out to manufacture some special line was very definitely aware of what he intended to make and how the work was to be done. He knew what he wanted. At the present time, in large plants men succeed to authority by transfer or by promotion and are very often without definite conceptions of the purposes for which the plant is working. Workers and foremen at the lower end of line organizations are so far from the "Little Father" or from the "Big Stick" who dictates all policies, who alone is responsible for organization, for delegation of power, and for supervision, that they are driven to create minor ideals and inspirations of their own, these being often at variance with the ideals of those above them. If all the ideals animating all the organization from top to bottom could be lined up so as to pull in the same straight line, the resultant would be a

Reprinted from the book, *The Twelve Principles of Efficiency,* by Harrington Emerson, Chapter III, pages 59–87. Published by The Engineering Magazine Company, New York, 1912. Used by permission of McGraw-Hill Book Company.

very powerful effort; but when these ideals pull in diverse directions, the resultant force may be insignificantly positive—may, in fact, be negative.

This condition of subsidiary deleterious and conflicting ideals is very common in all American plants, as well as great vagueness and uncertainty as to the major ideal, even among the higher officials, as we shall try to show by various examples which could be duplicated by every experienced manager in the country.

A handy man in a railroad shop examined cylinders for cracks. These were often so unimportant that they could be safely repaired by a patch, but in other cases a new cylinder had to be ordered. A patch may cost $30, a new cylinder $600. The handy man swelled with pride when his recommendation for a new cylinder was heeded. He boasted to his wife and fellows of the confidence placed in him and the importance of his work. When in doubt, he reported always in favor of a new cylinder; and it was easier to accept his recommendation than to institute a separate revisional examination to be made by a man scarcely better qualified. The ideals of economy and promptness were submerged, and the conflicting ideal of individual aggrandizement substituted.

A large plant was filled with machinery for turning out work. Some of these machines were automatic and some hand-operated. The automatic had been introduced to lessen expenses and delays. The superintendent of the department was an ardent patriot and churchman; not a man was employed by him who was not recruited from his own nationality and church. He had installed piece rates, singularly inappropriate, since volume of work fluctuated suddenly between wide limits. When work fell off, instead of doing it all on the automatics, he shut these down, and had it all done by hand so as to give employment to his piece workers. His ideals were not *"best product in shortest time at least expense,"* but *"largest amount of employment and reward to fellow-countrymen and co-religionists."* This superintendent, being unsupplied with ideals by the management, had created his own.

In another plant twenty-four men were working in the tool room. This was an excessive force, and the specialist in charge of tools allowed it gradually to shrink through resignations to eighteen men. Suddenly six new men reported for duty in the tool room, engaged by the general foreman. When the specialist interviewed him on the subject he stated: "My allowance for tool room is twenty-four men. If I get along without this number my allowance may be curtailed. Later when I need the men I may not be able to secure them. I propose to maintain the allowance whether there is work or not." It took a long time to convince this foreman:—

First, that twenty-four men were not needed.
Second, that if scheduled work made fifty men necessary he could have them.
Distorted ideals placed him in antagonism to the main purpose of the management.

In another plant, a general superintendent was very averse to any reduction of men below one thousand. He was anxious to turn out more work, was willing to curtail hours of the thousand employed, but to fall below one thousand, even though they voluntarily dropped out, seemed to him to be lowering his own rank since he had worked for years to reach the position of superintendency over a thousand men. Economy, efficiency, were all waived on account of a perverse ideal—personal pride.

The general superintendent of a plant employing twelve thousand mechanics was firmly convinced that the only way to turn out a large volume of work was to employ more men. He seemed to think that men could be piled into one side of the balance scale and volume of work into the other and that men would pull up the work by their gross weight. On one occasion he sent out an order that economy was not the object, but the production of output, and that the force was to be increased to the maximum. He ran up expenses $500,000 in five months and raised his unit costs far above what they had been, far above those of his competitors, far above what they retreated to when he was relieved of authority. A false numerical ideal worked at contrary purposes to true efficiency ideals.

The president of a great industrial corporation authorized standard-practice policies, then entered into contracts with clients on the basis of material, direct labor, and a percentage on direct labor. When it was pointed out to him that increased efficiency would mean fewer hours of direct labor, therefore less pay and less percentage for the same work, he promptly solved the difficulty by relieving the standard-practice advisor from the duty of offering further unpalatable advice, and by forbidding the application of efficiency methods to the shop in question.

In the early days of railroad construction all over the world, false conceptions and ideals greatly increased cost and left a legacy of inefficiency that centuries may not be long enough to obliterate.

The British engineers set up such high standards of grade, curvature, and double tracking, together with such low standards of clearance, as to double the initial cost of all British roads and curtail forever their capacity.

It is told of King Louis I of Bavaria that when he took his initial ride on the newly constructed first rail line in his kingdom, he expressed great disappointment that there was no tunnel, so the line was relocated and made to run through a hill.

Emperor Nicholas of Russia when deferentially asked by his engineers how the line was to be located between St. Petersburg and Moscow, took a ruler and pencil and ruled straight lines between the two cities. "That is the location, gentlemen!" It cost $337,000 a mile, the distance about 400 miles. The railways in Finland, where staff advice was heeded, cost $23,000 a mile.

Americans feel like smiling scoffingly at these mistakes, but was this arbitrary action any worse than that of a Secretary of the Navy who, without investigation and in spite of remonstrance by the naval board of construction, ordered the "Texas" built exactly according to the discordant purchased plans for two different vessels? No wonder the "Texas" was always a monstrosity! But it has at last served a really useful end under the name of "San Marcos" in being used as a target to test the accuracy and power of the big guns on the newer battleships.

What also shall we think of that American transcontinental road which having a water level between two points, 384 miles apart, deliberately abandoned the water level and put in 2,500 feet of mountain climbing and as many of descent between the same points, the officials after all failing to secure from a little western city the bonus for which they had sacrificed good location for all time.

In all these instances, from handy man with cracked cylinder to king, emperor, or knave ruling a railroad location, there is a definite ideal, however bad, consistently pursued; and when these ideals stand in dependent sequence, the result becomes exceedingly costly. The handy man orders a $600 cylinder instead of a $30 patch; his foreman, wishing to employ as many of his church members as possible, has the cylinder made on an inferior machine, with high piece rates; the general foreman fills the tool room with unnecessary men who become busy doing useless work at heavy expense in materials and overhead expense; the shop superintendent is content as he sees the men under him pass the one-thousand mark and joyfully acquiesces in the general superintendent's order to add fifty per cent to the force. Under this sequence, the making of an unnecessary $600 cylinder becomes almost a necessity and the handy man is promoted on account of his skill as a work provider. The 2,500 feet of mountain grade makes many additional locomotives necessary, so there are many more opportunities to make new cylinders instead of patching old ones.

These are examples of the cankering effect of low or lateral ideals, but perhaps even greater loss results from vague ideals and from personal impulse.

At the siege of Sebastopol the officers at dinner in the wardroom of a man-of-war were astounded to hear the big siege gun boom several times, with explosions of midshipmen's laughter afterward. Each firing of the gun cost $250. Investigation showed that bets were up between the middies as to which one could make a donkey move in the public square, and each was taking a shot in turn— with no damage to the donkey.

An engineer poured onto the ground a gallon of 40-cent oil in order to have the tinsmith solder a leak in a 15-cent can. A railroad track foreman and gang were recently seen burying under some ashes and dirt a 30-foot steel rail. It was less trouble to bury it than to pick it up and place it where it could be saved.

A young engineer in railroad service started out to spend some $750 for photographic apparatus, evidently laboring under the impression that if he only spent money enough he could overcome personal, meteorological, optical, and other limitations to good work.

The superintendent of a plant ordered a large automatic lathe to make crank pins from the solid bar. He had no ideals of his own, but vaguely felt that an automatic lathe ought to do cheaper work. When wire is cut into small screws it is the work that gives value, not the material; but in a crank pin it is the material that costs more than the work, and the cost of waste of new material on the automatic was greater than the total cost of scrap material, drop-forging, and turning by a boy under the old method.

The American mind is alert; men as individuals have been successful in proportion to their initiative; they have made great individual successes and also great individual failures.

It is not an accident that an American reporter was sent to find Livingston and that an American explorer forced his way to the North Pole. This reckless confidence in impulses, this reliance on individual initiative, is responsible for many failures; and even if wild advice is not always followed, it is alarming that it can be so confidently offered.

At the time of the planning of the Grand Trunk Pacific Railway, a brilliant young surveyor and railroad engineer wrote a thesis, urging that the gauge of this new line be made 30 feet, freight cars be made large enough to handle 1,000 tons, and all the buildings in the new villages, towns and cities be erected in standard cement sections. Happily this young man's power was not commensurate with his imagination, but it is not always so. Not only do individuals make tremendous blunders, but corporate bodies make greater ones, because, not being composed of specialists, they are not able to curb the initiative of a strong-willed leader. As a consequence, clearly defined ideals are lacking and this relative lack will have to be pointed out along general lines, using for illustration the seven wonders of the ancient world, the seven wonders of modern times, and in comparison with them seven great American enterprises.

There were seven ancient wonders of the world, each one of them a great work, nobly carried out. Even after the lapse of centuries, moderns of alien races can recognize and sympathize with the ideals that inspired these wonders. One of the tests of a definite ideal is that we can apprehend it even if we cannot always sympathize.

The oldest wonder-work of man is Egyptian—the great pyramid —at once a tomb and an astronomical instrument. The last ancient wonder was also Egyptian, the Pharos lighthouse at Alexandria to direct the floating commerce of the old world to this great city. One of the modern wonder-works is also Egyptian, the Suez Canal, so that through four millenniums Egypt has done a full share.

We can sympathize with the desire to have the largest and highest tomb ever constructed so that the bodies of king and of queen, preserved against decay, may lie in royal state until the time of resurrection. We can sympathize with the conception of the great lighthouse, built by King Ptolemy Philadelphos—even with the trick of the architect Sostratos, who engraved his own name in the solid stone, but hid it by a layer of perishable cement in which he engraved the king's name.

Of the remaining five ancient wonders one was the hanging gardens of Babylon—a peculiarly appropriate glorification of irrigated tropical vegetation which has always been able to support the densest population, a power that may in time turn the tide of civilization backward from Canada, Northern Europe and Northern Asia, back from Argentine to tropical America, to tropical islands. The other four wonders were Greek, one of them the temple of Diana at Ephesus, one the tomb of King Mausolus erected by his widow, one the Colossus of Rhodes, spanning with outstretched legs the entrance to the harbor, and the seventh the master work of Phidias, the gold-ivory statue of Jupiter at Olympia. There was faith or hope or love or beauty or civic pride in each of these seven wonders.

Of the seven modern wonder-works of the world, not one is American. One of them, 400 years old, had its inspiration in religion—St. Peter's at Rome, the largest church ever built; the second, 100 years old, is the greatest triumphal arch ever erected, commemorating the victories of the great conqueror Napoleon I; the other five are modern engineering works. It is typical of the changed ideal of the ages that only one of the ancient wonders was utilitarian, and only one of the modern wonders is religious, five being very distinctly utilitarian; yet noble ideals gave them all birth.

Of the utilitarian works the Suez Canal easily comes first. It shortens the sea route from northern Europe to the Orient by 5,000 miles, between certain ports more than half. The canal was begun in 1859, estimated to cost $30,000,000 and to be finished in 1864. Its actual cost was $80,000,000 and it was opened in 1869. The ideal was realized, but none of the other eleven efficiency principles* was thoroughly applied, most of them not at all; hence both the double time and trebled cost.

The next great engineering work was also French, the Eiffel tower, rising 1,000 feet into the air, at once the highest structure erected by man and the prototype of modern American steel construction, which as a matter of course followed when passenger elevators or lifts were made practical.

The third great wonder is the Firth of Forth bridge; cantilevers, similar to three pairs of great Eiffel towers, each pair joined at its base, each half stretching out horizontally 900 feet without end support. This bridge is massive in design because wind pressure is more dangerous than train load.

The fourth modern wonder is the St. Gotthard tunnel, 12 miles long, under the Alps. There was a Brenner railroad route over the Austrian Alps; a Mt. Cenis tunnel under the French Alps; but Italy,

---

* As stated in *The Twelve Principles of Efficiency,* the "other eleven" are: Common Sense; Competent Counsel; Discipline; The Fair Deal; Reliable, Immediate and Adequate Records; Despatching; Standards and Schedules; Standardized Conditions; Standardized Operations; Written Standard-Practice Instructions; and Efficiency Reward. See also page 185 herein.—EDITOR

Switzerland and Germany combined to divert the century-old trade between south and north to a shorter new route, the key to the situation being the long tunnel, more than twice as long as any American railroad tunnel. This enterprise almost failed because the workmen, hygienically neglected, died in great numbers, killed by an intestinal parasite similar to the hook-worm. The doctors ascribed the mortality to the work underground. The parasite has recently appeared in the United States, and may prove as serious a scourge as the hook-worm.

The seventh and last of the modern wonders are the twin cousin ships, the "Olympic" and the "Titanic," conceived and designed to restore to Great Britain the blue ribbon of the sea. Of these seven wonders one belongs to Italy, one jointly to Italy and Switzerland, three belong to France, and two to Great Britain. An ideal definitely conceived in advance and tenaciously realized is manifest in each, and in most of them other efficiency principles are applied, in some only in embryonic vestiges, in others in advanced form— notably in the two steamers, which as to cost, time of completion, and performance, realized expectations.

With these fourteen wonders, each with its own field, we may compare seven great American works of which none is religious, none a monument to beauty, while the utilitarian value of five of them is doubtful.

The Panama Canal, easily the costliest engineering work ever undertaken, is being prosecuted with vigor, and, thanks to the discovery of the yellow-fever mosquito and its suppression, a lock canal will be finished at a cost of about $600,000,000. Of twenty great minds selected by lot, no three would agree as to the ideal back of this great work. Mr. Roosevelt is entitled to speak with more authority than any one else, and his reasons for its building are also those of Goethe—that it was a work that some one would be tempted to undertake, some time, and that the United States was manifestly the proper party.

This is vague and uninspiring. The canal, in times of piping peace, when a navy is wanted for minor police duties only, ought indeed to lessen the need for a double fleet, one in each ocean;

but those who favor a strong American navy, capable of holding its own against such a combination as Great Britain and Japan, scoff at the canal as a substitute for a strong navy. They know full well that in case of war with strong maritime powers either entrance to the canal could be made exceedingly dangerous by floating mines, by submarines, by aeroplanes; that it might be easy to destroy the canal itself either by damaging the locks, damaging the dam of the Chagres River, or sinking some vessel in the canal. If, for self-protection, it is imperative for the United States to maintain maritime strength both in the Atlantic and Pacific, it is not safe to risk the national honor and supremacy on any such device as a canal trusting that it will work like a watch in war time.

The next in rank of great American engineering works are the new railroad terminals in the city of New York costing about $300,000,000.

There are engineers who consider big passenger terminals a survival of the time when English coaches started from some central hostelry. Central terminals are perhaps a convenience to through passengers, with trunks; never to local passengers without trunks. Passengers with trunks are very few, even in the fast through trains. It is possible that these great terminals have been built to accommodate the few hundred passengers who have trunks? The 500,000 people who go to and return from Coney Island on single hot summer holidays have not required great terminals; the million and a half of visitors handled on Chicago day at the Columbian Exposition did not require $100,000,000 terminals; the hundreds of thousands of passengers handled daily at 42nd Street subway or at Brooklyn Bridge have not required palatial terminals. In fact, these great crowds would neither gather nor could they be handled if they had to assemble at an initial terminal, and debouch from an arriving terminal, both far from their homes. Passengers want to be picked up at their doors, landed at their doors, like letters; they do not want the plan, now obsolete even in villages, of delivering themselves like letters at the central post-office and collecting themselves like letters from the general delivery or *poste restante*.

Nothing is more convenient than the present plan of checking trunks from house to house in cities far apart, for a charge of one dollar, nothing more convenient than to drop from business office in New York into subway ten minutes before train departure and go to Seattle, Portland, San Francisco or Los Angeles, winter or summer, needing neither hat, top coat, nor umbrella since the traveler is never without cover, and if transfer has to be made it is more comfortable and easier to make it from a Denver train to the Santa Fé flyer at La Junta, Colorado, with its station, than to make a similar change in a great New York, Chicago, Philadelphia, or Washington terminal. The great problem of city traffic is to secure distribution, to scatter foci, to dissolve congestion. Terminals of necessity create and increase congestion. Physically or financially, the ideals justifying these great terminal expenditures are not startlingly apparent. Material and maintenance charges on these great works, if distributed to each incoming and outgoing trunk, or even to each going and coming through passenger, would give a striking modern illustration of Horace's dictum that no artist makes a mountain travail to bring forth a mouse.

The Manhattan transfer station of the Pennsylvania Railroad, the 125th Street station of the New York Central Railroad, are as convenient as the big terminals are inconvenient. One wonders why one or both of these great companies did not acquire financing and directing control of the New York subways, run on them from every part of the city specially colored trains, gathering passengers at every express station, landing them directly at the transfer stations, where without long walk or loss of time, through and even local steam trains could be boarded to every part of the United States.

An arrangement of this kind would have added vastly to the convenience of the passengers, and would have saved a railroad investment of $300,000,000, since the subways are already paying institutions.

The third great American enterprise is the New York barge canal. Railroad men, keenly alert as to its folly, assert that the money to be spent in the barge canal would build, equip, and operate without freight charges a railroad between Buffalo and the Hudson, capable of handling ten times as much freight in the course of a year. A barge canal built by the State seems a roundabout way of curbing and limiting dreaded hypothetical railroad extortions, since the St. Lawrence River and Montreal route more or less fixes export rates from all American ports during the open season of navigation for canal and river.

The fourth great American projected undertaking is the improvement of internal waterways. It is assumed that the railroads are uncontrollable, although a single growl by the Interstate Commerce Commission causes a senseless decline of values in Wall Street. It is assumed by some that internal water transportation, subject to all the vague uncertainties of low water, flood, and frost, can be made so cheap as to bankrupt the railroads, although the Mississippi from St. Louis to the sea, open the year round, is paralleled by dividend-paying railroads. Railroad operation with its chronometer trains 99.97 per cent reliable between terminals 1,000 miles apart has in this respect realized an exalted and noble ideal not to be undermined and curtailed by the return to obsolescent canals and river highways.

Our fifth great proposed expenditure is for an American Navy. If there had been no "Maine" there would have been no Spanish war, no war expenditure of one thousand million dollars, no Philippine problem making us an Eastern Asiatic power when we have not yet solved a dozen simple elementary problems at home, such as living wages for sweat-shop workers, lack of employment, civic honesty and cleanliness.

Every battleship five years old is obsolescent. Today's and next year's development of flying machines may make every naval vessel as doomed as was chain and mail armor after the invention of gunpowder, as was the sailing corvette after the development of the steamship. Great Britain needs a navy and has kept up to date, has moreover coaling, repair and cable stations, indispensable to its effectiveness; but the value of great war navies to other nations— Germany, France, Russia, Italy, Argentina and the United States— has not yet been demonstrated; and to two of them, it has proved an added calamity in a losing war.

Nevertheless, being committed to a navy until such time as possible enemies are willing also to disarm, it is with great pride that the American can point to the efficiency of the modern American battleship, more efficient in action and operation than anything on a similar scale thus far evolved by man. Through the improvement of the dependent sequence of distance, accuracy, rapidity, and weight of salvo, the modern American battleship is three-thousand times as efficient as its forerunner thirteen years ago at the battle of Santiago.

Every one of these five great works commits one of our American besetting industrial sins—over-equipment—due to our mistrust of spiritual forces, reliance on material measures. It is almost assumed that if a mistake is gigantic enough it will become praiseworthy.

The sixth and seventh great American works are utilitarian, the subways in New York, and the elevator-served tall buildings everywhere. Even as to these, definite ideals have not been established and followed. Some of the tall buildings sacrifice utility to ornamentation, others are painfully ugly but admirably adapted, while a third class are both ornamental and convenient. As to the subways, in view of the fact that they are an independent system connecting with no other road, it is a pity that they were not made with 6-foot gauge and 12-foot wide double-deck coaches, that they were not built as double-deckers, thus giving 300 per cent greater seating capacity for the same length of platform and for a relatively small increase of initial expense.

It is not either the right or the privilege of the Efficiency Engineer to set up ideals of morality, goodness, or beauty, or to assume that his ideal of purpose is superior; but he has a right to expect that some definite and tangible ideal will be set up so that at the start its possible incompatibility with one or more of the efficiency principles may be pointed out. The ideals underlying British railroad construction are very clear: no grades, no curves, no grade crossings, double tracks, great passenger terminals, and capitalization of all betterments. Although five of these ideals are not compatible with common sense and were not adopted at the start by either practical colonials or Americans, the Efficiency Engineer can accept an estimate of $375,000 a mile, the cost of British railroads, and aid in giving the best result possible for the money, since these ideals are not incompatible with any efficiency principle except common sense.

There is one great American railroad genius, always an idealist, who has risen to the commanding position in the railroad world because he had definite ideals. He states that a railroad company is to be managed to earn dividends, that expenses are by the train mile and receipts are by the ton mile. In twenty years, on these three precepts, he has built up a dominant railroad system. He has developed the country through which his road ran, and lowered rates, because this gave him more ton miles. He has reduced grades and curvatures and used heavy locomotives and long trains because this reduced the cost per train mile. He has reached out for Oriental traffic because this not only gave more ton miles, but equalized traffic, thus lessening ton-mile cost. To each one of the three ideals—dividends, low mile cost, large volume of traffic—each of the other eleven principles could be applied and in unusual measures have been applied by James J. Hill.

Another great railroad executive, J. W. Kendrick, regarded disagreements with labor as consuming time and energy, destructive to peace, loyalty, and harmony, and he therefore resolved to set up a high standard of discipline based on the Fair Deal made attractive by an Efficiency Reward. Not a breath of labor trouble has occurred in six years in the departments to which these principles were applied, and the cost of each item of work has decreased, the standard of excellence has risen, the men have earned more money.

It is, however, in industrial companies smaller than the great railroads that in a few cases high ideals have been adopted.

The ideals of one company are that its customers shall be treated with absolute fairness, that its employees shall be of higher skill and be better paid than those of neighboring competitors, that they shall have permanence of employment. These ideals are an admirable foundation on which a very efficient organization has been built up, and while the managers have not consciously formulated and followed the eleven other efficiency principles, they are applying most of them.

The ideal of another company, to which they make their own profits subsidiary, is that their employees shall be able to lead wholesome New England village lives, the workers working near their homes, the fathers with leisure to retain leadership in their own families. An ideal of this kind is also an admirable foundation on which to build a highly efficient organization for, in corporations as in individuals, what is the profit of gaining the whole world if the soul is lost?

The president of an old and large plant near New York City stated with high-minded dignity the ideals under which he and his partners managed their business, not realizing how few managers had had time or opportunity to formulate such ideals, much less carry them into practice.

"We are not money-mad. We strive to be worthy sons of the worthy fathers who started this manufacturing business two generations ago. We wish to see our employees prosperous, well-paid, not overworked; we wish to surpass the world in the excellence of our product."

These are lofty, kindly, homely ideals and the Efficiency Engineer can frame this picture with all the other principles.

As to definite ideals, we could with profit learn from by-gone ages, although substituting other inspirations. Over one of the Greek temples the words were carved, "Know Thyself," for which we could substitute, "Know the Spirit Rather than the Externals of Your Business."

In the monasteries of a great religious order, everywhere was the inscription, "Remember that Death Comes." For this we can substitute, "Remember that We Must Endure." One great manager impressed on his workmen that there were just two ways of permanently raising men's wages. To obtain more from the purchaser, or to lessen unit cost of product by eliminating wastes.

The vagueness, the uncertainty, the aimlessness that characterizes employees is but an infiltration of the vagueness, uncertainty, aimlessness, that characterizes employers. There can be no legitimate conflict between rails and locomotive, between locomotive and its engineer and its firemen, no legitimate conflict between engineer and despatcher, no conflict between despatcher and time-table, although the time-table defines to a second the running time of a train going at extremest speed for a thousand miles or more.

If every manager would formulate his own ideals, promulgate them throughout his plant, post them everywhere, inoculate every official and every employee with them, industrial organizations could attain the same high degree of individual and aggregate excellence as a base-ball league. These ideals ought both specifically and by implication to include much that rational labor unions strive for; they ought as definitely to exclude ideals incompatible with efficiency even if labor unions mistakenly advocate them.

For the manager endowed with common sense but two courses are open. To set up his own ideals and reject all efficiency principles that do not accord with them, or to accept the organization and principles of efficiency and to create correspondingly high ideals.

ALEXANDER HAMILTON CHURCH

(1866–1936)

LEON PRATT ALFORD

(1877–1942)

THE STATEMENT of *The Principles of Management* which follows this introduction carries with it some of the air of controversy surrounding the subject in the first dozen years of this century. Frederick W. Taylor was deep in his crusade for the principles of scientific management. But many opposed his concepts, and others denied that any principles were even involved in his philosophy.

Alexander Hamilton Church and Leon Pratt Alford, co-authors, were in the latter group. They believed that Taylor was talking, not about principles, but about "a collection of axioms and an arbitrary combination of specific mechanisms" such as time study, task and bonus, and functional foremanship. They wanted to go deeper; and in the effort they came up with the proposition which follows. Their comments on the frequent lack of relationship between physical working conditions and morale provide a foretaste of Mayo's conclusions (pp. 377–408).

Church began his career in England as an electrical engineer, became a consultant in cost systems, and continued in this profession after moving to the United States at the turn of the century. Alford had just been appointed editor of *American Machinist* when he wrote the article with Church in 1912. He was widely known as an editor, author, educator, and consultant in the field of industrial management.

———————

THE PRINCIPLES OF MANAGEMENT

BY ALEXANDER H. CHURCH AND
L. P. ALFORD

An earnest attempt to discover and declare the basic regulative principles of management, with special reference to the shop and factory. The principles are:

> *The systematic use of experience.*

> *The economic control of effort.*

> *The promotion of personal effectiveness.*

THIS ARTICLE is intended as a contribution toward the fixing of a systematic basis for a definite art of management. It does not pretend to be either a dogmatic or a final statement of details. The stage which has been reached by the art of management is the outcome of a slow evolution during a period of at least 150 years.

The division of labor has been a well recognized principle since the days of Adam Smith, in the middle of the eighteenth century. The detailed study and analysis of processes began with the factory development of the textile trade, and had reached a high state

Reprinted from *American Machinist,* Volume 36, No. 22 (May 30, 1912), pages 857–861. Used by permission of *American Machinist.*

of evolution by 1832, as recorded in the writings of Charles Babbage.*

The considerable expansion of manufacturing operations during the last 20 years, owing to the enormous international commerce fostered by the steamship and the telegraph, and the uprise of an unprecedented civilized community of 100,000,000 people in America, has introduced much more complex problems than were known to the manufacturers of the nineteenth century, and has rendered the settlement of the art of management on well defined principles a matter of very great importance and urgency.

Many notable contributions to the question have been made of late years, yet it is not too much to say that their authors have been more occupied with urging special systems on the attention of the industrial world, than in developing the skeleton of a real scientific art of management.

In other words, many *solutions* of the problem of management have been offered, representing personal points of view, but these solutions are merely empirical combinations of methods, some good, others of distinctly doubtful value, and their importance is based rather on the authority possessed by their authors than on close logical reasoning.

Management is very far from having attained the dignity of a science at the present time. Yet it has progressed sufficiently for an orderly, though strictly tentative, statement of fundamental principles to be highly desirable. The logical development of these principles to the point where they touch practice may also be undertaken, and in the present paper this is all that is attempted.

The search for fundamental principles is, of course, of great practical importance. They would bring to light the gaps in our knowledge, and focus attention on the weakest links in our chain of practical applications. The mapping out of related fields of activity would become possible, so that every proposed improvement in method could be seen in its relation to the whole—a condition absent at the present time.

---

* See pages 17–34.—EDITOR

In Vol. 36, page 612,† Congressman W. C. Redfield ably outlines the present situation and need thus:

> But there has not yet been established a science of management. And yet, if a science were ever needed, meaning definite rules or principles, based on exact knowledge of facts, it is in this very matter of management.

No apology is therefore necessary for an attempt to formulate some definite basis on which to build a truly scientific art of management. The regulative principles of the art of management are three:

The systematic use of experience.
The economic control of effort.
The promotion of personal effectiveness.

If these three principles are correctly stated, then the scientific basis of management is capable of being derived from their development and extension.

THE FIRST PRINCIPLE—THE SYSTEMATIC USE OF EXPERIENCE

Experience is the knowledge of past attainment. It includes a knowledge of *what* has been done, and also *how* it has been done. It is inseparably associated with standards of performance, that is with the ideas of quantity and quality in relation to any particular method of doing something.

The great instrument of experience, which makes progress possible, is "comparison." By systematic use of experience is meant the careful analysis of what is about to be attempted, and its reference to existing records and standards of performance. In many cases it may be found that gaps in existing experience occur. In such cases the experimental determination of data may be undertaken, so that we have a full covering of the ground, either by

---

† The reference is to an earlier issue of *American Machinist.*—Editor

the experience of others or from our own experimental determinations.

In setting out to examine any work it is necessary to ask:

What experience, in the form of methods and standards of performance, already exists?

Is our performance equal to these standards?

Is it so far behind that it will pay to expend time, energy and money to approximate more nearly?

Are existing standards based upon the use of the most advanced practices and methods of the present day, or is there reason to suppose that experimental redetermination of such standards would show a new maximum of effectiveness?

In the experimental accumulation of experience the economic value of such experience must be kept in view. If the inquiry relates to operations which will be repeated many times, as in the processes of manufacturing staple articles, detailed experimental investigation may be worth while. In other cases it is well to consider the total economic value involved, the possible maximum that could be saved, and the probable cost of the investigation.

Experience tends to pass into traditional practice. That is its most useful form. Every kind of experience must pass into the mind of a man before it can be utilized practically; hence it follows that the new experience should be crystallized into new traditions of practice as fast as possible.

In the shop, men are not always running to textbooks to see if they are right—at least the competent practical man is not. Even if it be conceded that practice in the present day is all wrong, and needs to undergo exhaustive study and reform, this only means that we are engaged in developing new standards of practice, which will take the place of the old traditional practice, and will in turn, form a new tradition. The proper place for these new traditions or standards of practice is precisely the same place as where the old ones were kept, namely, in the minds and memories of those who do and are responsible for doing the work. Further, it is impossible to record it all—something must remain with the man.

New experience can be transmitted in one of two ways, either in minute instructions of which individual workers do not perceive the drift, or as a connected body of new practice. The latter form is the better, though it demands educational efforts somewhat apart from ordinary shop routine. Not until the new experience has become fixed as a habit will its full value be realized.

THE SECOND PRINCIPLE—THE ECONOMIC CONTROL OF EFFORT

Effort is experience in action. Before we can do we must think; that is, dig into our stores of experience relative to the proposed undertaking. Having taken thought, we proceed to action.

In order to produce organized action it is necessary to control effort in various ways. These are "division," "coordination," "conservation," and—in industrial undertakings—"remuneration." Most of the discussions about management are, in fact, discussions about the various methods and degrees of controlling effort and fixing its reward.

It is possible to manipulate effort so as to produce an organization of the utmost flexibility or on the other hand, one of hard and fast rigidity. In certain special cases, rigid organization is permissible, but in general manufacturing, flexibility is really essential.

By flexibility is meant the power of self-adjustment to unforeseen events.

The "division," "coordination," "conservation," and "remuneration of effort" will now be considered in the succeeding paragraphs.

Division of Effort

Division of effort is largely controlled by design. This is the principle of the unit part or component. Modern practice regards the complete machine or device as an aggregation of parts, and it is one test of efficiency when these parts come together in perfect shape, without requiring readjustment to correct faults of workmanship in their progress through the shops.

In modern manufacturing, design cannot be considered apart from operation. Not only must the exigencies of shape and dimensions with a view to economy in molding and machining be kept in view, but reduction of work by means of jigs, fixtures, etc., must be kept in mind. Usually also, standard dimensions, or fits, are a controlling feature in design.

All types of management are pretty much in agreement as to design. Concentration of attention on the unit part may be regarded as settled practice. There are, however, two important ways in which subsequent activities are built up. In one case the drawing sets things in motion; in the other case the model does it. Even a small characteristic like this tends to produce some variation in the type of organization, but consideration of these variations must be postponed.

It will be evident that design is a wholly independent function. It may be efficient or inefficient, quite apart from other functions. We may have very high efficiency of operation, for instance, and very poor design, or *vice versa*. As we proceed we shall see that all manufacturing operations consist of the combination of this with several other functions—all of which are independent, and contribute their quota of efficiency or inefficiency to the total result.

"Division of effort" is an universal principle throughout all the activities of manufacturing. Starting with design, which controls the maximum limit of operative division, it is usually found desirable that operation should also be divided into processes. These usually correspond to machines. To some extent they are controlled by "settings."

It is important to have as few settings as possible, as nothing else is so wasteful of time. One setting in a jig is, therefore, made to subserve several processes in some cases. In other cases one setting in a machine holds the work for a series of consecutive processes, which may be of a different character, as turning, boring, threading, etc., at one setting.

From this it is apparent that there are limiting considerations to the division of effort. It is not merely a question of dividing to the bitter end. There are cases in which it is better to combine operations, and in fact execute them simultaneously.

This is worthy of attention, because it will be found that in all the principles of management that have yet been ascertained the limiting conditions are not yet formulated. Every such principle has limitations and it is neither necessary nor advisable to push it to its farthest possible development. For example, the provision of jigs for repetition work and where it is required to secure dimensional relations of exactness, as in drilling holes, though a very old idea, has not yet been definitely settled as regards its limiting conditions, and there are frequent cases in which doubt exists whether the expenditure for such jigs was, after all, a wise one.

By many of the enthusiastic advocates of particular systems of management, the existence of limiting conditions is hardly suspected, consequently they ride their favorite hobby to exhaustion, till many useful ideas become discredited in the eyes of practical men. It is not enough to know that a principle can be applied— it is even more important to know when not to apply it.

Management cannot substantiate its claim to be a science until all these problems are cleared up. At present, it is not too much to say that very few of the problems of management have been recognized and defined, much less settled. Much of the present clamor is actually leading attention astray from the true essentials of the science of management.

The third great field of division of effort is in connection with administration or control. This is the great battleground of the systems at the present moment. Thus, to mention only two, we have Taylor's functional system, and Emerson's line-and-staff plan. Also we have the old method of simple, delegated authority in hierarchical form, from president to manager, manager to superintendent, superintendent to foremen and so on. Which is the best?

Obviously, the question cannot be answered until we have ascertained what principles have been applied in each case to produce these forms of organization, and what are the limiting conditions that control, or should control them. The subject is a tempting one, but it must be postponed until, at least, the remaining modes of manipulating effort have received attention.

Coordination of Effort

The coordination of effort is an inseparable counterpart of the division of effort. By coordination is meant the prearrangement of a number of separate efforts in such a manner as to produce a definite end. A still more perfect coordination is attempted when this end is to be attained in a definite time. Coordination in design means that unit parts are so designed that, ultimately, they fit together. Coordination in division of operations means that when all the operations are performed certain definite shape and dimension are given to the part. Both kinds of coordination are part of everyday practice, and are generally realized with a good percentage of success. Coordination of operations in regard to time, is, however, a more advanced matter, and in many plants is still in a very unsatisfactory stage.

The coordination of administrative effort is the most complex and debatable problem of all. The moment we begin to divide effort, we must also begin to provide for its coordination. Administrative effort does not possess the same tangibility or definiteness as do design and operation, because it is wholly made up of spheres of influence of personal authority.

Therefore, in proportion as we divide administrative effort (executive functions) its coordination becomes more difficult. The more we subdivide authority the less flexible becomes our organization.

There is a point midway between simple delegation of all authority and the method of analyzing it into component functions and handing out each of these functions to a separate man, that is probably the most effective way of dividing administrative effort. The limiting conditions to excessive functionalism can, however, already be seen as shown above.

Conservation of Effort

Effort requires not only to be divided and coordinated, but also conserved. The conservation of effort means proceeding along the line of least effort to attain a given end.

In regard to design, the conservation of effort implies standardization of tools and equipment. In regard to administration it means using only so much complexity of system as is absolutely necessary. The conservation of effort, though of very great practical importance, is so simple an idea that it hardly requires either emphasis or illustration, at this stage.

Remuneration of Effort

The remuneration of effort has very little relation to any of the other manipulations of effort, for these would still be necessary if no remuneration was offered at all. But as no plants are manned with staffs who work for the mere pleasure of working or "for their health," the question of remuneration is very important.

The Function of Comparison

It has already been remarked that the great instrument of experience is comparison. In practical matters, this is also a department of effort, and requires as careful treatment. It includes the comparison of actual product with set standards commonly termed "inspection," comparison of results as expressed in figures of various kinds, including works statistics, and cost accounts, as well as the accumulation of data of the efficiency of individuals with a view to justice in promotions.

Design is at the beginning of the chain of production and decides what is to be done. Comparison is at the end of the chain and records what has been done, and also in some cases decides whether it has been done according to design. The effort, or activity, devoted to comparison is, of course, subject to the general law of effort, and requires division, coordination, conservation, etc.; just like other branches of activity.

Although somewhat intimately connected in many cases with the mechanism of administration or control, it must be clearly perceived as a quite different kind of activity. Administration sets and keeps things going. Comparison merely records the results. The distinction is important, because it is quite possible to have an excellent system of comparison, and a wretched system of administration, and *vice versa.* Comparison is, therefore, one of the independent functions of manufacturing activity, and its efficiency is not interrelated with that of other functions.

THE THIRD PRINCIPLE—THE PROMOTION OF PERSONAL EFFECTIVENESS

The ideal plant is one which has good equipment, good methods, and good men. It is a comparatively modern discovery that the welfare of the plant and the welfare of its employees are closely connected. By welfare, we do not mean, however, the semi-philanthropic ideals which result in model villages and other "social welfare" experiments, but only the application of the principle of the "square deal" to working relations during working hours.

The Latin poet defined happiness as the possession of a healthy mind in a healthy body. The definition is perhaps a somewhat pagan one, but eminently practical at that. If the plant cannot secure these gifts for its people, it can at least see that all conditions shall be favorable, or at any rate, that they shall meet few conditions in their working hours inimical to either health of mind or body.

Remuneration stands, of course, at the head of these conditions, but it is not the only one, nor does it stand unconnected with others. In spite of Thomas Carlyle the "cash nexus" is far from being the only link between employer and employee, even today— that is, if he is wise. In every considerable organization *esprit de corps* is always latent, and if it remains latent or is turned into latent, or open, discontent it is a mark of the very worst management.

Every human being desires to feel that his work is important. Even the criminal frequently has pride in his criminality. With certain kinds of creative work the mere doing of it is associated with a high degree of personal satisfaction, because the author or the artist is only following out the law of his being.

The worst enemies of progress and contentment are those who are always crying from the house tops that mechanical work is dulling to the intellect, that men are becoming machines, and so on. It is a shock to any man to hear that his work is unimportant and destructive of the higher faculties. It may be so in certain cases, but it is not necessarily so. That largely depends on circumstances. The control of such circumstances is to some extent in the employer's hands.

Considered on the lowest platform the subject is one of importance, since all errors of policy have to be paid for, whether by an individual employer, or, in the case of a general practice, by the industry as a whole. It is one of the most hopeful signs of modern times that these matters are being actively discussed from many different points of view.

In proportion to the number of elements in a problem the difficulty of its solution augments. Personal effectiveness, and its favoring conditions, contain innumerable elements, many of which probably defy human analysis. Therefore, we must proceed modestly and cautiously on the path of discovery, and far from attempting to lay down the laws, it will be well if we succeed in observing the interplay of a few of the most obvious conditions of personal effectiveness.

To begin with, we must assume physical health. From this it is but a step to recognizing that shop conditions must be such that health can be conserved. This point is beginning to be understood, and modern shops avoid the dirt, darkness and obscurity and extremes of cold and heat that a generation ago were accepted as good business. We have progressed so far as to be aware that, on the contrary, they are very bad business. Closely allied is the question of affording facilities for personal cleanliness, dining halls for the midday meal and other auxiliaries to physical needs of shop existence. The most widespread application of this third principle today is in the safeguarding of machines and operations.

The real center of the problem is, however, not on the physical plane, or only incidentally so. The psychological elements are not so obvious, but they are much more important. As in most of the analyses we have made, it is observable that these two groups are nearly independent of one another; that is, their efficiency can vary independently. We may have very bad physical conditions and yet a fine *esprit de corps* or, on the other hand, a finely arranged modern shop and a sullen, discontented population within its walls.

The independence is not quite complete, since bad physical conditions must affect the psychological side to some extent, even though not observably. But on the other hand, the finest psychological adjustment will not make a dark shop light, or a cold shop warm.

Some of the conditions of personal effectiveness are these: The individual must feel leadership; have adequate encouragement and reward; be physically fit and under good physical conditions; and receive a definite allotment of responsibility.

These conditions apply not only to the operative force but to all grades of employees. In fact, some of them apply with greater urgency to the man "higher up" than to the actual worker. It is evident that they have, or should have, a considerable and controlling influence on the arrangements made for the division and coordination of administrative effort.

A good deal has been made by some of the modern schools of management doctrine of the claim that this or that system creates a fine spirit of cooperation between the plant and its men, but for the most part these claims are merely statements of a desirable end to be attained, and not indications of a method by which it can be attained.

The truth is, of course, that no single element of a system, or even a combination of half a dozen such elements as methods of payment, functionalized authority, etc., more than touches the fringe of the question. Highly organized systems may coexist with fine *esprit de corps,* but the latter is not dependent on any form of system or organization.

Of all the conditions controlling a fine working atmosphere, leadership probably plays the most important part. In warfare men prefer to serve under the general who wins battles, though that entails hardships without number and toil without end. In industrialism, mechanism is a mighty unimportant thing compared with an "old man" who is a born leader of men.

The weakness of one prominent school of management doctrine is that it pretends that it has superseded leadership, by substituting therefor elaborate mechanism. Such a contention betrays a complete misapprehension of how men are constituted, and of what the true functions of elaborate mechanism really are. All such mechanism is but a collection of mechanical tentacles or feelers, to enable the controlling mind and spirit of the management to be in several places at once. If the personality behind these tentacles is a feeble one, the mechanism will not supplement its deficiencies in the slightest degree.

This is not to say that such mechanism is useless; on the contrary, it is essential in the large-scale operations of modern industry, and it is, therefore, highly important that it should be carefully arranged and well balanced, but it is in itself inert and lifeless—a purely passive channel through which the capacities of leadership may exert themselves.

A favorite illustration of the folly of "perpetual motion" is the reflection that a pound will not lift a pound anyway, and that the chances of making it do so are not increased by putting gears, levers, and other mechanism between the first pound and the second one, however artfully and plausibly these may be arranged.

The same truth applies to the mechanism of the organization. All work is born of effort, and all effort is controlled by the personal reaction of one man on another; therefore it is evident that no greater results can be attained by putting a vast array of blanks, forms, cards and books between the first man and the second, however plausibly and artfully they are arranged.

In other words, organization and system are something forced on us by the necessities of the case, and that something has no virtue either in itself, or in any possible combination of its components. It does not add one single cubit to the stature of leadership, though, on the other hand, its absence or its bad arrangement may detract considerably from the full realization of what would otherwise be possible to leadership.

It is more than probable that types of organization depend for their success on their harmony with the particular type of leadership that is endeavoring to make use of them. This would explain why systems are successful in one case and fall down in what appears a similar case.

At the present stage of the analysis of management we can do no more than make a note of this. It must always be remembered, however, that organization is a tool, and that it is our duty to fit it to the leader, and not try to compress the leader to fit the system. Understanding of the limiting conditions of this part of the problem must be left to future progress to compass.

RECAPITULATION

This necessarily highly condensed and skeleton outline of the main relative principles of management must end here. It will be observed that we have enumerated three regulative principles dealing respectively with "experience," "effort" and "personal relationships." Effort is further subject to certain modes of action; namely, "division," "coordination," "conservation" and "remuneration." This action is applied in certain definite divisions: "Design," "administration," "operation" and "comparison."

The truth or error of these expansions of the three principles must rest on the idea that each of these subdivisions is independent of the others. One can have good division with bad coordination; a high degree of conservation with a faulty basis of remuneration. Similarly the practical applications are also independent. Good design may coexist with every subsequent inefficient element. Operation may be, and commonly is, well in advance of methods of administration. All these may be good, and yet the remaining function of comparison may be only rudimentary.

These considerations point to the fact that *these are not arbitrary or accidental classifications, but are really fundamental,* and can be used in the practical analysis of the activities of any business. Improving one of them does not improve the other, and may even in some cases be wholly wasted effort. This latter consideration shows why reorganizations sometimes fail of effect, and general efficiency is not improved.

Finally we have dealt cursorily with the question of personal relationships. In their very nature these are more nebulous and difficult of precise definition, yet the conditions of personal effectiveness enumerated also pass the test of independent functioning, inasmuch as any one of them may be at a maximum while the others are lower in the scale, or practically nonexistent.

It may be interesting to subjoin here a brief comparison of the chief principles put forward by Taylor and Emerson, and show their place in relation to this tentative attempt to formulate the fundamental and constructive principles of management.

Mr. Taylor's Principles

As pointed out in Vol. 35, page 108,‡ in an article entitled "Has Scientific Management Science?" Mr. Taylor's "scientific management"§ is a collection of axioms and an arbitrary combination of specific mechanisms rather than a body of principles. Among its leading features, time study, functional foremanship, standardization, planning in advance, and task-bonus may be selected as characteristic.

The place of time study is obviously under the first principle; namely, the systematic use of experience. It is a tool for supplementing and extending our experience, and its economic limitations have been discussed under that heading. Functional foremanship

---

‡ Again the reference is to *American Machinist.*—Editor
§ See pages 67–71.—Editor

is related to the principle of the economic control of effort, and particularly to the division of administrative effort.

Standardization belongs to the same principle, and its particular niche is under the head of conservation of effort, in an avoidance of complexity where uniformity and simplicity can be maintained. In reforming old industries, standardization usually means cutting down, but in new industries it means the avoidance of unnecessary kinds, sizes and methods. It means building up along the lines of least effort—either result flowing readily from acceptance of the sub-principle of the conservation of effort.

Planning in advance is largely an application of the coordination of effort. A certain amount of planning is inherent in every established routine, because the very idea of division of effort necessarily implies some measure of coordination. The necessity for preserving flexibility acts as a limiting condition to planning too elaborated and intensive.

Task-bonus is, of course, a special variety of application of remuneration of effort. Its value as a practical device must rest upon the degree to which it actually promotes personal effectiveness. It is one of many methods of remuneration, but the conditions to which this and the other methods apply in the most effective degree have not yet been studied and compared in any serious way.

One more point of Taylor's system may be mentioned. It is his claim that the science which underlies each act of each workman is so great that no workman is able to fully understand it (and presumably give it effect) without specific and very detailed guidance from above. This point has been covered by what has already been said on the subject of forming new traditions and habits based on the new knowledge that recent progress has given rise to.

This is obviously a case of applied systematic experience. If Mr. Taylor had in mind the use of his slide-rules in making this claim then it is obvious that the use of such slide-rules, where they are useful, should become as much a part of the man's working habit, as is the use of shifting gears or other devices for controlling the working of the machine.

Mr. Emerson's Principles

Emerson's twelve principles will not detain us long. His first principle, "clearly defined ideals,"|| is not especially an industrial principle. It is presupposed that a man knows what he wants, or he can do nothing successfully. It certainly comes, however, under the head of systematic use of experience, if we try to apply it practically. His second principle, "common sense," is hardly a principle at all. It is simply one of the basic conditions of all successful human endeavor, and might be ranked with "sound judgment," "perseverance" and other moral and mental attributes. It is not especially industrial.

His third principle, "competent counsel," must also be ranged under the systematic use of experience. It means from those best qualified to provide it. His fourth principle, "discipline," comes under the division of administrative effort.

One of the prime functions of administration is to secure discipline, that is, to prevent irregular activities which are not coordinated with the useful activities necessary to the work. Idleness, absence, disregard of instructions are examples of uncoordinated, and, therefore, harmful effort.

The fifth principle enunciated by Mr. Emerson is "the fair deal." This is a psychological matter belonging to the promotion of personal effectiveness. His sixth principle, "reliable and immediate records," is, of course, the function of comparison spoken of, though not the whole of it. The seventh principle, "dispatching," comes under, and in fact is, the practical mechanism of, the coordination of effort. The eighth, ninth and tenth principles, "standards and schedules," "standardized conditions" and "standardized operations," have been discussed under the Taylor system; so with the eleventh, "standard-practice instructions."

In these four cases standardization means conformity with the principle of conservation of effort, while standard practice instructions are a part of planning, and therefore of coordination of effort.

|| See page 158.—EDITOR

Finally we have the twelfth principle given by Mr. Emerson; namely, "efficiency reward," which is simply another phrase for "remuneration of effort."

These illustrations have been made to demonstrate that as far as can be seen at present the three fundamental principles formulated in this paper, with their derivatives, do actually find a place for all divisions which modern analysis of industrial working has brought to light.

The important point is, of course, that by stating and fixing what are believed to be the three basic and fundamental principles of industrial activity, and deriving the subordinate details from these in logical order, a beginning has been made toward finding a truly scientific basis for the art of management, on which all its prime facts can be built up, later, into a coherent and understandable system of theory and practice.

HENRI FAYOL

(1841-1925)

OF MANY ATTEMPTS to summarize the essence of management, Henri Fayol's *General Principles of Management*, which follows, stands the test of time as well as any other, and perhaps better. A part of a larger work, *General and Industrial Management*, it first appeared in 1916 in an industrial association bulletin in his native France.

The uniqueness of his *Principles* lies in a combination of practical wisdom and pithy, compressed style; Fayol was the Francis Bacon of management literature. His book was the fruit of more than 50 years' practice and study of management, and it ranges all the way from profound observations on the unity of command to penetrating comments on the irritations of memo writing. He used the same analytical approach as Taylor, but he developed it independently and applied it in a new and significant area—that of top management and administration.

Fayol spent his entire business career with a French industrial and mining concern, retiring as managing director after having made a notable success of reorganizing and expanding it. His last years were spent in furthering the idea, particularly in governmental circles, that administrative principles can and should be applied in all forms of human organization, not in business and industry alone.

GENERAL PRINCIPLES OF MANAGEMENT

BY HENRI FAYOL

THE MANAGERIAL FUNCTION finds its only outlet through the members of the organization (body corporate). Whilst the other functions bring into play material and machines the managerial function operates only on the personnel. The soundness and good working order of the body corporate depend on a certain number of conditions termed indiscriminately principles, laws, rules. For preference I shall adopt the term principles whilst dissociating it from any suggestion of rigidity, for there is nothing rigid or absolute in management affairs, it is all a question of proportion. Seldom do we have to apply the same principle twice in identical conditions; allowance must be made for different changing circumstances, for men just as different and changing and for many other variable elements.

Therefore principles are flexible and capable of adaptation to every need; it is a matter of knowing how to make use of them, which is a difficult art requiring intelligence, experience, decision and proportion. Compounded of tact and experience, proportion is one of the foremost attributes of the manager. There is no limit to the number of principles of management, every rule or managerial

Reprinted from the book, *General and Industrial Management,* by Henri Fayol, Chapter IV, pages 19–42. Translated from the French by Constance Storrs. Published by Sir Isaac Pitman & Sons, Ltd., London, 1949. Used by permission of Sir Isaac Pitman & Sons, Ltd.; and of Dunod, Paris, publisher of the original work and owner of the French copyright.

procedure which strengthens the body corporate or facilitates its functioning has a place among the principles so long, at least, as experience confirms its worthiness. A change in the state of affairs can be responsible for a change of rules which had been engendered by that state.

I am going to review some of the principles of management which I have most frequently had to apply; viz.—

1. Division of work.
2. Authority.
3. Discipline.
4. Unity of command.
5. Unity of direction.
6. Subordination of individual interests to the general interest.
7. Remuneration.
8. Centralization.
9. Scalar chain (line of authority).
10. Order.
11. Equity.
12. Stability of tenure of personnel.
13. Initiative.
14. Esprit de corps.

1. DIVISION OF WORK

Specialization belongs to the natural order; it is observable in the animal world, where the more highly developed the creature the more highly differentiated its organs; it is observable in human societies, where the more important the body corporate[1] the closer is the relationship between structure and function. As society grows, so new organs develop destined to replace the single one performing all functions in the primitive state.

---

[1] *"Body corporate."* Fayol's term "corps social," meaning all those engaged in a given corporate activity in any sphere, is best rendered by this somewhat unusual term because (*a*) it retains his implied biological metaphor; (*b*) it represents the structure as distinct from the process of organization. The term will be retained in all contexts where these two requirements have to be met. [*Translator's note.*]

The object of division of work is to produce more and better work with the same effort. The worker always on the same part, the manager concerned always with the same matters, acquire an ability, sureness, and accuracy which increase their output. Each change of work brings in its train an adaptation which reduces output. Division of work permits of reduction in the number of objects to which attention and effort must be directed and has been recognized as the best means of making use of individuals and groups of people. It is not merely applicable to technical work, but without exception to all work involving a more or less considerable number of people and demanding abilities of various types, and it results in specialization of functions and separation of powers. Although its advantages are universally recognized and although possibility of progress is inconceivable without the specialized work of learned men and artists, yet division of work has its limits which experience and a sense of proportion teach us may not be exceeded.

2. AUTHORITY AND RESPONSIBILITY

Authority is the right to give orders and the power to exact obedience. Distinction must be made between a manager's official authority deriving from office and personal authority, compounded of intelligence, experience, moral worth, ability to lead, past services, etc. In the make-up of a good head personal authority is the indispensable complement of official authority. Authority is not to be conceived of apart from responsibility, that is apart from sanction—reward or penalty—which goes with the exercise of power. Responsibility is a corollary of authority, it is its natural consequence and essential counterpart, and wheresoever authority is exercised responsibility arises.

The need for sanction, which has its origin in a sense of justice, is strengthened and increased by this consideration, that in the general interest useful actions have to be encouraged and their opposite discouraged. Application of sanction to acts of authority forms part of the conditions essential for good management, but it is generally difficult to effect, especially in large concerns. First, the degree of responsibility must be established and then the weight of the sanction. Now, it is relatively easy to establish a workman's responsibility for his acts and a scale of corresponding sanctions; in the case of a foreman it is somewhat difficult, and proportionately as one goes up the scalar chain of businesses, as work grows more complex, as the number of workers involved increases, as the final result is more remote, it is increasingly difficult to isolate the share of the initial act of authority in the ultimate result and to establish the degree of responsibility of the manager. The measurement of this responsibility and its equivalent in material terms elude all calculation.

Sanction, then, is a question of kind, custom, convention, and judging it one must take into account the action itself, the attendant circumstances and potential repercussions. Judgment demands high moral character, impartiality and firmness. If all these conditions are not fulfilled there is a danger that the sense of responsibility may disappear from the concern.

Responsibility valiantly undertaken and borne merits some consideration; it is a kind of courage everywhere much appreciated. Tangible proof of this exists in the salary level of some industrial leaders, which is much higher than that of civil servants of comparable rank but carrying no responsibility. Nevertheless, generally speaking, responsibility is feared as much as authority is sought after, and fear of responsibility paralyses much initiative and destroys many good qualities. A good leader should possess and infuse into those around him courage to accept responsibility.

The best safeguard against abuse of authority and against weakness on the part of a higher manager is personal integrity and particularly high moral character of such a manager, and this integrity, it is well known, is conferred neither by election nor ownership.

3. DISCIPLINE

Discipline is in essence obedience, application, energy, behaviour, and outward marks of respect observed in accordance with the standing agreements between the firm and its employees; whether these agreements have been freely debated or accepted without prior discussion, whether they be written or implicit, whether they derive from the wish of the parties to them or from rules and customs, it is these agreements which determine the formalities of discipline.

Discipline, being the outcome of different varying agreements, naturally appears under the most diverse forms; obligations of obedience, application, energy, behaviour, vary, in effect, from one firm to another, from one group of employees to another, from one time to another. Nevertheless, general opinion is deeply convinced that discipline is absolutely essential for the smooth running of business and that without discipline no enterprise could prosper.

This sentiment is very forcibly expressed in military handbooks, where it runs that "Discipline constitutes the chief strength of armies." I would approve unreservedly of this aphorism were it followed by this other, "Discipline is what leaders make it." The first one inspires respect for discipline, which is a good thing, but it tends to eclipse from view the responsibility of leaders, which is undesirable, for the state of discipline of any group of people depends essentially on the worthiness of its leaders.

When a defect in discipline is apparent or when relations between superiors and subordinates leave much to be desired, responsibility for this must not be cast heedlessly, and without going further afield, on the poor state of the team, because the ill mostly results from the ineptitude of the leaders. That, at all events, is what I have noted in various parts of France, for I have always found French workmen obedient and loyal provided they are ably led.

In the matter of influence upon discipline, agreements must be set side by side with command. It is important that they be clear and, as far as is possible, afford satisfaction to both sides. This is not easy. Proof of that exists in the great strikes of miners, railwaymen, and civil servants which, in these latter years, have jeopardized national life at home and elsewhere and which arose out of agreements in dispute or inadequate legislation.

For half a century a considerable change has been effected in the mode of agreements between a concern and its employees. The agreements of former days fixed by the employer alone are being replaced, in ever increasing measure, by understandings arrived at by discussion between an owner or group of owners and workers' associations. Thus each individual owner's responsibility has been reduced and is further diminished by increasingly frequent State intervention in labour problems. Nevertheless, the setting up of agreements binding a firm and its employees from which disciplinary formalities emanate, should remain one of the chief preoccupations of industrial heads.

The well-being of the concern does not permit, in cases of offence against discipline, of the neglect of certain sanctions capable of preventing or minimizing their recurrence. Experience and tact on the part of a manager are put to the proof in the choice and degree of sanctions to be used, such as remonstrances, warnings, fines, suspensions, demotion, dismissal. Individual people and attendant circumstances must be taken into account. In fine, discipline is respect for agreements which are directed at achieving obedience, application, energy, and the outward marks of respect. It is incumbent upon managers at high levels as much as upon humble employees, and the best means of establishing and maintaining it are—

1. Good superiors at all levels.
2. Agreements as clear and fair as possible.
3. Sanctions (penalties) judiciously applied.

4. UNITY OF COMMAND

For any action whatsoever, an employee should receive orders from one superior only. Such is the rule of unity of command, arising from general and ever-present necessity and wielding an influence on the conduct of affairs, which to my way of thinking is at least equal to any other principle whatsoever. Should it be violated, authority is undermined, discipline is in jeopardy, order disturbed and stability threatened. This rule seems fundamental to me and so I have given it the rank of principle. As soon as two superiors wield their authority over the same person or department, uneasiness makes itself felt and should the cause persist, the disorder increases, the malady takes on the appearance of an animal organism troubled by a foreign body, and the following consequences are to be observed: either the dual command ends in disappearance or elimination of one of the superiors and organic well-being is restored, or else the organism continues to wither away. In no case is there adaptation of the social organism to dual command.

Now dual command is extremely common and wreaks havoc in all concerns, large or small, in home and in State. The evil is all the more to be feared in that it worms its way into the social organism on the most plausible pretexts. For instance—

(a) In the hope of being better understood or gaining time or to put a stop forthwith to an undesirable practice, a superior S^2 may give orders directly to an employee E without going via the superior S^1. If this mistake is repeated there is dual command with its consequences, viz., hesitation on the part of the subordinate, irritation and dissatisfaction on the part of the superior set aside, and disorder in the work. It will be seen later that it is possible to by-pass the scalar chain when necessary, whilst avoiding the drawbacks of dual command.

(b) The desire to get away from the immediate necessity of dividing up authority as between two colleagues, two friends, two members of one family, results at times in dual command reigning at the top of a concern right from the outset. Exercising the same powers and having the same authority over the same men, the two colleagues end up inevitably with dual command and its consequences. Despite harsh lessons, instances of this sort are still numerous. New colleagues count on their mutual regard, common interest, and good sense to save them from every conflict, every serious disagreement and, save for rare exceptions, the illusion is short-lived. First an awkwardness makes itself felt, then a certain irritation and, in time, if dual command exists, even hatred. Men cannot bear dual command. A judicious assignment of duties would have reduced the danger without entirely banishing it, for between two superiors on the same footing there must always be some question ill-defined. But it is riding for a fall to set up a business organization with two superiors on equal footing without assigning duties and demarcating authority.

(*c*) Imperfect demarcation of departments also leads to dual command: two superiors issuing orders in a sphere which each thinks his own, constitutes dual command.

(*d*) Constant linking up as between different departments, natural intermeshing of functions, duties often badly defined, create an ever-present danger of dual command. If a knowledgeable superior does not put it in order, footholds are established which later upset and compromise the conduct of affairs.

In all human associations, in industry, commerce, army, home, State, dual command is a perpetual source of conflicts, very grave sometimes, which have special claim on the attention of superiors of all ranks.

5. UNITY OF DIRECTION

This principle is expressed as: one head and one plan for a group of activities having the same objective. It is the condition essential to unity of action, coordination of strength and focusing of effort. A body with two heads is in the social as in the animal sphere a monster, and has difficulty in surviving. Unity of direction (one head one plan) must not be confused with unity of command (one employee to have orders from one superior only). Unity of direction is provided for by sound organization of the body corporate, unity of command turns on the functioning of the personnel. Unity of command cannot exist without unity of direction, but does not flow from it.

6. SUBORDINATION OF INDIVIDUAL INTEREST TO GENERAL INTEREST

This principle calls to mind the fact that in a business the interest of one employee or group of employees should not prevail over that of the concern, that the interest of the home should come before that of its members and that the interest of the State should have pride over that of one citizen or group of citizens.

It seems that such an admonition should not need calling to mind. But ignorance, ambition, selfishness, laziness, weakness, and all human passions tend to cause the general interest to be lost sight of in favour of individual interest and a perpetual struggle has to be waged against them. Two interests of a different order, but claiming equal respect, confront each other and means must be found to reconcile them. That represents one of the great difficulties of management. Means of effecting it are—

1. Firmness and good example on the part of superiors.
2. Agreements as fair as is possible.
3. Constant supervision.

7. REMUNERATION OF PERSONNEL

Remuneration of personnel is the price of services rendered. It should be fair and, as far as is possible, afford satisfaction both to personnel and firm (employee and employer). The rate of remuneration depends, firstly, on circumstances independent of the employer's will and employee's worth, viz. cost of living, abundance or shortage of personnel, general business conditions, the economic position of the business, and after that it depends on the value of the employee and mode of payment adopted. Appreciation of the factors dependent on the employer's will and on the value of employees, demands a fairly good knowledge of business, judgment, and impartiality. Later on in connection with selecting personnel we shall deal with assessing the value of employees; here only the mode of payment is under consideration as a factor operating on remuneration. The method of payment can exercise considerable influence on business progress, so the choice of this method is an important problem. It is also a thorny problem which in practice has been solved in widely different ways, of which so far none has proved satisfactory. What is generally looked for in the method of payment is that—

1. It shall assure fair remuneration.
2. It shall encourage keenness by rewarding well-directed effort.
3. It shall not lead to over-payment going beyond reasonable limits.

I am going to examine briefly the modes of payment in use for workers, junior managers, and higher managers.

Workers

The various modes of payment in use for workers are—

1. Time rates.
2. Job rates.
3. Piece rates.

These three modes of payment may be combined and give rise to important variations by the introducton of bonuses, profit-sharing schemes, payment in kind, and non-financial incentives.

1. *Time Rates.* Under this system the workman sells the employer, in return for a pre-determined sum, a day's work under definite conditions. This system has the disadvantage of conducing to negligence and of demanding constant supervision. It is inevitable where the work done is not susceptible to measurement and in effect it is very common.

2. *Job Rates.* Here payment made turns upon the execution of a definite job set in advance and may be independent of the length of the job. When payment is due only on condition that the job be completed during the normal work spell, this method merges into time rate. Payment by daily job does not require as close a supervision as payment by the day, but it has the drawback of levelling the output of good workers down to that of mediocre ones. The good ones are not satisfied, because they feel that they could earn more; the mediocre ones find the task set too heavy.

3. *Piece Rates.* Here payment is related to work done and there is no limit. This system is often used in workshops where a large number of similar articles have to be made, and is found where the product can be measured by weight, length, or cubic

capacity, and in general is used wherever possible. It is criticized on the grounds of emphasizing quantity at the expense of quality and of provoking disagreements when rates have to be revised in the light of manufacturing improvements. Piece-work becomes contract work when applied to an important unit of work. To reduce the contractor's risk, sometimes there is added to the contract price a payment for each day's work done.

Generally, piece rates give rise to increased earnings which act for some time as a stimulus, then finally a system prevails in which this mode of payment gradually approximates to time rates for a pre-arranged sum.

The above three modes of payment are found in all large concerns; sometimes time rates prevail, sometimes one of the other two. In a workshop the same workman may be seen working now on piece rates, now on time rates. Each one of these methods has its advantages and drawbacks, and their effectiveness depends on circumstances and the ability of superiors. Neither method nor rate of payment absolves management from competence and tact, and keenness of workers and peaceful atmosphere of the workshop depend largely upon it.

Bonuses

To arouse the worker's interest in the smooth running of the business, sometimes an increment in the nature of a bonus is added to the time-, job- or piece-rate: for good time keeping, hard work, freedom from machine breakdown, output, cleanliness, etc. The relative importance, nature and qualifying conditions of these bonuses are very varied. There are to be found the small daily supplement, the monthly sum, the annual award, shares or portions of shares distributed to the most meritorious, and also even profit-sharing schemes such as, for example, certain monetary allocations distributed annually among workers in some large firms. Several French collieries started some years back the granting of a bonus proportional to profits distributed or to extra profits. No contract is required from the workers save that the earning of the bonus is subject to certain conditions, for instance, that there shall have been no strike during the year, or that absenteeism shall not have exceeded a given number of days. This type of bonus introduced an element of profit-sharing into miners' wages without any prior discussion as between workers and employer. The workman did not refuse a gift, largely gratuitous, on the part of the employer; that is, the contract was a unilateral one. Thanks to a successful trading period the yearly wages have been appreciably increased by the operation of the bonus. But what is to happen in lean times? This interesting procedure is as yet too new to be judged, but obviously it is no general solution of the problem.

In the mining industry there is another type of bonus, dependent upon the selling price of coal. The sliding scale of wages depending on a basic rate plus a bonus proportionate to the local selling price, which had long flourished in Wales, but was discontinued when minimum wages legislation came into force, is to-day the principle regulating the payment of miners in the Nord and Pas de Calais *départements,* and has also been adopted in the Loire region. This system established a certain fixed relationship between the prosperity of the colliery and the miner's wage. It is criticized on the grounds that it conduces to limitation of production in order to raise selling price. So we see it is necessary to have recourse to a variety of methods in order to settle wages questions. The problem is far from being settled to everyone's satisfaction and all solutions are hazardous.

Profit-Sharing

Workers. The idea of making workers share in profits is a very attractive one, and it would seem that it is from there that harmony as between Capital and Labour should come. But the practical formula for such sharing has not yet been found. Workers' profit-sharing has hitherto come up against insurmountable difficulties of application in the case of large concerns. Firstly, let us note that it cannot exist in enterprises having no monetary objective (State services, religions, philanthropic, scientific societies) and also that it is not possible in the case of businesses running at a loss. Thus profit-sharing is excluded from a great number of concerns. There remain the prosperous business concerns, and of these latter the desire to reconcile and harmonize workers' and employers' interests is nowhere so great as in French mining and metallurgical industries. Now, in these industries I know of no clear application of workers' profit-sharing, whence it may be concluded forthwith that the matter is difficult, if not impossible. It is very difficult indeed. Whether a business is making a profit or not the worker must have an immediate wage assured him, and a system which would make workers' payment depend entirely on eventual future profit is unworkable. But perhaps a part of wages might come from business profits. Let us see. Viewing all contingent factors, the worker's greater or lesser share of activity or ability in the final outcome of a large concern is impossible to assess and is, moreover, quite insignificant. The portion accruing to him of distributed dividend would at the most be a few centimes on a wage of five francs for instance, that is to say the smallest extra effort, the stroke of a pick or of a file operating directly on his wage, would prove of greater advantage to him. Hence the worker has no interest in being rewarded by a share in profits proportionate to the effect he has upon profits. It is worthy of note that in most large concerns, wages increases, operative now for some twenty years, represent a total sum greater than the amount of capital shared out. In effect, unmodified real profit-sharing by workers of large concerns has not yet entered the sphere of practical business politics.

Junior Managers.   Profit-sharing for foremen, superintendents, engineers, is scarcely more advanced than for workers. Nevertheless, the influence of these employées on the results of a business is quite considerable, and if they are not consistently interested in profits the only reason is that the basis for participation is difficult to establish. Doubtless managers have no need of monetary incentive to carry out their duties, but they are not indifferent to material satisfactions and it must be acknowledged that the hope of extra profit is capable of arousing their enthusiasm. So employees at middle levels should, where possible, be induced to have an interest in profits. It is relatively easy in businesses which are starting out or on trial, where exceptional effort can yield outstanding results. Sharing may then be applied to overall business profits or merely to the running of the particular department of the employee in question. When the business is of long standing and well run the zeal of a junior manager is scarcely apparent in the general outcome, and it is very hard to establish a useful basis on which he may participate. In fact, profit-sharing among junior managers in France is very rare in large concerns. Production or workshop output bonuses—not to be confused with profit-sharing—are much more common.

Higher Managers. It is necessary to go right up to top management to find a class of employee with frequent interest in the profits of large-scale French concerns. The head of the business, in view of his knowledge, ideas, and actions, exerts considerable influence on general results, so it is quite natural to try to provide him with an interest in them. Sometimes it is possible to establish a close connection between his personal activity and its effects. Nevertheless, generally speaking, there exist other influences quite independent of the personal capability of the manager which can influence results to a greater extent than can his personal activity. If the manager's salary were exclusively dependent upon profits, it might at times be reduced to nothing. There are besides, businesses being built up, wound up, or merely passing through temporary crisis, wherein management depends no less on talent than in the case of prosperous ones, and wherein profit-sharing cannot be a basis for remuneration for the manager. In fine, senior civil servants cannot be paid on a profit-sharing basis. Profit-sharing, then, for either managers or workers is not a general rule of remuneration. To sum up, then: profit-sharing is a mode of payment capable of giving excellent results in certain cases, but is not a general rule. It does not seem to me possible, at least for the present, to count on this mode of payment for appeasing conflict between Capital and Labour. Fortunately, there are other means which hitherto have been sufficient to maintain relative social quiet. Such methods have not lost their power and it is up to managers to study them, apply them, and make them work well.

Payment in Kind, Welfare Work, Non-financial Incentives

Whether wages are made up of money only or whether they include various additions such as heating, light, housing, food, is of little consequence provided that the employee be satisfied.

From another point of view, there is no doubt that a business will be better served in proportion as its employees are more energetic, better educated, more conscientious and more permanent. The employer should have regard, if merely in the interests of the business, for the health, strength, education, morale, and stability of his personnel. These elements of smooth running are not acquired in the workshop alone, they are formed and developed as well, and particularly, outside it, in the home and school, in civil and religious life. Therefore, the employer comes to be concerned with his employees outside the works and here the question of proportion comes up again. Opinion is greatly divided on this point. Certain unfortunate experiments have resulted in some employers stopping short their interest, at the works gate and at the regulation of wages. The majority consider that the employer's activity may be used to good purpose outside the factory confines provided that there be discretion and prudence, that it be sought after rather than imposed, be in keeping with the general level of education and taste of those concerned and that it have absolute respect for their liberty. It must be benevolent collaboration, not tyrannical stewardship, and therein lies an indispensable condition of success.

The employer's welfare activities may be of various kinds. In the works they bear on matters of hygiene and comfort: ventilation, lighting, cleanliness, canteen facilities. Outside the works they bear on housing accommodation, feeding, education, and training. Provident schemes come under this head.

Non-financial incentives only come in the case of large scale concerns and may be said to be almost exclusively in the realm of government work. Every mode of payment likely to make the personnel more valuable and improve its lot in life, and also to inspire keenness on the part of employees at all levels, should be a matter for managers' constant attention.

8. CENTRALIZATION

Like division of work, centralization belongs to the natural order; this turns on the fact that in every organism, animal or social, sensations converge towards the brain or directive part, and from the brain or directive part orders are sent out which set all parts of the organism in movement. Centralization is not a system of management good or bad of itself, capable of being adopted or discarded at the whim of managers or of circumstances; it is always present to a greater or less extent. The question of centralization or decentralization is a simple question of proportion, it is a matter of finding the optimum degree for the particular concern. In small firms, where the manager's orders go directly to subordinates there is absolute centralization; in large concerns, where a long scalar chain is interposed between manager and lower grades, orders and counter-information too have to go through a series of intermediaries. Each employee, intentionally or unintentionally, puts something of himself into the transmission and execution of orders and of information received too. He does not operate merely as a cog in a machine. What appropriate share of initiative may be left to intermediaries depends on the personal character of the manager, on his moral worth, on the reliability of his subordinates, and also on the condition of the business. The degree of centralization must vary according to different cases. The objective to pursue is the optimum utilization of all faculties of the personnel.

If the moral worth of the manager, his strength, intelligence, experience and swiftness of thought allow him to have a wide span of activities he will be able to carry centralization quite far and reduce his seconds in command to mere executive agents. If, conversely, he prefers to have greater recourse to the experience, opinions, and counsel of his colleagues whilst reserving to himself the privilege of giving general directives, he can effect considerable decentralization.

Seeing that both absolute and relative value of manager and employees are constantly changing, it is understandable that the degree of centralization or decentralization may itself vary constantly. It is a problem to be solved according to circumstances, to the best satisfaction of the interests involved. It arises, not only in the case of higher authority, but for superiors at all levels; and not one but can extend or confine, to some extent, his subordinates' initiative.

The finding of the measure which shall give the best overall yield: that is the problem of centralization or decentralization. Everything which goes to increase the importance of the subordinate's rôle is decentralization, everything which goes to reduce it is centralization.

9. SCALAR CHAIN

The scalar chain is the chain of superiors ranging from the ultimate authority to the lowest ranks. The line of authority is the route followed—via every link in the chain—by all communications which start from or go to the ultimate authority. This path is dictated both by the need for some transmission and by the principle of unity of command, but it is not always the swiftest. It is even at times disastrously lengthy in large concerns, notably in governmental ones. Now, there are many activities whose success turns on speedy execution, hence respect for the line of authority must be reconciled with the need for swift action.

Let us imagine that section F has to be put into contact with section P in a business whose scalar chain is represented by the double ladder $G–A–Q$ thus—

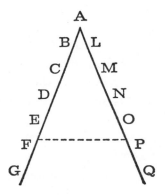

By following the line of authority the ladder must be climbed from F to A and then descended from A to P, stopping at each rung, then ascended again from P to A, and descended once more from A to F, in order to get back to the starting point. Evidently it is much simpler and quicker to go directly from F to P by making use of *FP* as a "gang plank" and that is what is most often done. The scalar principle will be safeguarded if managers E and O have authorized their respective subordinates F and P to treat directly, and the position will be fully regularized if F and P inform their respective superiors forthwith of what they have agreed upon. So long as F and P remain in agreement, and so long as their actions are approved by their immediate superiors, direct contact may be maintained, but from the instant that agreement ceases or there is no approval from the superiors direct contact comes to an end, and the scalar chain is straightway resumed. Such is the actual procedure to be observed in the great majority of businesses. It provides for the usual exercise of some measure of initiative at all levels of authority. In the small concern, the general interest, viz. that of the concern proper, is easy to grasp, and the employer is present to recall this interest to those tempted to lose sight of it. In government enterprise the general interest is such a complex, vast, remote thing, that it is not easy to get a clear idea of it, and for the majority of civil servants the employer is somewhat mythical and unless the sentiment of general interest be constantly revived by higher authority, it becomes blurred and weakened and each section tends to regard itself as its own aim and end and forgets that it is only a cog in a big machine, all of whose parts must work in concert. It becomes isolated, cloistered, aware only of the line of authority.

The use of the "gang plank" is simple, swift, sure. It allows the two employees F and P to deal at one sitting, and in a few hours, with some question or other which via the scalar chain would pass through twenty transmissions, inconvenience many people, involve masses of paper, lose weeks or months to get to a conclusion less satisfactory generally than the one which could have been obtained via direct contact as between F and P.

Is it possible that such practices, as ridiculous as they are devastating, could be in current use? Unfortunately there can be little doubt of it in government department affairs. It is usually acknowledged that the chief cause is fear of responsibility. I am rather of the opinion that it is insufficient executive capacity on the part of those in charge. If supreme authority A insisted that his assistants B and L made use of the "gang plank" themselves and made its use incumbent upon their subordinates C and M, the habit and courage of taking responsibility would be established and at the same time the custom of using the shortest path.

It is an error to depart needlessly from the line of authority, but it is an even greater one to keep to it when detriment to the business ensues. The latter may attain extreme gravity in certain conditions. When an employee is obliged to choose between the two practices, and it is impossible for him to take advice from his superior, he should be courageous enough and feel free enough to adopt the line dictated by the general interest. But for him to be in this frame of mind there must have been previous precedent, and his superiors must have set him the example—for example must always come from above.

10. ORDER

The formula is known in the case of material things, "A place for everything and everything in its place." The formula is the same for human order: "A place for everyone and everyone in his place."

Material Order. In accordance with the preceding definition, so that material order shall prevail, there must be a place appointed for each thing and each thing must be in its appointed place. Is that enough? Is it not also necessary that the place shall have been well chosen? The object of order must be avoidance of loss of material, and for this object to be completely realized not only must things be in their place suitably arranged but also the place must have been chosen so as to facilitate all activities as much as possible. If this last condition be unfulfilled, there is merely the appearance of order. Appearance of order may cover over real disorder. I have seen a works yard used as a store for steel ingots in which the material was well stacked, evenly arranged and clean and which gave a pleasing impression of orderliness. On close inspection it could be noted that the same heap included five or six types of steel intended for different manufacture all mixed up together. Whence useless handling, lost time, risk of mistakes because each thing was not in its place. It happens, on the other hand, that the appearance of disorder may actually be true order. Such is the case with papers scattered about at a master's whim which a well-meaning but incompetent servant re-arranges and stacks in neat piles. The master can no longer find his way about them. Perfect order presupposes a judiciously chosen place and the appearance of order is merely a false or imperfect image of real order. Cleanliness is a corollary of orderliness, there is no appointed place for dirt. A diagram representing the entire premises divided up into as many sections as there are employees responsible facilitates considerably the establishing and control of order.

Social Order. For social order to prevail in a concern there must, in accordance with the definition, be an appointed place for every employee and every employee be in his appointed place. Perfect order requires, further, that the place be suitable for the employee and the employee for the place—in English idiom, "The right man in the right place."

Thus understood, social order presupposes the successful execution of the two most difficult managerial activities: good organization and good selection. Once the posts essential to the smooth running of the business have been decided upon and those to fill such posts have been selected, each employee occupies that post wherein he can render most service. Such is perfect social order, "A place for each one and each one in his place." That appears simple, and naturally we are so anxious for it to be so that when we hear for the twentieth time a government departmental head assert this principle, we conjure up straightway a concept of perfect administration. This is a mirage.

Social order demands precise knowledge of the human requirements and resources of the concern and a constant balance between these requirements and resources. Now this balance is most difficult to establish and maintain and all the more difficult the bigger the business, and when it has been upset and individual interests resulted in neglect or sacrifice of the general interest, when ambition, nepotism, favouritism or merely ignorance has multiplied positions without good reason or filled them with incompetent employees, much talent and strength of will, and more persistence than current instability of ministerial appointments presupposes, are required in order to sweep away abuses and restore order.

As applied to government enterprise the principle of order, "A place for each one and each one in his place," takes on an astounding breadth. It means national responsibility towards each and all, everyone's destiny mapped out, national solidarity, the whole problem of society. I will stay no longer over this disturbing extension of the principle of order. In private businesses and especially in those of restricted scope it is easier to maintain proportion as between selection and requirements. As in the case of orderly material arrangement, a chart or plan makes the establishment and control of human arrangement much more easy. This represents the personnel in entirety, and all sections of the concern together with the people occupying them. This chart will come up again in the chapter on Organization.

11. EQUITY

Why equity and not justice? Justice is putting into execution established conventions, but conventions cannot foresee everything, they need to be interpreted or their inadequacy supplemented. For the personnel to be encouraged to carry out its duties with all the devotion and loyalty of which it is capable it must be treated with kindliness, and equity results from the combination of kindliness and justice. Equity excludes neither forcefulness nor sternness and the application of it requires much good sense, experience and good nature.

Desire for equity and equality of treatment are aspirations to be taken into account in dealing with employees. In order to satisfy these requirements as much as possible without neglecting any principle or losing sight of the general interest, the head of the business must frequently summon up his highest faculties. He should strive to instil a sense of equity throughout all levels of the scalar chain.

12. STABILITY OF TENURE OF PERSONNEL

Time is required for an employee to get used to new work and succeed in doing it well, always assuming that he possesses the requisite abilities. If when he has got used to it, or before then, he is moved, he will not have had time to render worthwhile service. If this be repeated indefinitely the work will never be properly done. The undesirable consequences of such insecurity of tenure are especially to be feared in large concerns, where the settling in of managers is generally a lengthy matter. Much time is needed indeed to get to know men and things in a large concern in order to be in a position to decide on a plan of action, to gain confidence in oneself, and inspire it in others. Hence it has often been recorded that a mediocre manager who stays is infinitely preferable to outstanding managers who merely come and go.

Generally the managerial personnel of prosperous concerns is stable, that of unsuccessful ones is unstable. Instability of tenure is at one and the same time cause and effect of bad running. The apprenticeship of a higher manager is generally a costly matter. Nevertheless, changes of personnel are inevitable; age, illness, retirement, death, disturb the human make-up of the firm; certain employees are no longer capable of carrying out their duties, whilst others become fit to assume greater responsibilities. In common with all the other principles, therefore, stability of tenure of personnel is also a question of proportion.

13. INITIATIVE

Thinking out a plan and ensuring its success is one of the keenest satisfactions for an intelligent man to experience. It is also one of the

most powerful stimulants of human endeavour. This power of thinking out and executing is what is called initiative, and freedom to
propose and to execute belongs too, each in its way, to initiative.
At all levels of the organizational ladder zeal and energy on the
part of employees are augmented by initiative. The initiative of
all, added to that of the manager, and supplementing it if need be,
represents a great source of strength for businesses. This is particularly apparent at difficult times; hence it is essential to encourage
and develop this capacity to the full.

Much tact and some integrity are required to inspire and maintain everyone's initiative, within the limits imposed, by respect for
authority and for discipline. The manager must be able to sacrifice
some personal vanity in order to grant this sort of satisfaction to
subordinates. Other things being equal, moreover, a manager able
to permit the exercise of initiative on the part of subordinates is
infinitely superior to one who cannot do so.

14. ESPRIT DE CORPS

"Union is strength." Business heads would do well to ponder
on this proverb. Harmony, union among the personnel of a concern,
is great strength in that concern. Effort, then, should be made to
establish it. Among the countless methods in use I will single out
specially one principle to be observed and two pitfalls to be avoided.
The principle to be observed is unity of command; the dangers
to be avoided are (*a*) a misguided interpretation of the motto
"divide and rule," (*b*) the abuse of written communications.

(*a*) *Personnel must not be split up.* Dividing enemy forces to
weaken them is clever, but dividing one's own team is a grave
sin against the business. Whether this error results from inadequate
managerial capacity or imperfect grasp of things, or from egoism
which sacrifices general interest to personal interest, it is always
reprehensible because harmful to the business. There is no merit
in sowing dissension among subordinates; any beginner can do it.
On the contrary, real talent is needed to coordinate effort, encourage keenness, use each man's abilities, and reward each one's

merit without arousing possible jealousies and disturbing harmonious relations.

(*b*) *Abuse of written communications.* In dealing with a business matter or giving an order which requires explanation to complete it, usually it is simpler and quicker to do so verbally than in writing. Besides, it is well known that differences and misunderstandings which a conversation could clear up, grow more bitter in writing. Thence it follows that, wherever possible, contacts should be verbal; there is a gain in speed, clarity and harmony. Nevertheless, it happens in some firms that employees of neighbouring departments with numerous points of contact, or even employees within a department, who could quite easily meet, only communicate with each other in writing. Hence arise increased work and complications and delays harmful to the business. At the same time, there is to be observed a certain animosity prevailing between different departments or different employees within a department. The system of written communications usually brings this result. There is a way of putting an end to this deplorable system and that is to forbid all communications in writing which could easily and advantageously be replaced by verbal ones. There again, we come up against a question of proportion.

It is not merely by the satisfactory results of harmony obtaining as between employees of the same department that the power of unity is shown: commercial agreements, unions, associations of every kind, play an important part in business management.

The part played by association has increased remarkably in half a century. I remember, in 1860, workers of primary industries without cohesion, without common bond, a veritable cloud of individual dust particles; and out of that the union has produced collective associations, meeting employers on equal terms. At that same time, bitter rivalry prevailed between large firms, closely similar, which has given place gradually to friendly relations, permitting of the settlement of most common interests by joint agreement. It is the beginning of a new era which already has profoundly modified both habits and ideas, and industrial heads should take this development into account.

*   *   *

There I bring to an end this review of principles, not because the list is exhausted—this list has no precise limits—but because to me it seems at the moment especially useful to endow management theory with a dozen or so well-established principles, on which it is appropriate to concentrate general discussion. The foregoing principles are those to which I have most often had recourse. I have simply expressed my personal opinion in connection with them. Are they to have a place in the management code which is to be built up? General discussion will show.

This code is indispensable. Be it a case of commerce, industry, politics, religion, war, or philanthropy, in every concern there is a management function to be performed, and for its performance there must be principles, that is to say acknowledged truths regarded as proven on which to rely. And it is the code which represents the sum total of these truths at any given moment.

Surprise might be expressed at the outset that the eternal moral principles, the laws of the Decalogue and Commandments of the Church are not sufficient guide for the manager, and that a special code is needed. The explanation is this: the higher laws of religious or moral order envisage the individual only, or else interests which are not of this world, whereas management principles aim at the success of associations of individuals and at the satisfying of economic interests. Given that the aim is different, it is not surprising that the means are not the same. There is no identity, so there is no contradiction. Without principles one is in darkness and chaos; interest, experience and proportion are still very handicapped, even with the best principles. The principle is the lighthouse fixing the bearings but it can only serve those who already know the way into port.

FRANK BUNKER GILBRETH

(1868–1924)

FRANK BUNKER GILBRETH paralleled Gantt (pp. 105–129) in his interest in human beings and human effort, applying to this interest an enormous capacity for organizing detail.

The result was the development of motion study as a basic management technique. In collaboration with his wife, Dr. Lillian Moller Gilbreth (who since his untimely death has carried on the work they began together), he also explored many other important new areas of management. A common characteristic of their thinking was emphasis on the employee as an individual, whose productivity depended on attitude, opportunity, and physical environment as much as on the use of correct methods and ideal equipment. The Gilbreths' "three-position plan of promotion," proposed in 1916, anticipated by almost 40 years what we now call systematic management development.

Gilbreth's early career was in construction, where the famous Gilbreth system of bricklaying was worked out. As he developed his ideas on improving methods, his interests broadened, and he became a consultant in management engineering. The following paper, presented at a management conference in Milan, Italy, in 1922, is a comprehensive statement of his beliefs, ranging from micro-motion study and "the one best way to do work" to the three-position plan of promotion and the effect of fatigue on productivity.

SCIENCE IN MANAGEMENT FOR THE ONE BEST WAY TO DO WORK

BY FRANK B. GILBRETH

Fallacy of the Drifting Process Toward Efficiency

In the past, progress in management has been made largely by the "drifting process." This drifting process is the slowest process. The drifting process has never once led to the One Best Way to do work—*never once*. Everybody knows this, yet only a small percentage of the world is applying science to methods of work and to management, as has been done to so many of her material things.

Actual Measurement Should Be the Basis for Decisions for Obtaining Efficiency

Times have changed, and are changing, and the engineer has now shown how greater changes for progress in methods of work and in management can be made in a year than have formerly been made in centuries. For greatest results, the best of present practice must be recorded, measured, judged, and conserved. In

Reprinted from the pamphlet, *Science in Management for the One Best Way to Do Work,* by Frank B. Gilbreth. Published by Società Umanitaria, Milan, 1923. Paper presented at IIIème Conférence Internationale de Psychotechnique Appliqué à l'Orientation Professionelle, Milan, Italy, October 2–4, 1922. Original pamphlet made available through the courtesy of the Gilbreth Collection, Engineering Library, Purdue University, Lafayette, Indiana. Used by permission of Mrs. Lillian M. Gilbreth.

the past, there has been no nation which has attempted to standardize, as a result of measurement, the best that is known regarding methods of work and management.

A Nation Should Measure and Inventory Its Efficiency

This is the age of measurement.

An epoch in the development of a nation is marked when it inventories its efficiency and gathers detailed records of successful methods and devices for doing work, in order that all may use the One Best Way available, or extant, wherever it be found, and improve constantly and cumulatively from the best that is known at any time; but unless measurement is applied, and the causes and reasons for success or efficiency are recorded sufficiently in detail for others than those who did the recording to understand, real, constant, cumulative, and lasting progress cannot result.

Thoroughness Is Necessary

It is necessary not only to observe present conditions carefully but to *"think things through,"* to get back to fundamentals, and to ask not only *what* is efficient but *how* and *why* it is efficient, and what can be standardized that will automatically cause the conditions that will enable those efficient happenings to exist continuously, to be permanent and repetitive.

Science of Management Tells the "What," "How," and "Why"

It is for this reason that the science of management is an indispensable aid in understanding and using efficiency methods and devices,—because it tells *what* is efficient, decides exactly *how* efficient it is, and explains the *why*.

The Science of Management consists of applying measurement to management and of abiding by results of measurement. National prosperity can be maintained only if it measures its development and plans its progress as a result of this measurement.

Purpose of This Paper

It is the purpose of this paper to show why the science of management forms an important part in attaining, and especially in maintaining, national prosperity.

How Scientific Management Got Its Name

"Scientific Management" is merely a name for an attempt to enlist science in the solving of the complicated problem of increasing the productivity of all for the greatest good of the greatest number and for justice, increased opportunity, comfort, and happiness for all. As it is known to-day, it dates in the minds of most people from the time when successful methods of work were investigated in America, and especially when the Interstate Commerce Commission and Congress were holding hearings on the claims, merits, and possibilities of the Taylor* and other systems of management in relation to increases in efficiency, particularly of the railroads in opposition to proposed increases of railroad freight rates.

In planning the hearings before the Interstate Commerce Commission, it was found desirable to decide upon a short title, or name, by which the subject of "Science applied to management" could be identified and discussed. At a small meeting of a few of the early advocates of the movement at which we were present, prior to the hearings, Mr. Louis Brandeis, now Justice Brandeis, who advocated better management instead of increasing freight rates, presented the need for such a name. The term "Scientific Management" was finally decided upon as being suitable, free from personal entanglements, and embodying the underlying ideas of this new "decision by measurement" type of management. As a consequence, the name "Scientific Management" was used and was flashed and mailed around the world by news and technical writers, although the name "measured functional management," suggested

---

* See pages 55–103.—EDITOR

at the time, would perhaps have been better for the cause of science in management, as well as being more appropriate and more truly descriptive.

The "Science of Management" includes much more than what is included in the term "Scientific Management."

Age and Origin of Early Attempts at Definite and Systematic Management

The science of management far antedates Taylor and the other leaders of the movement of this generation. We find it well under way in the work of Babbage and of Adam Smith. In 1776 Adam Smith wrote "An Inquiry into the Nature and Cause of the Wealth of Nations," a masterpiece for its time and in many respects still a masterpiece not only of economics but of industrial efficiency. In 1832 Charles Babbage,† in his "Economy of Machinery and Manufacture," gave not only a masterly description and discussion of conditions in industry at that time but a model method of studying such conditions. These clear thinkers and finished writers were able to put into words thoughts that intelligent men everywhere had been working toward and struggling to express and use for ages. Learned men were also giving this subject their attention in France and Italy, as is clearly seen in the works of Coulomb and in the handbook of Leonardo da Vinci.

Management has for centuries been a subject that held popular attention, the complicated managerial problems of pay systems and cooperation being clearly described in the Parable of the Vineyard. It is not surprising that management has always been an essential element of work and of production.

Ancient Records of Methods of Management

All existing records of methods in arts and trades show unmistakable signs of an advanced development in management and

---

† See pages 17–34.—EDITOR

motion study, as may be seen even in the sculptured pictures of the Assyrian, Babylonian, and Egyptian monuments, executed in the dawn of written history, which show a certain type of efficiency and which may well have served not only as records but also as teaching devices. In these records there are numerous examples of recognition of the factor of rhythm as a variable of motions and of efficiency. In many instances these records show that the different kinds and classes of workers were distinguishable by their different kinds of dress. The records show, in part, the accepted and apparently highly standardized methods of enforcing order of those days,—for the gang bosses are repeatedly shown as each possessing one large club and two long daggers. The large club is poised in the air in the right hand, and one long dagger in the left, and the second dagger is always so located and positioned that it can be grasped with the shortest and quickest motions, in case at any time it was desired in the hand more than was the club.

Units, Methods and Devices for Judging Management

We cannot properly compare, or "rate," or judge management without *measurement*. For constant, cumulative improvement and progress, this measurement of efficiency and management must consider three factors: namely,—first, the units to measure, the numerical measures of which indicate the quality of management; second, the methods of measuring, the measures of which, in many different units, determine their value and desirability; third, the measuring devices, the measures of which determine their desirability as tools of measuring. The *unit* selected indicates the results desired to be achieved or eliminated. The *method* used shows the state of perfection of the theory. The *device* shows the existing state of the practice.

To be efficient, the units must be as elementary as possible and selected with special regard to their facilitating the holding of all units constant except the one which is being measured at that time. The units should foster accuracy and be readily transferable for the solving of other, similar problems. The *method* must insist on such a degree of accuracy as the results desired demand. Any error should be toward the practice of too great accuracy, because of the possibility of utilizing accurate records for many more problems than the original one for which they were specially intended. For the same reason, the devices must attain as great a degree of accuracy as is possible, but must be as cheap and available as is consistent with such accuracy. As far as possible, these devices must be free from human error.

Example of Selection of Wrong Unit of Management

For a definite illustration of the importance of this, consider the original records of Assyrian and Egyptian management already referred to and still available to the world in the British Museum. These records show that the *unit* to be measured selected by these ancient managers was improperly and unwisely chosen. This unit considered, apparently, the amount of time worked and, secondarily, *the amount of output accomplished,* the emphasis being upon the amount of effort exerted, rather than upon the continuity of effort. The quality of output was judged from the standpoint of the finished work and not the method by which it was done. The human element was not only not considered, but the subject was apparently discarded as being entirely unworthy of attention. Apparently there was not the least consideration given to measuring any units that reduce fatigue or labor turnover, for the workers were drafted and impressed in accordance with royal edicts which were issued in some cases, after a careful census of the inhabitants had been taken.[1] Their "employment psychology" was apparently based upon no such scheme as dismissal for disobedience, insubordination, or lack of cooperation. Their plan was apparently to make a horrible example of each act that the ever present gang boss considered a breach of discipline. This practice can be paralleled in some organizations to-day, but public sentiment prevents going so near the limit as was apparently customary in ancient times.

Human life, in the earliest records of management, was the

---

[1] King, Willford, "The Elements of Statistical Method," page 2.

cheapest of commodities, and work was done either by slaves of foreign extraction, or by [native?] slaves, or the equivalent of slaves, or prisoners of war, who were undergoing punishment or who belonged to a class expected to live lives of drudgery.

Ethics, Not Science, Furnish Standards of Right and Wrong

We note that while science is not called upon to furnish a standard of right and wrong, this being the task of ethics, science can be utilized for measuring the data submitted and comparing them to the established standard, and publishing the facts for all to see. Such a standard having been determined, it is thus possible to judge whether the units, methods, and devices selected are ethical or otherwise.

The Best Unit for Science to Use to Measure Ethical Standards Is a Minute of Happiness

In scientific management the most constructive, desirable, successful, and ethical unit of measurement is a "Minute of Happiness," [2] here or hereafter. In many instances a reward hereafter has been found sufficient for obtaining the workers' best efforts, serving instead of the customary wage in money for that kind and quantity of output in the vicinity.

Obviously, other things being equal, that which affects favorably the largest number of people will cause the greatest quantity of happiness minutes. It must be remembered that to enlist the ability and zeal of those fitted to lead an aggregation or organization to greatest success, sufficient motivation must be offered; or the *one best leader*, as desired in each division of the organization, will devote his efforts and time to something which will bring him what he thinks will be greater returns.

This brings us to the great problem of "pay for results," the

---

[2] See "Fatigue Study," Routledge & Co., London; "Etude des mouvements appliqué," Dunod, Paris; "Ermüdungsstudien," Berlin.

discussion of which is out of place in this paper. For further details of this, see Chapter entitled "Incentives in Psychology of Management."

A method in management is ethical when it gives those concerned a square deal. Even the *devices* can be judged as honest or dishonest, as well as accurate or inaccurate, and condemned as unethical, as the spying stop-watch book has been where it disregards or infringes human rights.

Science Determines Units of Efficiency

While the science of management may not determine standards of right and wrong, it can, and actually does, determine standards of efficiency, such as the One Best Way to learn, do, or teach any kind of work. In its most approved and advanced forms, the science of management has been more just and ethical in defining the subject matter of implied, as well as actual, contracts between employer and employee based upon "pay for results" than has any other form of management.

To determine these standards of just and ethical procedure, management must, first, *conserve the best of the past;* second, *organize the present;* and, third, *forecast and plan for the future.*

It has often been thought that the science of management, like some unfortunate improperly prepared and planned attempts in "Scientific Management," is a destructive force,—a critical force, —that aims to do away with whatever exists, root and branch, and to start something entirely new on a new foundation. This is not the case at all when the management is installed by one who properly understands it. The aim of the science of management is to submit to measurement what already exists in the plant under examination, in order to discover and conserve those things which are worth keeping and perpetuating.

When this is not done, there is always an astounding unnecessary waste, because time and individual conditions and differences bring to pass many standards, customs, and methods of great value, which could be utilized with profit. It must not be forgotten that nothing is exempt from inspection and judgment by measurement because of its aim or its long use as a standard, and that sometimes things which are of less than no value have been allowed to go on continuously for years because no one has had the combination of the thought, the desire, and the proper authority to make a change. On the other hand, a method or a device that has worked satisfactorily for many years should be most carefully investigated, in order that the demands which it fulfills, as well as the manner in which it fulfills them, may be most carefully estimated. "Hold fast to that which is good" might well be a slogan of the science of management, though it is not generally understood to be one.

Recognition of Some Laws of Motion Study by the People of the Stone Age as Shown by Their Implements

Scores of definite instances illustrating the above can be cited from existing evidences of tool efficiency in the days of the stone age, due consideration being given to the handicap that stone instead of metal was the material of which these tools were made. The tools of the expert workmen of that age, found in the archaeological museums of the world, indicate certain features relating to motion study, fatigue study, and causes of skill—developed during the many thousands of years of the stone age—that have not been equalled or appreciated as yet, even by the designers, makers, and users of the later bronze tools or of the steel tools of to-day. The reason for this is that the tool designers of to-day have not actually had these tools in their hands and examined them from the standpoint of the laws of motion study, fatigue study, and standardization. Such definite instances should be recognized, measured, and recorded in the survey of all existing evidences of the One Best Way to do work.

Types of Surveys for Efficiency

Systematizing and organizing all existing desirable conditions calls for a careful survey which can also assist in conservation. A survey may be anything from a more or less unsystematic record or list of what occurs to what is known as a technical survey, made by experts who are experienced in finding, recording, and using data. Such surveys as those made by the Russell Sage Foundation, under the brilliant leadership of Dr. Leonard Ayers, furnish an excellent example of what a scientific survey is and can accomplish. The advantage of having a survey made by someone in the plant is that the making of the survey is of itself a highly educative process. The advantage of having the survey made by a survey expert is that he is already trained to note minute likenesses and differences. He is able not only to record what exists but also to deduce valuable recommendations for improvement from his experience in similar problems in other organizations, particularly regarding the adoption of fewer and better standards and methods for the same kind of work.

Everything Should Be Standardized and All Standards Noted in The Survey

This does not mean fewer standards for different kinds of work. On the contrary, the best results come only when everything is standardized down to the smallest and most insignificant details. This means that decisions on often repeated questions should be standardized wherever possible. For example: Before starting to work one's first minute on a typewriter, calculating or accounting machine, the decisions as to which fingers shall strike each individual key should be standardized and settled, once and for all.

A Survey Should Record "What Is" Separate from "What Should Be" or "Will Be"

It is almost impossible for the amateur survey maker to give an unprejudiced record of what occurs, not only because of his limited experiences, but also because he is constantly tempted to put down not that which he actually does but, rather, that which he obviously ought to do or would like to do, or what he thinks he does, or what he thinks will be the method in the near future,—or something in some degree different from a survey of what actually is being done. The ideal conditions exist when as many members of the organization as possible make an amateur survey, each of his own work, as part of and in accordance with a complete outline in process chart form; and when, to supplement this, a survey expert makes a survey of the entire plant and organization in order to "check up" and supplement the individual surveys and individual process charts.

Surveying, Classifying and Filing Information

A most important part of the organization work of the science of management consists of planning, gathering, arranging, and systematizing all this and similar information and filing it under a complete interrelated mnemonic classification filing system. This is specially adapted for all existing and all future notes and information specifically related to any work in question and classified and subclassified by subject, so that all data differing by one variable only are as nearly contiguous as possible. In this way, related matter comes automatically to the attention of the searcher, even if he does not suspect the existence of such information, in accordance with the laws of modern filing of information.

It is possible that much of this organizing of information and of the methods and processes throughout the plant can be done without the aid of a professional expert in the science of management. By this we mean that all successful and progressive plants of to-day have undoubtedly systematized their procedure to some extent. However, the science of management is fortunate in being able to provide the complete skeleton and mechanism for handling all procedure, with units, methods, and devices already standardized for visualizing, filing, and using. This means that both materials and information can be stored or used with ease.

Filing, Connecting and Visualizing Interrelations of Separate Pieces Of Information

A cursory study of many types of management charts will illustrate this very clearly. For example, take the typical organization chart, showing methods of visualizing and grouping responsibilities and lines of authority and counsel. Take, for example, our functional organization chart, illustrating grouped inter-related sub-divisions of the Taylor system, which recognizes the functional division of the planning from the performing and which shows plainly such divisions as the "what," "who," "where," "when," "how," "why," and "how much" of the problem. Take, again, our sub-functional chart, which shows the various types of work or sub-functions that are performed under each function. Take, for example, a typical chart of our three-position plan of promotion. See also the chapter on "Units, Methods and Devices," in "Applied Motion Study," which shows the financial and promotion relations of each type of work to every other type, and exactly along which regular and optional or exceptional-principle lines the employee must advance to reach any predetermined function. Take our master and individual process charts, which show the various stages in the manufacture of the product. These are but a few of many charts which show how information is recorded, grouped, visualized, and filed, and which indicate the degree to which it is available when needed.

A close study of these charts shows that in every case they depict logical and definite relationships; that is, they show the relation of cause to effect, and they give the valid cause for each desired effect. They conform not only to the laws of logic but to those of psychology, and of least waste in education, in that they afford the best method of imparting ideas and facts and of memorizing the information. Here, again, it is impossible for an organization to do much for itself in putting its information into a more orderly state. In fact, a series of more or less complete charts, showing, in comparable form, possible and planned changes, may be made a most valuable by-product of the survey.

Facts as Shown by the Surveys and Collected Information Must Be Faced

It requires something like courage for one to record and study the actual existing conditions in his own plant, whether in chart form or not, and to record the present and proposed future position of each and of every member of the organization engaged in management,—his present and probable titles and functions; the work that he actually does now; the work that he could or should do; and the relation of his work to that of the other members of that branch of the organization. It takes courage to walk personally with open mind and eyes through one's plant and to cause to have made and to study the actual records and charts of the various processes. These should begin where the requisition for raw material originates and the material enters the plant, and end as the finished product leaves the plant for transportation elsewhere. In the case of a blank form, these start with the first filling-in and state exactly, step by step, workplace by workplace, where it goes when it reposes in or travels through current or obsolete files; who or what transports it there; why it goes to each place; how long it remains there; what happens to it there; when, where, and with what it is inspected and over-inspected for quantity or quality, or both, etc.

The Best Way Is Always the Simplest Way After It Is Learned

By studying these things one realizes, as never before, the ramifications of and the many complications that beset even the simplest problems in production, and how numerous the instances are which are handled in a complicated way simply because there is no definite system recorder in detail for maintaining the simplest way.

It must not be forgotten also that "putting things in order" implies two things; first, getting them *into* the place desired; second, getting them *out of* the place without delay when they are needed. In most cases, the important thing is to be able to get the thing out and ready for use in the shortest amount of time possible when it is needed. The test of the efficiency of "filing," for example, is not in how short a time can any specific item be put into a resting place, but rather in how short a time can it be found and taken from its resting, or storage, place to the place where it is to be used. As an example of this let us consider the repair and storage of tools.

A Tool Room Must Be Completely Standardized for Best Results

The advantage of a tool room, under the most scientifically planned practice, is that a tool can be taken to the workplace a short time before it is needed, in that predetermined standard condition described by the written and otherwise recorded standard as essential to doing the best work in the shortest amount of time possible. True, it takes time to have the tool carried to the tool room, to have it inspected to see if it complies in every respect with the requirements of the written standards and, if it does not, to have it put into the standardized condition, then re-inspected and put away.

With a few standardized exceptions, which are also thoroughly provided for, each tool should be stored in the tool room when not in use, and when stored should be so placed in the tool rack (1) that the part showing its working condition will be most easily seen during the regular inspection and over-inspection trips arranged on the exception principle for an executive; (2) that it can be taken out in the shortest amount of time possible; and (3) that it conforms, while in storage in the tool room, to the laws of least waste for the motion cycle elements, such as "search," "find," "select," "grasp," [3] just as it does while being used. If at any time it is not in the condition that has been standardized and specified in writing, it is not to be put into storage until so conditioned and again inspected. When it conforms to the written standard made for that tool, it is to be put away in the standard position, which is the easiest way, after the tool bin has been constructed in accordance with the requirements of the standard.

The cost of the time of sharpening, conditioning, transporting, storing, and inspecting is as nothing compared with the benefits,—direct and indirect,—resulting from putting this standardized, properly sharpened and conditioned, automaticity-causing tool in the hand of the worker at the moment when he needs it; and the assurance that, as a result, he will be able to perform his part of the production schedule and program in the expected and allotted time.

---

[3] See chapter on "Motion Study for Crippled Soldiers" in the book "Motion Study for the Handicapped," Routledge, London.

The Astounding Loss to the World by Reason of Lack of Appreciation of the Part That Proper Tools Play in the One Best Way to Do Work

The hindrance to the productivity of all nations due to those in responsible charge of workers neither understanding the needs for, nor the solutions of, the problem of maintaining the best tools constantly in the proper condition undoubtedly amounts in money to more than an average of twenty per cent of the payroll of the world's workers. We have estimated this figure carefully, and we believe that 20% is much below the true amount. The resulting figures are astounding. Some people are so constituted that they cannot look wastes squarely in the face, simply because these wastes are astoundingly large. As an example of this, last year we stated that the loss in the United States due to unnecessary fatigue of all workers is a matter of hundreds of millions of pounds sterling per year. However, after due consideration one of the officers of the National Safety Council, a great organization for the prevention of accidents and unnecessary fatigue, in their official organ said our statement was reasonable and unanswerable.

These facts, when visualized in actual total money waste, are astounding, but we have seen many cases in motion study laboratory investigations of some of the best organizations where the loss has been more than fifty per cent of the workers' payroll, and we know of organizations where it is probably more. The motion study variable of automaticity is so important that it is better to have all one kind of an inferior class of tools in perfect condition than to have some first and some second class tools in varying states of condition.

The Quality of Tools Is Not Changed by Reason of Their Having Originated Outside of One's Own Country

One thing that hinders efficiency and fosters the continuation of the deplorably inefficient system of *"drifting toward efficiency"* is that in practically all nations there is evidence of the belief that it is something resembling a lack of patriotism and loyalty to acknowledge that any other nations have better tools than has one's own nation. Nevertheless, the facts bear out the economic law that those nations as a whole, and those parts of nations in particular which have paid the highest wages continuously for long periods, have the best tools with which to work. If a worker is paid low enough wages, it matters comparatively little what kind of tools he has, from a cost standpoint, but if his wages are unusually high, his managers and foremen insist that he be provided with the most suitable tools obtainable.

Motion Study Laboratories for Research in the World's Tools Should Be at the Disposal of Every Earnest Worker

The difference in tools is everywhere so evident that it would pay any nation, any city, or even any Employers' Board of Trade or Workers' Association to be ever cognizant of the best tools and best methods of conditioning tools, regardless of whence the necessary information must come. Any organization is lucky that can obtain a man, at almost any price, who can analyze tools from the motion study, fatigue study, and skill study standpoint, instead of relying upon the prejudice and preference of workers, due to habit and dexterity in spite of their wrong and poor tools, which influence their attempts to be perfectly fair in their judgment.

Tool Study Applies to All Departments

At present, first cost is the test of tools. Even a broom is made to that width which will sell to best advantage, not sweep with fewest motions. Where is the broom maker who has had his broom's motion studied? The same general criticism applies to many other tools. The maker of tools is not the only one asleep. How many executives have provided sweepers with a properly selected assortment of different-sized brooms to be used by the same sweeper in different parts of the sweeping? How many great organizations have furnished their purchasing departments with clearly circumscribed super-standards for tools to be purchased? No large organization can avoid losing money that has not hundreds of such standards for its purchasing department. This does not mean merely for hatchets, saws, and wrenches. It means everything down to the smallest item used,—that automaticity may be achieved for big outputs and least fatigue. Our clients have invariably been surprised when they have seen the simple money-saving standards that could be substituted for their unsystematized practices. The executive who does not also, personally, use a dictating machine instead of a stenographer exclusively, thus enabling his typist to earn higher wages because of his and her higher outputs; the man who still prefers the old-fashioned razor because he has neither personally acquired automaticity with the one best safety razor, nor counted the relative number of motions while shaving; the man who has not accustomed himself to walking on the one best kind of rubber heels and noted carefully the extra amount of work which he is capable of performing because he is less fatigued—these are examples of the types who cannot be expected to realize the amount of money that the world is losing by reason of its workers not being provided with the *best tools in proper condition.*

This is not a matter to be decided by a few minutes' consideration, for a short time review of this subject will give the same sort of decision as that of the American Indian who tried sleeping with one feather between his head and the rock that supported it. His conclusion was, you remember, that sleeping on a bed full of feathers would give him a similar disastrous result, proportionate to the relative number of feathers used. All mankind is prone to say, as did this Indian, "You can't change my mind. I've tried it." It must be remembered that a *trial is not a trial until the condition of automaticity has been achieved, and even then measurement must be used instead of judgment.* There are still many men who act as though it were as necessary to be present personally when their boots are cleaned as it is for them to be personally present when they are shaved.

The Subject of Tool Study Is Too Large for This Paper

This paper is not the place to describe in detail the differences in output of contented workers, both in the shops and in the offices, when they are furnished with super-standardized tools, maintained in condition in the One Best Way, and in sufficient quantity and with proper routines that will eliminate delays. Super-standardized tools permit learning their use in less time—a point of great importance to the learner and the nation. Super-practice with few tools makes greater skill in the same time. It also makes sooner the state of automaticity which is the greatest free asset of the worker. This gives more time for learning the use of more tools.

Letter Files Are Tools of the Mental Worker and Are Subject To All the Laws of Tool Study

The hindrance due to improperly standardized and operated tool systems is a no more flagrant example of causes of inefficiency than is the method of handling of letters for and by executives in the majority of organizations.

The value of the time taken to put a letter properly into the file is trifling compared with the value of the time required to find that letter and place it before the man at the moment he requires it if the letter is not filed in the One Best Way together with related information.

It is not expedient to write here the details of the necessity nor the process of having all letters in all departments put away properly into the files within one day from the day that they are received, regardless of the size of the organization, nor is it wise to start any argument about the possibility of this with those executives who have not seen it done in great organizations as well as in small ones.

It is not wise to dwell here upon the usual and customary arguments to the effect that a letter cannot be filed until after it has been answered, nor to discuss the admission that, in many files, filing means "probably lost" or "lost for a long time."

It is also not wise to dwell here upon the unnecessary delay and the cost of the ordinary routine in organizations where inefficient routing, filing systems, and handling of inward and outward correspondence testify to a general lack of appreciation of the fact that the usual practice to be found almost everywhere was not designed by the methods of motion study but, on the contrary, appears to be designed with the idea of *making* motions instead of *saving* them.

The Cost per Piece for Handling Mail Should Be Watched

It will pay any organization to have a careful record made of the cost of handling each piece of mail. The results of such a cost investigation have never, in our experience, failed to turn doubters of the value of the science of management into enthusiastic exponents, at least so far as process charts and a standardized standing order system are concerned.

Present Methods Should Be Visualized and Compared with Planned Methods

We note here only the importance of visualizing, measuring, and comparing the existing methods with a well-thought-out logical plan for all details of administration. We emphasize, as we must repeatedly, the benefits of specific standard mechanisms and installations, such as those referred to in the two examples just given, as a stimulus to thought and imitation. They are a starting point from which improvements are to be made and suggestions and inventions considered; and must be understood, installed, and working smoothly before real progress can be assured.

Watching for Indications of the Probable Trend of Events

The third function of management, following conservation and organization, is the forecasting of and planning for the trend of future developments. The study of statistics in graphical form shows that a careful investigation and comparison of the past and the present permits the prediction of at least the *trend* of future developments. Elderton, King, Secrist,—among the recent writers on statistics,—make this extremely plain even to the lay mind. The admirable books and papers of such men as Brinton and the Graphical Standards Committee show exactly how to present statistics graphically and not only *what* can be done but *how* it can be done, in the simplest and most impressive fashion.

*Graphs of the Past and Present Measurements Indicate the Trends
Of Similar Events in the Future*

A careful study of the past history and the present practice in
a plant will enable one, to some extent, to predict future development or at least show present trends. It will probably be said that
much of this development depends on conditions peculiar to the
individual plant, upon the prosperity of the country, upon the business and labor conditions, upon the demand for the product, and
upon all sorts of outside factors. This is undoubtedly true, but two
things should be said:

1. A man should be able to estimate what he will do if conditions
   remain the same as they are at present;
2. He should be prepared to meet almost any emergency by some
   planned-for expedient in his program.

The science of management is fortunate in being able not only
to forecast a trend for any individual enterprise more scientifically
than can be done without scientific management, but also in being
able to tell what the trend *ought to be,* as well as what it probably
will be. Thus, it is possible to plan ahead for such action as may
be desirable only when the quantity plotted falls outside the zone
of exclusion on the graphical exception-principle charts,[4] and present the case for action to an executive on the exception principle,
automatically notifying the executive whose rank is comparable with
the quantity of deviation.

*Preparedness for Meeting Emergencies and Other Exceptions
From Class*

Scientific Management is also fortunate in having definite and
proved methods with which to meet an emergency. Such terms as
"automatic notification," "exception principle," "zones of exclusion,"
"elasticity station," "standard deviation," "Flying Squadron in Man-

---

[4] See "Graphical Control on the Exception Principle for Executives," A. S. M. E.

agement," represent the standardized methods already provided
for meeting and handling the unexpected. Perhaps it might better
be said, "expecting the unexpected to happen" and getting ready to
handle it when it does occur. After all, statistics seem to show that
"chance" is really no longer "chance" but happens fairly closely in
accordance with the laws of expected variation from the normal
curve of the class.

Planning for Probable Development

Much can be said of the value of statistics in assisting in the
making of correct decisions regarding lines of probable development and planning accordingly. Take, for an actual example of this,
the future need for and the building of a great Western University.
A loyal citizen, a regent of the University, instituted a competition,
which was engaged in by architects from many countries, to plan
for the development of the buildings and grounds of this University.
Every department of the University outlined its present and future
needs; everyone interested in the University contributed information as to its possible, probable, and desired development. All of
these data were assembled and studied, and the resulting needs
were met by the foremost leaders in their professions. The plans made
were far ahead of the requirements at the time. Their effect, however, has been extremely successful. Not only has such development
as has taken place in the twenty years since then followed the lines
wisely laid down at that time, but undoubtedly much has found
its way into the resources of the University, because those who had
things to contribute knew that what they gave would be utilized
in a directed, orderly fashion. As a result, these plans have served
as a stimulus, as well as a conserving and guiding force, and have
probably exceeded even the usefulness that their donor expected
of them.

In the same way the science of management is already equipped
to supply a plan for the development of an industry or an organization. It is able not only to meet the general demands but to consider
the individual differences of the organization. The early recognition

of the trend, the laying out of this plan, and the adaptation of the methods of the science to the individual needs is not work for an untrained, inexperienced executive, although such can be found in charge of this responsible work almost everywhere. The literature of the subject of management contains the necessary information, but only the trained thinker and installer can use this information for the betterment of the plant. In some plants to-day management has developed to such a stage that experts are now at work making surveys, organizing, and forecasting the trend of future development. However, the majority of plants are as yet in an earlier stage, where the chief necessities are to arouse interest in progress in the plant towards better management; to make every member of the organization, in all fields of the work, *think* along the lines of measurement in management; and to stimulate the plant to take such preliminary steps as it can for itself.

Procedure of the Preliminary Stage of the Transitory Period in Management

We are informed on good authority that it is the belief of many of the leaders of thought in Europe that the majority of the plants abroad require most of all information as to the best procedure in this preliminary stage. We are, therefore, and by request, making this paper very definite and specific in its description of what can wisely be done in the first stages of thinking along the lines of the science of management and of preparing to make measurement and accept its results.

Visualizing the Problem

With this thought in mind, we shall review what we have already said on the subject, to emphasize the importance, in all three stages, of visualizing the problem. Charts, photographs, graphs, and other methods of recording have, as their prime object, presenting the existing state of things to the eye in the clearest possible way.

Those not intimately acquainted with present-day investigations in education scarcely realize how many more people learn easier through their eyes than through their ears, or their muscles, or other sense avenues. Through our work with the crippled and blinded, especially the crippled and blinded soldier, we are now able to substitute the use of the other senses for the use of sight.[5] It still remains to be said, however, that the sighted in a large majority of cases learn things easiest through the eye. While we supplement eye teaching with teaching through the ear and teaching through the kinesthetic sensations,—as in the use of motion models[6] —we always stress the importance of visualization. Therefore, in the preliminary stage of introducing the science of management into a plant, we endeavour in every possible way to visualize the problems and to make the process of teaching visual.

So far we have outlined the relation of scientific management to the *past,* to the *present,* and to the *future* of the plant. It is now well to outline its relation to other existing activities. The science of management owes the chief part of its development to the work of the engineer. The leaders in the field have all been engineers,— the leaders both in the theory and in the practice,—and at the present time the installers are largely also recruited from the field of engineering. This is undoubtedly because the engineer has been accustomed, from his earliest instruction, to deal with measurement and to abide by the results of measurement. The engineer has, however, been ready and glad to acknowledge and is increasingly willing to acknowledge the value of cooperation in other fields.

Cooperation Stimulates Progress

The science of management profits by using the results of other already existing activities. It must, of course, test these activities, not only for their validity, but for their usefulness in the field of

---

[5] See "Motion Study for the Handicapped," page 147.

[6] See "Applied M. S.," page 91; Macmillan & Co., N. Y.; "Etude des mouvements appliqué," chap. VI, Dunod, Paris; "Angewandte Bewegungsstudien." Berlin.

management. It has, in this way, tested and cooperated with findings in the field of safety, of vocational guidance,[7] of betterment work, of teaching,—both in full-time schools and colleges and in part-time and continuation schools,—in the work of the industrial schools and institutes; in the work done by the public libraries; in fact, in all work done by teaching, betterment, philanthropic, and clinical activities in the community.

More than this, the engineer has welcomed investigators and thinkers in other lines into the field of management. The work of testing and investigating materials of all kinds is not new. The engineer has gladly cooperated with the chemist, the physicist, and with all other scientists whose work leads them into the field of materials. Increasingly, also, the engineer is cooperating with, and inviting into management, the educator, the physiologist, the psychologist,[8] the psychiatrist, and other scientists engaged in what are known as the human sciences—also, the economist and the statistician.

Cooperation with Psychologist

The cooperation with the psychologist has been especially valuable, and it is a matter for congratulation that increasingly bodies of psychologists are devoting themselves to intensive study of the problems of industry. Courses in psychology are being introduced into the curriculum of the engineer. The fact that psychology is devoting itself to such a great extent to industrial problems insures teaching of young engineers that will be most profitable and allow them with the least expenditure of time to apply the results of the teaching to their individual problems.

It may be argued that scientific management as recorded in literature does not always show the influence of, or the results of, the cooperation that we advocate. To which the reply may be

---

[7] See "Publications of National Safety Council," Chicago, Meyer Bloomfield.

[8] "Psychology of Management," Macmillan & Co., New York; German Edition, "Verwaltungs-psychologie" by I. M. Witte, published by Verlag des Vereins Deutscher Ingenieure.

made that we are not here discussing so-called "Scientific Management," some instances of which are unquestionably in many respects faulty, but *the science of management*. The theory of management is evidently on the right trend if it is based upon science or upon accurate measurement.

The technique is often the honest though imperfect attempt to carry out that which is misunderstood to be the theory, and the practice does not always live up even to what is recognized and conceded to be best in the technique.

Lack of Cooperation Causes Unnecessary Wastes

But what we must emphasize here is not so much that cooperation does not exist as that an enormous waste occurs when it does not exist. The duplication and reduplication of effort is a pitiful waste of time and effort. Sometimes this is unavoidable, as it was in our own case, when after years of painstaking effort in devising many different methods for the photography of time and motion we discovered, too late to prove of use, though not too late to prove of interest and inspiration, the remarkable work of the French genius, Marey.‡ His work, unfortunately, had never been at our disposal until we had reinvented and abandoned many of its processes because they were unsuitable for our work. We finally invented and perfected our own units, methods, and devices for the solution of our problems and for their application to the needs in hand.

Management has many times experienced a similar waste of effort, as was the case in the early evolution of stop-watch time study without the proper knowledge of educational psychology and statistics.[9] Doubtless other fields have experienced a similar waste through failing to cooperate with management, but comments along

---

[9] See "Time Study and Motion Study as Fundamental Factors in Planning and Control." Taylor Society, N. Y.

---

‡ The reference may possibly be to Jules Etienne Marey, 1830–1904, student of physiology, medicine, and photography.—EDITOR

these lines will come more appropriately from thinkers and investigators in those fields.

The Management Should Cooperate with Outside Efforts to Increase Efficiency

As for the practical application, in making an investigation in any particular field we urge cooperation with all existing activities in the community, but it is not possible to list all of these. There are already functioning numerous philanthropic, social service, social, and other agencies engaged in betterment work who are glad to cooperate in many phases of the subject. For example: housing, feeding, lighting, heating, entertaining, insurance, service of doctor, dentist, and nurse, safety, social service, psychiatric clinic, the giving of psychological and fitness tests, together with all the educational forms of service. There are also the libraries,—those housed in permanent habitations and the traveling libraries,—the foreman's meeting held under such auspices as those of the Y. M. C. A. Again, there are the existing unions and other labor bodies, and all their many-sided activities.

It is a waste to install any new activity in a plant, or to assist in getting such activity going in the plant, if it can be handled better through cooperation with some already existing outside activity. Nothing but accurate measurement can determine whether the activity is better handled inside or outside the plant. The subject must come under serious consideration, and the waste of duplication must be eliminated, for it is expensive not only in direct cost but in indirect cost, because it encourages a practice which is unprofitable, uncooperative, and unscientific.

It may be urged that such cooperation often does away with the "personal element," with the development of individuality, and with the "personal interest" in these activities. Very true. In such case, let the value of these mentioned traits be measured, and if their value proves to be greater than the value of other things gained through cooperation, by all means conserve the individuality, the personal element, but do not refuse to subject the problem under consideration to measurement.

Here again, we note the importance of *units* of measurement and their relation to the ethical side of the problem. We must be careful to make it plain that by cooperation we mean "working together" in the old fashioned sense of the word, and that we do not attach any socialistic or other significance to the word. "Cooperation" is always used in this sense of "working together for the common good" in the literature, the theory, and the practice of the science of management.

Efficiency Is Not Limited Merely to the Production of Goods

In order to set about this work of installing the science of management in the preliminary stage in a plant with the least handicap, it is necessary to be forearmed with information as to the field of such application. The science of management has, in the past, done its most important work in the field of production—and this for several reasons. The leaders in the movement were primarily interested in production. It was their life work; and it is still with difficulty that most engineers can be persuaded that production is not the great work of the world. At times, marketing, distribution, and other types of work may seem, for the moment, to hold the most important place; but, in the long run, *production is the universal need of all times.*

Because of the importance of production, and because the leaders were in the field of production, the vocabulary of the science of management is the vocabulary of production. More than this, because Dr. Taylor was an engineer engaged chiefly in machine shop work and primarily interested in the machine shop, much of the terminology of management today appears to fit the needs of the machine shop rather than the needs for explaining the theory and the phenomena of management in general. For this reason, many have had the mistaken idea that the science of management applies only to production, and others have had the equally wrong notion that it applies only, or at least best, to work in the machine shop.

Precise Measurement for Finding the One Best Way in the Work Of Executives and Office Work

This latter idea has not been common recently due to the growth of the literature of the movement, telling of micromotion studies of work of executives and managers themselves and of the standardization by photography and writing, and of the organization in the field, in the office, in accounting, in distribution, in sales, in advertising, in the hospi als and other institutions. This literature is becoming lengthy and important. As a matter of fact, since the early days management has been applied in all these fields and also in fields entirely outside the industries, as in the professions of surgery and nursing, ard even in the sports.

Office and All Other Kinds of Mental Work Can Be Done More Efficiently, and Are Subject to the Same Laws as Work in the Shop

The office end is perhaps receiving special prominence, since the extensive micromotion and chronocyclegraph studies which we made in 1912 again proved, and beyond argument, that the underlying principles of obtaining and maintaining the One Best Way in office work are identical to those in any other work, so far as analysis, planning, routing, motion study, fatigue study, waste elimination, standardization, large outputs, management, and control are concerned. Further, the side of distribution is receiving great emphasis because of the need, nowadays, for consideration of this subject.

It is a sign of the times that the economist is arguing that the great waste of the war must ultimately be compensated for by extra production, at the same time that the manufacturers are unable to find a ready market for their wares, and while also there is much unemployment.

The Taylor Society, the Society of Industrial Engineers, and the Management Section of The American Society of Mechanical Engineers, all of them organizations in America for the study of problems of management, are now carefully collecting and exchanging data for the consideration of the special problems of distribution and salesmanship, and in the near future we may expect results which will be of international value.

The Super-Standardization of Everything, Every Tool, Every Practice, Every Process, Down to the Most Insignificant Item, Is Necessary for the Greatest Efficiency

We have thus far pointed out the need for and the advisability of applying the science of management to all work. We have explained the advantages of the preliminary survey which presents a record of existing conditions and existing needs. What is the next step to be considered? Undoubtedly the selection of *units* to be measured and some knowledge of methods and of devices which make the measurements, so that the best practice may be known and the tools, machines, equipment, and surrounding conditions, down to the smallest item, may be super-standardized; that automaticity, the great variable of motion study, may be enlisted to increase skill and production and decrease fatigue.

Motion Study, Fatigue Study, Skill and Time Study Are Indispensable for Determining the One Best Way to Do Work

Motion study, fatigue study, skill study, and time study are methods of measurement under the science of management, and *without them it is absolutely impossible to find the One Best Way to do work,* or to make and enforce the super-standards and programs for the benefit of all. These have application in every field, are closely related, and must receive attention at the proper periods in the installation of scientific methods of management.

Motion Study

Motion study is a method of increasing the efficiency of the worker. It is the science of determining and perpetuating the scheme of perfection; the performing of the One Best Way to do work.

Fatigue Study

Fatigue study is a first step in motion study. It is the investigation of the causes and opportunities for the elimination of unnecessary fatigue, and the provision of rest from necessary fatigue. It is unreasonable to expect to obtain hearty cooperation in matters where the workers have not received proper consideration as to the elimination of their unnecessary fatigue.

Skill Study

Skill study is an inquiry into the causes of, and the best way of acquiring and transferring, skill. It is a subject that affects everyone, whether he is apprentice, journeyman, laborer, manager, employer, or stockholder,—and also the consumer. The accuracy of the *method of working* leads to the accuracy of the resulting workmanship. Too much emphasis during the learning period cannot be laid upon the importance of correcting the erroneous practice of saving material at the expense of later interference of habits of motions, and the postponement of the day of utilization of automaticity of decision as well as motions. In no other way can super-standardization of tools and working conditions be enforced so well as by putting the emphasis on the accuracy of methods to be used from the beginning. In no other way can such rapid fitness for promotion be achieved. In no other way can the best way known be improved by those who have the greatest craft skill and craft knowledge. We advocate the transference to other work of all trade teachers who do not appreciate this scientific fact as a prime requisite for fitness to teach the beginners in the arts, trades, and crafts. The practice of allowing the *average* method to be taught by the *average* teacher should be discouraged and abolished wherever possible, and the practice of having the One Best Way taught by the *best teacher available* should be encouraged by everyone.

There have been no careful and systematized attempts by any nation to collect information about skill, similar to the attempt to find the best wheat, yet the field for synthesizing elements of skill offers opportunities of more importance to mankind than the cross fertilizations resulting in Marquis Wheat. There has been no nation or city that has had a definite system for conserving such information if it were offered to it. Rarely can a man be found who is able to distinguish skill of method from high speed of output in arts and crafts and trades. The workers of the world can now *make* anything. Let the emphasis *now*, during the learning process, be on the *method and not on the accuracy of the resulting product.* This is a problem in psychology, but apparently very few psychologists have more than a remote idea of what it is, yet it has been already proved by measurement, time and again, and solved to the point of standardization.

The best way to conserve the skill of the passing generations profitably is to establish a special department for encouraging the disclosure of unpatentable information, particularly regarding skill study; a department in the patent office should operate on the lines of a modern suggestion system in a motion study laboratory, with all the refinements of the present patent office, and subject to nearly all the same general principles and laws. This would furnish incentive, encouragement, and recognition, as well as a market for ideas pertaining to skill and to methods thought for the time being to represent the One Best Way to do work. Awards for disclosing full information regarding new and useful improvements in skill, which are not patentable, should be paid to the "Inventor" instead of requiring the "Inventor" to pay a fee, as is the custom in all patent offices, when he acquires exclusive rights to make and sell his invention for a term of years. Such a department could not be properly organized by anyone who does not know motion study and the methods of measuring its subdivisions and psychological variables. Neither could it be handled by anyone who does not know that *the One Best Way means the best way at present obtainable.* Nor could it be properly maintained by anyone who persists in believing that the individual differences in any one group of properly placed workers, due to heredity, are as great as their differences due to habit, education, wrong teaching, and automaticity.

It is to be expected that there will be a large number of people who will say that any such arrangement could not possibly work out in actual practice. Our answer is that it *is* already working in several very large organizations with such remarkable results that we venture to predict that a nation could afford to install it and could look for great benefits, even though it were muddled.

Time Study

Time study is the art of determining "how long it takes to do work" or, stated in other words, "how much work can be done in a given time." Time is a variable of motion study, and correct time study is a subdivision and a by-product of micromotion study.[10] Time study should never be confused with motion study. They are quite distinct. Neither should *correct* time study, which is the by-product of photographically recorded times, free from personal error, be confused with the inaccurate non-method recording stop watch time study.

Development of Motion Study and Time Study

The development of motion study and time study in their relation to each other, and to fatigue study, serves—as we have already shown—as an example not only of how much slower the methods and devices are developed than is the theory, but also of the ultimate development of methods and devices that fulfil the requirements and needs, once these are thoroughly understood. We find the practice of timing work early in the history of management. Dr. Taylor said he first received his idea of taking times from Mr. Wentworth, a teacher of his at Phillips Academy, Exeter, New Hampshire. Be this as it may, Dr. Taylor is undoubtedly, as he has

---

[10] See Engineering & Industrial Management, "Time Study and Motion Study as Fundamental Factors in Planning and Control: An Indictment of Stop Watch Time Study." Also Bulletin of the Taylor Society.

been called, "The Father of Time Study." He was, undoubtedly, the first who had the idea of timing the work cycles and frequent rest periods separately, thus being able to predetermine with greater accuracy than it had hitherto been done how long it would take to do work. Time study should be used for making reasonable, achievable schedules and programs, according to which all can plan. In no other way can everyone assist in making the largest outputs. Time tables are necessary for railroads for greatest service to themselves and to the public, not for speeding the trains up to the point of destruction.

In spite of the fact that Taylor had no better device than the stop watch, his idea marked a great step forward in management, the full possibilities of which are little realized due to psychological defects of presentation and to objections which have nothing to do with the merit and value of the underlying principle involved. This great step of timing the work periods and the rest periods separately is *the* feature that distinguishes Taylor's plan of timing for prophesying how long it would take to do work from all the work of his predecessors. It is still so important that many great engineers continue to confuse time study with motion study, although the two are entirely different and even Dr. Taylor's theory must not be confused with his practice. The two must be analyzed and criticized separately.

Secret Time Study Is Worthless and Should Never Under Any Circumstances Be Practiced

Timing of work was done by Taylor, and by some of his immediate followers, by the use of a stop watch. In the early days some secret timing of work was undoubtedly done, as the stop-watch book, described and repudiated in Taylor's "Shop Management" and in other works, shows.

It was sooner or later realized by most of its former advocators that secret time study is despised by the worker, that it never fosters hearty cooperation and therefore is valueless; and such time study was abandoned. There is, however, an additional reason for never making or using secret time study which, alone, should have been sufficient reason for dispensing with it from the very first. The times recorded are valueless, as they time a method and a rate of speed of motions at which the worker did not and could not cooperate, for the obvious reason that he had no knowledge that he was being timed.[11] There is no possibility of ever finding the One Best Way to do work by means of "secret" time study, neither is there any chance of determining causes of skill by its use. Any time records derived from "secret" time study are not worth the paper upon which they are written, to say nothing of the value of the time of the secret times observer.

Motion Study Antedates Time Study

From our first interest in the subject of management, which began in 1885, we have specialized in motion study and the One Best Way to do the work; that is, in studying the motions made by the worker in doing his work and endeavouring to eliminate useless motions and to reduce the number of motions and the effort and resulting fatigue to the lowest amount possible. Since it so happened that heavy stone, concrete, brick, and steel construction, and more than a dozen other trades, formed an essential element of the specially provided practical part of the training of one of the writers in preparing to become a construction engineer, the early intensive applications of motion study were actually made under the most practical everyday conditions in those fields, under the constant training of the best mechanics obtainable, specially selected and assigned by the employer for the writer's intensive training for special progress.

Transference of Skill Is Possible

We have always believed that the writer's ability to earn more than the journeyman's pay in more than a dozen different trades

---

[11] See Chapter on "Motion Study Instruments of Precision" in "Applied Motion Study," Macmillan Co.

was wholly due to the emphasis he placed upon transference of skill in the motions themselves, and that his progress in apprenticeship, his being made foreman before the expiration of the time of his apprenticeship, then superintendent at the expiration of his apprenticeship, and then highest of all the employees in the entire organization was due to his practice of submitting all of his working problems to the analytical method of motion study.

"How Long It Takes to Do Work" Is Not So Important as "How To Do It in the One Best Way"

Through our acquaintance with Dr. Taylor, we first recognized the importance of prophesying the time it takes to do work in order to make schedules and programs. While we still recognize the importance of knowing the time it takes to do work, it should always be realized that the problem of prophesying the times of doing work will probably never have the importance of the problem of the One Best Way to do work.

We desire to emphasize again that the time required by any method is quite unimportant as compared with making the correct sequence of cycle sub-divisions, the problem of least waste in energy involved, and the quality of the resulting product. However, we have always strenuously insisted that if times are recorded, they must be times of the smallest elements and they must be recorded with accuracy, if they are to be of permanent value. The micromotion process of motion study and its indirect by-product, photographically recorded time study, coupled with a search for greater information than merely what the eye can see and more permanent records regarding the actual behaviour and the exact motions used, whether or not at the time the records are made there is knowledge enough to recognise and appreciate the information, is the outcome of this theory and practice.

At the present time, while we advocate the use of the stop watch as a part of the preliminary education of the young engineer,[12] in order that he may appreciate the value and possibilities of the

---

[12] See "Motion Study and Time Study."

more accurate methods of micromotion study, in all our work we use the micromotion method, as we find it is vastly superior to stop-watch time study not only from the standpoint of accuracy and permanent value but also from the standpoint of low cost, and especially from the standpoint of educational value, particularly the preservation of the best that has been done for future learners.

Chronocyclegraphs Record Effects of Psychological Variables on The Elements of Behaviour as Shown in Paths of Motion

Where it is desired to study the paths and the elements of the motion, and particularly the phenomena of skill, such as habit, con-flict of habits, automaticity, distraction, and other psychological and motion study variables, we supplement micromotion study with the chronocyclegraph method of making records. Chronocycle-graphs were invented as a result of realizing the need for some form of recapitulation of the motions shown in the individual frames of the micromotion film. In no other way has the effect of one or more psychological variables been shown so plainly as by the cycle-graph method. In fact, the synthetic stereochronocyclegraph has already been used by us in research on the motion study variable of automaticity wherever data on the subject could be found, including studies of the motions of epileptics in seizures. The result-ing analyses[13] have completely confirmed the opinions expressed in 1910 regarding our practice in teaching the trades and have proved again, to our own satisfaction, that "the present apprentice-ship system is pitiful and criminal from the apprentice's standpoint, ridiculous from a modern system standpoint, and there is no word that describes its wastefulness from an economic standpoint." [14]

Chronocyclegraphs Can Be Made at the Same Cost as Amateur Snapshots

It has been said by some that the chronocyclegraph method is a scientific refinement of great accuracy which no manager should

---

[13] See Paper by Dr. Damon.
[14] See "Motion Study," page 41.

countenance in practice, because it deals with the minutiae of motions, but when it is realized that cyclegraphs can be made in a minute with even the cheapest of cameras, at a cost of a few cents, and that they furnish a permanent record that proves the fallacy of present methods, no further proof of their practicability is needed. These cyclegraph records assist in visualizing better methods. The actual results prove that there is no sound argument against them.[15]

Interpretation of Chronocyclegraphs Requires Knowledge of Motion Study

They are, however, of little use in the hands of those who do not understand how to read and interpret them and compare the behaviour of different demonstrators and workers under different conditions. Cyclegraphs are of greatest value only when they are made of the method of the most efficient worker demonstrating the One Best Way to do work. In no way, however, do they supplant or become a substitute for the usual procedure under the micromotion methods.

A Fatigue Survey Is the First Step in Fatigue Study

As an indispensable adjunct to all motion study and time study we have fatigue study, which, as we have already said, is really the first step in motion study. In the description of the making of a survey we spoke of the importance of a fatigue survey as a part of the general survey of the entire plant. We advise taking up this subject very early in the process of diagnosis and analysis, in order to enlist the self-interest and hearty cooperation of every member of the organisation, as fatigue elimination is a subject upon which all can agree, for there are no interests against it. It is a very tangible, practical subject, easily visualized, and will pay big returns on the time and money invested.

In the making of the fatigue survey, we recommend record-

---

[15] Chronocyclegraph Motion Devices for Measuring Achievement, "Applied Motion Study," Chapter V, Macmillan Co., N. Y.; Etude des mouvements appliqué, Chap. V; Angewandte Bewegungsstudien, Berlin.

ing everything that has ever been done to eliminate unnecessary fatigue and recording every idea for super-standardization of that which will cause less fatigue and greater comfort to the workers, for in no other way can the management start a new era of cooperation throughout the plant so successfully. There is no more practical way of actually fostering that first and greatest law for durable satisfactions of life and success in management, namely, "The Golden Rule." There is some misunderstanding as to the reduction of fatigue through motion study. The prime aim of motion study is not to reduce the total amount of fatigue, although that of course is *very* desirable, but to eliminate that part of fatigue which is unnecessary, which does no one any good, and which reduces productivity and therefore earning power. Only by scientific investigation can it be determined how much fatigue any individual worker can endure day after day, without injury.

If there is any question about the matter, our own recommended practice is to "provide facilities for rest, whether it is thought to be needed or not." The great thing in Fatigue Study, in which every one can participate, is to eliminate useless, unnecessary, unproductive fatigue, wherever possible, throughout the entire plant.

There Is Too Little Attention Given to the Great Waste of Unnecessary Fatigue

It is surprising to read the interesting and valuable literature on the subject of fatigue, and the making of investigations in fatigue, and to note how little thought has been directed toward the most important and most easily corrected waste, the *elimination of unnecessary fatigue*. Measurements of the periodicity and length of rest intervals and of the effects of overtime and night work—these are important and must be considered also; but emphasis on the old-fashioned method for cutting out or reducing unnecessary fatigue is essential, and this is absent, or practically absent, in the literature of fatigue, and absent also in a large percentage of all plants in all the countries we have visited.

Enforcing Repetitive Unproductive and Uninteresting Motions Spoils Men for Real Work Later

It is interesting to note that the amount of unnecessary fatigue and indifference to the problem of fatigue existing is a good index of the civilization, education, general efficiency, and culture of a country, and of the intelligence and ethical standing of those in authority, whether in the factory, services, school, home, hospital, or other public institution. Such a deadening circle as selecting buttons to be polished, and polishing the button selected, should be eliminated everywhere or supplemented by work that stimulates the workers' brains and that fits them for promotion, or at least for transference to other more remunerative life works. Repetitive unnecessary motions that do not lead to valuable by-products, or to knowledge of the science of motion study, are deteriorating to the brain and insulting to the intelligence, and at best lead to habits of inefficient motions and inefficient processes of thought.

Never forget that fatigue study and the actual elimination of unnecessary fatigue *pays in actual money savings*. It pays in greater cooperation, which always means lower costs.

Employers Should Be Made to Provide Seats for All Workers So That They May Utilize Their Periods of Unavoidable Delay for Rest

Any country that seriously desires to help its working people to produce larger outputs with less fatigue and with more comfort and greater public health is recommended to tax the owner of each individual work place that has not provided a suitable seat for occupancy during periods of "unavoidable delay." Each time that we have made this proposal we have had submitted to us a list of trades at which some one believes such practice not to be practical. We come to our recommendations after many years spent in the careful study of this subject, and we suggest that emphasis be put first on the places where it is easy to install chairs. The balance of the cases will then be found to be suitable also for the same treatment. If a worker desires to loaf it is better that he should also at the same time rest instead of adopting a make-believe work and a ca' canny policy. The general law of "making each industry pay the bill" has invariably caused invention to do away with the reason for the bill, although there may also be attempts temporarily to pass the tax on to the consumer by means of adding the amount to the price of the product. This, however, is always followed by an attempt to save the price of the tax.

A Comfortable Chair Will Permit Larger Outputs with Less Fatigue

It is invariably astonishing to see how many places can be supplied with special-problem and special-purpose chairs and stools, and how many kinds of work can be done alternately sitting and standing that have always been considered as standing jobs, when incentive to invention is brought to bear, and—most fortunately—*invariably with greater productivity as well as greater comfort* to the worker.

Only those who have studied the problems of the One Best Way to do work realize the increases in outputs, wages, and profits resulting from the elimination of unnecessary fatigue. We realize that this recommendation to tax each work place that is not provided with a proper seat specially designed for the kind of work done sounds radical. We have tried every other form of education, including maintaining a small museum for exhibits of devices for eliminating unnecessary fatigue, but the progress has been altogether too slow to satisfy us. The public must be made to think along the lines of eliminating unnecessary fatigue as a source of national health, as well as for their own health and comfort. We started the Fatigue Day Campaign in 1913. Professor Henry F. Spooner was the first to cooperate on a large scale in England, and each year he has addressed his students on the costs and discomforts of unnecessary fatigue. The Society of Industrial Engineers through its Fatigue Elimination Committee, of which Prof. Spooner is a member and of which one of the authors is Chairman, is arousing public interest wherever possible on the subject of the Elimination of Unnecessary

Fatigue. The Society, the Committee, and the Chairman will welcome cooperation on this subject. Membership in the Society is not a prerequisite for full opportunities for cooperation.

Professor George Blessing, head of the Mechanical Engineering Department at Swarthmore College and now with the Rockefeller interests, was the first to do noteworthy work in celebrating this "first Monday in December," or "Fatigue Elimination Day," in a college. He wrote a most interesting lecture to his students regarding the possibilities of eliminating unnecessary fatigue in his own and their daily lives, beginning with the automatic time clock and an electrical device that opens the furnace draft door before he and his family arise in the morning, and ending with the well-known advantages from an anti-fatigue standpoint of rubber heels on shoes for all members of the family, which every student of motion study and fatigue study knows to be an important factor in helping anyone to do more walking and standing with less fatigue.

Rubber Heels Eliminate Unnecessary Fatigue

This factor of cushioning the feet of workers is so important that where rubber heels are too expensive for general use by them, similar but by no means such good results have in a measure been obtained by wearing, even in warm weather, extra-heavy woollen socks and wooden-soled shoes.

Fatigue investigation cannot be too definite and concrete; no item is too small to consider; for the problem, to be successful, must be educational. It must be constantly emphasized that small individual outputs are often due largely to the discomfort and the fatigue of the worker. Fatigue investigations should consider also types of lighting and heating and its closely allied factor, accident prevention in the plant. Fear of accidents and constant watchfulness and unflagging attention to keep from being caught in an accident are very fatiguing, and it is now recognized that there is no sharp dividing line between accident prevention and fatigue prevention. Description photographs and other records of chairs—particularly special-purpose chairs, such as three-way stools,[16]

---

[16] See "Transactions Society of Industrial Engineers," 1920.

foot rests, fatigue-eliminating work desks, individual tables, or work benches—are valuable; and these should include, wherever possible, some estimate of the fatigue prevented.

Workers Have Not Done Their Bit in Eliminating Their Own Unnecessary Fatigue or in Disseminating Information About It

While the workers get immediate and ultimate comfort and satisfaction from the results of eliminating unnecessary fatigue, they have done less for themselves and for each other in this important subject than have the managers and the employers. There is an interesting reason for this, however. Workers have little time and opportunity for gaining scientific knowledge of the underlying causes of unnecessary fatigue, or of the best practice of fatigue elimination, or of the comparative fatigue-eliminating qualities of the various pieces of equipment or chairs which they use. This is proved without the question of a doubt through our own personal experience.

Executives Have Failed to Provide and Practise What They Preach

It is also remarkable to find that some of the executives, who have been most conscientious and insistent on providing the least fatiguing work places, so neglect their own work places that they become examples to be avoided.

Labor Will Cooperate

If a square deal is assured, there is no doubt that labor will cooperate in every advance in the science of management affecting industry.

Labor Is Studying the Science of Economics Today

Labor has representatives today who have enrolled as students in the science of economics. They have recently again had it proved conclusively to them that neither strikes, lockouts, nor high pay and short hours furnish the permanent panacea for the working man's troubles. They have found that there is no permanent and cumulative improvement in the working man's conditions unless the higher pay and the shorter hours are accompanied with maximum production per man and the consequent low unit costs of manufacture, marketing, and distribution. This seeming paradox of high wages and low unit costs is not a contradiction at all. On the contrary, it is this combination that the science of management makes possible. A most valuable unit of measurement for comparing the quality of different managements is the amount that the wages are higher, and, at the same time, the costs are lower in one organization than in another, or under one regime than under another. When this is realized, hearty and strenuous cooperation between the management and the workers will be the rule and not the exception, and he who wastes either time, effort, or material will be treated as the enemy of all.

Economists Know That All Must Share in Paying for Any and All Wastes

Economists have known for a long time that the benefits from the elimination of every kind of individual and public waste of time, material, and human effort sooner or later are distributed to everyone, and the more savings of time and materials and the greater productivity the better the chance of having the benefits of the savings distributed sooner or later to everybody. All students of economics, in and out of the ranks of labor, realize that labor's prospects increase with the quality of the management, and it is for their interests especially to have all that science can offer applied to management.

It would seem reasonable to expect that all countries suffering from the wastes of war ought to realize this fact and begin by insisting upon the reorganization of their governmental departments and the rearrangement of inter-departmental relations in accordance with the best practices of scientific management to suit their present and future needs, instead of continuing the ill-fitting, outgrown, and unnecessarily wasteful traditional methods of organization and work handed down from times of different conditions.

Unfortunately, those on the outside, who nevertheless have to pay the bill, have insufficient power and realization of the facts, and those on the inside are also uninformed, although they are quite satisfied; yet the loss from waste of any kind is passed on to all, and the costs of the totals of inefficiency are well nigh unbearable in all countries at the present time.

The results of actual practice of motion study and science in management in large commercial and industrial organizations show beyond argument or doubt that the amount of money needed for taxes is actually small as compared with the amount of savings that can be made by motion study, scientific organization and management.

Science in Management Is a Unifying Force Because It Is Applicable To All Fields of Endeavor

It perhaps never has been sufficiently emphasized that the science of management may serve as a great unifying force in industry. Because most students in management are specialists and are forced to be interested in any specialized field of their individual life work, if industry as a whole is to succeed, management has often been thought of largely in terms of application to specific fields. However, it must be recognized that when the producers of raw materials, the producers of machines and manufactured products, the users of the products, and all the other producers in the country are thinking along lines of waste elimination and the science of management for obtaining the One Best Way and condition of doing work, a new type of cooperation will result, and an enormous amount of waste will be automatically, progressively, and constantly eliminated, if transferable information regarding the units of management is recorded. Take for the simplest sort of an illustration the question of *glare spots,* as induced for example by nickel parts of office devices and highly polished and varnished desks in highly lighted offices.

When the maker of equipment and also the public realize that glare spots and reflection prevent the user from achieving his full quota of possible production without unnecessary fatigue and perhaps also eye strain, when the user and the employer of the equipment know that the glare spots cut down production and cause unnecessary fatigue, these glare spots will be eliminated as being against good salesmanship and good practice. These highly polished surfaces are a matter of false ideas of what is demanded by the buyers of the product. They serve the short temporary demand of salesmanship, based on measuring the wrong units of what is desired in order to make sales, on wrong psychology, on selling something that is "bright and new and shiny," not something that is efficient,—and they remain, to hinder the user, because of his mental inertia or ignorance of the conditions that hinder or permit the One Best Way to do work. The workers in most factories do not note the handicap of glare spots, because they have seen everywhere and have become accustomed to seeing workers at benches facing the bright sky through the window. The one who locates the benches against the windows instead of at or about right angles to windows probably does so because of his belief that the amount of floor space utilized is a more important unit to measure than visual acuity, fatigue, and quantity of resulting output.

When dark walls are painted white to enforce cleanliness, and to insure the proper amount and more even distribution of light for employees; when shiny metals, varnish, paint, and other glare spots are dulled so that the worker will not be handicapped by unnecessary eye strain; when scientifically designed chairs and seats are made to suit the needs of the individual user, with at least as much attention and regard as is given to fitting collars on horses, instead of the usual and customary practice of providing chairs for the indefinite, non-existing "average man," then there will be a good beginning in creating standards that will be transferable to, and usable by, all organizations that desire to cooperate. Great progress has already been made in the design of some types of chairs by the American Posture League.

Summary

We desire to emphasize the following:

First,—the thought that the science of management is for everybody, everywhere, in every line of work, and that its underlying principles are those of education itself; that parts of it are teachable even in the lower grades of the schools; that the theory and practice of the One Best Way in sports is identical to that in the trades, industries, and in all kinds of work.

Second,—the idea that while the application of the fine points of the science,—the critical work,—must be done by an expert, some of the preliminary steps can be taken by anyone, anywhere.

Third,—that ultimately all successful establishments will be run along scientific lines, and that therefore everything done from this time onward should be in the line of adjusting the past and present along predetermined scientific plans, in order to determine the trend of, and plan for, the future. This is vitally important, for science is now applied to all work, and plants and organizations which have been and are run on rule-of-thumb, traditional, or "pure salesmanship" bases will have more difficulty in surviving in the future.

Greatest national prosperity depends upon greatest individual training in knowledge and in ability to contribute toward the public welfare. Such contributions may be, and often have been, more or less haphazard and still result in good. However, to be most profitable, activity must be planned and *directed,* must have ability, experience, and knowledge behind it. It must be based on measurement and willingness to abide by the result of measurement. Nothing will stand for a long time and continue to exist and to give satisfaction unless there is a real reason for its so doing. It may stand for a long while because no one has changed it, but the day of comparison and struggle for survival will come, and unless it can show logical reason for its existence, it must go.

Therefore, development of national prosperity that is to have permanent stability, that is to be evolution and not revolution, that is to attain and perpetuate the all-essential element of maintenance, does depend upon science, upon measurement; and it is for this reason that the science of management is an essential factor in the development of national prosperity, of international prosperity, and of the prosperity of the whole world.

The psychologist, who has done so much not only in his own field but in cooperating with others, can do much to further this development, and will doubtless prove not only an eloquent advocate but also an untiring participant in better management.

OLIVER SHELDON

(1894–1951)

No MORE stirring, prophetic statement of the mission and responsibility of management has ever been made than that in the closing chapter of *The Philosophy of Management,* which follows. It was written by Oliver Sheldon, British management man, and published in 1923.

Sheldon confined his definition of management to the area of manufacturing, and he subordinated it to another function, administration. Nevertheless, he saw clearly the professional aspects of management that are gaining major attention today. It was from this standpoint that he presented a "suggested creed, as it were, by which the practice of management in the future shall be governed." His insistence that industry exists to serve the community would have gratified Gantt (p. 105).

Sheldon began and ended his business career with Rowntree & Co., Ltd., English chocolate manufacturers, where his principal activity was liaison and coordinating work among the many Rowntree associated and subsidiary companies. He worked closely with B. S. Rowntree, for many years head of the company and an outstanding pioneer in management methods.

A PROFESSIONAL CREED FOR MANAGEMENT

BY OLIVER SHELDON

IN A BOOK of this character, it is not intended to analyse and weigh up the various schemes promulgated for the moulding of industry, either by means revolutionary or evolutionary, into a form fundamentally different from the shape it assumes at present. In any event, all such schemes must necessarily be largely manufactured of the tissue of dreams, since, though in some cases they may be based squarely enough upon the facts of to-day, they cannot by any conceivable means take adequately into account the circumstances and the influences which will affect our kaleidoscopic society as it moves forward towards the dawns of days to come. He who sets himself either to design a future form of industry or to conjure up a vision of what industry may yet become, faces a problem not of logical construction or of scientific planning, but of continual adjustment and adaptation to circumstances which cannot be foretold. The value of such schemes is rather that they may trace the outline of our ideals, and thus mayhap can guide our progress. But that our progress will lead us to any prefigured land of promise is as improbable as the existence of Utopia itself.

Therefore, though the thoughts of the more daring and speculative may fare ahead of the times, to set before us social systems wherein our present ills have vanished, the thoughts of others, who

Reprinted from the book, *The Philosophy of Management*, by Oliver Sheldon, Chapter VIII, pages 280–291. Published by Sir Isaac Pitman & Sons, Ltd., London, 1923. Used by permission of the publisher.

offer gifts of no less value to future generations, may well, whilst accepting the criticism of being opportunistic, take only into consideration the immediate tendencies in the area where forecasts bear some chance of realization. For such as these, the analysis of the present provides as large a scope as the uncharted future offers to others.

The present form of industry is determined, in a broad sense, by the interplay of forces and tendencies, both within and without industry. The main forces, outside industry, which to-day appear to be exercising the greatest effect upon the evolution of the industrial structure, may be summarized as, firstly, the action of the State, viewed not as the whole of organized society, but as one of several forms of social organization; secondly, the attitude of the general public in the capacity of consumers and critics; thirdly, education; fourthly, foreign competition and foreign trade conditions; and fifthly, finance. The main forces affecting industry from within are, firstly, the position and progress of Labour; secondly, the progress of science in management, organization and manufacturing technique.

With none of these are we immediately concerned, save one— the progress of science in management and organization. In management we have the one stable element in our process of evolution. Whether the State continues increasingly to circumscribe the activities of industry, or leaves it to shoulder its own way into the future; whether foreign competition overwhelms us or compels us radically to reconstruct the form of our industry; whether the consciousness, on the part of society, of its responsibility for those who toil for it develops, as education proceeds, or becomes less insistent as industry grows more complex; whether, indeed, the means of production come to be owned by the State or continue in the hands of private Capital—no matter what the changes, management as a function remains constant. There is no conceivable structure of industry—whether we take the self-governing and self-ownership conception of Syndicalism, the State ownership and Government management of State Socialism, the Guild management and State ownership of Guild Socialism, or the Soviet system as exemplified in Russia to-day—there is no structure where management does not fulfil approximately the same functions as under the present system in this country. Every scheme for the reconstruction of industry is concerned primarily with the ownership of the means of production and, only as incidental to that, with the management of industry. Whether the managers of the factories are appointed, as on the Soviet model, by the Minister or local representative of the "Supreme Council of Political Economy"; or, as visualized by the Guild Socialists, by a National Guild composed of representatives of all those engaged, whether on manual, technical or intellectual work, in the particular industry; or, as under our present system, by the acting representatives of the private capitalistic owners, will not materially affect the duties they have to perform. Each system will, of course, occasion different relations between management and labour, management and ownership, management and State, management and the organized consumers, but the functions of management will remain much the same under each régime. Efficiency engineers will still be necessary, whether State, Guild or Syndicalist Committee is in supreme command. Management is as inherent in the composition of industry as Labour. By virtue of its functions, moreover, it is that element in industry which, whatever changes may come, will be charged with the piloting of the ship through the waters of change. A firmly established body of management, therefore, is the greatest safeguard against disruptive change.

Looking immediately ahead, the two major forces making for change, with which management has to deal, are Labour and Science. The greater the changes these forces portend, the greater the responsibility of management for the safe pilotage of the vessel. The activities of these two forces indicate most surely that the sea which has to be traversed in the years ahead will be far from placid. Labour, viewed either as an organized entity or as a heaving, throbbing movement of the times, is wedded to progress. Chafing at the restrictions of economic logic, it grounds its faith upon a profound moral reconstruction of society. It steps forward into the future, deeply assured that, despite the abstractions of economists, statisticians and politicians, the days to come will witness a revision of the ethical principles of our social order. It is convinced by neither argument nor experience. It clings to its faith in a new world of justice; it thinks upon the moral plane. It trusts to progress, primarily and fundamentally, not because progress means more material advantages and a wider and higher field for human intelligence, but rather because it promises a state of society in which the principles governing the form and conduct of society shall be founded upon neither expediency nor force but upon what is morally right. Amid the whirling of widely divergent movements and manifold philosophies, its ultimate goal is clearly established. Its discontent is neither of mind nor of body, but of spirit. It demands a constant impulse to go forward, it resents every setback and hindrance.

Science is similarly imbued with the forward-looking mind. It subjects every established precedent to dispassionate research. It is continually amending our methods both of manufacture and of management. It impels us to a higher and still higher standard of efficiency. It installs method in the place of chaos, laws in the place of "rule-of-thumb," knowledge in the place of ignorance. It sifts our experience, analyses our practices, and puts to new purpose our energies. It devises machines for our manual work, new methods for our procedure in management, new forms of our organization. It experiments, compares, tests, standardizes, organizes and rebuilds. It regards no standard as final, no method as ideal, no sphere as sacred. It applies its analytical process to both the things and the men of production. Without partiality, it marshals facts, discovers principles, and unhesitatingly applies them. It improves quality, decreases cost, designs products, and effects economies. It holds efficiency to be not the negative virtue of eliminating what is wasteful, but the positive virtue of building up what is the best. In its own sphere, it spells as great an era of change and progress as does the restless mentality of Labour in the sphere of human relations. Neither is content with the *status quo;* both insist upon growth and renovation.

As for the forces outside industry, a greater exercise of regulatory activity by the State, a greater concern on the part of all grades of the community in the conduct of industry, a steady uplift of the general intelligence, a more menacing assult upon our industrial supremacy as a nation, and a greater complication, or, alternatively, prodigious disruption of the powers of finance— these, in their effect upon industry, promise at least no stagnation, no respite from the strain of progressive change.

Amid the waters, blown stormy by the blast of all these forces, management stands at the helm of industry. Labour may bring about a change in its composition and relations; Science in its methods and materials, but neither can change its functions. The man at the wheel may be replaced, may be put under a new authority, may be regarded differently by the crew, and may work with different instruments in a different way, but the functions performed remain constant, essential under every conceivable circumstance. It is important, therefore, that we should devise a philosophy of management, a code of principles, scientifically determined and generally accepted, to act as a guide, by reason of its foundation upon ultimate things, for the daily practice of the profession. The adoption of this or that principle in this or that plant will avail but little. Management must link up all its practitioners into one body, pursuing a common end, conscious of a common purpose, actuated by a common motive, adhering to a corporate creed, governed by common laws of practice, sharing a common fund of knowledge. Without this not only have we no guarantee of efficiency, no hope of concerted effort, but also no assurance of stability.

It may be a fitting conclusion, therefore, to state as concisely as possible a suggested codification of such a philosophy, not with any hope that it will be adopted as it stands, but rather that it may form a concrete beginning, in the criticism and explanation, elaboration and amendment of which some acceptable creed may be ultimately arrived at which shall govern the practice of management in the future.

A PHILOSOPHY OF INDUSTRIAL MANAGEMENT

I

Industry exists to provide the commodities and services which are necessary for the good life of the community, in whatever volume they are required. These commodities and services must be furnished at the lowest prices compatible with an adequate standard of quality, and distributed in such a way as directly or indirectly to promote the highest ends of the community.

II

Industrial management, in a broad sense, is the function, practised by whatever persons or classes, responsible for the direction of industry to the above end. It must, therefore, be governed by certain principles inherent in the motive of service to the community.

Such principles are—

Firstly, that the policies, conditions, and methods of industry shall conduce to communal well-being. It is therefore part of the task of management to value such policies, conditions, and methods, by an ethical measure.

Secondly, that, in this ethical valuation, management shall endeavour to interpret the highest moral sanction of the community as a whole, as distinct from any sanction resting upon group or class interests, or, in other words, shall attempt to give practical effect to those ideals of social justice which would generally be accepted by the most unbiased portion of communal opinion.

Thirdly, that, though the community, expressing itself through some representative organization, is, consequently, the ultimate authority in the determination of such matters as legitimate wages and profits, it is for management, as an integral and a highly trained part of the community, to take the initiative, so far as possible within its own sphere, in raising the general ethical standard and conception of social justice.

III

Management, as a comprehensive division of industry, is to be distinguished on the one hand from Capital, and, on the other hand, from Labour. It is divisible into three main parts—

ADMINISTRATION, which is concerned in the determination of corporate policy, the coordination of finance, production and distribution, the settlement of the compass of the organization, and the ultimate control of the executive;

MANAGEMENT proper, which is concerned in the execution of policy, within the limits set up by Administration, and the employment of the organization for the particular objects set before it; and

ORGANIZATION, which is the process of so combining the work which individuals or groups have to perform with the faculties necessary for its execution that the duties, so formed, provide the best channels for the efficient, systematic, positive and coordinated application of effort.

IV

It is for Management, while maintaining industry upon an economic basis, to achieve the object for which it exists by the development of efficiency—both personal or human efficiency, in the workers, in the managerial staff, and in the relations between the two, and impersonal efficiency, in the methods and material conditions of the factory.

V

Such efficiency is, in general, to be developed by Management—

Firstly, through the treatment of all features in every field of industry by the scientific method of analysis and the synthetical use of established knowledge, with the object of determining standards of operative and managerial practice; the application of the accepted sciences to those features of industry to which they are applicable; and the gradual formation and subsequent elaboration of a science of management, as distinct from those accepted sciences which, in practice, it employs; and

Secondly, through the development of the human potentialities of all those who serve industry, in a cooperation consequent upon the common acceptance of a definite motive and ideal in industry, and through the pursuit of that policy, as affecting the human agent in production, which a social responsibility to the community imposes.

VI

Efficiency in management by these general means is, in the first instance, dependent upon a structure of organization, based upon a detailed analysis of the work to be done and the faculties requisite for doing it, and built up on the principle of combining related activities in such a way as to allow for the economical practice, progressive development, and constant coordination of all such activities.

VII

Apart from Finance, which is primarily concerned in the provision and usage of Capital, and Administration, which determines the field and ultimately controls and coordinates the activities of Management proper, the various activities of Management proper are divisible, on the above principle, into the following functions—

Firstly, those functions essential to the inception of manufacture—

DESIGN (Purchasing), or that group of activities which determines the final character of the product and specifies and provides the material for its manufacture; and

EQUIPMENT, or that group of activities which provides and maintains the necessary means of production.

Secondly, the function dealing with the actual production, i.e. with all those activities whereby skill and effort are applied to the transformation of the material into the finished product. This function may broadly be described as MANUFACTURE.

Thirdly, those functions comprising the work necessary to facilitate the manufacture of the product—

TRANSPORT, or that group of activities which connects up the various units of production, stores or moves the material between the processes of manufacture, and provides the means of transportation for each function;

PLANNING, or that group of activities which determines the volume and progress of work;

COMPARISON, or that group of activities which analyses the work of each function and compares the records of its activities with the scientific standards set up for each function;

LABOUR, or that group of activities concerned in the application and maintenance of the human agent in production, and the promotion of cooperation between all engaged in production.

Fourthly, those functions comprising the work necessary for the distribution of the product—

SALES PLANNING, or that group of activities which determines, according to the data available, the policy and methods of distribution; and

SALES EXECUTION, or that group of activities which disposes of and actually distributes the product.

VIII

The use of the scientific method to ensure the most economical utilization of the impersonal factors—or, of the personal factors regarded purely as productive units—in industry, involves in particular—

Firstly, the development of research and accurate measurement in each branch of activity which management undertakes or controls, followed by experiments upon or deductions from the data established by such research;

Secondly, the preparation and use of precise definitions and statements of what actually constitutes each item of work in each function;

Thirdly, the determination, after the analysis of the constituent parts of any activity and their synthetical reconstruction, of reference and working standards, both for manufacture and for management, representing, for the present, a justifiable and precise appraisement of desirable achievement; and

Fourthly, the institution of the necessary supervision, authority, and machinery to ensure the application of, adherence to, and improvement upon such standards, the measurement of actual practice by such standards, and their utilization for planning the most economical mode of production and management.

IX

The application of that policy, which responsibility to the community imposes, involves certain practices as regards the human agent in production, whether by hand or by brain. These may be enumerated as follows—

Firstly, in the relation of such human agent to the community— (a) the recognition of and cooperation with such forms of association as may be founded for the furtherance of the ends of those engaged in industry, provided such ends are not held, by the community, to be deleterious to communal well-being; and (b) the facilitation, within the necessary economic limits of the conduct of industry, of the exercise by the individual, in his own self-development, of his higher faculties for the better service of the community.

Secondly, in the relation of such human agent to his industrial work—the promotion of individual and corporate effectiveness of effort, by the stimulus of a compelling leadership and an equitable discipline, in turn developing a corporate spirit of loyalty and high endeavour; by the provision of such training as will qualify the individual effectively to carry out his work, whilst at the same time furthering his general mental capacity; by the provision for each individual of work as far as possible calling for the exercise of his best ability, and in any event suited to his type of mentality; by the provision of conditions, both material and spiritual, conducive to the highest working efficiency; by the provision of legitimate and equitable incentives to and opportunities for the exercise of interest, both in the particular task of the individual and the general policy and progress of the business; and by the cultivation of cooperation, as a working principle, among all concerned in the activities of production.

Thirdly, in the relation of such human agent to his life as an individual—(*a*) the provision of means whereby all concerned may share in the determination and maintenance of the conditions under which work is to be conducted; (*b*) the provision of the means requisite to furnish a standard of living appropriate to a civilized community; (*c*) an allowance of leisure adequate for the maintenance of bodily and mental health and the development of individual capacity both as workers and as citizens; (*d*) the provision of security for efficient workers from the hardships incidental to involuntary unemployment due to trade conditions or other unfavourable circumstances; (*e*) the provision of a share in industrial prosperity proportionate to the share taken in the promotion of such prosperity; and (*f*) the conduct of the relations arising in the course of industrial activities in a strict spirit of equity.

X

By the elaboration of Standards, on the impersonal side of industry, through the analytical and synthetical methods of Science, and by the deductive determination of the principles and methods of management on the personal or human side, it is the aim of those practising management to evolve, by a sharing of knowledge and experience, irrespective of trade and business divisions, a SCIENCE OF INDUSTRIAL MANAGEMENT, distinct alike from the sciences it employs and the technique of any particular industry, for the several purposes of forming a code to govern the general conduct of industry, of raising the general level and providing a standard measure of managerial efficiency, of formulating the basis for further development and improvement, and of instituting a standard as a necessary qualification for the practice of the profession.

MARY PARKER FOLLETT

(1868–1933)

THE MANAGEMENT WRITING of Mary Parker Follett is so filled with profound truth and practical help, and yet is so simple and direct, that making selections from it is a major problem. This Boston-born social worker used common occurrences, familiar to every executive, as points of departure for developing management principles; thereby she gave them a realism and an immediacy which make them extremely convincing.

In the following paper on business management as a profession, Miss Follett argues that the scientific method can be applied to human relations problems, thus carrying matters beyond the limits set by Sheldon (pp. 265–277).

The second two excerpts presented here are from a series of lectures Miss Follett gave at the University of London just before her death in 1933. They represent a final summing up of her thinking. The ideas offered in *The Essentials of Leadership* (pp. 295–308) are by now widely accepted. *Coordination* (pp. 309–324) discusses a basic management problem for which there can never be a complete solution. Her "third way" of dealing with the differences that arise in the coordinating process has unusual interest today when so much attention is being given to creativity in management.

While her viewpoint and language have special appeal to managers, Miss Follett was not a manager herself. But her ideas, expressed in books and lectures, led many business men to seek her counsel on problems involving personal and group relationships, the area where she made her major contribution to management thinking.

———————

MANAGEMENT AS A PROFESSION

BY M. P. FOLLETT

THE WORD "profession" connotes for most people a foundation of *science* and a motive of *service*. That is, a profession is said to rest on the basis of a proved body of knowledge, and such knowledge is supposed to be used in the service of others rather than merely for one's own purposes. Let us tonight ask ourselves two questions: (1) How far does business management rest on scientific foundations? (2) What are the next steps to be taken in order that business management shall become more scientific?

Present Signs of a Scientific Basis for Business Management

We have many indications that scientific method is being more and more applied to business management. First, of course, is the development of so-called "scientific management" which, after its early stages, began to concern itself with the technique of management as well as with the technique of operating.

Secondly, there is the increasing tendency toward specialized, or what is being called functionalized, management. Functionalized management has, indeed, not yet been carried far. In some cases the only sign we see of it, beyond the recognition that different

Reprinted from the book, *Business Management as a Profession*, edited by Henry C. Metcalf, Chapter IV, pages 73–87. Published by A. W. Shaw Company, Chicago, 1927. Paper presented at October 1925 conference of Bureau of Personnel Administration, New York, N. Y. Used by permission of McGraw-Hill Book Company.

departments require different kinds of knowledge, different kinds of ability, is the employing of experts for special problems. In other cases a further step is taken and a planning department is created; but the powers given to planning departments vary greatly from plant to plant—some take up only occasional problems as they are asked, some are only advisory bodies. Yet in most plants the functionalization of management is a process which in one way or another has gained a good deal of ground recently. That is, the fact is very generally accepted that different types of problems require different bodies of knowledge.

In the third place, arbitrary authority is diminishing, surely an indication that more value is being put on scientific method. The tendency today is to vest authority in the person who has most knowledge of the matter in question and most skill in applying that knowledge. Hiring, for instance, is now based on certain principles and special knowledge. The job of hiring is given to those who have that knowledge. It is not assumed by some one by virtue of a certain position.

Perhaps nowhere do we see more clearly the advance of business management toward becoming a profession than in our conception of the requirements of the administrative head. It would be interesting to take some firm and note how one duty after another has in recent years passed from the president to various experts, down to that most recent addition to many businesses, the economic adviser. One president, of whom I inquired what he thought exactly his job to be, said to me: "I can't define my job in terms of specific duties because I can't tell what special duty which I have today may be given at any moment to some one better able than I to handle it." One of the interesting things about that remark (there are several) is that he recognized that some one might handle some of his duties better than he could; and yet he is an exceedingly able man. He saw that some particular task might develop a special technique and that men might be trained as experts in that technique.

The stereotype of the successful business man is indeed changing. The image of the masterful man carrying all before him by the sheer force of his personality has largely disappeared. One good result of this is that we now consider that executive leadership can in part (remember, I say only "in part") be learned. Sheldon* calls executive leadership "an intangible capacity." I do not wholly agree. Some one else says it is "beyond human calculation." There are many things, we hope, which have not yet been calculated which are not beyond calculation. I think that one of the hopes for business management lies in the fact that executive leadership is capable of analysis and that men can be trained to occupy such positions. I do not, of course, mean every man; but not every man can become a doctor or an architect. I mean that for business management, exactly as for other professions, training is gaining in importance over mere personality. I know a man who told me ten or fifteen years ago that he relied on his personality in business dealings. He has not made a success of his business. It was once thought that the executive's work rested largely on "hunch," and his subordinates' on obeying—no science in either case. The administrative head who relies first on the magic shortcut of "hunch," and secondly on his adroitness or masterfulness in getting others to accept his "hunch," is, I believe, about to be superseded by a man of different type.

Can you not remember the picture we used to have of the man in the swivel chair? A trembling subordinate enters, states his problem; snap goes the decision from the chair. This man disappears only for another to enter. And so it goes. The massive brain in the swivel chair all day communicates to his followers his special knowledge. An excellent plan if—there seem to be too many if's in the way! And so we resort to the humbler method of scientific research, the method of all the professions.

But with this agreed to, there is another misconception in regard to the administrative head. Many writers speak as if he were only the glue to hold together all these departments and functions of our big modern plants. As the need of coordination is daily and hourly felt in these vast, complex organizations, it is said that the

---

* See pages 265–277.—EDITOR

president must do the coordinating. True; but I think that coordination is very different from matching up the pieces of a picture puzzle, to change our metaphor. Later, I am going to say just what I think it is; but let me say now that those of us who think of the administrative head as more than a mere coordinator and those of us who think that administrative decisions should rest on more than "hunch" (although "hunch," too, is important) are thinking of scientific foundations for business management.

A significant indication of the different type of management required today is the fact that managers are somewhat less inclined to justify their behavior by a claim of abstract "rights." An employer used to say, "I have a right to treat my men so and so." Or, "My behavior in this matter is perfectly reasonable." Today there are many who are more inclined to say: "If I treat my men so and so, how will they behave? *Why* will they behave in that way?" It takes far more science to understand human beings—and their "rights"—than to proclaim loudly our own rights and reasonableness.

We have a very interesting indication of the new demand made upon management in the fact that the idea, which is everywhere gaining ground, that we may have greater conscious control of our lives is seen in the business world most significantly. For example, those fatalistic rhythms, business cycles, are now considered susceptible to study, not as mysteries wholly beyond the comprehension of man. Again, take unemployment. Consider the steel industry. There you have an imperishable commodity. Moreover, you can calculate pretty well the demand. And you have rather permanently located firms and mills. There seems no reason, therefore, why the steel industry should not eventually be stabilized. Every time we take a problem out of the unsolvable class and put it into the solvable, and work at it as such, we are helping to put business management on a scientific basis. Mr. John Maynard Keynes, in an address last summer, spoke of the three great epochs of history described by Dr. John R. Commons,† and stated his belief that

---

† John Rogers Commons, 1862–1945. American economist, educator, and author. Also had considerable influence in labor legislation.—EDITOR

we are on the threshold of the third of those epochs. The first of these was the era of scarcity, which came to an end in about the fifteenth century. Next came the era of abundance, the dominating idea of which was the doctrine of *laissez faire*. Finally, there has come the era of stabilization upon which we are now entering and in which the doctrine of *laissez faire* must be abandoned in favor of deliberate, conscious control of economic forces for the sake of the general social good.

Many people today think of business not as a game of chance, not as a speculative enterprise depending on rising and falling markets, but as largely controllable. The mysteriousness of business is in fact disappearing as knowledge in regard to business methods steadily increases.

This is seen in the increased sense of responsibility for failure. You know the old excuses if a business failed or was not getting on well: the hard terms of bankers, the unscrupulousness of competitors, the abominable behavior of trade unions. I think that today there is less inclination to take refuge in such excuses; that there is a tendency to seek the difficulty in the running of the business. There is greater frankness in facing difficulties and a keener zest in overcoming them. You know, perhaps, the story of little Mary who was naughty and was told by her mother to go into the next room and ask God to forgive her. When she came back her mother said, "Did you do what I told you to?" And received the reply, "Yes, I did; and God said, 'Mercy me, little Mary, I know heaps worse'n you.'" Many an employer takes this attitude, but their numbers are diminishing.

Moreover, many of the points disputed with trade unions, many points which both sides have thought to be legitimate fighting issues, are now considered problems which we should try to solve. To increase wages without increasing price is sometimes a solvable problem. Wherever thinking takes the place of fighting, we have a striking indication that management is coming to rest on scientific foundations. In international relations—but I have only to mention that term for you to see the analogy, for you to see the barbarous stage we are yet in, in international relations. Business men have the chance to lead the world in substituting thinking for fighting. And business men are thinking. One of the things I have been most struck with in the last four or five years has been the vitality of the thinking of business men. I said last winter to a professor of philosophy, "Do you realize that you philosophers have got to look to your laurels, that business men are doing some very valuable thinking and may get ahead of you?" And he acknowledged this fully and generously, which I thought was a significant concession.

Finally, management, not bankers nor stockholders, is now seen to be the fundamental element in industry. It is good management that draws credit, that draws workers, that draws customers. Moreover, whatever changes come, whether industry is owned by individual capitalists or by the state or by the workers, it will always have to be managed. Management is a permanent function of business.

There are many circumstances, let us note in concluding the first part of this talk, which are impelling us toward a truly scientific management: (1) efficient management has to take the place of that exploitation of our natural resources whose day is now nearly over; (2) keener competition; (3) scarcity of labor; (4) a broader conception of the ethics of human relations; (5) the growing idea of business as a public service which carries with it a sense of responsibility for its efficient conduct.

What Are the Next Steps Toward Making Business Management More Scientific?

Recognizing that business management is every day coming more and more to rest on scientific foundations, what has it yet to do? First, the scientific standard must be applied to the whole of business management; it is now often applied to only one part. Business management includes: (1) on the technical side, as it is usually called, a knowledge of production and distribution, and (2) on the personnel side, a knowledge of how to deal fairly and fruitfully with one's fellows. While the first has been recognized as a matter

capable of being taught, the latter has been often thought to be
a gift which some men possess and some do not. That is, one part
of business management rested on science; the other part, it was
thought, never could. Oliver Sheldon says: "Broadly, management
is concerned with two primary elements—things and men. The
former element is susceptible to scientific treatment, the latter is
not."[1] And again: "Where human beings are concerned, scientific
principles may be so much waste paper."[2] If we believed that, we
should not be here tonight in a Bureau of Personnel Administration.
Let us take that statement—that human relations are not susceptible of scientific treatment—and ask what scientific treatment is.
Science has been defined as "knowledge gained by systematic
observation, experiment, and reasoning; knowledge coordinated,
arranged and systematized." Can we not accumulate in regard
to human relations knowledge gained by systematic observation,
experiment, and reasoning? Can we not coordinate, arrange, and
systematize that knowledge? I think we can.

Sheldon says further: "There may be a science of costing, of
transportation, of operation, but there can be no science of cooperation."[3] The reason we are here studying human relations in
industry is that we believe there can be a science of cooperation.
By this I mean that cooperation is not, and this I insist on, merely
a matter of good intentions, of kindly feeling. It must be based
on these, but you cannot have successful cooperation until you
have worked out the methods of cooperation—by experiment after
experiment, by a comparing of experiments, by a pooling of results.
Not everyone who cries "Cooperation, cooperation!" . . . It is my
plea above everything else that we learn *how* to cooperate. Of
course, one may have a special aptitude for dealing with men as
others may have for dealing with machines, but there is as much
to learn in the one case as in the other.

---

1 Oliver Sheldon, *Bulletin of Taylor Society*, Vol. 8, No. 6, December, 1913, p. 211.
2 Oliver Sheldon, *The Philosophy of Management* (London, Sir Isaac Pitman &
Sons, Ltd., 1923), p. 36. [See pp. 265–277.—EDITOR]
3 *Ibid.*, p. 35.

In all our study of personnel work, however, we should remember that we can never wholly separate the human and the mechanical problem. This would seem too obvious to mention if we did not so often see that separation made. Go back to that sentence of Sheldon's: "There may be a science of costing, of transportation, of operation, but there can be no science of cooperation." But take Sheldon's own illustration, that of transportation. The engineering part of transportation is not the larger part. Please note that I do not say it is a small part. It is a large part, and it is the dramatic part, and it is the part we have done well, and yet the chief part of transportation is the personal thing. Every one knows that the main difficulty about transportation is that there have not always been sensible working arrangements between the men concerned. But you all see every day that the study of human relations in business and the study of technique of operating are bound up together. You know that the way the worker is treated affects output. You know that the routing of materials and the maintenance of machines is a matter partly of human relations. You know, I hope, that there is danger in "putting in" personnel work if it is super-added instead of being woven through the plant. You remember the man who wanted to know something about Chinese metaphysics and so looked up China in the encyclopedia and then metaphysics, and put them together. We shall not have much better success if we try merely to add personnel work. Even although there is, as I certainly believe there should be, a special personnel department run by a trained expert, yet it seems to me that every executive should make some study of personnel work a part of that broad foundation which is today increasingly felt to be necessary for the business man.

If, then, one of the first things to be done to make business management more scientific is to apply scientific methods to those problems of management which involve human relations, another requirement is that we should make an analysis of managers' jobs somewhat corresponding to the analysis of workers' jobs in the Taylor system. We need to get away from tradition, prejudice, stereotypes, guesswork, and find the factual basis for managerial jobs. We know, for instance, what has been accomplished in elimination of waste by scientific methods of research and experiment applied to operating, to probable demand for commodities, and so on. I believe that this has to be carried further, and that managerial waste, administrative waste, should be given the same research and experiment. How this can be done, I shall take up later.

The next step business management should take is to organize the body of knowledge on which it should rest. We have defined science as an organized body of exact knowledge. That is, scientific method consists of two parts: (1) research, and (2) the organization of the knowledge obtained by research. The importance of research, of continued research, receives every year fuller and fuller appreciation from business men; but methods of organizing the results of such research have not kept pace with this appreciation. While business management is collecting more and more exact knowledge, while it is observing more keenly, experimenting more widely, it has not yet gone far in organizing this knowledge. We have drawn a good many conclusions, have thought out certain principles, but have not always seen the relation between these conclusions or these principles.

I have not time to speak here of more than one way of organizing in industrial plants our accumulating knowledge in regard to executive technique. There should be, I think, in every plant, an official, one of whose duties should be to classify and interpret managerial experience with the aid of the carefully kept records which should be required of every executive. From such classification and interpretation of experience—this experience which in essentials repeats itself so often from time to time, from department to department, from plant to plant—it would be possible to draw useful conclusions. The importance of this procedure becomes more obvious when we remember that having experience and profiting by experience are two different matters. Experience may leave us with mistaken notions, with prejudice or suspicion.

A serious drawback to a fuller understanding of and utilization of executive experience is that we have at present (1) no systematic follow-up of decisions, of new methods, of experiments in managing;

and (2) no carefully worked out system of recording. Poorly kept records, or the absence of any systematic recording, are partly responsible for what seems in some plants like a stagnant management, and in all plants for certain leaks in management. For instance, the fact that we have no follow-up for executive decisions with a comparing of results—a procedure necessary before business management can be considered fully on a scientific basis—is partly a deficiency in recording. The fact that an executive, if he wishes to introduce a certain method (not in operating but in management itself), cannot find in any records whether that method has been tried before or anything like it, and what the results have been, is a serious deficiency in recording. If an executive is facing a certain problem, he should be able to find out: (1) whether other executives have had to meet similar problems, (2) how they met them, (3) what the results were. It seems to me very unfortunate that it is possible for one man to say to another, as I heard some one say at the suggestion of a new method, "I believe our department tried that a few years ago, but I've forgotten what we thought of it."

I have heard it said that the Harvard football team was put on its feet when Percy Haughton introduced the system of recording football experience. After that, if some one thought he had a brilliant idea that such and such a play could be tried on Yale, the first thing done was to examine the records; and it might be found that that play had been tried two years before and failed. It might even be discovered why it had failed. This system of recording—I believe it already existed at Yale—was Mr. Haughton's great contribution to Harvard football. Because of it, the team could not, at any rate, go on making the same mistakes.

The recording of executive experience, which will probably need a technique somewhat different from that used for the rest of business recording, should have, I think, our immediate attention. The system of both recording and reporting should be such that records and reports can be quickly mastered, and thus be practically useful to all, instead of buried underneath their own verbiage, length, and lack of systematization. And there should be required from every executive, training in the technique of keeping records and making reports.

But we need more than records. We need a new journal, or a new department in some present journal; we need sifted bibliographies of reports; ways of getting information from other parts of the country, from other countries; above all, we need executive conferences with carefully worked out methods for comparing experience which has been scientifically recorded, analyzed, and organized. When many different plants are willing to share with one another the results of their experience, then we shall have business policies based on wider data than those of the present.

The Graduate School of Business Administration and the Bureau of Business Research of Harvard University are now collecting cases of business policy, thus opening the way for classifying and cross-indexing. Harvard has, of course, been able to get hold of a very small number of cases, but this seems to be a valuable and significant undertaking.

I have been interested also in what a certain recent committee, with representatives from various firms, deliberately stated as its object: "the comparison of experience." I should like to know how frank and full their exchange of experience was; but any attempt of this kind is interesting, indicating, as it does, the attitude on the part of those participating that they expect to gain more by working together than they will lose (the old idea) by allowing other firms to gain any intimate knowledge of their affairs.

Moreover, not only should we analyze and compare our experience, but we should deliberately experiment. We should make experiments, observe experiments, compare and discuss these with each other, and see what consensus we can come to in our conclusions. For this we should be wholly frank with one another. If we have the scientific attitude toward our work, we shall be willing to tell our failures. I heard of a man who made an ice machine which did not work, and the following conversation took place between him and a friend he met:

FRIEND: "I was sorry to hear your experiment was a failure!"
MAN: "Who told you it was a failure?"

FRIEND: "Why, I heard your ice machine wouldn't work."
MAN: "Oh, that was true enough, but it was a great success as an experiment. You can learn as much from your failures as from your successes."

From such experimenting and from the comparison of experience, I think certain standards would emerge. But we should remember that, as no Taylorite thinks there is anything final in "standardization," so we should not aim at a static standardization of managerial method, executive technique. We should make use of all available present experience, knowing that experience and our learning from it should be equally continuous matters.

If science gives us research and experimentation as its two chief methods, it at the same time shows us that nothing is too small to claim our attention. There is nothing unimportant in business procedure. For instance, I spoke above of record keeping. I know a firm where they tell me that they are not getting nearly so much advantage as they should from their records because they have not yet worked out a system of cross-indexing. Yet to some, cross-indexing may not seem to be of great importance. I know a man who says frequently about this detail or that, "Oh, that doesn't matter." Everything matters to the scientist. The following incident ͡ems to me to have some significance. I told a man that I was working at the technique of the business interview, at which he seemed rather amused and said, "I guess most business men know how to conduct interviews." It was evident that he thought he did—but he is a man who has never risen above a small position. Later, I said the same thing to a clever man in a good position, a New York man, by the way. I said it a little hesitatingly, for I thought he too might consider it beneath his notice, but he was much interested and asked if he might see my paper when finished.

I have spoken of the classification of experience, the organizing of knowledge, as one of the necessary preliminaries to putting business management on a scientific basis. This organized body of knowledge tends at first to remain in the hands of a few. Measures should be taken to make it accessible to the whole managerial force. There should be opportunities for the training of executives through talks, suggested readings (including journals on management), through wisely led discussion groups and conferences, through managers' associations, foremen's associations, and the like. The organized knowledge of managerial methods which many of the higher officials possess should spread to the lower executives. In some cases, the higher official does not even think of this as part of his responsibility. He will say to a subordinate, "Here is what I want done; I don't care how you do it, that's up to you." Indeed, many an official has prided himself on this way of dealing with subordinates. But this is changing. It is part of the Taylor system that standards and methods for each worker's job are made accessible to the worker; also knowledge of the quality of work expected, which is shown him by specifications or drawings. Some such system should be developed for management. To develop it might be made part of that analysis of managerial jobs which I spoke of a few moments ago. Indeed, more and more of the higher executives are seeing now that managers' jobs as well as workers' jobs are capable of carrying with them accepted standards and methods.

Of course, it is recognized that many of these standards and methods need the sanction of custom rather than of authority, that they should be indicated rather than prescribed, also that much more elasticity should be allowed than in the detailed instructions of the Taylor system—but this all part of that large subject, the method of training executives. Possibly in time, as business organization develops, we shall have an official for executives corresponding to the functional foreman who is sometimes known as the "methods instructor," an official whose duty it will be to see that certain managerial methods are understood and followed, as it is the duty of the functional foreman to see that certain operating methods are understood and followed. But I should not advocate this unless the executives were allowed fullest opportunity for contributing to such prescribed methods. The development of managerial technique has been thought by some to involve the risk of crushing originality, the danger of taking away initiative. I think that, rightly managed, it should give executives increased opportunity for the fruitful exercise of initiative and originality, for it is they themselves who must develop this technique even if helped by experts. The choice here presented is not that between originality and a mechanical system, but between a haphazard, hit-or-miss way of performing executive duties and a scientifically determined procedure.

Yet when business management has gained something of an accepted technique, there still remains, as part of the training of executives, the acquiring of skill in its application. Managerial skill cannot be painted on the outside of executives; it has to go deeper than that. Like manual workers, managerial workers have to acquire certain habits and attitudes. And just as in the case of manual workers, for the acquisition of these habits and attitudes three conditions must be given: (1) detailed information in regard to a new method; (2) the stimulus to adopt this method; and (3) the opportunity to practice it so that it may become a habit.

A business man tells me that I should emphasize the last point particularly. He says that his firm has been weak just here; that they have done more preaching than giving opportunity for practice. He says: "We've given them a lecture on piano playing and then put them on the concert stage. This winter we are going to try to invent ways of giving real practice to foremen so that a set of habits can be formed." No subject is more important than the training of executives, but as it is a subject which would require an evening for the most superficial consideration, we cannot speak further of it tonight. Let me just say, however, as a hint of what I shall elaborate later, that if you wish to train yourself for higher executive positions, the first thing for you to decide is what you are training for. Ability to dominate or manipulate others? That ought to be easy enough, since most of the magazines advertise sure ways of developing something they call "personality." But I am convinced that the first essential of business success is the capacity for organized thinking.

In conclusion: What does all this imply in regard to the profession of business management? It means that men must prepare themselves as seriously for this profession as for any other. They must realize that they, as all professional men, are assuming grave responsibilities, that they are to take a creative part in one of the large functions of society, a part which, I believe, only trained and disciplined men can in the future hope to take with success.

THE ESSENTIALS OF LEADERSHIP

BY M. P. FOLLETT

I HAVE TRIED to show you certain changes which are creeping into our thinking on business management. As I have said, in the more progressively managed businesses an order was no longer an arbitrary command but—the law of the situation. A week ago I defined authority as something which could not really be conferred on someone, but as a power which inhered in the job. Now I want to show the difference between the theory of leadership long accepted and a conception which is being forced on our attention by the way in which business is today conducted.

What I call the old-fashioned theory of leadership is well illustrated by a study made a few years ago by two psychologists. They worked out a list of questions by which to test leadership ability. Here are some of the questions:

At a reception or tea do you try to meet the important persons present?

At a lecture or entertainment do you go forward and take a front seat?

Reprinted from the book, *Freedom and Co-ordination,* by Mary Parker Follett, Chapter IV, pages 47–60; edited by L. Urwick. Published by Management Publications Trust, Ltd., London, 1949. Lecture delivered at Department of Business Administration, London School of Economics and Political Science, in January and February 1933. Used by permission of the editor, of The University of London, and of Sir Isaac Pitman & Sons, Ltd.

At a hairdresser's are you persuaded to try a new shampoo or are you able to resist?

If you make purchases at Woolworth's, are you ashamed to have your friends know it?

If you are at a stupid party, do you try to inject life into it?

If you hold an opinion the reverse of which the lecturer has expressed, do you usually volunteer your opinion?

Do you find it difficult to say No when a salesman is trying to sell you something?

What do you do when someone tries to push in ahead of you in a line at the box office?

When you see someone in a public place whom you think you have met, do you go up to him and enquire whether you have met?

And so on—there were a good many more. But what on earth has all this to do with leadership? I think nothing whatever. These psychologists were making tests, they said, for aggressiveness, assuming that aggressiveness and leadership are synonymous, assuming that you cannot be a good leader unless you are aggressive, masterful, dominating. But I think, not only that these characteristics are not the qualities essential to leadership, but, on the contrary, that they often militate directly against leadership. I knew a boy who was very decidedly the boss of his gang all through his youthful days. That boy is now forty-eight years old. He has not risen in his business or shown any power of leadership in his community. And I do not think that this has been in spite of his dominating traits, but because of them.

But I cannot blame the psychologists too much, for in the business world too there has been an idea long prevalent that self-assertion, pugnacity even, are necessary to leadership. Or at any rate, the leader is usually supposed to be one who has a compelling personality, who can impose his own will on others, can make others do what he wants done.

One writer says that running a business is like managing an unruly horse, a simile I particularly dislike. Another writer says, "The successful business man feels at his best in giving orders. . . . The business man tends to lay down the law—he feels himself to be an individual source of energy." While this is undoubtedly true of many business men, yet there are many today of whom it is not true. It is no longer the universally accepted type of administrative leadership. We saw two weeks ago that in scientifically managed plants, with their planning departments, their experts, their staff officials, their trained managers of the line, few "orders" are given in the old sense of the word. When therefore we are told that large-scale ability means masterfulness and autocratic will, some of us wish to reply: But that is the theory of the past, it is not what we find today in the best-managed industries.

This does not however denote that less leadership is required than formerly, but a different kind. Let me take two illustrations, one of the foreman, one of the salesman. We find in those plants where there is little order-giving of the old kind, where the right order is found by research, that the foreman is not only as important but more important than formerly. He is by no means less of a leader; indeed he has more opportunities for leadership in the sense of that word which is now coming to be accepted by many. This is because his time is freed for more constructive work. With the more explicitly defined requirements made upon him—requirements in regard to time, quality of work and methods —he has a greater responsibility for group accomplishment. In order to meet the standards set for group accomplishment, he is developing a technique very different from the old foreman technique. The foreman today does not merely deal with trouble, he forestalls trouble. In fact we don't think much of a foreman who is always dealing with trouble; we feel that if he were doing his job properly, there wouldn't be so much trouble. The job of the head of any unit—foreman or head of department—is to see that conditions (machines, materials, etc.) are right, to see that instructions are understood, and to see that workers are trained to carry out the instructions, trained to use the methods which have been decided on as best. The test of a foreman now is not how good he is at bossing, but how little bossing he has to do, because of the training of his men and the organisation of their work.

Now take the salesman. If the foreman was supposed to dominate by aggressiveness, the salesman was supposed to dominate by persuasiveness. Consider the different demand made on salesmen today. Salesmen are being chosen less and less for their powers of persuasion, but for their general intelligence, for their knowledge of the goods handled, and for their ability to teach prospective customers the best way to use the goods. A business man said to me: "The training of salesmen . . . is being carried on with increasing elaboration, and always with more emphasis on knowledge of the product and its uses, and distinctly less on the technique of persuasion. . . ." For the firms who sell production equipment, this means sending men who sometimes act as consulting engineers for their customers.

We find this same doctrine taught in the salesmanship classes held in the big shops. The shop assistants are told not to over-persuade a customer, else when the customer gets home she may be sorry she has bought that article and may not come to that shop again. The saleswoman may have made one sale and lost a dozen by her persuasiveness. Her job is to know her goods and to study the needs of her customer.

To dominate, either by a masterful or a persuasive personality, is going out of fashion. People advertise courses in what they call "applied psychology" and promise that they will teach you how to develop your personality and thus become leaders, but wiser teachers say to their students, "Forget your personality, learn your job."

What then are the requisites of leadership? First, a thorough knowledge of your job. And this fact is keenly appreciated today as business is becoming a profession and business management a science. Men train themselves to become heads of departments or staff officials by learning all that goes with the particular position they wish to attain.

Consider the influence which it is possible for the cost accountant to exercise because of his special knowledge. Where there is cost-accounting and unit budgeting, the cost accountant is in a position to know more about the effect of a change in price than anyone else. His analyses and his interpretations may dictate policy to the chief executive.

Moreover, we find leadership in many places besides these more obvious ones, and this is just because men are learning special techniques and therefore naturally lead in those situations. The chairman of a committee may not occupy a high official position or be a man of forceful personality, but he may know how to guide discussion effectively, that is, he may know the technique of *his* job. Or consider the industrial-relations-man now maintained in so many industries. This man is an adept at conciliation. He has a large and elaborate technique for that at his command.

When it is a case of instruction, the teacher is the leader. Yet a good instructor may be a poor foreman. Again, some men can make people produce, and some are good at following up quality who could never make people produce.

There is also individual leadership which may come to the fore irrespective of any particular position; of two girls on a machine, one may be the leader. We often see individual leadership, that is, leadership irrespective of position, springing up in a committee. There was an instance of this in a sales committee. The chairman of the committee was the sales manager, Smith. Smith was narrow but not obstinate. Not being obstinate, Jones was able to get Smith to soften his opinion on the particular matter in question, and there was then an integration of the opinion of that committee around Jones' leadership.

I think it is of great importance to recognise that leadership is sometimes in one place and sometimes in another. For it tends to prevent apathy among under-executives. It makes them much more alert if they realise that they have many chances of leadership before they are advanced to positions which carry with them definitely, officially, leadership. Moreover, if such occasional leadership is exercised with moderation without claiming too much for oneself, without encroaching on anyone's official position, it may mean that person will be advanced to an official position of leadership.

But let us look further at the essentials of leadership. Of the greatest importance is the ability to grasp a total situation. The chief mistake in thinking of leadership as resting wholly on personality lies probably in the fact that the executive leader is not a leader of men only but of something we are learning to call the total situation. This includes facts, present and potential, aims and purposes and men. Out of a welter of facts, experience, desires, aims, the leader must find the unifying thread. He must see a whole, not a mere kaleidoscope of pieces. He must see the relation between all the different factors in a situation. The higher up you go, the more ability you have to have of this kind, because you have a wider range of facts from which to seize the relations. The foreman has a certain range—a comparatively small number of facts and small number of people. The head of a sub-department has a wider range; the head of a department a wider still, the general manager the widest of all. One of the principal functions of the general manager is to organise all the scattered forces of the business. The higher railway officials may not understand railway accounting, design of rolling stock, and assignment of rates as well as their expert assistants, but they know how to use their knowledge, how to relate it, how to make a total situation.

The leader then is one who can organise the experience of the group—whether it be the small group of the foreman, the larger group of the department, or the whole plant—can organise the experience of the group and thus get the full power of the group. The leader makes the team. This is pre-eminently the leadership quality—the ability to organise all the forces there are in an enterprise and make them serve a common purpose. Men with this ability create a group power rather than express a personal power. They penetrate to the subtlest connections of the forces at their command, and make all these forces available and most effectively available for the accomplishment of their purpose.

Some writers tell us that the leader should represent the accumulated knowledge and experience of his particular group, but I think he should go far beyond this. It is true that the able executive learns from everyone around him, but it is also true that he is far more than the depository where the wisdom of the group collects. When leadership rises to genius it has the power of transforming, of transforming experience into power. And that is what experience is for, to be made into power. The great leader creates as well as directs power. The essence of leadership is to create control, and that is what the world needs today, control of small situations or of our world situation.

I have said that the leader must understand the situation, must see it as a whole, must see the inter-relation of all the parts. He must do more than this. He must see the evolving situation, the developing situation. His wisdom, his judgment, is used, not on a situation that is stationary, but on one that is changing all the time. The ablest administrators do not merely draw logical conclusions from the array of facts of the past which their expert assistants bring to them, they have a vision of the future. To be sure, business estimates are always, or should be, based on the probable future conditions. Sales policy, for instance, is guided not only by past sales but by probable future sales. The leader, however, must see all the future trends and unite them. Business is always developing. Decisions have to anticipate the development. You remember how Alice in Wonderland had to run as fast as she could in order to stand still. That is a commonplace to every business man. And it is up to the general manager to see that his executives are running as fast as they can. Not, you understand, working as hard as they can—that is taken for granted—but anticipating as far as they can.

This insight into the future we usually call in business anticipating. But anticipating means more than forecasting or predicting. It means far more than meeting the next situation, it means making the next situation. If you will watch decisions, you will find that the highest grade decision does not have to do merely with the situation with which it is directly concerned. It is always the sign of the second-rate man when the decision merely meets the present situation. It is the left-over in a decision which gives it the greatest value. It is the carry-over in a decision which helps develop the situation in the way we wish it to be developed. In business we are always passing from one significant moment to another significant moment, and the leader's task is pre-eminently to understand the moment of passing. The leader sees one situation melting into another and has learned the mastery of that moment. We usually have the situation we make—no one sentence is more pregnant with meaning for business success. This is why the leader's task is so difficult, why the great leader requires great qualities—the most delicate and sensitive perceptions, imagination and insight, and at the same time courage and faith.

The leader should have the spirit of adventure, but the spirit of adventure need not mean the temperament of the gambler. It should be the pioneer spirit which blazes new trails. The insight to see possible new paths, the courage to try them, the judgment to measure results—these are the qualifications of the leader.

And now let me speak to you for a moment of something which seems to me of the utmost importance, but which has been far too little considered, and that is the part of the followers in the leadership situation. Their part is not merely to follow, they have a very active part to play and that is to keep the leader in control of a situation. Let us not think that we are either leaders or—nothing of much importance. As one of those led we have a part in leadership. In no aspect of our subject do we see a greater discrepancy between theory and practice than here. The definition given over and over again of the leader is one who can induce others to follow him. Or that meaning is taken for granted and the question is asked: "What is the technique by which a leader keeps his followers in line?" Some political scientists discuss why men obey or do not obey, why they tend to lead or to follow, as if leading and following were the essence of leadership. I think that following is a very small part of what the other members of a group have to do. I think that these authors are writing of theory, of words, of stereotypes of the past, that they are, at any rate, not noticing the changes that are going on in business thinking and business practice. If we want to treat these questions realistically, we shall watch what is actually happening, and what I see happening in some places is that the members of a group are not so much following a leader as helping to keep him in control of a situation.

How do we see this being done? For one thing, in looking at almost any business we see many suggestions coming up from below. We find sub-executives trying to get upper executives to instal mechanical improvements, to try a new chemical process, to adopt a plan for increasing incentives for workers, and so on. The upper executives try to persuade the general manager and the general manager the board of directors. We have heard a good deal in the past about the consent of the governed; we have now in modern business much that might be called the consent of the governing, the suggestions coming from below and those at the top consenting. I am not trying to imitate Shaw and Chesterton and being paradoxical; there is actually a change going on in business practice in this respect which I want to emphasise to you at every point.

How else may a man help to keep those above him in control? He may, instead of trying to "get by" on something, instead of covering up his difficulties so that no one will know he is having any, inform his chief of his problems, tell him the things he is not succeeding in as well as all his wonderful achievements. His chief will respect him just as much for his failures as for his successes if he himself takes the right attitude towards them.

Another way is to take a wrong order back for correction. It may have been an error, or it may be that it was all right once, but that it must be changed to meet changing conditions. The worker has not met his responsibility by merely obeying. Many a worker thinks that the pointing out of a wrong order is a gratuitous thing on his part, a favour he generously confers but which he need not because it is not really his job, his job is to obey. As a matter of fact, however, obeying is only a small part of his job. One general manager told me that what they disliked in his factory was what they called there the Yes, yes man. The intelligent leader, this man said, does not want the kind of follower who thinks of his job only in terms of passive obedience.

But there is following. Leader and followers are both following the invisible leader—the common purpose. The best executives put this common purpose clearly before their group. While leadership depends on depth of conviction and the power coming therefrom, there must also be the ability to share that conviction with others, the ability to make purpose articulate. And then that common purpose becomes the leader. And I believe that we are coming more and more to act, whatever our theories, on our faith in the power of this invisible leader. Loyalty to the invisible leader gives us the strongest possible bond of union, establishes a sympathy which is not a sentimental but a dynamic sympathy.

Moreover, when both leader and followers are obeying the same demand, you have instead of a passive, an active, self-willed obedience. The men on a fishing smack are all good fellows together, call each other by their first names, yet one is captain and the others obey him; but it is an intelligent, alert, self-willed obedience.

The best leaders get their orders obeyed because they too are obeying. Sincerity more than aggressiveness is a quality of leadership.

If the leader should teach his followers their part in the leadership situation, how to help keep their chief in control, he has another duty equally important. He has to teach them how to control the situations for which they are specifically responsible. This is an essential part of leadership and a part recognised today. We have a good illustration of this in the relation between upper executives and heads of departments in those firms where the Budget is used as a tool of control. Suppose an upper executive is dissatisfied with the work of a department. When this happens it is either because quality is too poor or costs are too high. The old method of procedure was for the upper executive simply to blame the head of the department. But in a plant where the departments are budgeted, an upper executive can ask the head of a department to sit down with him and consider the matter. The Budget objectifies the whole situation. It is possible for an upper executive to get the head of the department to find out himself where the difficulty lies and to make him give himself the necessary orders to meet the situation.

Many are coming to think that the job of a man higher up is not to make decisions for his subordinates but to teach them how to handle their problems themselves, teach them how to make their own decisions. The best leader does not persuade men to follow his will. He shows them what it is necessary for them to do in order to meet their responsibility, a responsibility which has been explicitly defined to them. Such a leader is not one who wishes to do people's thinking for them, but one who trains them to think for themselves.

Indeed the best leaders try to train their followers themselves to become leaders. A second-rate executive will often try to suppress leadership because he fears it may rival his own. I have seen several instances of this. But the first-rate executive tries to develop leadership in those under him. He does not want men who are subservient to him, men who render him an unthinking obedience. While therefore there are still men who try to surround themselves with docile servants—you all know that type—the ablest men today have a larger aim, they wish to be leaders of leaders. This does not mean that they abandon one iota of power. But the great leader tries also to develop power wherever he can among those who work with him, and then he gathers all this power and uses it as the energising force of a progressing enterprise.

If any of you think I have underestimated the personal side of leadership, let me point out that I have spoken against only that conception which emphasises the dominating, the masterful man. I most certainly believe that many personal qualities enter into leadership—tenacity, sincerity, fair dealings with all, steadfastness of purpose, depth of conviction, control of temper, tact, steadiness in stormy periods, ability to meet emergencies, power to draw forth and develop the latent possibilities of others, and so on. There are many more. There is, for instance, the force of example on which we cannot lay too great stress. If workers have to work overtime, their head should be willing to do the same. In every way he must show that he is willing to do what he urges on others.

One winter I went yachting with some friends in the inland waterways of the southern part of the United States. On one occasion our pilot led us astray and we found ourselves one night aground in a Carolina swamp. Obviously the only thing to do was to try to push the boat off, but the crew refused, saying that the swamps in that region were infested with rattlesnakes. The owner of the yacht offered not a word of remonstrance, but turned instantly and jumped overboard. Every member of the crew followed.

So please remember that I do not underestimate what is called the personal side of leadership, indeed there is much in this paper, by implication, on that side. And do not think that I underestimate the importance of the man at the top. No one could put more importance on top leadership than I do, as I shall try to show you next week when we consider the part of the chief executive in that intricate system of human relationship which business has now become.

I might say as a summary of this talk that we have three kinds of leadership: the leadership of position, the leadership of personality and the leadership of function. My claim for modern industry is that in the best managed plants the leadership of function is tending to have more weight and the leadership of mere position or of mere personality less.

Please note that I say only a tendency. I am aware how often a situation is controlled by a man either because his position gives him the whip hand and he uses it, or because he knows how to play politics. My only thesis is that in the more progressively managed businesses there is a tendency for the control of a particular situation to go to the man with the largest knowledge of that situation, to him who can grasp and organise its essential elements, who understands its total significance, who can see it through—who can see length as well as breadth—rather than to one with merely a dominating personality or in virtue of his official position.

And that thought brings me to my conclusion. The chief thing I have wanted to do in this hour is to explode a long-held superstition. We have heard repeated again and again in the past, "Leaders are born, not made." I read the other day, "Leadership is a capacity that cannot be acquired." I believe that leadership can, in part, be learned. I hope you will not let anyone persuade you that it cannot be. The man who thinks leadership cannot be learned will probably remain in a subordinate position. The man who believes it can be, will go to work and learn it. He may not ever be president of the company, but he can rise from where he is.

Moreover, if leadership could not be learned, our large, complex businesses would not have much chance of success, for they require able leadership in many places, not only in the president's chair.

Leadership is a part of business management and there is a rapidly developing technique for every aspect of the administration and management of a business.

I urge you then, instead of accepting the idea that there is something mysterious about leadership, to analyse it. I think that then you cannot fail to see that there are many aspects of it which can be acquired. For instance, a part of leadership is all that makes you get on most successfully in your direct contacts with people— how and when to praise, how and when to point out mistakes, what attitude to take toward failures. All this can of course be learned. The first thing to do is to discover what is necessary for leadership and then to try to acquire by various methods those essentials. Even those personal characteristics with which we were endowed by birth can often be changed. For instance, vitality, energy, physical endurance, are usually necessary for leadership, but even this is not always beyond us. Theodore Roosevelt was a delicate lad and yet became an explorer, a Rough Rider, a fighter, and by his own determined efforts. You have seen timid boys become self-confident. You have seen bumptious little boys have all that taken out of them by their schoolmasters.

Leadership is not the "intangible," the "incalculable" thing we have often seen it described. It is capable of being analysed into its different elements, and many of these elements can be acquired and become part of one's equipment.

My paper has been concerned with functional leadership and with multiple leadership. Our present historians and biographers are strengthening the conception of multiple leadership by showing us that in order to understand any epoch we must take into account the lesser leaders. They tell us also that the number of these lesser leaders has been so steadily increasing that one of the most outstanding facts of our life today is a widely diffused leadership. Wells goes further and says that his hope for the future depends on a still more widely diffused leadership. In the past, he says, we depended on a single great leader . . . today many men and women must help to lead. In the past, he says, Aristotle led the world in science, today there are thousands of scientists each making his contribution.

Industry gives to men and women the chance for leadership, the chance to make their contribution to what all agree is the thing most needed in the world today.

Business used to be thought of as trading, managing as manipulating. Both ideas are now changing. Business is becoming a profession and management a science and an art. This means that men must prepare themselves for business as seriously as for any other profession. They must realise that they, as all professional men, are assuming grave responsibilities, that they are to take a creative part in one of the large functions of society, a part which, I believe, only trained and disciplined men can in the future hope to take with success.

COORDINATION

BY M. P. FOLLETT

I HAVE SAID that we find responsibility for management shot all through a business, that we find some degree of authority all along the line, that leadership can be exercised by many people besides the top executive. All this is now being increasingly recognised, and the crux of business organisation is how to join these varied responsibilities, these scattered authorities, these different kinds of leadership. For a business, to be a going concern, must be unified. The fair test of business administration, of industrial organisation, is whether you have a business with all its parts so coordinated, so moving together in their closely knit and adjusting activities, so linking, inter-locking, inter-relating, that they make a working unit, not a congeries of separate pieces. In the businesses I have studied, the greatest weakness is in the relation of departments. The efficiency of many plants is lowered by an imperfectly worked-out system of coordination. In some cases all the coordination there is depends on the degree of friendliness existing between the heads of departments, on whether they are willing to consult; sometimes it depends on the mere chance of two men coming up to town on the same train every morning.

Reprinted from the book, *Freedom and Co-ordination,* by Mary Parker Follett, Chapter V, pages 61–76; edited by L. Urwick. Published by Management Publications Trust, Ltd., London, 1949. Lecture delivered at Department of Business Administration, London School of Economics and Political Science, in January and February 1933. Used by permission of the editor, of the University of London, and of Sir Isaac Pitman & Sons, Ltd.

I spoke to you last week of a recent conference here in London of Works Managers and Sales Managers. The object of the conference was to discuss ways in which Works Managers and Sales Managers could work more closely together. We heard a great deal about the lack of cooperation between them. We heard a great deal of the necessity of understanding each other's problems, that the production department should know more of customers' demands, why they liked one product, why they complained of another; that the sales department, on the other hand, should know more of the difficulties of production, the difficulty, for instance, of producing what the customer wants within the price the customer is willing to pay. And so on. Many instances were given of the way in which Sales Managers and Works Managers could help each other by a greater understanding of each other's work. We heard that neither side should lead, that they should work together, that they should make a team.

I thought this one of the best conferences I had ever attended. I thought it was bound to do a lot of good. But one thought persisted uppermost in my mind all day and just at the end of the afternoon one man voiced this thought when he rose and said: "But surely coordination is a problem of management." There was no discussion of this point and quite rightly. These were Works Managers and Sales Managers and they were considering how, as industry is generally organised, they could cooperate more effectively. But surely it is obvious that many of the capital suggestions made at that Conference, suggestions for voluntary cooperation, were things that could be required of the sales and production department. Two men thought it desirable that the heads of these departments should lunch together frequently. One trembles to think of the success of industry depending on such a mere chance as that. Surely regular meetings between production department and sales department could be required at which they could inform each other of all the things which were mentioned at this conference as essential each should know of the other.

And indeed a good many companies are considering coordination a question of management and organisation and the problem is met in different ways. In some cases regular meetings between departments are required. Some companies have a coordinating department whose special function it is to bring into closer relation the work of the various departments. Some have a planning department which serves also as a coordinating agency. A department of sales research, separate from the selling department as such, may act as a link with production. Research as to future lines of production must necessarily be linked up with sales research. The merchandise department to a certain extent links production and sales. And so on. I give these merely as illustrations. If I were to describe to you all the ways in which coordination is being effected in industry that would be a talk on organisation, and, besides the fact that that would take all winter, it is not what I have undertaken to do. I have, therefore, chosen three things which seem to me to make for the greater unity of an enterprise. I might express this more forcefully and say that I think they embody the fundamental principle of unity.

One, which I consider a very important trend in business management, is a system of cross-functioning between the different departments. Let me take, as providing an example of this trend, the Telephone Company of which I have already spoken to you, although of course there are many other companies which would do equally well for illustration. Here we find the four departments —traffic, engineering, commercial and plant—conferring with one another and all together. These conferences are often informal but they are expected of all officials. Each department is expected to get in touch with certain others. The district traffic manager asks the wire chief from the plant department to talk some matter over with him, or if it is a commercial matter, he calls in the commercial manager of that district, or if it is a question of blue prints or costs, he asks the engineering department if they will send a man over. They may settle it among themselves. If not, the district traffic manager puts the matter up to the superintendent of the traffic department. The superintendent of the traffic department may consult the superintendent of the plant or the commercial department.

Here, you see, we have a combination of going both across the line and up the line. When one of the exchanges was cut in two (such questions come up every day, I mention this only because it occurred while I was making my investigation), the question came up whether to cut thirty-five a day or five hundred in a blanket order one night. This affected all four departments—traffic, engineering, commercial and plant. They agreed after discussion on the blanket order. If they had disagreed they would have taken it up to the general superintendent of each department—up the line, note. Then the four superintendents would have consulted, now across the line. If they had agreed the matter would have ended there. If not, it would have had to go to the General Manager—up the line.

This combination of across and up exists, as I have said, in many plants today. Many businesses are now organised in such a way that you do not have an ascending and descending ladder of authority. You have a degree of cross-functioning, of inter-relation of departments, which means a horizontal rather than a vertical authority. That means in this case that a problem which occurs at X which concerns Y does not have to be taken up the line from X and then taken down the line to Y.

A telephone company sells service rather than a product, but you can have the same cross-functioning anywhere. If you have it in a company which both manufactures and sells a product, instead of all that the selling department knows of customers' demands going up the line to the general manager and then going down the line from him to the manufacturing department, and the problems of the manufacturing department going up the line to the general manager and then from him down the line to the sales department, instead of this you can have a system of cross-relations which gives opportunity for direct contact between Sales Manager and Production Manager. Where you have this direct contact there is much less chance of misunderstanding, there is opportunity of explaining problems and difficulties each to the other. This seems to me very important. Direct contact of the responsible people concerned is, indeed, one of the four vital principles of organisation which I shall speak of later.

I should like to say incidentally that where we see a horizontal rather than a vertical authority, we have another proof of what I said two weeks ago, namely that we are now finding in business practice less of that kind of authority which puts one man over another. We have conferences of parallel heads.

But there are companies who get this horizontal authority, as I have called it, by another method. These companies think that the methods which I have been describing to you, where each man decides for himself when he needs to discuss a matter with another, are not sufficient for the steadily continuous binding together of the different parts of a business. These companies, therefore, have a system of committees composed of men who have closely related problems who meet regularly to discuss these problems. I do not, however, propose to consider the question of committees in industry here, it is too large and too controversial a subject. I mention them because they are a form of cross-functioning, and cross-functioning was one of the ways of unifying a business of which I wished to speak to you.

But all this matter of consultation, of discussion of problems, whether it be done officially and formally or informally, means that there will be constantly antagonistic policies, antagonistic methods, confronting each other, each wanting right of way. Before we can hope for the most effective coordination, we shall have to learn how best to deal with all the differences of opinion that arise day by day, hour by hour, in any enterprise. They may be between the members of the Board of Directors, between executives, or between executives and workers, but daily they tend to produce discord, daily they threaten to be a disintegrating influence, if we do not know the best method of dealing with them. This seems to me of the utmost importance and I shall therefore spend a larger part of my hour considering this point.

There are three ways of settling differences: by domination, by compromise, or by integration. Domination, obviously, is a victory of one side over the other. This is not usually successful in the long run for the side that is defeated will simply wait for its chance to dominate. The second way, that of compromise, we understand well, for that is the way we settle most of our controversies—each side gives up a little in order to have peace. Both these ways are unsatisfactory. In dominating, only one side gets what it wants; in compromise neither side gets what it wants. We are continually hearing compromise praised. That is the accepted, the approved, way of ending controversy, yet no one really wants to compromise, because that means giving up part of what he wants. Is there any other way of dealing with difference?

There is a way beginning now to be recognised at least and sometimes followed, the way of integration. Let me take first a very simple illustration. In a University library one day, in one of the smaller rooms, someone wanted the window open, I wanted it shut. We opened the window in the next room where no one was sitting. There was no compromise because we both got all we really wanted. For I did not want a closed room. I simply did not want the north wind to blow directly on me; and he, the man in the room with me, did not want that particular window open, he merely wanted more air in the room. Integration means finding a third way which will include both what A wishes and what B wishes, a way in which neither side has had to sacrifice anything.

Let us take another illustration. A Dairymen's Cooperative League almost went to pieces on the question of precedence in unloading cans at a creamery platform. The creamery was on the side of a hill. The men who came down the hill thought they should not be asked to wait on a downgrade and that therefore they should unload first. The men who came up the hill thought equally that they should unload first. They had a hot row about it, so hot that it almost broke up the League. Both sides, you see, were thinking of just those two possibilities: should the uphillers or downhillers unload first? But then an outsider suggested that the position of the platform should be changed so that uphillers and downhillers could unload at the same time. This suggestion was accepted by both sides. Both were happy. But neither was happy because he had got his way. They had found a third way. Integration involves invention, the finding of the third way, and the clever thing is to recognise this and not to let one's thinking stay within the boundaries of two alternatives which are mutually exclusive. In other words, never let yourself be bullied by an either-or situation. Never think you must agree to either this or that. Find a third way.

And the extraordinarily interesting thing about this is that the third way means progress. In domination you stay where you are. In compromise likewise you deal with no new values. By integration something new has emerged, the third way, something beyond the either-or.

Take now an illustration from business. I am making a good deal of this point because I think it about the most important thing in the world. If you go into business you will have to integrate with someone almost every day. When you marry you surely will. And can we have any peace between nations until we learn this? We all recognise that Germany is right in wanting equality of status, and France right in wanting security. International states must discover how both these objects can be attained.

Now for my illustration from industry. The purchasing agent in a factory said that he had found a material for a certain product which he could buy at less cost than that being used. The head of the manufacturing department said that the cheaper material would not produce as good results, he preferred to keep to the material then in use. What was to be done? The general manager at first thought he had a struggle on his hands between these two men, but then he met the difficulty by suggesting that the purchasing agent should continue his hunt for a cheaper material, but should try to find one which would fill the requirements of the head of the manufacturing department. The purchasing agent succeeded in doing this and both he and the head of the manufacturing department were satisfied. This could not have happened if they had stayed within an either-or situation, if they had thought that either the purchasing agent must have his way or the head of the manufacturing department his way. And that integration was obviously good for the business. If the purchasing agent had had his way, quality would have suffered. If the head of the manufacturing department had had his way, costs would have remained unnecessarily high. But as it was, they got at the same time quality and reduced costs. The integration created something new. Hence difference can be constructive rather than destructive if we know what to do with it. It may be a sign of health, a prophecy of progress.

I have told you what I think integration is and how necessary it is in business. I have not spoken of how to get integration, but I will speak further of this. For the moment all that I can do is to point out that there *is* a technique for integration. And the person who should know most about this is the chief executive. I think that books on business management sometimes make a mistake here, for they sometimes tell us that in the case of a difference of opinion between executives, the chief executive acts as arbitrator, decides between the executives. But I know chief executives who do not decide between their executives. And let me say here, what perhaps I should have called your attention to before, that in these talks I am not moralising to you, telling you what I think ought to be done, or theorising to you, telling you what I think might be done, I am merely telling you the things I have seen in practice in industry. And I am saying now that I know chief executives who do not act as umpire and decide between their executives. They try to integrate the different points of view, for they know that if they take A's and reject B's, they will lose whatever advantage there might be in B's view. The clever administrator wants to get the advantage of both A's and B's views and so he tries to secure such an interplay of their different experience and different knowledge as will bring them into cooperating agreement.

If a chief executive cannot integrate the different policies in his business, that is, if he cannot make his executives unite wholeheartedly on a certain policy, the suppressions will work underground and be a very strong factor against the success of his business. For suppression means dissatisfaction, and that dissatisfaction will go on working underneath and increasing, and may crop up at any moment in some place where we least desire to see it, in some place where it will give us more trouble than if we had dealt with it in the first instance.

We find the same thing in cases of disputes between nations. The nation which has had a decision go against it in an arbitrated matter, simply waits for some further chance of getting what it wants, and during that time, embittered by its disappointment and its sense of unfair dealing, the trouble grows.

Professor Brierley of Oxford, who, I have been told, is the best international lawyer in England, goes to Geneva and urges the method of integration. He tries to convince people that this is better than arbitration. He of course is not, any more than any of us, opposed to arbitration. We all recognise that arbitration is better than war. But there is something even better than arbitration offering. The best business practice is on this point in line with the best modern thinking in general.

Of course you will understand that all I have said on this subject in regard to the general manager applies equally to any executive who has conflicting suggestions made to him by under executives or to a foreman who has the conflicting claims of two workmen to deal with. Many in such positions are coming to see that it is better not to decide between, but to try when possible to integrate the conflicting claims. It is not always possible, that must be fully recognised, but many are coming to think that it is well worth trying, that when it is possible the gains are great.

I have so far been speaking chiefly of the coordination of departments, or of departments and the regular staff officials. But there is another correlation to be made, that between executive and expert—the expert who is a staff official, or the expert who may not be a regular staff official. And just here there is an important change going on, hardly noticed as yet, a change in regard to the place of an expert in a business, a change indeed in regard to our conception of his function—advice. We used to think that the different heads gave orders, that the various experts gave advice, but we have seen emerging in recent years something which is neither orders nor advice. This is an extraordinarily interesting point. For instance, a staff man, an expert, may be responsible for seeing that machines are taken care of, but the line man, the man, that is, at the head of a department, takes care of them. Now suppose the staff man tells a line man that a certain machine needs attention. Is that an order? No, because the line man does not take orders from this man. Is it then advice? No, because one of the characteristics of advice, as we have been accustomed to use that word, is that advice can be rejected, and this cannot be rejected without taking it higher up. The line man, the man in charge of that department, has either to attend to the machine or else take the matter to someone higher up the line.

You see why I think this so extraordinarily interesting. It is because something is coming into business which is neither orders nor advice, and we have not any word for it yet.

It is not advice as we have been accustomed to use that word, for in ordinary usage advice involves a take-it-or-leave-it attitude. If I ask a friend to give me his advice about something, we both have a take-it-or-leave-it attitude about what he may say. That is, I do not feel any obligation to take his advice and he does not expect me to feel any obligation in the matter. But those who give advice in business are usually such an integral part of the organisation that one cannot have a take-it-or-leave-it attitude towards their suggestions.

Yet we do not want the executive to be dominated by the expert. While the executive should give every possible value to the information of the expert, no executive should abdicate thinking because of the expert. The expert's opinion should not be allowed automatically to become a decision. On the other hand, full recognition should be given to the part the expert plays in decision making. Our problem is to find a method by which the opinion of the expert does not coerce and yet enters integrally into the situation. Our problem is to find a way by which the specialist's kind of knowledge and the executive's kind of knowledge can be joined. And the method should, I think, be one I have already advocated, that of integration.

And I should like to point out that when there is a difference of opinion with an expert, we often take that method without realising that we are doing so. Let me try to make this clear by a very simple illustration. An electrician comes to wire my house for electric lighting. I say that I want it done in a certain way. He says that there are mechanical difficulties about doing it in that way. I suggest another way. He tells me that the laws in regard to safeguarding against fire do not permit that way. Then he tells me how he thinks it shall be done. Do I accept his suggestions? No, because I have a very decided objection for aesthetic reasons or reasons of convenience. We continue our discussion until we find a way which meets the mechanical difficulties and the laws in regard to fire safeguards and at the same time satisfies me.

Now I believe the reason that we integrate so often with the expert without knowing that we are doing such a difficult thing as I am told integration is, is that we do not usually think of our relation with the expert as that of a fight. We expect to be able to unite a difference of opinion with him. We have gone to him for that purpose.

So with the general manager or any executive. They recognise that the specialist has one kind of knowledge and they another and they expect to be able to unite them.

To conclude then a matter so important that it should have a whole paper to itself, namely, the expert's place in business organisation, I should say that the tendency is in recent years to give the expert a real place in the game. Lord Cecil said the other day: "The expert must be on tap but not on top." Well, I certainly do not want him on top, but I think he is coming to be a more constituent part of an enterprise than is implied by saying that he must be merely on tap. Any study of business administration shows us that the expert in industry is not merely on tap when the executive wants to turn him on to a question, but that he is becoming an integral part of the decision-making machinery.

I have spoken of two things which will help to unify a business, namely, some system of cross-functioning and an understanding of integration. There remains a third equally important and bound up with the other two. Present business practice shows an increased

sense of collective responsibility. One evidence of this has a special
interest for us. Many companies have now what is called a functional form of organisation. This in itself makes a joint responsibility imperative. The functional development in industry means, as
you know, that in many plants we have now, in addition to the
different departments, a number of special functions recognised,
each of which serves all the departments. For instance, formerly
the head of each department looked after its own machines; now
the equipment department looks after the machines in all the departments. Formerly each department dealt with its own labour
problems; now we have a labour manager who deals with labour
problems in all the departments. Purchasing has become a special
function; the purchasing department purchases for all the manufacturing processes. And so on.

Now what new demand is made on us in the way of joint
responsibilities by the functional development in industry? Suppose the head of the production department wants a new machine.
Before the degree of specialisation which we have now come to,
this man would have made his decision himself, and then made
his recommendations to the general manager. Now in those plants
where there is a special department for mechanical equipment, the
head of this special department and the head of the manufacturing
department have to agree before the recommendation can go to
the general manager. They share the responsibility.

Such instances might be multiplied indefinitely. Is it the head
of a production department who is responsible for the quality of
a food product or is it the consulting chemist? Or both together?
Or if a certain method proves a failure, who is responsible? The
expert who suggested it? Or the head of the department who accepted it? Or both?

This interlocking responsibility exists indeed under any form of
organisation, but we have much more of it wherever the functional
form has been introduced.

You will have noticed that the Telephone Company I spoke of
has a functional form of organisation, for it is organised both by

areas, the different districts, and by functions—traffic, engineering, etc.

A second tendency in present business practice which is helping to increase the sense of collective responsibility is the development of group responsibility. In a certain large shop all the men on the lifts have regular meetings at which are considered how this department, the men who run the lifts, can help the general manager, can help the charge office, can help the floor superintendent, can help the information bureau, and so on. I knew another instance where the drivers of the delivery vans undertook as a group certain responsibilities toward the firm.

You remember the little girls in the chocolate factory who were shown how their work affected the sale of chocolate and hence the success of the whole business. A salesman in the north of England told me that he had reckoned that there were seventy men whose continuation in their jobs depended on the number of sales he made. Such awareness of interdependence is surely an asset for any business.

A man said to me once, a man working on a salary as the head of a department in a factory, "I'm no wage-earner, working so many hours a day; if I wake up at midnight and have an idea that might benefit the factory, it belongs to the factory." That was a very proper sentiment for him to have, but his implication was that wage-earners would not feel this. Organisation engineers, however, expert organisers who go into a business to organise or re-organise are paying a good deal of attention to this point. They are trying to devise ways by which everyone concerned in an enterprise should feel responsible for its success.

And wherever men or groups think of themselves not only as responsible for their own work, but as sharing in a responsibility for the whole enterprise, there is much greater chance of success for that enterprise. Take the question of waste and think how often we have failed to cure that. Over and over again in the past we have heard it said to workmen, "If this were your material, you wouldn't waste it," and over and over again that admonition has failed to produce any results. But when you can develop a sense of collective responsibility then you find that the workman is more careful of material, that he saves time in lost motions, in talking over his grievances, that he helps the new hand by explaining things to him, and so on.

We have been preached to times without number that everyone should do conscientiously his particular piece of work, and this has perhaps tended to make us forget that we are also responsible for the whole. This is a very interesting point. There was an amusing story in *Punch* a few weeks ago, amusing but suggesting a very fundamental truth. A man said that he wanted to get rid of the feeling that he owed money to America and for his part he was thinking of washing out his debt. He had divided the amount of the American debt by the number of inhabitants in Great Britain and he found that each individual owed America twelve shillings, and he was going to send Mr. Hoover twelve shillings and be through with the matter. Of course this was meant to be merely amusing, but it is interesting, is it not, to think that he could not be through with the matter by sending Mr. Hoover twelve shillings, that he could not thus wash out his debt to America, that after he had sent his twelve shillings he would have been exactly as much in debt to America as before. *Punch* gave us a profound truth there, for we cannot get rid of our joint obligation by finding the fraction of our own therein, because our own part is not a fraction of the whole, it is in a sense the whole. Wherever you have a joint responsibility, it can only be met jointly.

I have now spoken of three things which will help to unify a business—an understanding of integration as a method of settling differences, some system of cross-functioning, and a sense of collective responsibility. Let me now give an example which will illustrate all three of these. Suppose a firm is selling Frigidaires. The production department has decided on a certain design, best from the engineering point of view. If the production and sales departments of that firm are given opportunities of consulting together, the sales department may say: "Yes, that's a nice tidy design, but my customers tell me that the dishes they use in which to put food away do not fit that design so well as if your ice cubes were in this place and your shelves in that." But then the engineering department might have a good deal to say about condensation of moisture, direction of draughts for the passing off of odours, and so on. What has to be done obviously is to find a design which will satisfy both the engineers' requirements and customers' demand. Neither must be given up, they must find a third way.

Think also of the different ways of looking at the question of the amount of electricity consumed. The engineer's job is to see that his Frigidaire does the greatest amount of work on the least amount of electricity. But then the salesman's point of view on this matter is that he must be able to tell customers that the Frigidaire of this firm does not consume any more electricity than some other make. But then the engineer may say to him, "Can't you show your customers that for a little more electricity with our make they get better service?" And so it may go, backwards and forwards, each modifying the other until we have a truly integrated plan for a Frigidaire.

In regard to my second point, the advantage of some form of cross-functioning is obvious here. When you have a purely up and down the line system of management, those who sell Frigidaires have to take all their requirements up to the general manager and he communicates them, if he considers them worth-while suggestions, to the production department. And in the same way the production department takes its problems up to the general manager and he may pass them down to the sales department. But then you lose all the advantage of that first-hand contact, that process of backwards and forwards, that process of reciprocal modification.

Again, the third point of this paper, collective responsibility, is also very well illustrated, I think, by the Frigidaire case. It has often been thought in the past, as I pointed out a few moments ago, when I told the story from *Punch,* that I need be concerned only with doing my part well. It has been taken as self-evident, as a mere matter of arithmetic like 2 and 2 making 4, that if everyone does his best, then all will go well. But one of the most interesting things in the world is that this is not true, although on the face of it it may seem indisputable. Collective responsibility is not something you get by adding up one by one all the different responsibilities. Collective responsibility is not a matter of adding but of interweaving, a matter of the reciprocal modification brought about by the interweaving. It is not a matter of aggregation but of integration.

We see this very clearly in the Frigidaire illustration. A Frigidaire company needs much more from its salesmen than that they shall know how to sell, much more from its engineers than that they shall know how to design. These two departments must know how to integrate their different kinds of knowledge and experience. It isn't enough—I cannot repeat too often, since the success of any enterprise depends largely on an understanding of this point—it isn't enough to do my part well and leave the matter there. My obligation by no means stops at that point. I must study how my part fits into every other part and change my work if necessary so that all parts can work harmoniously and effectively together.

The most important thing to remember about unity is—that there is no such thing. There is only unifying. You cannot get unity and expect it to last a day—or five minutes. Every man in a business should be taking part in a certain process and that process is unifying. Every man's success in business depends largely, I believe, on whether he can learn something of this process, which is one neither of subordination nor of domination, but of each man learning to fit his work into that of every other in a spirit of cooperation, in an understanding of the methods of cooperation.

HARRY ARTHUR HOPF

(1882–1949)

MORE THAN THIRTY YEARS ago, Harry Arthur Hopf proposed "optimology: the science of the optimum" as the next great step in developing a science of management. While the term failed to catch on at the time, the thinking behind it, as revealed in *Management and the Optimum,* is fundamental. This paper, which follows, was prepared for the 1935 meeting of the International Committee of Scientific Management in London. It shows the broad sweep of Hopf's mind, from historical allusions through literary references to detailed mathematical formulas. In 1938, for distinguished service to the cause of management, the CIOS gold medal was awarded him, the first American to receive it.

Hopf was born in England and came to the United States at 16. He held positions in life insurance and manufacturing companies, and in 1922 formed his own management consulting firm. His death occurred just as the electronic computer arrived on the management scene to make practicable the vast amount of data processing required in applying his "science of the optimum."

Hopf was a strong advocate of long-range corporate planning, a technique that was widely held to be impossible if not heretical at the time of this paper. In the interests of brevity, the "numerous examples" mentioned in the summary have been omitted.

MANAGEMENT AND THE OPTIMUM

BY HARRY ARTHUR HOPF

Summary

It is the thesis of this paper that the time is ripe for transformation of
the science of management into a new and much more inclusive science
—optimology, the science of the optimum. The author argues that the
practice of management has reached its fruition in the creation of vast
combinations of men, methods, and money which must inevitably defeat
their own ends and lead to ultimate disaster. By numerous examples from
his practice as a management engineer, he shows how, by failure to
achieve and maintain optimal conditions, many business enterprises have
sustained losses or met failure.

Defining the optimum as that state of development of a business enterprise which tends to perpetuate an equilibrium among the factors of size,
cost, and human capacity and thus to promote in the highest degree
regular realization of the business objectives, the author describes how,
in the field of life insurance, he has made extensive measurements of
business results and managerial capacity and established optimal areas
of operation for ten large companies. He suggests that, by the application
of similar techniques, the optimum can and should be ascertained for
every business enterprise.

I. Introductory

Among the most profound problems with which society must
concern itself under present-day conditions is that relating to the

---

Reprinted from the pamphlet, *Management and the Optimum,* by Harry Arthur
Hopf. Privately printed. Copyright © 1935 by Harry Arthur Hopf. Paper presented at
Sixth International Congress for Scientific Management, London, July 1935. Used
by permission of Mrs. Rita H. Hopf.

determination, achievement, and maintenance of optimal conditions in all types of organized human enterprise. The overwhelming economic disaster, from the effects of which the world is still suffering, halted with ruthless force an era of unparalleled expansion which, in the United States of America at least, assumed proportions indicative of a belief in the feasibility of unlimited growth and unchecked size.

As we falteringly proceed upon the road to recovery, we are faced with new political, social, and economic trends and doctrines which are evidently destined to bring into being forms of organization and control without precedent in our experience, and to call for qualities of cooperation and joint action on the part of business men, engineers, social scientists, Government officials, Labour representatives, and others, far beyond any need of the past. Having, then, narrowly escaped complete destruction upon the rock of Scylla, are we now being drawn with increasing force into the whirlpool of Charybdis?

In the proposal and institution of the bewildering number of measures which, taken together, constitute the substance of the New Deal in the United States, qualities of supreme courage and audacity have been revealed. Whatever we may conclude about the practicability of the host of ideas advanced under the head of planned economic control on a national scale, we must recognize, if not admire, the capacity for visualization of all-embracing, theoretical concepts possessed by their authors. But the furious vortex of new theories and opinions which threatens to engulf us in our well-nigh frantic endeavour to escape from the punitive consequences of our heedless economic striving, has tended to obscure the possibility that the very number, complexity, and size of the new agencies which owe their existence mainly to the fertility of the political brain, may comprise the seed from which in due season will sprout the stems of another disaster even more frightful in its effects than the one which we are now endeavouring to surmount.

Adam Smith who, in opposition to the mercantilist planning of his day, advocated "the simple and obvious system of natural liberty," or the doctrine of "laissez-faire," as it soon became known, held to the view that the wealth of the nation will increase most rapidly if every individual is left free to conduct his own affairs as he sees fit. Irrespective of the applicability of this doctrine under present-day conditions, we cannot but admit that, as Mitchell[1] has pointed out, "in the countries which have given wide scope to private initiative since Adam Smith presented his momentous argument for laissez-faire, the masses of mankind attained a higher degree of material comfort and a larger increase of liberty than at any earlier time of which we have knowledge, or under any other form of organization which mankind has tried out in practice."

If we analyse dispassionately the forces of expansion which have manifested themselves since the beginning of the twentieth century, and with particular effect in the decade following the World War, we are convinced that until lately the predominant characteristic of the American scene has been worship at the shrine of size. Is the type of thinking that could justify our gigantic business institutions and could contemplate with approval what thoughtful students have come to regard as the menace associated with great size to be expressed and perpetuated in the post-depression forms of organization? In all this seething that goes under the name of the New Deal and creates laws and regulations that bewilder and baffle even our best minds, is it not meet that we pause long enough to weigh calmly the possibilities of success and failure attaching to the management problems involved?

It is because of a profound conviction that, for an indefinite period to come, the solution of the economic problems of this country will have to be sought through reconstitution of all types of organized human enterprise on levels of simplicity and scope low enough to permit readily of coordination and control, that consideration of the rôle of management and what it can and should do to create and preserve optimal conditions in the individual

---

[1] Mitchell, Wesley C.: *The Social Sciences and National Planning;* an Address delivered at the Annual Meeting of the American Association for the Advancement of Science, Pittsburgh, 1 January, 1935.

business enterprise appears to be a timely and worth-while undertaking.

II. *Defining Certain Important Concepts*

In order to facilitate understanding of the subject to be discussed, it is desirable to set forth initially definitions of four concepts of basic importance; i.e., management, optimum, organization, and break-even point.

Despite many definitions advanced by others, the author has elected to define management as "the direction of a business enterprise, through the planning, organizing, coordinating, and controlling of its human and material resources, toward the achievement of a predetermined objective." This definition, it will be seen, places the emphasis upon the dynamic aspects of management; in other words, it views management as an art, but, it should be added, with complete acceptance of the scientific foundations upon which the art must rest.

With respect to the optimum, the second concept, it should be stated, first of all, that in the evolution of every business enterprise those who direct its affairs should recognize the necessity of determining reasonable dimensions to which it should conform, and of devising organization patterns which will facilitate effective control through the use of human agencies.

The optimum may be defined as that state of development of a business enterprise which, when reached and maintained, tends to perpetuate an equilibrium among the factors of size, cost, and human capacity, and thus to promote, in the highest degree, regular realization of the business objectives.

Definition of the third concept, organization, should turn upon the fact that it represents both a process and a condition. In the former sense, the elements of the structure are subject to combination, development, and adaptation, as required by evolution and growth; in the latter, the structure itself is regarded as an instrument to be employed by management in the furtherance of its aims. The dynamics of organization enter vitally into the problem of achieving and maintaining the optimum.

The break-even point, the fourth and last concept to be defined, calls for somewhat more extended explanation. The conduct of every business enterprise involves the incurring of two classes of operating expense: constant and variable. The former represents what is commonly termed "overhead" (insurance, taxes, rent, interest, salaries of executives, etc.), and the latter the "direct" items of expense (materials, labour, freight, commissions, etc.). Obviously there can be no such thing as profitable operation unless and until the volume of sales currently realized reaches dimensions yielding an income in excess of the aggregate of the constant and variable costs. The point at which this condition occurs—different for each business considered and subject to change within any given business—is known as the break-even point (or "tote Punkt," as the Germans designate it). It is of the greatest consequence to the success of a business enterprise that the break-even point represent at all times a readily attainable level, and that during periods of shrinking business volume expense commitments will allow of commensurate downward revisions in the break-even point.

It will serve to definitize the discussion and prevent it from assuming too broad a scope for present purposes, if the author states that he will concern himself here with treatment of the factors which influence the management of the individual enterprise in its struggle to achieve mastery over the controllable phases of its progress. The problem of adapting the enterprise to meet the uncontrollable factors of economic change is not dealt with in this discussion, although its importance is conceded.

III. *Theory and Practice in Planning*

The English economist Marshall begins Book V of his *Principles of Economics* as follows: "A business firm grows and attains great strength, and afterwards perhaps stagnates and decays; and at the turning-point there is a balance, or equilibrium, of the forces of life and decay."[2] How to promote the progress of a business organ-

---

[2] Marshall, Alfred: *Principles of Economics*, 8th Edition, p. 323, published by Macmillan & Co., Ltd.

ization so that growth will continue and strength increase to the greatest possible degree, worsting the forces of stagnation and decay, is one of the chief objectives of management.

The length of life of a business institution is determined by so many extraneous factors that it is futile to generalize concerning them. One may, however, conclude that the settled conditions which surround the older civilizations, such as those of England and France, constitute influences promotive of the longevity of business organizations. Indeed, it is quite common, in England especially, to observe flourishing businesses whose ages range from a century to a century and a half, or more. In America, on the other hand, very few businesses have as yet survived a century of existence, a fact traceable most likely to the peculiar economic history of the country, characterized as it has been by rapid development of almost limitless natural resources and the demonstration of remarkable inventive genius, combining to result in the unparalleled industrial, commercial, and financial expansion of the last fifty years. Under such unprecedented conditions, distinguished by extraordinary manifestations of a universal spirit of enterprise, business mortality was bound to be high. It is a well-known fact that of the enormous number of business failures which have been a constant concomitant of our economic development, a large part, possibly over 50 per cent., have been caused by faulty management (including as one outstanding factor, lack of capital).

In considering the influence of planning upon the achievement and maintenance of an optimum, we note at once that often the initial planning—that which is done in connection with the establishment of the business—results in placing insurmountable obstacles on the path to success, and thus in frustrating permanently the realization of optimal conditions. It is to planning at that stage that this discussion will be restricted, eliminating from consideration the constant process of planning that enters into the very heart of the activities of a business once it has been launched upon its career. The following cases, drawn from the author's experience as a management engineer, will illustrate the great importance of initial planning.

Case 1. A newly built brewery, with a capacity of 350,000 barrels per annum, undertook to compete in satisfying the recently legalized demand for beer. After a year or more of operation, it turned out that to meet the break-even point, sales of nearly 240,000 barrels would have to be secured. The spread between the break-even point and capacity was too small to permit of the realization of a satisfactory profit; the optimum lay well beyond production capacity, and reduction in the break-even point could be accomplished only at the cost of seriously curtailing an elaborate sales promotion and advertising programme. Faulty initial planning had caused the building of too small a brewery, and disturbed economic conditions prevented the raising of additional capital to finance new plant construction. The strong prospect of ultimate failure now faces this organization.

Case 2. A so-called "parking" garage, of the ramp type, was constructed on a plot of ground in the vicinity of the main business thoroughfare of a populous eastern city. Capacity represented 800 motor-cars, but experience covering a two-year period of operation revealed that a patronage of not more than 300 cars per day could regularly be relied upon. This volume of business was 100 cars below that required to reach the break-even point, and despite the sale of accessories, as well as of gasoline and oil, it became impossible to bridge the gap.

An intelligent analysis made in the planning stage would have disclosed the absurdity of building a structure with the capacity indicated; the promoters were led astray by the value of the ground which, in their judgment, called for the erection of an enormous building. The crux of the problem, however, lay in the patronage to be anticipated; because of general traffic density and consequent police regulations, even optimistic calculations as to patronage, based upon readily obtainable figures regarding flow of traffic, would have failed to justify the project as carried out. Under such unfavourable conditions, the establishment soon found itself in the hands of a receiver, with consequent severe loss to the original investors.

Case 3. A company was established for the manufacture and

sale of reproductions of period furniture. An expensive head office and show-rooms were maintained in a metropolitan city while a fine factory building was erected in a smaller city in a neighbouring state. The operating costs included heavy charges for a relatively small volume of production, as well as for large commissions to interior decorators, through whose influence much of the output was marketed. There was an utter lack of flexibility and adjustability to changing conditions; the high break-even point prohibited a satisfactory profit except under most favourable circumstances; inflated prices exposed the organization to constant attacks by resourceful competitors.

In practically every phase of the undertaking, poor initial planning had produced severe handicaps; while the furniture made was distinctive and of high quality, the market simply was not broad enough to absorb it in the requisite volume at the price levels maintained. Soon the bankers stepped in and took control; in their desire to retrieve losses they attempted to market cheaper and cheaper lines, backed by blatant advertising. Failure and liquidation of the business were the inevitable outcome.

By way of comment upon the three cases presented, it may be said that technical ability was nowhere at fault. The brewery was supplied with an exceedingly competent brewmaster; the garage was managed by an executive who had been identified for many years with the industry; the chief executive of the furniture company was an authority in the field, and he was supported by a group of master-craftsmen. In each instance, however, there was present a strong speculative instinct, unsupported by thorough grounding in fundamentals of management, and seeking only the satisfaction of a profit urge.

Correct initial planning in the case of the brewery would have dictated the establishment of an adequate spread between the break-even point and plant capacity, and would have determined an attainable area of optimal relationships. In this case, success could in all probability have been achieved only by building a much larger plant and taking advantage of every opportunity for reducing manufacturing and selling costs. The obvious hazard to be met lay in the fact that strong competitive influences working in the direction of price-cutting practices could be overcome only by providing a safety factor in the form of a relatively low break-even point.

With respect to the garage, all the vital facts forming a basis for sound planning could have been ascertained beforehand. The apparently favourable location of the plot of ground, however, blinded the promoters to the dangerous implications of the heavy carrying charges required for land and building, and they optimistically concluded that no difficulty would be experienced in obtaining ample patronage. It would have been much safer and far more sensible if a structure of half the size had been erected, and the remaining area of the plot had been utilized for outside parking facilities, at nominal charges, or, indeed, for some business not at all connected with the major enterprise. The undertaking, as established, was doomed to failure from its very inception.

As for the furniture company, the erection of a special factory building at a distance from the head office was an over-ambitious undertaking that could have been justified only on the assumption of a large and constant demand for the product. Plenty of inexpensive and suitable factory space, amid excellent surroundings, could have been secured within a half-hour's travelling distance from the head office. Since the product was manufactured practically to order, a much closer relation could have been maintained between volume of orders and extent of manufacturing facilities. When the enterprise finally collapsed, several of the former factory employés banded together and began in a most modest way to create furniture identical with that previously manufactured. They did this at their own risk in a small suburban shop and workroom, and at the last accounts they appeared to be making the venture pay, in spite of inevitable fluctuations in the number of orders received. Craftsmanship is their chief asset, and it requires only a small volume of business to enable them to make a decent profit.

Much that could be said about planning has not come to expression in the discussion of the three cases presented. Entering into the major aspects of planning and intimately associated with its manifestations, are the processes of analysis, simplification, and standardization. The ultimate realization of optimal conditions in a business enterprise is predicated upon adequate employment of these processes, not alone at the inception of the enterprise, but at all stages of its evolution. The assurance of reaching an optimum will, however, derive its main strength, as we have seen, from sound planning *ab initio,* and here perhaps the most important decision to be made turns upon the ultimate size to which the business should aspire.

As Beste[3] so convincingly points out, the maintenance of optimal conditions requires that some businesses remain small, others adhere to moderate size, and still others deliberately aim to achieve great size. Finally, in certain types of business, the optimum may be realized in all three categories of size. It is for those who perform the initial planning to bring keen understanding and a broad perspective to the determination of the question of size so that the immense consequence of this factor upon the success of the enterprise may be turned to profit.

IV. Theory and Practice in Organizing

Underlying every form of business enterprise there will be found an organization structure, or framework, which is designed to provide the necessary foundation for the activities to be carried on. In comparatively rare instances will the structure be well adapted to the attainment of the objectives it is intended to promote. More often it will turn out to be fixed or rigid in character, and lagging far behind current conditions and requirements. Indeed, in numerous instances the structure will be so poorly devised that it will constitute a formidable interference to constructive accomplishment.

Now, it cannot be too often emphasized that organization is but a means to an end, and not the end in itself. It is a continuous

---

[3] Beste, Theodor: *Die optimale Betriebsgrösse als betriebswirtschaftliches Problem,* published by G. A. Gloeckner, Leipzig, 1933.

process that depends for its success upon the maintenance of such degrees of combination, development, and adaptation of the structural elements as will keep the business machine moving swiftly, surely, and without frictional losses toward its appointed objectives. Sound organization expresses recognition of the fact that purpose and conditions are controlling considerations, and that the design of the structure must be adapted to them.

Analysis of the influence of organizing upon the optimum at first leads to the conclusion that at all stages of size of a business enterprise a plan of organization can be devised that will adapt itself effectively to existing requirements. But when one probes further into the question, it often becomes apparent that where adaptation to requirements exists, it has been the resultant, not of a conscious process of organizing, but mainly of fortuitous circumstances. It will be recognized that the influence of the factor of personnel in shaping the process is great; where one encounters instances of optimal conditions of organization, it frequently turns out that they are referable to a welding of the human elements that has proceeded without the assistance of a well-ordered plan, and has been dominated by psychological adjustments of varied character.

Study of the organization structures of hundreds of business enterprises, both in America and abroad, has convinced the author that in many instances they reflect the forces of personality and power rather than the logic and strength of proper structural relationships. In this fact lies the explanation for the ultimate arrival of such enterprises at a plateau of progress from which emergence more often follows a downward than an upward curve. That a business cannot permanently occupy levels of effectiveness higher than those clearly determined by the capacity of its executives is self-evident, but it is not generally understood that the influence of superior organization upon the accomplishments of mediocre executives can raise the enterprise to heights not otherwise attainable.

Without embarking upon an extended discussion of the principles of organization, it is pertinent to state that the chief obstacle to achievement of optimal conditions, as far as organization is concerned, is the unwillingness of top executives to delegate authority. "Place the power of decision as close as possible to the point where action originates," is one of the ten commandments of organization. But in how many business institutions is this commandment observed? A few cases, again drawn from the author's experience, will serve to illustrate the influence of organizing upon the evolution of a business towards optimal conditions.

Case 4. A chain-store company, composed of several hundred widely scattered outlets, was dominated by the founder, who possessed financial control and acted as chairman of the board. The organization was separated into six major divisions. The division heads reported to the president, but were subject also to instructions, often conflicting in character, issued by the chairman. In view of the general uncertainty of the division heads as to their respective authorities and prerogatives, they permitted themselves to act individually only upon matters of minor consequence, and left all other decisions to the executive committee, of which they, together with the president, were members. As an indication of the atrophying effect of this procedure upon the evolution of organization, it may be noted that an analysis of over 2,200 decisions recorded in the minute books of the executive committee during a two-year period, revealed that nearly nine-tenths should never have been presented to the committee at all, but should have been disposed of by individual action. The damaging effect of this condition upon operating results in the stores may well be imagined.

It was evident that drastic action was required to save the organization from gradual disintegration and to provide a sound foundation for the programme of expansion to which the business stood committed. After much discussion, a policy of decentralization was approved. This carried with it the creation of a regional plan of organization predicated upon the establishment of several divisions, each composed of 100 stores. Within each division, four districts of 25 stores were created, and each was placed in charge of a superintendent, who reported direct to the division manager. The staff of each division manager was organized to include specialists representing the major functions of the organization. The division managers, together with one of the vice-presidents at the head office, constituted an advisory committee which met bi-monthly for exchange of views concerning operating needs and results.

The head office organization was reconstituted into two groups, Administration and Operation, and each was placed in charge of a vice-president, supported by several officials of lesser rank. In place of the executive committee, a new committee with the same name was organized, but its membership was limited to the president, as chairman, the chairman of the board (*ex-officio*), and the vice-presidents in charge of administration and operation. This committee dealt only with questions of major policy relating to the organization as a whole. In the manner here described, elements of simplicity and freedom of action were introduced into the organization. It was not long before the beneficial effects of the changes made themselves felt throughout the entire institution in a sound distribution of the executive burden, a quickening of the tempo of performance, and a universal feeling of confidence that expressed itself in greatly increased initiative of the rank and file.

Case 5. In a retail merchandizing company, owned and managed by three partners, no attempt had ever been made to proceed according to sound principles of organization. The business had prospered for a long time, but competition was beginning to make serious inroads upon its volume of sales; frequent style changes finally caused loss of ground and led to a condition of profitless operation. The outstanding organization faults discerned upon investigation were (*a*) lack of a planned structure, (*b*) failure to establish clear-cut lines of authority and to hold specific individuals responsible for results, (*c*) failure to adhere to those meagre lines of authority which had been evolved by the mere passage of time.

The first corrective step taken was to separate the organization into three divisions, place each in charge of a competent official, and appoint one of the three partners as general manager, with full authority to operate the business. The next step was to educate the entire organization to the necessity of adhering strictly to the new lines of authority and to impress upon the other two partners the wisdom of pursuing a policy of non-interference with the jurisdiction of the general manager. The third step was to organize and institute comprehensive market analyses and sales-promotion activities, with special reference to the recapture of lost customers and attraction of new ones.

It soon became evident that the combined effect of these three steps was to arrest the unfavourable trends that had manifested themselves. With other improvements instituted, and the entire organization responding loyally to the new order of things, operating results rapidly showed marked gains and, at the end of the first year under the new plan of organization, a handsome profit was realized.

Case 6. A drug company, operating five retail stores and engaged also in the manufacture and wholesale distribution of many preparations under its own trademark, fell into difficulties upon the death of its founder. The latter, a man of unusual ability and aggressiveness, had built up the business almost single-handedly; with some of the profits of former years he had erected an expensive manufacturing plant and warehouse shortly before his death. As long as the founder was there to direct the business, its affairs prospered, despite the fact that there was hardly a semblance of organization to aid him and his half-dozen associated executives. With his passing, however, the extent to which his personality had dominated the business at once became painfully evident. The widow, who held control and had made herself president, permitted all important matters to be determined by her lawyer, a man ignorant of the business and devoid of experience in management.

It was obvious that several serious drawbacks would have to be overcome if the business was to be continued on a basis that would protect the capital invested and yield a stable profit. First of all, either the manufacturing plant and warehouse, with capacities designed to meet the needs of a great many retail outlets, would have to be disposed of, or an aggressive chain-store development —for which capital was utterly lacking—would have to be undertaken. Secondly, the wholesale division would have to be expanded, but strongly entrenched competitors of national standing and ample resources would undoubtedly prove a stumbling-block to any such effort. Thirdly, if the plant was abandoned, retail policies would have to be changed, and one or more of the stores closed. Last, a practical plan of organization would have to be designed, and the widow and her lawyer eliminated from the situation as operating factors.

Fortunately, at this juncture an opportunity presented itself to sell the plant at a satisfactory price and to retain the warehouse space at a low rental. This unexpected turn of events greatly eased the financial situation with which the company was confronted; the determination was, therefore, reached to continue the whole-sale and retail divisions of the business, and to preserve as much as possible the value of the goodwill attaching to the trademark owned.

A simple plan of organization was adopted; one of the executives with much experience in the business was made president; other executives were placed in charge of various divisions, and store managers were given a profit-sharing interest. The business ultimately turned the corner, but its condition prior to reorganization had been such as to prohibit the attainment of an optimum because sound organization was completely lacking and no equilibrium was possible among the manufacturing, wholesale, and retail activities, each of which, in fact, stood in the way of the proper development of the others.

It is clear from the three cases described that in each instance the influence of organizing upon the progress of the business was tremendous. If space permitted, additional illustrations could be cited of the evil effects of such organization faults as over-elaboration, unwarranted sub-division of activities, unjustifiable extremes of functionalization, excessive departmentalization, etc. Experience has shown each of these faults to be an important contributory factor to the failure of many businesses to achieve optimal conditions of development. Their influence is subtle and not easily discerned; it is made more compelling by the fact that even where there is the will to organize soundly, this is often frustrated by a clash between the points of view of ownership and management—

especially when the two rôles are merged in one and the same person or group—with ownership usually dominant and scant regard accorded to such abstract considerations as sound principles of organization.

V. *Theory and Practice in Coordinating*

As business institutions grow in size, problems of coordination multiply. Regardless of the character of the organization pattern in effect, twilight zones, indicating the need for coordination, often develop between functions or departments. In large businesses, lack of coordination frequently manifests itself in the relations between head offices and their branches, and leads to conditions of confusion and friction. Similar observations may be made with respect to the relations between the so-called staff and line functions; authority of knowledge and power of action, when possessed by different individuals, cannot be readily coordinated to secure the best results. Again, clashes of personality, so common among incumbents of higher positions, not infrequently constitute a difficulty traceable, in part at least, to lack of coordination of authorities and responsibilities. Finally, wherever economy, dispatch, and smoothness of procedures are conspicuous by their absence, faulty coordination, regardless of other causes, is sure to be found at the root of the difficulties encountered.

It has long been the author's conclusion that even the most carefully designed organization plans ordinarily fail to take adequately into account the need for supplying some form of coordination, whether tangible or intangible, that may be relied upon to cement all the elements whose presence is necessary to the success of a business. Perhaps this grave shortcoming may be explained by the statement that coordination is essentially a motive force utilized by human beings, and that it is, therefore, difficult of definition and not readily reduced to a set of rules. If the word is to be defined in general terms, it may be said to be a resultant of the processes of integration, cooperation, and motivation. Recognition of the human implications which pervade all of these concepts will do much to overcome the limitations inherent in the organizing process. It is certainly a conservative statement to say that the influence of coordinating over the achievement and maintenance of optimal conditions is exceeded by no other single factor. A few illustrations from the author's experience will serve to substantiate the points of view here advanced.

Case 7. An educational institution of the "correspondence" type was concerned over the mounting number of withdrawals among its many thousands of students in different parts of the world. The affairs of the institution were organized on a functional basis, the main divisions of its activities being Sales, Finance, Education, and Service. Its salesmen specialized in the handling of individual courses; therefore, they could make no attempt to furnish sound guidance to prospective students at the time of enrolment. Each of the four main divisions dealt independently with students, and there was not even an awareness of the importance of co-ordinating their activities so that consistent and individualized treatment could be given to students and their problems.

Study of the situation revealed that the future of the institution depended upon recognition of the individual student as an organic unity and upon coordination of the various dealings with him in such a manner that each would effectively supplement the others. It was quite clear that by persistently working at cross-purposes, the four divisions had destroyed much of the goodwill that had been built up when the number of students was smaller, and that their tactics were actually driving students away from the institution.

Corrective measures took the form of reorganization on the unit plan. Exhaustive experimentation revealed that 10,000 accounts represented the optimal size of a unit; i.e., the size which permitted the best integration of the activities performed by the representatives of the various divisions having regular dealings with the students. In place of four or five separate card records previously maintained, one master card was designed, on which all the significant facts concerning each account were brought together; thereafter, no detail, however unimportant, entering into dealings with students was attended to without first scanning the entire picture revealed by the master card.

This method of operation, which called for the establishment of a number of parallel units, proved of particular value in familiarizing members of a unit with the personal problems of students. After the new plan of organization had been in effect for some time, student mortality began to drop, collection of tuition instalments was considerably accelerated, the quality of lesson papers improved noticeably, and a marked increase in the interest of staff members in exploiting all the possibilities of the plan was manifested.

Case 8. In one of the large administrative departments of the Government, which had expanded to enormous size during the World War, the work had accumulated to such an extent that the authorities were importuned to sanction an unprecedented increase in the number of employés as the only means of coping with the problem. The department was organized on a functional basis; while this had proved practicable when only a few score employés, who could readily familiarize themselves with the various phases of the work, were involved, it became an utter impossibility after the staff had risen to approximately 3,700 persons.

Apart from a steady lengthening of the time required to perform the work cycle—an infallible sign of lack of coordination—the routines were so disjointed that it was a frequent occurrence for divisions or sections dealing with phases of the same transaction to reach conflicting decisions. The situation was complicated by the attitude of the official in charge, who was imbued with the notion that importance was commensurate with size, a point of view which led him to frown upon any attempts to solve operating difficulties in a fundamental manner.

There was unmistakable evidence that the organization pattern was at fault and that departmentalization would have to be substituted for functionalization if an enduring solution of the problem was to be achieved. Moreover, it was shown that by taking steps to bring related lines of work together in organized form and to coordinate it on all levels through the creation of parallel operating units, instead of having to add several hundred employés, an even greater number could be eliminated.

A report embodying recommendations based upon these findings was presented to the official in charge; while it was under consideration the Armistice was declared, and the resulting collapse of work in the department rendered definite action on the report unnecessary. What would have happened to the recommendations had the war continued another six months will always remain an interesting speculation.

Case 9. A group of executives, who had been identified with the management of a business enterprise since its inception a generation ago, had had the gratifying experience of achieving a success far beyond their most optimistic expectations. The men were endowed with organizing talent to only a limited extent; they were preponderantly of the technical type, hence engrossed largely in detail and slow to adjust their points of view to the increasing need for coordination of the various parts of the business they had built up.

With the passage of time, they became more and more wedded to the early patterns with which they were familiar, and ultimately held almost fanatically to the belief that the perpetuation of their nationwide business depended chiefly upon the extent to which authority, knowledge, and action were concentrated at the head office. Worship of form, reinforced by extreme application of principles of standardization, was substituted for creative utilization of fundamentals of organization. In consequence, scores of the younger executives, stationed both at the head office and in the field, gradually found themselves faced with the fact that their own development and progress were being materially restricted.

Analysis of the conditions described demonstrated that it had become increasingly difficult to do justice to the management problems presented by relying wholly upon coordination through the head office instead of granting a reasonable degree of freedom of action to the field forces. The company had outgrown that type of organization and was running the risk of experiencing diminishing returns by continuing to adhere to it. A new organization pattern, based upon decentralization of authorities, responsibilities, and activities, appeared to be the chief vehicle for creating more flexible conditions. In practice, this pattern would divide the area of operations into several self-contained regions, each with its own head office charged with the responsibility of coordinating the activities of the district offices in the territory over which it had control. In this way transactions would be expedited, service to customers would be greatly improved, and the field executives, for the most part seasoned men of long experience and thoroughly acquainted with every department of the business, would be given an incentive to increased effort.

To accomplish such a result, it would, however, be necessary to reorganize the head office of the enterprise upon a purely functional basis, to transfer to the regional offices many of the activities which had been centralized at the head office, to vest field executives with a degree of authority commensurate with the responsibilities assumed by them, and to teach the chief executives of the company to appreciate the value of receiving control information and figures in place of the flood of detailed reports which descended regularly upon the head office from the field.

Recommendations designed to accomplish the changes indicated were presented to the group of chief executives. While certain steps were taken to improve existing conditions, wholehearted approval of the new scheme of relationships proposed calls for a process of education which can be accomplished only with the passage of time. The transitional stage in which the enterprise now finds itself will either eventuate in diminishing returns or benefit by application of the points of view of the younger executives, who are free from the hampering influences of tradition and able to evaluate existing problems in terms of the needs and opportunities of the future.

The three cases discussed present certain aspects upon which it will be worth while to dwell in summarizing the discussion of the influence of coordinating. In each instance, it is fair to say that the executives concerned were singularly lacking in the power of synthesis. They had apparently acquired little from their experience, except a mastery of the facts with which they were called upon to deal in their daily work. They could readily interpret their relations with others in terms of working understandings which had grown up among them and their immediate associates; but to project their minds beyond was difficult—to form an objective and dispassionate view regarding the many elements embraced in the areas which they were in a position to influence, impossible.

In one important respect, the impulse to action, the cases differed radically from one another. The educational institution was brought to a realization of the need for action by the fact that its operating costs were mounting and its student income was dropping rapidly. Something had to be done to reverse the trends if disaster was to be avoided. Consequently, it did not require the exercise of great pressure to secure adoption of the new plan of organization. The Government official would undoubtedly have proved a hard nut to crack if termination of the war had not automatically removed the problem from the realm of consideration. He lacked the ability to relate the part to the whole, which is a *sine qua non* of co-ordination; moreover, his over-developed ego would have made it extremely difficult for him to take an impersonal view of the remedies suggested. As for the third case, a condition of long-continued business prosperity and a singular record of immunity to the drastic effects of the depression, joined to an autocracy of ownership, educational lacunae, and strongly provincial points of view, constituted inhibiting influences that might have raised effective barriers to coordination in the case of executives of even greater ability and vision than those in question. Accordingly, the impulse to comprehensive action was not present; in all likelihood, it will not be created until the extreme of growth or the imminence of severe loss presents itself. In either eventuality, the organization will have lost much valuable time in making the necessary adjustments.

If coordinating, as one of the instruments essential to achievement of the optimum, is to be adequately and constructively utilized, there must be recognition of the fact that the need for its use occurs on even the lowest level of the organization hierarchy. In the ascent to successively higher levels, the need becomes more and more acute, until, finally, at the apex of the business pyramid, the presence or absence of coordination is apt to make the difference between ultimate success and failure. Certain it is that, wherever business enterprises have demonstrated their ability to attain and to perpetuate the optimum in their affairs, highly developed conditions of coordination will invariably be found in effect. Indubitably it will also be true in such cases that the influence of coordinating has been brought to bear chiefly upon the human factor, and that the processes of integration, cooperation, and motivation have been interpreted in human terms. One cannot help admiring the mind of a Schmoller[4] who, over a generation ago, perceived all this, and expressed it in much better terms.

VI. Theory and Practice in Controlling

Among the chief objectives of management is the exercise of purposive and successful control. In the light of this statement, control may at first blush be regarded as a terminal function, standing in a dependent relationship to planning, organizing, and coordinating, the three instruments of management thus far discussed. Granted that there is some substance to this point of view, and that the more effectively these instruments are utilized the more certain and firm a foundation is erected for exercise of the control function, it will nevertheless appear from mature reflection that control, provided the term be not too narrowly defined, is entitled to be regarded as an independent instrument in furthering the objectives of management.

In order to prevent misunderstanding, it is advisable to state that control, in the sense here employed, has nothing to do with political, legal, or financial considerations, or with questions of ownership. Brushing these possible interpretations aside, it may be explained that within the framework of the present discussion, and having in

---

[4] Schmoller, Gustav: *Grundriss der allgemeinen Volkswirtschaftslehre,* vol. I, par. 143, pp. 514–21; published by Duncker & Humblot, München-Leipzig, 1900.

mind the definition of management previously given, control expresses itself through the processes of supervision, measurement of performance, and maintenance of standards. Thus it will be seen that control is a dynamic concept, and that in operation it tends to keep the enterprise upon the appointed course, to provide it with the proper momentum, to determine its rate of progress, and to evaluate the operating results produced.

The onward march of industry, from small beginnings to great size, has been accompanied at all stages by perplexing questions of control. Indeed, in the period which has elapsed since the turn of the century, such questions have assumed particular prominence in view of the magnitude and complexity of the great corporations which have become characteristic of the economic order in which we live. It is widely recognized by students of the problem that human development has not kept pace with corporate size, and that therefore even the most finely conceived processes of control as yet made available are inadequate for the purpose of determining, achieving, and maintaining the optimum. While the last word has not yet been said upon this subject, it is certainly demonstrable that when institutions such as banks, life insurance companies, public utilities, mail order houses, department stores, and great concerns in industrial fields pass a certain stage in their development, something seems to happen to them that is in the nature of decreasing success, if not, indeed, of pronounced loss.[5]

It is impossible to generalize with respect to the causes responsible for such reversals, but we do know that supervision often breaks down because it is placed in the hands of technicians whose ability to deal with things far outweighs their capacity for controlling the human beings for whose success they are responsible. Moreover, we are aware that, despite the era of "scientific" management in which we are living, comparatively little has been done in the field of measuring performance in general, and practically nothing in evaluating scientifically the results produced by comparable groups

---

[5] The author desires the statement made in this sentence to be construed as applying only to conditions in the United States of America. He doubts not, however, that conditions in many European countries would justify similar observations.

of executives. As for maintenance of standards, rarely are executives furnished with valid norms, qualitatively and quantitatively expressed, and hardly ever is recognition given to the need for differentiating adequately between controllable and non-controllable conditions affecting performance. It is a regrettable fact that these shortcomings exist; to a great extent they are preventable, but the author questions whether much progress will be made with their eradication until a new generation of executives appears upon the scene, endowed with sufficient intelligence and scientific training to understand, accept, and practise the principles underlying optimal relations.

The following cases, drawn from the author's experience, are cited to illustrate the influence of controlling upon the attainment of optimal conditions.

Case 10. A chain of hotels, composed of leading establishments in a score or more of the larger cities of the country, had been organized by a group of promoters, some of whom were unfamiliar with the hotel business. In establishing the chain, the organizers followed the plan of enlisting local financial support through making appeals to local pride and emphasizing the value of the holding company's great experience and purchasing power. During the expansion period affairs prospered moderately, although even under the most favourable circumstances some of the hotels failed to establish a consistent record of satisfactory earnings. When general business conditions gave indications of declining, the chain of hotels was among the first to suffer, and revenues fell sharply.

Upon investigation, the situation proved to be quite involved. Location severely handicapped one hotel; another was being eclipsed by a competitor with a more modern building; a third, erected in the heyday of prosperity, was so extravagantly constructed and furnished that the carrying charges and maintenance costs were preposterous; a fourth was badly adapted to the needs of the class of guests that could be expected to patronize it, and a variety of difficulties faced other members of the chain. In short, the whole distorted picture led one to wonder what, besides greed for profits, had induced the promoters to assemble the chain.

It was evident that the holding company almost completely lacked control over the situation. Despite the fact that some of the organizers who possessed experience in hotel management were devoting a large part of their time to the supervision of individual hotels, nothing tangible was accomplished except to make the hotel managers feel that their authority was restricted. Absentee control through operating reports was ineffective, for the figures reached headquarters too late for anything but post-mortems, and these often lacked valuable interpretative statements on the part of those in a position to supply the facts.

It became increasingly clear that no plan of organization and control could be devised to do justice to the critical conditions which soon developed, and that the most sensible plan would be to make drastic reductions in the number of hotels managed, retaining only those that gave substantial promise of satisfactory earnings with the return of normal conditions. Even this step resulted merely in postponing, not averting, ultimate receivership.

Case 11. A life insurance company of considerable size, and with a long history of service, found itself compelled by force of circumstances to make a number of changes in the personnel of its executive staff during a comparatively short period of time. Serious interruptions to the continuity of administrative policies necessarily resulted, but the board of directors was so unaware of the condition that when the office of president was made vacant by death, they selected as the new incumbent a capable executive who was a lawyer by profession and without experience in the life insurance business.

The new administration of which this man found himself the leader was naturally alert to the necessity of safeguarding the investments of the company, but had no pronounced convictions with respect to control of sales, either as to volume or quality. The sales department was in charge of a very aggressive executive, who was constantly appealing to his field men for more and more volume, and was given practically free rein in the matter of spending money to produce new business. No budget was in existence; no cost data were compiled; operating standards were conspicuous by their absence; home office expenses were constantly on the increase. Soon it became evident that the extravagant expenditures of the company were beginning to make inroads on its surplus; one of the more conservative executives suggested the adoption of an economy programme involving substantial curtailment of operating expense.

The majority of the departments were found upon investigation to be conducting their activities without regard for expense control. When a department head desired to enlarge his force of employés, his requisition for new clerks was usually honoured without question; expenditures for printing and supplies exceeded all previous figures; the most elaborate installations of furniture and office machinery were everywhere in evidence; despite an abundance of office space, there was talk about the necessity for erecting a new building so as to provide more suitable and commodious quarters to cope with the great growth expected in new business.

The net result of the survey was to uncover opportunities for savings running into hundreds of thousands of dollars per annum. It required prolonged argument, however, to convince department heads of the validity of the recommendations applying to their own departments and to gain acceptance of the programme of improvement. It is a striking fact that in the entire institution there was not a single measure available, much less in use, that could be classified as sound and worth while for purposes of control.

Case 12. An old and conservative financial institution whose trust department administered estates running into many hundreds of millions of dollars in value, succumbed to the lure of expansion during the post-war prosperity period and developed its commercial banking business on a rather large scale. In rapid succession, it acquired ownership of several other banking institutions and converted them into branches. Apart from the difficulty of applying operating policies consistently to all phases of its activities, the parent company had also to contend with perplexing questions of control which grew out of the expansion programme.

Its method of meeting this situation was to deploy its man

power from time to time with the objective of making a frontal attack upon as many problems as could be isolated. There was very little semblance of organization; the principal executives were slaves to detail; regular meetings of all the officers constituted the chief means of facilitating concurrence of judgement and action. Presently the trustees of the institution became concerned over mounting costs and diminishing profits, and determined to make a comprehensive investigation.

The analysis pointed unmistakably to the conclusion that traditional points of view, the calibre of executives, the divergent objectives of the component units of the organization, all militated against successful operation. Moreover, supervision left much to be desired; little information existed in organized form to facilitate measurement of the performance of the various departments and branches, and operating standards had not been devised to any extent. It was possible to obtain a rough idea of operating costs, but much information necessary to the establishment of a sound cost system was either wholly lacking or in such form as to require considerable recasting before it could be utilized.

The first effort in the direction of control was to subject the branches to the acid test of results. This revealed that several of them were suffering losses and, because of location, competition, and other factors, should be discontinued. The next step was to analyse the accounts of the remaining branches, so as to determine a schedule of service charges to be levied on the great number of small accounts handled in order to prevent loss to the institution. The information obtained from this study proved conclusively that the policy of the institution with respect to such accounts would have to be sharply revised.

General policies and objectives of the company were then scrutinized, and the consideration given them brought into focus the importance of devising an organization plan that would furnish the basis for exercise of effective control. Many changes of constructive character were instituted. However, even with the introduction of effective control factors, theretofore conspicuous by their absence, it was found that optimal conditions of operation could be experienced only on a level of size much lower than that to which the institution had aspired.

Some general comments on the three cases presented are now appropriate. In each instance the principal executive was untrained in the field of business he assumed to control. The president of the holding company was a stock promoter, not a hotel man; the president of the life insurance company was a lawyer, not a life insurance man; the president of the financial institution was a trust company, not a commercial banking, executive. It would seem that these men should have recognized their lack of experience, and therefore have been all the more concerned about establishing sound processes of control. As it was, the affairs of the organizations for which they were responsible simply flooded past them, for no constructive process was employed in the selection of matters brought to their attention, and there were marked limitations to what they could encompass in the course of the day's work.

How could intelligent and effective supervision be exercised under such circumstances? All three men were adepts at figures, but their judgement could not rise superior to the quality and extent of the information furnished them. Budgets of a kind were in effect in the hotel organization, but the life insurance president was persuaded that in his business a budget could not be made to work, a point of view widely held by life insurance executives, but fallacious and apt to prove extremely costly to the business in the long run. As for the trust company president, his ideas regarding budgets were nebulous, and expressed largely in terms of ineffectual attempts at expense control. Of the three organizations, only the hotel business made a pretence of using standards, but these were of the rule-of-thumb variety, and failed entirely to take into account modifications necessitated by differing local conditions.

To refer in these cases to an optimum attainable through management was justifiable only on the assumption that the executives concerned would develop a perception of the importance of the influence of controlling over the accomplishment of an optimum. As may be inferred from what has been stated, this was wellnigh impossible; hence, the three organizations were deprived of the use of instruments of control that would undoubtedly have proved of great value in guiding their affairs.

VII. *Measuring Size, Cost, and Human Capacity*

In the evolution of the theme here presented, it is appropriate now to turn from qualitative to quantitative considerations—or from philosophy to mathematics—and to give a demonstration of how a process of measurement has been employed in determining the optimum in a specific field of business. For this purpose the author has chosen to borrow a few illustrations from the results of a comprehensive research project concerning the measurement of management in the life insurance field[6] in which he has been actively engaged for the past seven years.[7] In gathering and analysing the material used in this study, the author has attempted to measure the influence of size upon operating results, and to establish the extent of relation between these two factors and human capacity. In other words, the author has sought, by means of mathematical and statistical procedures, to determine the optimum by establishing the point, or points, of equilibrium among size, cost, and human capacity. The relation between size and cost will be considered first.

After a great deal of experimentation with various measures, the author concluded that the most valid manner in which to express the factor of size was by means of total actuarial net premiums paid annually. Cost, he decided, should be defined as the net cost to policyholders resulting from a balancing of all

---

[6] This field was chosen because of (1) the ready availability of the needed research material in the published annual reports of the insurance commissioner of New York; (2) the possibility of selecting companies characterized by a high degree of comparability; and (3) the fact that since 1907 the salaries of executives of all companies admitted to do business in New York State have been published in the official reports.

[7] It is anticipated that the completed work will be published by Harper & Bros., under the title *Measuring Management*, some time during 1936. [The manuscript had not been completed at the time of Dr. Hopf's death.—EDITOR]

items of operating income and expense.[8] Based on these definitions, the ratio of cost to size

$$\frac{\text{net cost to policyholders}}{\text{total actuarial net premiums}}$$

was accepted as constituting a valid, objective measure of company accomplishment.

Ten comparable companies were selected for intensive study. A preliminary analysis of the data pertaining to these companies revealed that the net cost to policyholders was a negative function of company size, when measured as indicated above; in other words, the larger the company, the lower, on the whole, the net cost. For the ten companies combined, the Spearman coefficient (ρ) for the two factors for the period 1906–29 was $-\cdot72$. This relation could not, however, be regarded as infinite; it was unthinkable that net cost would continue indefinitely to decline with increase in the size of a company. It was to be expected that at some point in a company's experience the net cost ratio would flatten out. Conceivably, after a certain point of decline in net cost had been reached, further increase in the size of a company might cease to be an advantage, and might, even, become a disadvantage; under such circumstances net cost would turn upward. In that event, it could be said that a point of optimal relation between company size and net cost had been reached and passed. That point would establish the maximum size of the company in relation to the fundamentally important factor of net cost to policyholders.

In order to test the validity of this reasoning, the appropriate series of paired values for the largest three companies were plotted,

---

[8] Readers not conversant with the significance of technical life insurance terms, may inform themselves concerning the manner in which the factors used for measuring purposes were constructed by referring to an address delivered by the author under the title of "Measuring Management in Life Insurance." It will be found in the *Proceedings of the Eleventh Annual Conference of the Life Office Management Association,* held at Hartford, Conn., 1–3 October, 1934. Copies may be obtained from the Executive Secretary, Frank L. Rowland, 110 E. 42nd Street, New York, U.S.A. [As of 1970 this organization is at 100 Park Avenue.—Editor]

and third-degree parabolas were fitted to the data. The derived equations were found to be:

For Company Alpha: $y = 106 - \cdot73x + \cdot0061x^2$
For Company Beta: $y = 106\cdot6 - \cdot833x + \cdot0103x^2$
For Company Gamma: $y = 104\cdot5 - \cdot595x + \cdot007221x^2$

Diagrams 1, 2, and 3 illustrate this parabolic relationship between net cost and company size. In each case, it will be noted, net cost declined with increase in size of the company, but only

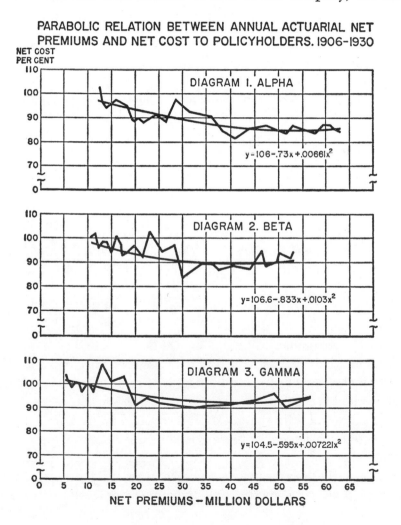

PARABOLIC RELATION BETWEEN ANNUAL ACTUARIAL NET PREMIUMS AND NET COST TO POLICYHOLDERS. 1906-1930

to a certain point. Thereafter, net cost increased with the size of the company; in other words, in relation to net cost, the optimal size had been reached and passed.

Naturally, the optima lie in different areas on the scales of the different companies, for the ranges of experience of the companies are different. Nevertheless, all the companies display obedience to one rule; i.e., growth in size is subject to certain limiting forces. With respect to these forces, an optimum may be attained. Beyond that optimum, further growth becomes a detriment.

The following is offered as a test of the conclusion just expressed. During the course of the researches made it was observed that the negative correlation between company size and net cost was referable mainly to the relative advantage of the larger companies with respect to operating expense. Selecting administrative expenses as those most directly subject to control by management (commissions paid to agents, which account for a material portion of the expenses of a life insurance company, are a direct function of the extent of its operations and therefore less readily controlled), the author paired them with the corresponding amounts of annual actuarial net premiums as measures of size. In order to make the test as representative as possible, Alpha, the largest of the ten companies, Epsilon, a medium-sized company, and Kappa, the smallest company, were chosen. In each case the computations yielded well-defined optimal points of relation between company size and administrative expense.

Again, as may be seen from Diagrams 4, 5, and 6, the optima are located in different areas on the scales of the different companies. Each of the companies, differing in size and experience, is subject to the limitations of size at a different stage of development. The operation of a law of ultimate limitation of size is, however, clearly demonstrated in each case.

Let us now consider the question whether there is a limit to the capacity of management as there is to company size. Is there a point of most effective operation by management? Is there a stage of optimal contribution by management to operating results? In attempting to answer these queries, the author confesses with regret

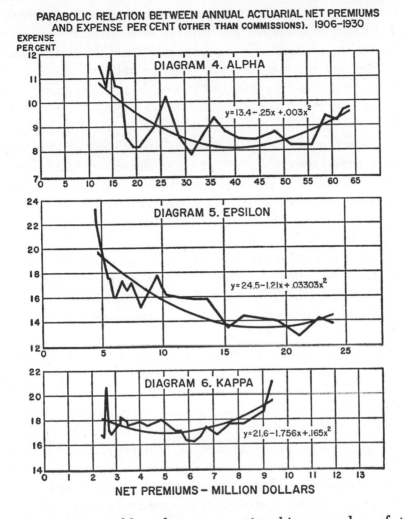

PARABOLIC RELATION BETWEEN ANNUAL ACTUARIAL NET PREMIUMS
AND EXPENSE PER CENT (OTHER THAN COMMISSIONS). 1906-1930

EXPENSE
PER CENT

DIAGRAM 4. ALPHA

$y = 13.4 - .25x + .003x^2$

DIAGRAM 5. EPSILON

$y = 24.5 - 1.21x + .03303x^2$

DIAGRAM 6. KAPPA

$y = 21.6 - 1.756x + .165x^2$

NET PREMIUMS – MILLION DOLLARS

that it was impossible, when prosecuting his researches of the human factor, to obtain sufficient psychological data pertaining to the executive personnel of the ten life insurance companies to prove revealing with respect to innate managerial capacity. Therefore, he had to content himself with such objective factors as age, experience, education, promotional progression, etc. With respect to these, a vast amount of data was accumulated, relating to over five hundred executives who had been associated with the companies at one time or another throughout a twenty-five-year period.

Correlation of the factors of average age of executive appointees, and the ratio of administrative expense to actuarial net premiums, indicated the existence of a parabolic relation of the same nature as that disclosed for company size and the ratio of administrative expense. In the case of the largest four of the ten companies studied, the equation for age and administrative expense is $y = 16.28 - .262x + .0031x^2$. From collateral studies it appeared that business achievement, as measured in terms of smoothness of year-to-year change, varied inversely with the age of the executives. As a result of those studies, the conclusion seemed warranted that the older the executives grew, the less able were they to direct or to control the forces that determined annual net sales; the less able were they, apparently, to adjust themselves to the exigencies of rapidly changing times. That is what seems to be implied by the foregoing equation, also. However, in this connexion it is necessary to take into account the factor of experience, which is obviously correlative with age, and to determine whether that factor is not the more sensitive of the two.

For average length of experience with the company in any capacity, for all executives of all ten companies combined (see Diagram 7), the equation is: $y = 31 - 1.193x + .01996x^2$; it may be interpreted as follows: with an increase in the average length of company experience of the total executive personnel, the administrative expense ratio tends to decline, but only up to a certain point; after that point is reached, the expense ratio begins to rise. In the instance considered the point is not clearly defined, but this fact may be attributed to the counterbalancing influence of the heterogeneity of the data.

Similar findings present themselves when the length of experience of the major executives only is related to the average administrative expense ratio of the ten companies. For the relation of length of service of the major executives in any capacity with the company and the administrative expense ratio, the following parabolic equation is obtained: $y = 27.79 - .85x + .0121x^2$. Here the constants are relatively high (the average y equals only 14.387), and the point at which the upward turn of the curve occurs is not

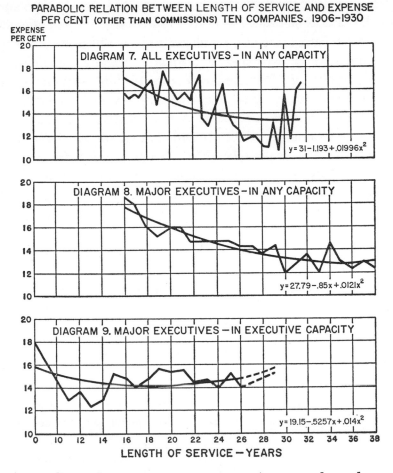

PARABOLIC RELATION BETWEEN LENGTH OF SERVICE AND EXPENSE
PER CENT (OTHER THAN COMMISSIONS) TEN COMPANIES. 1906-1930

EXPENSE
PER CENT

DIAGRAM 7. ALL EXECUTIVES – IN ANY CAPACITY

$y = 31 - 1.193 + .01996x^2$

DIAGRAM 8. MAJOR EXECUTIVES – IN ANY CAPACITY

$y = 27.79 - .85x + .0121x^2$

DIAGRAM 9. MAJOR EXECUTIVES – IN EXECUTIVE CAPACITY

$y = 19.15 - .5257x + .014x^2$

LENGTH OF SERVICE – YEARS

yet forcefully indicated (see Diagram 8). But when the same
calculations are made for the average *executive* experience of the
major executives, a much more definitive picture of relation, one
in line with earlier findings, is obtained. The equation now becomes:
$y = 19.15 - .5257x + .014x^2$, and the turn of the curve is clearly defined at the point indicating an average of twenty years of executive
experience (see Diagram 9).

That the curve turns upward at this point does not mean that
twenty years of executive experience is the optimum for any one of
the companies studied, for, as previously stated, the calculations
were based on the combined experience of ten different companies,

covering a period of twenty-five years. The curve does demonstrate the existence of a law of average relation between the average length in years of executive experience of the major executives of a company and its average administrative expense ratio. What the particular point of change in direction of this relation is for a given company for a given period of its business experience must be determined on the basis of the specific data for that company.

It is now justifiable to affirm, with regard to the field covered by the study, the general law that, beyond a certain point, age and length of experience constitute limiting factors in the influence of managerial capacity upon company accomplishment. In any company, after a certain average age has been reached and a given average length of experience attained, the managerial personnel loses in effectiveness, and may even exert an adverse influence over company progress.

The author is conscious of the attenuated and technical character of the material presented in this section; but if he has succeeded in conveying to the reader an appreciation of the validity of the methods of measurement employed to determine the optimum in the life insurance field, the material will have served its purpose. Those who may be particularly interested in pursuing inquiries concerning the findings of the research project or the techniques employed will be able to do so upon publication of the completed report.

It will be recalled that the author's approach to discussion of management and the optimum was from the point of view of limiting himself to treatment of the factors which influence the management of the individual enterprise in its struggle to achieve mastery over the *controllable* phases of its progress. When we consider the factors of size, cost, and human capacity, it must be conceded that they have both controllable and non-controllable aspects, and that determination of the relative importance of these in a given case is likely to constitute a perplexing problem.

We may postulate that it is the natural aim of management, in striving for attainment of the optimum, to extend its influence over as large an effective area as possible, while endeavouring concurrently to reduce to a minimum the need for adjustment to non-controllable factors. It will be interesting in this connexion to picture briefly current conditions in the life insurance field, with special regard for the factors of size, cost, and human capacity.

Several of the companies in the United States have attained dimensions that may be characterized only as enormous; indeed, in one instance, size has reached such proportions that thoughtful students in increasing number are beginning to view it as potentially a menace to society. Fortunately, fidelity to the responsibilities and implications of trusteeship is exceedingly high among the directors and officers of these great institutions. At the other extreme, there are many life insurance companies so small that there is really no economic justification for their existence. In a number of cases, convincing mathematical demonstrations of this fact can be made. Whether large, medium-sized, or small, no American life insurance company of which the author has knowledge has consciously tried to achieve and adhere to the optimum, as the highest expression of service to policyholders.

Considering the factor of cost, it may be pointed out that competition has naturally tended to bring this subject to the fore, and thus to impress upon the minds of life insurance executives the wisdom of maintaining effective cost control; moreover, requirements of State insurance departments and the commendable prudence of the executives of the better-managed companies have had similar influences. By and large in the life insurance field, however, there is as yet to be discerned only an inadequate application of the principle that increasing volume should be accompanied by decreasing unit costs. In a measure this is due to the commission form of payment of agents, whose remuneration constitutes so great a portion of expense. Abandonment of this archaic and unintelligent method in favour of an enlightened and justifiable system of compensation represents the next great reform which will come in the life insurance field.

Finally, human capacity. It is, indeed, strange that in a field which requires for its successful development so much in the way of scientific attainment and technical and executive ability, the selection of major executives is, and has always been, dominated by the rule of seniority. European readers need hardly be told that the breeding of a bureaucracy is almost certain to be the outcome of such a practice. Where sheer ability in management, as the term is here defined, is exemplified by life insurance executives, it is grounded quite as often in personal attributes as in experience. To lay a broader foundation for the achievement and maintenance of optimal relations in this field, the author believes that a limited tenure of office on the part of major executives and an adequate demonstration of ability to think and act in terms of management are prime essentials. Mediocrity may or may not prove a persistent phenomenon of life insurance management, but the vast army of policyholders will be served best if the personal experience of life insurance executives is gradually supplemented by a growing ability and inclination to view management in its relation to the optimum and to translate this accomplishment into concrete action.

VIII. *Optimology: The Science of the Optimum*[9]

Science is organized knowledge; it is the product of the synthesis of facts derived from observations, experimentation, and measurement. Science embraces generalizations, theories, and laws that are attainable and verifiable; no field of human knowledge which fails to meet these tests can be called scientific. "Science pays back to life what it has borrowed from experience";[10] it serves mankind by promoting its welfare. The disciples of science seek to discover the truth; to them science is exact, for it represents the "I know," as opposed to the "I think" or the "I believe." Moreover, in their eyes, as the French put it: "Savoir, c'est prévoir; prévoir, c'est pourvoir" [to know is to foresee; to foresee is to make provision]!

[9] In this final section, the author seeks to give expression to points of view inspired by a life-long endeavour to assist in developing scientific foundations of management, by intimate association with the management movement since its very inception, and by consistently maintained freedom from allegiance to any particular school of thought.

[10] Bliss, Henry Evelyn: *The Organization of Knowledge*, p. 212; published by Henry Holt & Company, New York, 1929.

When Taylor and his associates appeared before the Interstate Commerce Commission, during the autumn of 1910, and testified concerning their theories, activities, and accomplishments, technical literature was suddenly enriched, in most dramatic fashion, by a new concept, "scientific management." The public was conversant enough with management in the abstract, but it was at first startled, then attracted, and finally completely overwhelmed, for the time being, by the implications and possibilities of this new idea.

What the general public did not know, and never took the trouble to find out, was how the term "scientific management" came to be coined, and to what extent the use of the word "scientific" was justified. To-day, all who are familiar with the history of the Taylor system know that the term was devised in rather casual fashion by those who testified at the Interstate Commerce Commission hearings, because they realized the need for a uniform designation of the principles and techniques whose merit they were extolling. In naming them, Taylor and his associates hit upon a singularly unfortunate and quite inappropriate combination of words. Used separately, they represented easily recognizable concepts, but, taken together, they constituted, in the opinion of this author at least, a decidedly unwarranted assumption.

These men meant by "management," not the sum total of functions that a business enterprise is called upon to perform, but only the concededly important area of production, and not even always every phase of that function. What they described as "scientific" was the product of long years of research which, while it did ultimately reach a scientific stage, at that time included so many unintegrated phases that it could hardly be said to have achieved a quality of synthesis warranting the appellation employed. In justice to their pioneer work, it should be added that Taylor and his associates certainly aided in formulating the beginnings of a new philosophy.

"Scientific management" and its companion concept, "efficiency," became catch-words that fired their users and hearers with varying emotions. With the advent of the World War, scientific management spread to Europe, and especially to France, where it became known as "le système Taylor" and, more formally, as "l'organisation scientifique du travail." [11] It was at a time when Fayol, the great French engineer, had laid the foundations for the preparation and publication of his monumental study on industrial and general administration. This first appeared in print in a bulletin of the Société de l'Industrie Minérale, issued in 1916, and reprinted in book form in 1920.[12] Fayol was, of course, familiar with the system of management advocated by Taylor. In spite of the fact that he could not bring himself to accept it wholeheartedly, he had admiration for Taylor's accomplishments and expressed it in language that may well be repeated here:

> "Mes réserves sur l'organisation scientifique ou administrative de Taylor ne m'empêchent point d'admirer l'inventeur des aciers à coupe rapide, le créateur de procédés minutieux et précis des conditions dans lesquelles s'exécute le travail de l'ouvrier, l'industriel énergique et ingénieux qui, après avoir fait des découvertes, n'a reculé devant aucun effort et aucun ennui pour les faire entrer dans le domaine de la pratique, et le publiciste infatigable qui a tenu à faire profiter le public de ses essais et de ses expériences. Nous pouvons souhaiter que l'exemple du grand ingénieur américain soit suivi à cet égard par beaucoup de nos compatriotes."[13]

In the literature of scientific management, one may search far without discovering a characterization of Taylor that is more in accord with the truth.

---

[11] In later years, French engineers gradually began to substitute the phrase, "l'organisation rationelle du travail," evidently because of a reaction of unfavourable character to the continued use of the word "scientifique." *Vide* Urwick, L.: *The Meaning of Rationalization;* published by Nisbet & Co., Ltd., London, 1929.

[12] Fayol, Henri: *Administration Industrielle et Générale; Dunod,* éditeur, Paris, 1920. [See pages 215–241.—EDITOR.]

[13] Fayol, *op. cit.,* pp. 98–9. [Translation: "My reservations as regards Taylor's scientific or functional management do not prevent me from admiring the inventor of high-speed steel, the pioneer of minute and precise methods in conditions of work, the energetic and adept industrialist who, having made discoveries, shrank from no effort nor spared any pains to make them of practical application, and the tireless propagandist who meant the world to profit from his trials and experiments. We may hope that the example of the great American engineer may be followed in this respect by many of our own fellow countrymen."]

After the World War, European countries in increasing number concerned themselves with scientific management. Germany found ways of adapting "Wissentschaftliche (or Wirtschaftliche) Betriebsführung" [scientific, or economic management][14] to her peculiar needs and requirements but, paralleling and ultimately overshadowing scientific management, the concept of "Rationalisierung" came into vogue and spread with amazing rapidity from Germany to other European countries. The aims of rationalization were far broader in scope than those of scientific management but, in general, they were substantially alike. Where the two movements stood in sharp contrast was in respect of the form of attack employed. Whereas rationalization was based upon cooperative endeavour on a broad scale,[15] scientific management, and, indeed, the whole movement of which it was a part, was animated by distinctively individualistic tendencies which only in recent years have been gradually giving way to an era of cooperation.

The beginning of such an era in America may be said to have been signalized by the formation of the National Management Council of the U.S.A.,* an advisory body for the advancement of the management movement whose membership is composed of eleven associations and societies in the field.[16]

If the author has dwelt somewhat upon scientific management, it is in order to lead up to the statement that to-day it has become largely an historic concept relating to an industrial period that

---

14 Thanks to the flexibility of its vocabulary, the German language, better than any other with which the author is familiar, makes exactness of translation of the term "scientific management" possible.

15 *Vide Handbuch der Rationalisierung,* 3rd Edition, published by the Reichskuratorium für Wirtschaftlichkeit, Berlin, 1932. On the seventh page of the "Geleitwort" [preface] appears the following statement: "Aber eine Arbeitsmethode kann empfohlen werden, das ist die *Gemeinschaftsarbeit.*" [But there is one method of work that can be recommended, namely, cooperative endeavor.]

16 *Vide* Hopf, Harry Arthur: *The Management Movement at the Cross-roads;* an Address delivered at the Preliminary Organization Meeting of the National Management Council, 20 December, 1932; privately printed.

---

* Now the Council for International Progress in Management.—EDITOR

must now be regarded as closed. To what extent scientific management must bear a share of the responsibility for making possible the enormous expansion that led finally to the collapse of 1929 is wholly a matter of conjecture. That it was founded upon considerations attaching to an expanding economy, and was more or less instrumental in creating the greatly enhanced production results that ultimately destroyed the economic equilibrium, are conclusions that appear tenable.

In America, where scientific management had its origin, the term is losing steadily in importance. One may well agree with the appraisal made some years ago by a qualified German observer[17] who, in the introduction to a life of Taylor, stated as follows: "Heute sind Namen und System (i.e., Taylor System) in den Augen vieler ein überwundener Standpunkt" [today, in the eyes of many, both name and system (i.e., Taylor System) represent an outmoded viewpoint]. In spite of its waning influence, scientific management still furnishes a ready peg upon which many a propagandist with greater capacity for salesmanship than for science may hang the alleged scientific doctrine, principle, or system which he seeks to exploit. Thus we have such curious concatenations as "the X method of scientific marketing management"; "the Y method of scientific office management"; "the Z method of scientific production management"; "the A system of scientific budgeting"; "the B plan of scientific salary control"; "the C principle of scientific sales quotas," etc., in each of which we must visualize the name of an individual in place of the letter of the alphabet used. Why all this "scientific" pother, which is so patently misleading? Indeed, when a field of knowledge is truly scientific, do we have to designate it so? Do we, for example, speak of scientific mathematics, scientific physics, scientific botany, scientific chemistry, etc.?

We may appropriately think in terms of a science of management, but in so doing it is of the utmost consequence that we strive to furnish justification for the establishment and evolution of such a science by envisaging it increasingly in terms of optimal relations of factors. Of what avail is it in the long run to develop

---

[17] Witte, I. M.: *F. W. Taylor—der Vater Wirtschaftlicher Betriebsführung;* published by C. E. Poeschel, Stuttgart, 1928.

a science of management if its teachings translate themselves into practice chiefly in the form of vaster and ever vaster combinations of men, methods, and money which inevitably defeat their own ends? Is the science of management to furnish mankind merely with tools whose use will lead to ultimate disaster? Or is management susceptible of transformation into an agency of almost limitless possibilities of service to society, into a science that may appropriately be termed *optimology: the science of the optimum?*

The next great step in management is to raise synthesis from the level of functional, to that of structural, thinking. To view dispassionately and with complete objectivity every facet of the management problem of a large business enterprise is at present a faculty that very few business executives possess. The chief distinction to be drawn between Fayol and Taylor is that the former could and did develop such a perspective, whereas the latter, in spite of his brilliant accomplishments, did not push synthesis much beyond the boundaries of the production function. Exponents of divergent schools of thought in management, both failed to reveal in their writing an appreciation of the significance of the optimum; but of the two, Fayol, more than Taylor, possessed the type of mind and philosophic approach that would have manifested complete sympathy with the concept of optimal relationships.

Optimology has as its principal task the analysis and measurement, by scientific means, of all facts, experiences, techniques, processes, and trends in any field of human effort and their classification and codification, with the objectives in view of defining for a given enterprise the level of optimal relations to which it should aspire, and of providing it constantly with reliable data through the use of which the progress made in realizing and adhering to the optimum may be determined.

With regard to the three factors of size, cost, and human capacity, optimology aims to bring about much the same transformation of points of view, the same "complete mental revolution," as was insisted upon by Taylor [18] in the case of the applica-

---

[18] *Vide* Taylor's testimony at the hearings of the Special Committee of the House of Representatives, reprinted in the *Bulletin of the Taylor Society*, vol. XI, Nos. 3 and 4 (pp. 102–3), June–August, 1926. [See page 68.—EDITOR]

tion of principles of scientific management. Optimology seeks to associate with the concepts of changing size, cost, and human capacity that appertain to an enterprise, a philosophic acceptance of the likelihood that, through proper planning, organizing, coordinating, and controlling, a condition may ultimately be achieved that will represent the optimum, and that it is in conformity with the most enlightened considerations of economic and social character for management to direct the enterprise toward such a goal.

The art of management will perfect a union with optimology when its practitioners orient themselves with respect to the philosophy, techniques, and economic aims that underlie the new science in the making and accept its teachings without material reservations. Obviously, a tremendous task lies ahead in the industrial field alone, for it will take many years to devise valid measures of management and related factors for any considerable number of lines of business [19]; until the requisite data are produced, approaches to the determination of various optima must be left to qualitative rather than quantitative processes. In this connexion, perpetuation of the clash of opinion in an area where science can and should prevail is a contingency that is much to be deplored.

As the interest of economists, engineers, and other students of industrial and social trends rivets itself upon inspection and interpretation of organized human enterprise, it is indeed stimulating to observe the extent to which the problem of the optimum engages consideration. We may well leave a Spengler [20] to his macabre reflections and turn with relief and encouragement to Robinson,[21]

---

[19] Such results as the author may have been able to achieve through his researches in the single field of life insurance cannot possibly reflect the tremendous amount of labour involved in laying the necessary foundations. It is in the vast mass of data produced that was later found to be without scientific value that an index to the factors of time and effort may be discovered.

[20] Spengler, Oswald: *Der Mensch und die Technik*, published by C. H. Beck'sche Verlagsbuchhandlung, München, 1932. *Vide* p. 78: "Alles Organische erliegt der um sich greifenden Organisation" [everything organic is strangled in the grip of organization]. Also p. 88: "Nur Träumer glauben an Auswege. Optimismus ist Feigheit" [only dreamers believe in a way out; optimism is cowardice].

[21] Robinson, E. A. G.: *The Structure of Competitive Industry*, published by Nisbet & Co., Ltd., London, 1931.

who has performed a brilliant piece of analysis in considering
the principal phases of the optimum from the point of view of an
economist, and to Sheldon,[22] whose masterpiece, written a dozen
years ago, delineates a philosophy that points definitely in the
direction of the optimum.

In the German literature it is possible to go back to Schmoller[23]
for most interesting discussions and almost prophetic forecasts of
the evolution of industrial undertakings. But to the Russian, Bogdanow,[24] apparently belongs the priority in establishing, in a monumental work of two volumes, what is described in the German
translation as *Allgemeine Organisationslehre-Tektologie*. To read
this work constitutes a formidable intellectual challenge; it is
painted upon an enormous canvas, and is Spenglerian in its erudi-
tion, but decidedly anti-Spenglerian in its militancy. Possibly the
following quotation, which is the last paragraph of vol. I, part
II (p. 86), will convey to the reader an indication of the thesis,
advanced by Bogdanow:

"Die Tektologie ist eine allgemeine Naturlehre. Sie ist jetzt erst
im Entstehen begriffen. Da aber die gesamte organisatorische Er-
fahrung der Menschheit in ihr Gebiet fällt, muss ihre Entwicklung
einen stürmischen revolutionären Charakter annehmen, weil sie
selbst ihrer Natur nach revolutionär ist. Das Aufblühen dieser Wis-
senschaft wird ein Zeichen dafür sein, dass die Menschen die
bewusste Herrschaft über die äussere und die soziale Natur sowie
die unbeschränkte Möglichkeit gewonnen haben, die Aufgaben der
Praxis und Theorie wissenschaftlich planmässig zu lösen."†

---

[22] Sheldon, Oliver: *The Philosophy of Management,* published by Sir Isaac Pitman & Sons, Ltd., London, 1923. [See pages 265–277.—EDITOR]

[23] Schmoller, Gustav: *op. cit.,* vol. 1, par. 144.

[24] Bogdanow, A. (Professor an der Universität Moskau): *Allgemeine Organisationslehre-Tektologie;* published by Organisation Verlagsgesellschaft m.b.H., Berlin,
1926 (1913).

---

† Translation: "Tectology is a comprehensive natural theory. It is only now beginning to be understood. But since all of man's knowledge of organization falls
within its orbit, its development must take on a stormy, revolutionary character, be-

In striking contrast to Bogdanow's generalizations are the specific reasoning and approach employed by Ermanski.[25] In a brief dissertation of six or seven printed pages, he begins by questioning whether fundamental principles of scientific organization of work exist, and then proceeds to give a remarkable demonstration of philosophico-mathematical character concerning the principle of the optimum. It is the author's belief that nowhere in the literature of management is a finer piece of scientific reasoning to be discovered; indeed, he attributes to his first reading of Ermanski's dissertation in 1927 a direct stimulus to his since-sustained interest in the question of the optimum.

In general, the German literature contains an abundance of references to the optimum, for it seems to be a problem that has a peculiar interest, if not fascination, for the German mind. So we find Beste's work, previously cited, a masterly discussion of the subject, and perhaps the most comprehensive and understandable treatment provided by any author; it is, indeed, a scholarly and penetrating work that should be translated into other languages so as to make it as widely known as possible. Von Beckerath,[26] in his *Der Moderne Industrialismus*, presents a very illuminating discussion of the factor of size of industrial enterprises, and considers specifically five main principles of modern business management, as follows: (*a*) division of labour; (*b*) mechanization; (*c*) optimum size of the plant; (*d*) optimum utilization of capacity;

---

cause it is itself revolutionary by nature. The flowering of this theory will be a sign that man has won conscious dominion over the external and social [forces of] nature, as well as the unlimited ability to solve the tasks of theory and practice systematically and scientifically."

---

[25] Ermanski, J.: "Existieren grundlegende Principien der wissenschaftlichen Organisation der Arbeit? Worin bestehen dieselben?" [Do fundamental principles of the scientific organization of work exist? Of what do they consist?] *Proceedings of Third International Congress for Scientific Management*, pp. 770–5; Rome, 1927.

[26] Von Beckerath, Herbert: (English translation) *Modern Industrial Organization: an Economic Interpretation*, 48 ff. and 82 ff.; published by McGraw-Hill Book Company, Inc., New York and London, 1933.

(*e*) optimum and constant relationship between the different elements and sections of the plant. This is an interesting analysis, reflecting the views of a prominent German authority on the extent to which the optimum enters into the warp and woof of management.

No reference to the German literature concerning the optimum would be adequate without mention of Werner Sombart, the great German economist, and his *Der Moderne Kapitalismus*, which first appeared in 1902, was republished in enlarged and revised form in 1916 and, after incorporation of additional material, was finally completed in 1926. With great learning, brilliancy of style, and fertility of ideas, Sombart allowed his philosophic mind to penetrate to the depths of his subject, and his viewpoints and conclusions with respect to the optimum constitute contributions of illuminating character to the literature relating to this question.

In the United States consideration of optimal relations is still very much an academic matter. Accordingly, the literature dealing with management is practically devoid of references to the optimum and, if one wishes to inform himself, it becomes necessary to examine the writings of economists and to fall back upon what has been published abroad. Naturally, considerable thought has been devoted in the United States to problems incident to size, but, until the pressure of the sequelæ of economic disaster induced gradual changes in traditional points of view, solution of such problems was habitually sought in terms of still greater size, and little, if any, thought was devoted to the study of optimal values. Without wishing to detract from the importance or significance of other American works, the author will content himself with a reference to only two that seem to him to be of special interest in connexion with the theme here presented.

Secrist,[27] in a study of the operations of thousands of business firms in a number of fields of business activity, comes to the following conclusion: "Mediocrity tends to prevail in the conduct of

---

[27] Secrist, Horace: *The Triumph of Mediocrity in Business*, p. 7; published by Bureau of Business Research, Northwestern University, Chicago, Ill., 1933.

competitive business. This is the conclusion to which this study of the costs (expenses) and profits of thousands of firms unmistakably points. Such is the price which industrial (trade) freedom brings— a freedom to enter business, to continue operations, or finally in the face of hazards to drop out, or to seek new fields."

Clark,[28] in his brilliant study of overhead costs, which established his reputation as an economist, has this to say in bringing his study to a conclusion:

"So at the end, without further apology, we may end our study with a curious wonder at the intricacies of the financial-economic machinery which man has built. Man did not design them; they are rather the unintended by-products of the inventions which he did design to serve his supposed needs. These unintended by-products he does not even understand. They appear with all the force of living things with purposes foreign to those of mankind, because they act in ways which man does not understand and did not plan. No man has as yet comprehended them completely. Yet we do know enough to offer some prospect of controlling them, though we must wellnigh remake ourselves and our industrial organization in the process. And so we may look forward, not without hope, to the task of taming the New Leviathan. The stakes are heavy, for if we do not tame him, he may devour us."

Here are two thoughtful and authoritative statements over which we may well ponder; both go right to the heart of considerations affecting the optimum.

In concluding this discussion of "Management and the Optimum" the author can do no better than to reproduce at this point his own conception of an approach to the formulation of a technique for determining optimal size and relations which he ventured to present during the course of a discussion of the subject at a meeting of the Taylor Society in 1930.[29] At that time, he offered the following suggestions:

---

[28] Clark, John Maurice: *Studies in the Economics of Overhead Costs*, pp. 486–7; published by the University of Chicago Press, Chicago, Ill., 1923.

[29] *Vide Bulletin of the Taylor Society*, vol. XV, No. 1, pp. 28–9, February, 1930.

1. Establish the objectives of the business in comprehensive terms;
2. Define those general policies which should be followed regardless of operating conditions or results;
3. Define the task of management in human terms;
4. Staff the executive group with members who are competent to perform successfully the tasks assigned to them;
5. Furnish the executive group with standards of accomplishment by which performance can be accurately measured;
6. Study operating results and establish trends of accomplishment;
7. Adjust the rate of replacement of members of the executive group in line with requirements for maintaining the standards set;
8. Consider particularly the factor of age in its relation to productive capacity of executives;
9. Analyse all dynamic elements so as to discern the possible operation of the law of diminishing returns with respect to any element, substituting measurement for judgement, wherever possible;
10. Establish the optimal size of organization at the level at which the most favourable operating results can be secured, within the limits of the predetermined objectives and policies and without causing an executive overload at any point of the organization.

In the last analysis, the problem of establishing an optimal size of organization resolves itself into the ascertainment of that level of effectiveness on which all the vital factors are so perfectly balanced and executive talent and capacity are so purposefully and successfully employed, that maximum service and profit possibilities are regularly realized. The fact that such a goal is difficult of attainment is no reason for not recognizing its existence and, at least, striving to approach it.

GEORGE ELTON MAYO

(1880–1949)

FROM his studies of industrial workers on their jobs, George Elton Mayo concluded that a sense of participation and a feeling of being a member of a team are stronger motivating forces than economic self-interest, lighting, rest periods, and similar material influences. Thus he provided research evidence of the need to understand human motivations and group reactions in getting things done through people; and he opened up an immense new area for study, one which has scarcely been touched and from which few management principles have yet been drawn.

Mayo was an Australian who taught logic, philosophy, and ethics until he came to the United States and entered industrial research in 1922. In 1926 he was appointed associate professor of industrial research at the Harvard Business School, and from 1929 to 1947 he held the chair in that subject. It was early in this period that the famous Hawthorne studies were made.

Mayo in "The First Inquiry," which follows, describes a puzzling problem in a textile mill and touches on the far-reaching implications that lay in its solution. "Hawthorne and the Western Electric Company: Some Further Comments on the Interview Experiment" (pp. 389–408) is an account of the methods Mayo and his associates used in one of the most famous industrial relations studies and of the conclusions they reached.

THE FIRST INQUIRY

BY ELTON MAYO

ECONOMIC THEORY in its human aspect is woefully insufficient; indeed it is absurd. Humanity is not adequately described as a horde of individuals, each actuated by self-interest, each fighting his neighbor for the scarce material of survival. Realization that such theories completely falsify the normal human scene drives us back to study of particular human situations. *Knowledge-of-acquaintance* of the actual event, intimate understanding of the complexity of human relationships, must precede the formulation of alternatives to current economic abstractions. This is the clinical method, the necessary preliminary to laboratory investigation. Only when clinically tested by successful treatment can a diagnosis be safely developed toward logical elaboration and laboratory experiment.

The first inquiry we undertook ran headlong into illustration of the insufficiency of the assumption that individual self-interest actually operates as adequate incentive. Rather more than twenty years ago we were asked to discover, if possible, the causes of a high labor turnover in the mule-spinning department of a textile

Reprinted from the book, *The Social Problems of an Industrial Civilization*, by Elton Mayo, Chapter III, pages 59–67. Published by Division of Research, Graduate School of Business Administration, Harvard University, Boston, 1945. Copyright © 1945 by the President and Fellows of Harvard College. Used by permission of the publisher.

mill near Philadelphia.[1] The general labor situation elsewhere in the plant seemed highly satisfactory; the employers were unusually enlightened and humane; the work was exceedingly well organized in respect of operations and the company was generally regarded as an extremely successful venture. But the president and his director of personnel were much troubled by the situation in the mule-spinning department. Whereas the general labor turnover in other departments was estimated to be approximately 5% or 6% per annum, in the spinning department the turnover was estimated at approximately 250%. That is to say, about 100 men had to be taken on every year in order to keep about 40 working. And the difficulty tended to be most acute when the factory was busily employed and most in need of men.

Several firms of efficiency engineers had been consulted; these firms had instituted altogether four financial incentive schemes. And these schemes had been a total failure; labor turnover had not dropped one point, nor had production improved: it was almost as a last resort that the firm consulted a university. Although other plants in the vicinity had apparently drifted into acceptance of low morale amongst mule spinners as inevitable, the president of this company refused to believe that the situation was beyond remedy.

On a first inspection the conditions of work in the department did not seem to differ in any general respect from conditions elsewhere in the mill. For some time Saturday work had been discontinued throughout the plant, so that the work week was of 50 hours—five days of 10 hours, two shifts of 5 hours each separated by a 45-minute lunch interval. The mule-spinner attendant was known as a piecer; his work involved walking up and down a long alley, perhaps 30 yards or more, on either side of which a machine head was operating spinning frames. These frames moved back and forth stretching yarn taken from the carding machines, twisting it, and rolling it up on cops. The number of frames operated

---

[1] For a more detailed account of this inquiry, see Elton Mayo, "Revery and Industrial Fatigue," *Personnel Journal,* Vol. III, No. 8, December, 1924, pp. 273–281.

by a machine head varied from 10 to 14. All had to be closely watched; threads constantly broke and had to be pieced together. The number of piecers in an alley, usually two or three, varied according to the kind of yarn being spun. To an observer the work looked monotonous—walking up and down an alley twisting together broken threads. The only variation in work occurred when a machine head was stopped in order to doff or to replace some spools.

Dr. S. D. Ludlum, professor of neuropsychiatry in the graduate school of medicine in the University of Pennsylvania, was of immense aid to us at this stage as later in the study. He arranged that a registered nurse, one of our group, should be able to relate her small clinic for minor troubles in the plant direct to the Polyclinic Hospital in Philadelphia. Serious cases she referred to the hospital clinicians; minor injuries, a cut or splinter, she could deal with herself. This arrangement seemed to do away with any need for further explanation. Workers gratefully accepted the services of the nurse and, in some instances, the further clinical aid of the hospital. These services were real and understandable. From the first the mule spinners formed a large part of the nurse's regular callers—and either when at work or in the clinic talked to her and to us quite freely. It was of course clearly understood that nothing said to any of us was ever repeated to anyone in the plant.

As the men began to talk to us, the picture of the situation developed quite differently from that obtained at first inspection. We discovered that almost every piecer suffered from foot trouble of one or another kind for which he apparently knew no effective remedy. Many also claimed neuritis in various localities of arms, shoulders, or legs. But above and beyond all this, the striking fact was the uniformly pessimistic nature of the preoccupations of these workers while at work. To this there seemed no exception: their own opinion of their work was low, even lower than the estimate of mule spinning held by other workers in the plant. We discovered also that the job was essentially solitary: there might be three workers in an alley, but the amount of communication between them in a day was almost nil. One might be piecing threads together here; another, 20 yards away. And the doffing process when it took place involved rapid work with a minimum of communication. Some of the men were young—in the twenties; others were in the fifties—all alike claimed that they were too fatigued to enjoy social evenings after work. Occasionally a worker would flare out into apparently unreasonable anger and incontinently leave his job.

The whole group was characterized by a species of strongly held loyalty to the company president. He had been a colonel in the regular United States Army and had seen active service both before and during the First World War. Many of the workers had been in the trenches in France under his immediate command and had the highest opinion of him; they had come with him from his regiment to the textile mill. Perhaps for this reason their pessimistic moods showed no anger against "The Colonel" or "the company." For the most part the individual seemed to be almost melancholic about himself; this mood alternated with spurts of rage against some immediate supervisor.

After some discussion the management permitted us to experiment with rest periods—two of 10 minutes' length in the morning and two again in the afternoon. We arranged these rests so that the work period should be divided thus: 2 hours' work, 10 minutes' rest; 1½ hours' work, 10 minutes' rest; and a final work period of 1 hour and 10 minutes. The actual uninterrupted work period thus diminished in morning and afternoon. In these rest periods the workers were permitted to lie down; we instructed them in the best method of securing the maximum of muscular relaxation. We encouraged them to sleep for 10 minutes and most of them were able to do so.

We began with one team of piecers, about one-third of the total number, and the results were encouraging from the outset. The men themselves were pleased and interested; they speedily adopted the method of rest we advised. The effect was immediate —symptoms of melancholy preoccupation almost wholly disappeared, the labor turnover came to an end, production was maintained, and the morale generally improved. Such immediate effects could not be attributed to the mere elimination of physical fatigue. This was confirmed by the fact that an almost equivalent improvement showed itself in the work of the other two-thirds of the piecers. These men had discussed the experiment at lunch time with their fellows and were confident that "The Colonel" would extend the system to them if it were found satisfactory. And in the October of that year, 1923, this expectation was fulfilled; the management, pleased with the improved condition of the men and the work, decided to extend the rest period system to include the entire personnel of the spinning department. This made it possible for us to do what we could not do before—to measure the effect of the rest periods upon the productivity of the department.

Until October, 1923, the spinning department had never earned a bonus under one of the incentive systems introduced; in October and for the months recorded thereafter, with one interesting exception, the spinners consistently earned a bonus in addition to their wages. I have elsewhere described the bonus plan[2] and shall not repeat this detail here. Enough to say that, if the production of the department in any month exceeded 75% of a carefully calculated possibility, every spinner was paid an excess percentage of his flat-rate wage equivalent to the average excess percentage of production over 75%. Thus a monthly man-hour efficiency of 80% meant a 5% bonus on his monthly wage to every employee in the department. As said above, no fraction of bonus had ever been earned by the department. We were unable to get figures showing the average productivity of the department before October, 1923, when the experiment proper began; but it was generally admitted by executives and supervisors that production had never been above an approximate 70%.

The period from October, 1923, to mid-February, 1924, inclusive, showed a surprising change. The mental and physical condition of the men continued to improve, and, whereas the financial incentive of the bonus had not operated to stimulate production while they felt fatigued, they were now pleased by the fact that under

---

[2] Elton Mayo, "Revery and Industrial Fatigue," loc. cit.

conditions of work that seemed much easier they were earning bonuses as never before. The system was not, however, altogether satisfactory at this time. The immediate supervisors had never liked the sight of workers lying asleep on sacks while the mules were running; it occurred to one of them that the men should be made to "earn" their rest periods. That is to say, a task was set and, if finished within a given time, the men had their rest. For the most part, the workers had three or four rests every day and the innovation worked well enough. For example, the monthly average of productivity ran as follows:

		Efficiency	Bonus
October,	1923	79½%	4½%
November,	"	78¾	3¾
December,	"	82	7
January,	1924	78¾	3¾
February,	"	80¼	5¼

This, for workers who had never before earned a bonus, meant much.

This general condition continued until Friday, February 15, when in response to a heavy demand for goods the supervisor who had introduced the idea of earned rest periods ordered the whole system abandoned. Within five days production fell to a point lower that it had been for months. And on February 22, we found that the old pessimistic preoccupations had returned in full force, thus coinciding almost exactly with the drop in production. The executive officer in charge ordered the resumption of the rest period system on Monday, February 25; this was done, but the idea of earned rest periods was also reinstated even more strongly than before. At this point, the workers gave every symptom of profound discouragement; they professed a belief that the system would be discontinued before long. In spite of this, the daily record for March showed definite improvement, but the general average for the month was back at the old point, 70%.

At this point the president of the company, "The Colonel," took charge. His military service had taught him two important things —one, to care for his men, and, two, not to be afraid of making decisions. He called a conference in his office to discuss the remarkable diminution from 80% to 70% in the department's productive efficiency. We were able to point out that in March there had been a recrudescence of absenteeism, an ill that had notably diminished in the October to February period. This meant that the men were taking their rest periods in the form of "missed" days, a proceeding that did not greatly remedy their condition and that produced chaos in the plant. We put it therefore that the question was not whether a certain proportion of their working time was to be given up to rest. We pointed out that they took the rest, whether it was given them or not. We were asking that a less proportion should be thus allotted, but that it should be done systematically. Furthermore, we were able to claim that the whole rest period system had never had a fair trial. In other words, it had not been possible for a worker to know as he entered the factory in the morning that he was assured of his four rests in the day.

In order to test our claim, the president ordered that during the month of April the spinning mules should be shut down for 10 minutes at a time four times a day and that all hands from the floor supervisor down should rest as they had been instructed to do. There was some difficulty in securing the requisite amount of floor space for approximately 40 men to lie down by their machines and in securing sufficient sacking to provide for their comfort. With the exception of the president himself, there were few who believed that this drastic alteration of method could result in increased production. The men themselves believed that 40 minutes lost by 40 men per day during a whole month could not be recovered. They pointed out that the machines could not be "speeded up" and that there was no other way of recovering the lost time. In spite of this general belief, the returns for April showed an improvement on March.[3] The March production-efficiency figure had been 70%, the April figure was 77½%. This, while it represented a 7½% gain in the company's rating, was actually a 10% gain. The men had had their rests, the pessimism had again dis-

---

[3] Ibid.

appeared; simultaneously, their morale had much improved, absenteeism had diminished, and every worker had earned a 2½% bonus on his wages. In the month of May and thereafter, the president ordered a return to the system of alternating rest periods, with this important difference: that each group of three men in an alley was to determine for itself the method of alternation, the understanding being that every worker was to have four such rest periods daily and regularly. In the month of May, the average efficiency of man-hour production was 80¼%. In June it reached the then record high figure of 85%. During the following three months the department maintained its improved capacity: July, 82%; August, 83½%; September, 86½%.

It is interesting to observe the difference that an absolute certainty of a minimum number of rest periods made. The months from April to September differed from the preceding months in this respect and they revealed a steady progress. Mondays and Fridays were no longer the worst days in the week. The irregularity reported in May was due to the fact that the spinning mules were constantly "running away from the cards," that is, outdistancing the carding machines which supplied them with spooled yarn. By June, the company had put in two new carding machines, and June was as steadily above 85% as March was below 75%.

The investigation began with a question as to the cause of a very high labor turnover. In the 12 months of experiment there was no labor turnover at all. This does not mean that no worker left the factory—during a period of trade slackness, some were laid off, one at least moved his place of residence and found work elsewhere, another was found to be phthisical and sent to the country. But the former problem of a highly emotional labor turnover ceased to exist. The factory began to hold its mule spinners and no longer had difficulty in maintaining a full complement in times of rushed work. The attitude of management to the innovation was revealed in the fact that the company purchased army cots for the workers to rest upon. When these cots proved unequal to the wear and tear, management installed a bed and mattress at the end of each alley as provision for the workers' adequate rest. And the workers developed the habit of sleeping for the last three rest periods of the day, the late morning rest and both afternoon rests. Experience seemed to show that the benefit was directly proportionate to the completeness of the relaxation—hence the beds. Several years later, the president of the company said publicly that from this time the labor turnover sank to an approximate 5% or 6% per annum and stayed there until the mules were taken out and ring spinning substituted.

At the time when we completed our part in this work, we were sure that we had not wholly discovered the causes of the high labor turnover. We could not even attribute the change to the mere introduction of rest periods; inevitably many other changes had been simultaneously introduced. For example, we had listened carefully and with full attention to anything a worker wished to say, whatever the character of his comment. In addition to this, we —supported by the president—had demonstrated an interest in what was said by the introduction of experimental changes, by instruction in the best methods of relaxation. The Colonel also had demonstrated unmistakably a sincere interest in his workers' welfare; he had lived up to his Army reputation. The supervisor who instituted the earning of rest periods was swept aside by the president and the company—thereby "placing" the company's attitude in the minds of its workers.

But, in addition to this—and we did not see this clearly at the time—the president had effected another important change. He had helped to transform a horde of "solitaries" into a social group. In May, 1924, he placed the control of rest periods squarely in the hands of the workers in an alley with no one to say them nay. This led to consultation, not only between individuals, but between alleys throughout the group—and to a feeling of responsibility directly to the president. And the general social changes effected were astonishing—even in relationships outside the factory. One worker told us with great surprise that he had begun taking his wife to "movies" in the evenings, a thing he had not done for years. Another, equally to his surprise, gave up a habit of spending alcoholic week ends on bootleg liquor. In general the change was complex, and the difficulty of assigning the part played in it by various aspects of the experiment impossible to resolve. We should have liked to experiment further, but this desire—probably wisely in the circumstances—was disallowed. Thus the inquiry left us with many questions unanswered, but it pointed a direction for further studies, the results of which later proved helpful in reinterpreting the data of this first investigation.

But we had moved onwards. The efficiency experts had not consulted the workers; they regarded workers' statements as exaggerated or due to misconception of the facts and therefore to be ignored. Yet to ignore an important symptom—whatever its character—on supposedly moral grounds is preposterous. The "expert" assumptions of rabble hypothesis* and individual self-interest as a basis for diagnosis led nowhere. On the other hand, careful and pedestrian consideration of the workers' situation taken as part of a clinical diagnosis led us to results so surprising that we could at the time only partly explain them.

---

* Defined by Mayo in an earlier chapter of *The Social Problems of an Industrial Civilization* as the assumption that "mankind is a horde of unorganized individuals actuated by self-interest."—EDITOR

HAWTHORNE AND THE WESTERN ELECTRIC COMPANY

Some Further Comments on the Interview Experiment

BY ELTON MAYO

THE CASES selected for discussion in these chapters must not be supposed to be a report of all the work done by the Industrial Research Department of Harvard University. Any such conception would be very far from the truth; at some future time my colleagues will present reports of many other studies that will vie in interest with those here described. The selection of a case has been based upon the extent to which the experience developed our insight into, or understanding of, a particular industrial situation; those inquiries are presented that seem notably to have helped the department to move forward in its thinking. And, of these, the most signal instance is probably the five years and more spent in active collaboration with officers of the Western Electric Company at Hawthorne. In Philadelphia we had been fortunate in finding as president of a company an Army colonel who was not afraid

Reprinted from the book, *The Social Problems of an Industrial Civilization*, by Elton Mayo, Chapter IV, pages 68–86. Published by Division of Research, Graduate School of Business Administration, Harvard University, Boston, 1945. Copyright © 1945 by the President and Fellows of Harvard College. Used by permission of the publisher.

of a crucial experiment, and, having experimented, was also not afraid to act on the result—even though his action seemed to the workers to be in their favor. Furthermore, he deemed it proper to give the workers control of their rest periods, thereby securing for him and his company an eager and spontaneous loyalty. We were equally fortunate in finding at Hawthorne a group of engineers who ranked as first-rate in matters of applied science or of organized industrial operation, but who wished to find out why human cooperation could not be as exactly and as accurately determined by the administrative organization.

I shall make no attempt to describe at length that which has been already and fully described. The interested public is well acquainted with *Management and the Worker*, the official account of the whole range of experiments, by my colleagues F. J. Roethlisberger of Harvard University and William J. Dickson of the Western Electric Company. The same public has not yet discovered *The Industrial Worker*,[1] by another colleague, T. North Whitehead. This is unfortunate, for the beginning of an answer to many problems significant for administration in the next decade is recorded in its pages. I refer to the problems involved in the making and adaptive re-making of working teams, the importance of which for collaboration in postwar years is still too little realized. Assuming that readers who wish to do so can consult these books, I have confined my remarks here to some comments upon the general development of the series of experiments.

A highly competent group of Western Electric engineers refused to accept defeat when experiments to demonstrate the effect of illumination on work seemed to lead nowhere. The conditions of scientific experiment had apparently been fulfilled—experimental room, control room; changes introduced one at a time; all other conditions held steady. And the results were perplexing: Roethlisberger gives two instances—lighting improved in the experimental room, production went up; but it rose also in the control room. The

---

[1] Cambridge, Harvard University Press, 1938, 2 vols.

opposite of this: lighting diminished from 10 to 3 foot-candles in the experimental room and production again went up; simultaneously in the control room, with illumination constant, production also rose.[2] Many other experiments, and all inconclusive; yet it had seemed so easy to determine the effect of illumination on work.

In matters of mechanics or chemistry the modern engineer knows how to set about the improvement of process or the redress of error. But the determination of optimum working conditions for the human being is left largely to dogma and tradition, guess, or quasi-philosophical argument. In modern large-scale industry the three persistent problems of management are:

1. The application of science and technical skill to some material good or product.
2. The systematic ordering of operations.
3. The organization of teamwork—that is, of sustained cooperation.

The last must take account of the need for continual reorganization of teamwork as operating conditions are changed in an *adaptive* society.

The first of these holds enormous prestige and interest and is the subject of continuous experiment. The second is well developed in practice. The third, by comparison with the other two, is almost wholly neglected. Yet it remains true that if these three are out of balance, the organization as a whole will not be successful. The first two operate to make an industry *effective*, in Chester Barnard's phrase; the third, to make it *efficient*. For the larger and more complex the institution, the more dependent is it upon the whole-hearted cooperation of every member of the group.

This was not altogether the attitude of Mr. G. A. Pennock and his colleagues when they set up the experimental "test room." But the illumination fiasco had made them alert to the need that very careful records should be kept of everything that happened in the

2 *Management and Morale*, pp. 9–10.

room in addition to the obvious engineering and industrial devices.[3] Their observations therefore included not only records of industrial and engineering changes but also records of physiological or medical changes, and, in a sense, of social and anthropological. This last took the form of a "log" that gave as full an account as possible of the actual events of every day, a record that proved most useful to Whitehead when he was re-measuring the recording tapes and recalculating the changes in productive output. He was able to relate eccentricities of the output curve to the actual situation at a given time—that is to say, to the events of a specific day or week.

First Phase—The Test Room

The facts are by now well known. Briefly restated, the test room began its inquiry by, first, attempting to secure the active collaboration of the workers. This took some time but was gradually successful, especially after the retirement of the original first and second workers and after the new worker at the second bench had assumed informal leadership of the group. From this point on, the evidence presented by Whitehead or Roethlisberger and Dickson seems to show that the individual workers became a team, wholeheartedly committed to the project. Second, the conditions of work were changed one at a time: rest periods of different numbers and length, shorter working day, shorter working week, food with soup or coffee in the morning break. And the results seemed satisfactory: slowly at first, but later with increasing certainty, the output record (used as an index of well-being) mounted. Simultaneously the girls claimed that they felt less fatigued, felt that they were not making any special effort. Whether these claims were accurate or no, they at least indicated increased contentment with the general situation in the test room by comparison with the

---

[3] For a full account of the experimental setup, see F. J. Roethlisberger and William J. Dickson, *Management and the Worker,* and T. North Whitehead, *The Industrial Worker*, Vol. I.

department outside. At every point in the program, the workers had been consulted with respect to proposed changes; they had arrived at the point of free expression of ideas and feelings to management. And it had been arranged thus that the twelfth experimental change should be a return to the original conditions of work—no rest periods, no midmorning lunch, no shortened day or week. It had also been arranged that, after 12 weeks of this, the group should return to the conditions of Period 7, a 15-minute midmorning break with lunch and a 10-minute midafternoon rest. The story is now well known: in Period 12 the daily and weekly output rose to a point higher than at any other time (the hourly rate adjusted itself downward by a small fraction), and in the whole 12 weeks "there was no downward trend." In the following period, the return to the conditions of work as in the seventh experimental change, the output curve soared to even greater heights: this thirteenth period lasted for 31 weeks.

These periods, 12 and 13, made it evident that increments of production could not be related point for point to the experimental changes introduced. Some major change was taking place that was chiefly responsible for the index of improved conditions—the steadily increasing output. Period 12—but for minor qualifications, such as "personal time out"—ignored the nominal return to original conditions of work and the output curve continued its upward passage. Put in other words, there was no actual return to original conditions. This served to bring another fact to the attention of the observers. Periods 7, 10, and 13 had nominally the same working conditions, as above described—15-minute rest and lunch in midmorning, 10-minute rest in the afternoon. But the average weekly output for each girl was:

> Period 7—2,500 units
> Period 10—2,800 units
> Period 13—3,000 units

Periods 3 and 12 resembled each other also in that both required a full day's work without rest periods. But here also the difference of average weekly output for each girl was:

Period   3—less than 2,500 units
Period 12—more than 2,900 units

Here then was a situation comparable perhaps with the illumination experiment, certainly suggestive of the Philadelphia experience where improved conditions for one team of mule spinners were reflected in improved morale not only in the experimental team but in the two other teams who had received no such benefit.

This interesting, and indeed amusing, result has been so often discussed that I need make no mystery of it now. I have often heard my colleague Roethlisberger declare that the major experimental change was introduced when those in charge sought to hold the situation humanly steady (in the interest of critical changes to be introduced) by getting the cooperation of the workers. What actually happened was that six individuals became a team and the team gave itself wholeheartedly and spontaneously to cooperation in the experiment. The consequence was that they felt themselves to be participating freely and without afterthought, and were happy in the knowledge that they were working without coercion from above or limitation from below. They were themselves astonished at the consequence, for they felt they were working under less pressure than ever before: and in this, their feelings and performance echoed that of the mule spinners.

Here then are two topics which deserve the closest attention of all those engaged in administrative work—the organization of working teams and the free participation of such teams in the task and purpose of the organization as it directly affects them in their daily round.

Second Phase—The Interview Program

But such conclusions were not possible at the time: the major change, the question as to the exact difference between conditions of work in the test room and in the plant departments, remained something of a mystery. Officers of the company determined to "take another look" at departments outside the test room—this, with the idea that something quite important was there to be observed, something to which the experiment should have made them alert. So the interview program was introduced.

It was speedily discovered that the question-and-answer type of interview was useless in the situation. Workers wished to talk, and to talk freely under the seal of professional confidence (which was never abused) to someone who seemed representative of the company or who seemed, by his very attitude, to carry authority. The experience itself was unusual; there are few people in this world who have had the experience of finding someone intelligent, attentive, and eager to listen without interruption to all that he or she has to say. But to arrive at this point it became necessary to train interviewers how to listen, how to avoid interruption or the giving of advice, how generally to avoid anything that might put an end to free expression in an individual instance. Some approximate rules to guide the interviewer in his work were therefore set down. These were, more or less, as follows:[4]

1. Give your whole attention to the person interviewed, and make it evident that you are doing so.
2. Listen—don't talk.
3. Never argue; never give advice.
4. Listen to:
   (*a*) What he wants to say.
   (*b*) What he does not want to say.
   (*c*) What he cannot say without help.
5. As you listen, plot out tentatively and for subsequent correction the pattern (personal) that is being set before you. To test this, from time to time summarize what has been said and present for comment (e.g., "Is this what you are telling me?"). Always do this with the greatest caution, that is, clarify but do not add or twist.

---

[4] For a full discussion of this type of interview, see F. J. Roethlisberger and William J. Dickson, op. cit., Chap. XIII. For a more summary and perhaps less technical discussion, see George C. Homans, *Fatigue of Workers* (New York, Reinhold Publishing Corporation, 1941).

6. Remember that everything said must be considered a personal confidence and not divulged to anyone. (This does not prevent discussion of a situation between professional colleagues. Nor does it prevent some form of public report when due precaution has been taken.)

It must not be thought that this type of interviewing is easily learned. It is true that some persons, men and women alike, have a natural flair for the work, but, even with them, there tends to be an early period of discouragement, a feeling of futility, through which the experience and coaching of a senior interviewer must carry them. The important rules in the interview (important, that is, for the development of high skill) are two. First, Rule 4 that indicates the need to help the individual interviewed to articulate expression of an idea or attitude that he has not before expressed; and, second, Rule 5 which indicates the need from time to time to summarize what has been said and to present it for comment. Once equipped to do this effectively, interviewers develop very considerable skill. But, let me say again, this skill is not easily acquired. It demands of the interviewer a real capacity to follow the contours of another person's thinking, to understand the meaning for him of what he says.

I do not believe that any member of the research group or its associates had anticipated the immediate response that would be forthcoming to the introduction of such an interview program. Such comments as "This is the best thing the Company has ever done," or "The Company should have done this long ago," were frequently heard. It was as if workers had been awaiting an opportunity for expressing freely and without afterthought their feelings on a great variety of modern situations, not by any means limited to the various departments of the plant. To find an intelligent person who was not only eager to listen but also anxious to help to expression ideas and feelings but dimly understood—this, for many thousand persons, was an experience without precedent in the modern world.

In a former statement I named two questions that inevitably

presented themselves to the interviewing group in these early stages
of the study:

1. Is some experience which might be described as an experience of personal futility a common incident of industrial organization for work?
2. Does life in a modern industrial city, in some unrealized way, predis-
   pose workers to obsessive response?[5]

And I said that these two questions "in some form" continued
to preoccupy those in charge of the research until the conclusion of
the study.[6]

After twelve years of further study (not yet concluded), there
are certain developments that demand attention. For example, I
had not fully realized in 1932, when the above was written, how
profoundly the social structure of civilization has been shaken by
scientific, engineering, and industrial development. This radical
change—the passage from an established to an adaptive social order
—has brought into being a host of new and unanticipated problems for management and for the individual worker. The management problem appears at its acutest in the work of the supervisor.
No longer does the supervisor work with a team of persons that he
has known for many years or perhaps a lifetime; he is leader of a
group of individuals that forms and disappears almost as he watches
it. Now it is difficult, if not impossible, to relate oneself to a working group one by one; it is relatively easy to do so if they are
already a fully constituted team. A communication from the supervisor, for example, in the latter instance has to be made to one
person only with the appropriate instructions; the individual will
pass it on and work it out with the team. In the former instance,
it has to be repeated to every individual and may often be misunderstood.

But for the individual worker the problem is really much more

---

[5] Elton Mayo, *The Human Problems of an Industrial Civilization* (New York, The
Macmillan Company, 1933; reprinted by Division of Research, Harvard Business
School, 1946), p. 114.
[6] Ibid.

serious. He has suffered a profound loss of security and certainty in his actual living and in the background of his thinking. For all of us the feeling of security and certainty derives always from assured membership of a group. If this is lost, no monetary gain, no job guarantee, can be sufficient compensation. Where groups change ceaselessly as jobs and mechanical processes change, the individual inevitably experiences a sense of void, of emptiness, where his fathers knew the joy of comradeship and security. And in such situation, his anxieties—many, no doubt, irrational or ill-founded —increase and he becomes more difficult both to fellow workers and to supervisor. The extreme of this is perhaps rarely encountered as yet, but increasingly we move in this direction as the tempo of industrial change is speeded by scientific and technical discovery.

In the first chapter of this book I have claimed that scientific method has a dual approach—represented in medicine by the clinic and the laboratory. In the clinic one studies the whole situation with two ends in view: first, to develop intimate knowledge of and skill in handling the facts, and, second, on the basis of such a skill to separate those aspects of the situation that skill has shown to be closely related for detailed laboratory study. When a study based upon laboratory method fails, or partially fails, because some essential factor has been unknowingly and arbitrarily excluded, the investigator, if he is wise, returns to clinical study of the entire situation to get some hint as to the nature of the excluded determinant. The members of the research division at Hawthorne, after the twelfth experimental period in the test room, were faced by just such a situation and knew it. The so-called interview program represented for them a return from the laboratory to clinical study. And, as in all clinical study, there was no immediate and welcome revelation of a single discarded determinant: there was rather a slow progress from one observation to another, all of them important —but only gradually building up into a single complex finding. This slow development has been elsewhere described, in *Management and the Worker;* one can however attempt a succinct résumé of the various observations, more or less as they occurred.

Officers of the company had prepared a short statement, a few sentences, to be repeated to the individual interviewed before the conversation began. This statement was designed to assure the worker that nothing he said would be repeated to his supervisors or to any company official outside the interviewing group. In many instances, the worker waved this aside and began to talk freely and at once. What doubts there were seemed to be resident in the interviewers rather than in those interviewed. Many workers, I cannot say the majority for we have no statistics, seemed to have something "on their minds," in ordinary phrase, about which they wished to talk freely to a competent listener. And these topics were by no means confined to matters affecting the company. This was, I think, the first observation that emerged from the mass of interviews reported daily. The research group began to talk about the need for *"emotional release"* and the great advantage that accrued to the individual when he had "talked off" his problem. The topics varied greatly. One worker two years before had been sharply reprimanded by his supervisor for not working as usual: in interview he wished to explain that on the night preceding the day of the incident his wife and child had both died, apparently unexpectedly. At the time he was unable to explain; afterwards he had no opportunity to do so. He told the story dramatically and in great detail; there was no doubt whatever that telling it thus benefited him greatly. But this story naturally was exceptional; more often a worker would speak of his family and domestic situation, of his church, of his relations with other members of the working group—quite usually the topic of which he spoke presented itself to him as a problem difficult for him to resolve. This led to the next successive illumination for the inquiry. It became manifest that, whatever the problem, it was partly, and sometimes wholly, determined by the attitude of the individual worker. And this defect or distortion of attitude was consequent on his past experience or his present situation, or, more usually, on both at once. One woman worker, for example, discovered for herself during an interview that her dislike of a certain supervisor was based upon a fancied resemblance to a detested stepfather. Small wonder that the same supervisor had warned the interviewer that she was "difficult to handle." But the discovery by the worker that her dislike was wholly irrational eased the situation considerably.[7] This type of case led the interviewing group to study carefully each worker's *personal situation* and attitude. These two phrases "emotional release" and "personal situation" became convenient titles for the first phases of observation and seemed to resume for the interviewers the effective work they were doing. It was at this point that a change began to show itself in the study and in the conception of the study.

The original interviewers, in these days, after sixteen years of industrial experience, are emphatic on the point that the first cases singled out for report were special cases—individuals—and not representative either of the working group or of the interviews generally. It is estimated that such cases did not number more than an approximate two per cent of the twenty thousand persons originally interviewed. Probably this error of emphasis was inevitable and for two reasons: first, the dramatic changes that occur in such instances seemed good evidence of the efficacy of the method, and, second, this type of interviewing had to be insisted upon as *necessary to the training of a skilled interviewer.* This last still holds good; a skilled interviewer must have passed through the stage of careful and observant listening to what an individual says and to all that he says. This stage of an interviewing program closely resembles the therapeutic method and its triumphs are apt to be therapeutic. And I do not believe that the study would have been equipped to advance further if it had failed to observe the great benefit of emotional release and the extent to which every individual's problems are conditioned by his personal history and situation. Indeed, even when one has advanced beyond the merely psychotherapeutic study of individuals to study of industrial groups, one has to beware of distortions similar in kind to those named; one has to know how to deal with such problems. The first phase of the interview program cannot therefore be discarded; it

---

[7] F. J. Roethlisberger and William J. Dickson, op. cit., pp. 307–310.

still retains its original importance. But industrial studies must nevertheless move beyond the individual in need of therapy. And this is the more true when the change from established routines to adaptive changes of routine seems generally to carry a consequence of loss of security for many persons.

A change of attitude in the research group came gradually. The close study of individuals continued, but in combination with an equally close study of groups. An early incident did much to set the new pattern for inquiry. One of the earliest questions proposed before the original test room experiment began was a question as to the fatigue involved in this or that type of work. Later a foreman of high reputation, no doubt with this in mind, came to the research group, now for the most part engaged in interviewing, and asserted that the girls in his department worked hard all day at their machines and must be considerably fatigued by the evening; he wanted an inquiry. Now the interviewers had discovered that this working group claimed a habit of doing most of their work in the morning period and "taking things easy" during the afternoon. The foreman obviously realized nothing of this, and it was therefore fortunate that the two possibilities could be directly tested. The officer in charge of the research made a quiet arrangement with the engineers to measure during a period the amount of electric current used by the group to operate its machines; this quantity indicated the over-all amount of work being done. The results of this test wholly supported the statements made by the girls in interview; far more current was used in the morning period than during the afternoon. And the attention of the research group was, by this and other incidents, thus redirected to a fact already known to them, namely, that the working group as a whole actually determined the output of individual workers by reference to a standard, predetermined but never clearly stated, that represented the group conception of a fair day's work. This standard was rarely, if ever, in accord with the standards of the efficiency engineers.

The final experiment, reported under the title of the Bank Wiring Observation Room, was set up to extend and confirm these observations.[8] Simultaneously it was realized that these facts did not in any way imply low working morale as suggested by such phrases as "restriction of output." On the contrary, the failure of free communication between management and workers in modern large-scale industry leads inevitably to the exercise of caution by the working group until such time as it knows clearly the range and meaning of changes imposed from above. The enthusiasm of the efficiency engineer for the organization of operations is excellent; his attempt to resume problems of cooperation under this heading is not. At the moment, he attempts to solve the many human difficulties involved in wholehearted cooperation by organizing the organization of organization without any reference whatever to workers themselves. This procedure inevitably blocks communication and defeats his own admirable purpose.[9]

This observation, important as it is, was not however the leading point for the interviewers. The existence and influence of the group —those in active daily relationship with one another—became the important fact. The industrial interviewer must learn to distinguish and specify, as he listens to what a worker says, references to "personal" or group situations. More often than not, the special case, the individual who talks himself out of a gross distortion, is a solitary—one who has not "made the team." The usual interview, on the other hand, though not by any means free from distortion, is speaking as much for the working group as for the person. The influence of the communication in the interview, therefore, is not limited to the individual but extends to the group.

Two girl workers in a large industry were recently offered "upgrading"; to accept would mean leaving their group and taking a job in another department: they refused. Then representatives of the union put some pressure on them, claiming that, if they continued to refuse, the union organizers "might just as well give

---

[8] F. J. Roethlisberger and William J. Dickson, op. cit., Part IV, pp. 379 ff.

[9] For further evidence on this point, see Stanley B. Mathewson, *Restriction of Output among Unorganized Workers,* and also Elton Mayo, *The Human Problems of an Industrial Civilization,* pp. 119–121.

up" their efforts. With reluctance the girls reversed their decision and accepted the upgrading. Both girls at once needed the attention of an interviewer: they had liked the former group in which they had earned informal membership. Both felt adjustment to a new group and a novel situation as involving effort and private discontent. From both much was learned of the intimate organization and common practices of their groups, and their adjustments to their new groups were eased, thereby effectively helping reconstitute the teamwork in those groups.

In another recent interview a girl of eighteen protested to an interviewer that her mother was continually urging her to ask Mr. X, her supervisor, for a "raise." She had refused, but her loyalty to her mother and the pressure the latter exerted were affecting her work and her relations at work. She talked her situation out with an interviewer, and it became clear that to her a "raise" would mean departure from her daily companions and associates. Although not immediately relevant, it is interesting to note that, after explaining the situation at length to the interviewer, she was able to present her case dispassionately to her mother—without exaggeration or protest. The mother immediately understood and abandoned pressure for advancement, and the girl returned to effective work. This last instance illustrates one way in which the interview clears lines of communication of emotional blockage—within as without the plant. But this is not my immediate topic; my point is rather that the age-old human desire for persistence of human association will seriously complicate the development of an adaptive society if we cannot devise systematic methods of easing individuals from one group of associates into another.

But such an observation was not possible in the earliest inquiry. The important fact brought to the attention of the research division was that the ordinary conception of management-worker relation as existing between company officials, on the one hand, and an unspecified number of individuals, on the other, is utterly mistaken. Management, in any continuously successful plant, is not related to single workers but always to working groups. In every department that continues to operate, the workers have—whether aware of it or not—formed themselves into a group with appropriate customs, duties, routines, even rituals; and management succeeds (or fails) in proportion as it is accepted without reservation by the group as authority and leader. This, for example, occurred in the relay assembly test room at Hawthorne. Management, by consultation with the girl workers, by clear explanation of the proposed experiments and the reasons for them, by accepting the workers' verdict in special instances, unwittingly scored a success in two most important human matters—the girls became a self-governing team, and a team that cooperated wholeheartedly with management. The test room was responsible for many important findings —rest periods, hours of work, food, and the like: but the most important finding of all was unquestionably in the general area of teamwork and cooperation.

It was at this time that the research division published, for private circulation within the company, a monograph entitled "Complaints and Grievances." Careful description of many varied situations within the interviewers' experience showed that an articulate complaint only rarely, if ever, gave any logical clue to the grievance in which it had origin; this applied at least as strongly to groups as to individuals. Whereas economists and industry generally *tend to concentrate upon the complaint and upon logical inferences from its articulate statement* as an appropriate procedure, the interviewing group had learned almost to ignore, except as symptom, the—sometimes noisy—manifestation of discomfort and to study the situation anew to gain knowledge of its source. Diagnosis rather than argument became the proper method of procedure.

It is possible to quote an illustration from a recently published book, *China Enters the Machine Age.*[10] When industries had to be moved, during this war, from Shanghai and the Chinese coast to Kunming in the interior of China, the actual operation of an industry still depended for the most part on skilled workers who

---

[10] Shih Kuo-heng (Cambridge, Harvard University Press, 1944).

were refugees from Shanghai and elsewhere. These skilled workers knew their importance to the work and gained considerable prestige from it; nevertheless discontent was rife among them. Evidence of this was manifested by the continual, deliberate breaking of crockery in the company mess hall and complaints about the quality of the food provided. Yet this food was much better than could have been obtained outside the plant—especially at the prices charged. And in interview the individual workers admitted freely that the food was good and could not rightly be made the subject of complaint. But the relationship between the skilled workers as a group and the *Chih Yuan*—the executive and supervisory officers—was exceedingly unsatisfactory.

Many of these officers—the *Chih Yuan*—have been trained in the United States—enough at least to set a pattern for the whole group. Now in America we have learned in actual practice to accept the rabble hypothesis* with reservations. But the logical Chinese student of engineering or economics, knowing nothing of these practical reservations, returns to his own country convinced that the workman who is not wholly responsive to the "financial incentive" is a troublemaker and a nuisance. And the Chinese worker lives up to this conviction by breaking plates.[11] Acceptance of the complaint about the food and collective bargaining of a logical type conducted at that level would surely have been useless.

Yet this is what industry, not only in China, does every day, with the high sanction of State authority and the alleged aid of lawyers and economists. In their behavior and their statements, economists indicate that they accept the rabble hypothesis and its dismal corollary of financial incentive as the only effective human motive. They substitute a logical hypothesis of small practical value for the actual facts.

---

[11] Ibid., Chap. VIII, pp. 111–127; also Chap. X, pp. 151–153.

---

* See footnote, page 388.—EDITOR

The insight gained by the interviewing group, on the other hand, cannot be described as substituting irrational for rational motive, emotion for logic. On the contrary, it implies a need for competent study of complaints and the grievances that provoke them, a need for knowledge of the actual facts rather than acceptance of an outdated theory. It is amusing that certain industrialists, rigidly disciplined in economic theory, attempt to shrug off the Hawthorne studies as "theoretic." Actually the shoe is on the other foot; Hawthorne has restudied the facts without prejudice, whereas the critics have unquestioningly accepted that theory of man which had its vogue in the nineteenth century and has already outlived its usefulness.

The Hawthorne interview program has moved far since its beginning in 1929. Originally designed to study the comfort of workers in their work as a mass of individuals, it has come to clear specification of the relation of working groups to management as one of the fundamental problems of large-scale industry. It was indeed this study that first enabled us to assert that the third major preoccupation of management must be that of organizing teamwork, that is to say, of developing and sustaining cooperation.

In summary, certain entirely practical discoveries must be enumerated.

First, the early discovery that the interview aids the individual to get rid of useless emotional complications and to state his problem clearly. He is thus enabled to give himself good advice—a procedure far more effective than advice accepted from another. I have already given instances of this in discussing "emotional release" and the influence on individual attitude of personal history and personal situation.

Second, the interview has demonstrated its capacity to aid the individual to associate more easily, more satisfactorily, with other persons—fellow workers or supervisors—with whom he is in daily contact.

Third, the interview not only helps the individual to collaborate better with his own group of workers, it also develops his desire and capacity to work better with management. In this it resembles somewhat the action of the Philadelphia colonel.[12] Someone, the interviewer, representing (for the worker) the plant organization outside his own group, has aided him to work better with his own group. This is the beginning of the necessary double loyalty— to his own group and to the larger organization. It remains only for management to make wise use of this beginning.

Fourth, beyond all this, interviewing possesses immense importance for the training of administrators in the difficult future that faces this continent and the world. It has been said that the interviewer has no authority and takes no action. Action can only be taken by the proper authority and through the formally constituted line of authority. The interviewer, however, contributes much to the facilitation of communication both up and down that line. He does this, first, by clearing away emotional distortion and exaggeration; second, his work manifestly aids to exact and objective statement the grievance that lies beyond the various complaints.

Work of this kind is immensely effective in the development of maturity of attitude and judgment in the intelligent and sensitive young men and women who give time to it. The subordination of oneself, of one's opinions and ideas, of the very human desire to give gratuitous advice, the subordination of all these to an intelligent effort to help another express ideas and feelings that he cannot easily express is, in itself, a most desirable education. As a preparation for the exercise of administrative responsibility, it is better than anything offered in a present university curriculum. It is no doubt necessary to train young men and women to present their knowledge and ideas with lucidity. But, if they are to be administrators, it is far more necessary to train them to listen carefully to what others say. Only he who knows how to help other persons to adequate expression can develop the many qualities demanded by a real maturity of judgment.

Finally, there remains the claim made above that the interview has proved to be the source of information of great objective value

---

[12] Chap. III, supra. [See pp. 379–388.—EDITOR]

to management. The three persistent problems of modern large-scale industry have been stated as:

1. The application of science and technical skill to a material product.
2. The systematization of operations.
3. The organization of sustained cooperation.

When a representative of management claims that interview results are merely personal or subjective—and there are many who still echo this claim—he is actually telling us that he has himself been trained to give all his attention to the first and second problems, technical skill and the systematic ordering of operations; he does not realize that he has also been trained to ignore the third problem completely. For such persons, information on a problem, the existence of which they do not realize, is no information. It is no doubt in consequence of this ignorance or induced blindness that strikes or other difficulties so frequently occur in unexpected places. The interview method is the only method extant[13] that can contribute reasonably accurate information, or indeed any information, as to the extent of the actual cooperation between workers—teamwork—that obtains in a given department, and beyond this, the extent to which this cooperation includes management policy or is wary of it. The Hawthorne inquiry at least specified these most important industrial issues and made some tentative steps toward the development of a method of diagnosis and treatment in particular cases.

---

[13] We realize that there are at present in industry many individuals possessed of high skill in the actual handling of human situations. This skill usually derives from their own experience, is intuitive, and is not easily communicable.

CHESTER IRVING BARNARD

(1 8 8 6 – 1 9 6 1)

CHESTER BARNARD took up where Henri Fayol (p. 187) left off. Barnard not only believed that management principles could be applied to any type of organization in any field; he also proved it in practice.

During his career he managed business, governmental, educational, and philanthropic organizations with uniform success, notably as president of the New Jersey Bell Telephone Company from 1927 to 1948, and as president of the Rockefeller Foundation and General Education Board from 1948 until his retirement in 1952. In the Second World War he also served as national president of the United Service Organizations, a job he called "the most difficult single organization task in my experience." But his management beliefs and practices stood the test here, too.

Barnard, however, was much more than a successful executive. With his scholarly mind, he was a pioneer in developing the philosophical groundwork of management, and in laying it he went deep into sociology, psychology, and abstract reasoning. Thus much of his masterwork, *The Functions of the Executive,* is difficult to read—if Fayol is the Francis Bacon of management literature, Barnard is surely its Thorstein Veblen. Nevertheless, the book is well worth the effort of study by the practicing manager, and the chapter from it that follows is unusually direct in style. This is also true of "The Nature of Leadership" (p. 432), which sums up Barnard's thinking on what he regards as the key factor in all organizational activity.

THE THEORY OF AUTHORITY

BY CHESTER I. BARNARD

IN this chapter we consider a subject which in one aspect relates to the "willingness of individuals to contribute to organizations," the element of organization presented in the preceding chapter; and in a second aspect is the most general phase of the element "communication."

I. The Source of Authority

If it is true that all complex organizations consist of aggregations of unit organizations and have grown only from unit organizations, we may reasonably postulate that, whatever the nature of authority, it is inherent in the simple organization unit; and that a correct theory of authority must be consistent with what is essentially true of these unit organizations. We shall, therefore, regard the observations which we can make of the actual conditions as at first a source for discovering what is essential in elementary and simple organizations.

Now a most significant fact of general observation relative to authority is the extent to which it is ineffective in specific instances. It is so ineffective that the violation of authority is accepted as a matter of course and its implications are not considered. It is true that we are sometimes appalled at the extent of major criminal activities; but we pass over very lightly the universal violations, particularly of sumptuary laws, which are as "valid" as any others. Even clauses of constitutions and statutes carrying them "into effect," such as the Eighteenth Amendment, are violated in wholesale degrees.

Violation of law is not, however, peculiar to our own country. I observed recently in a totalitarian state under a dictator, where personal liberty is supposed to be at a minimum and arbitrary authority at a maximum, many violations of positive law or edict, some of them open and on a wide scale; and I was reliably informed of others.

Nor is this condition peculiar to the authority of the state. It is likewise true of the authority of churches. The Ten Commandments and the prescriptions and prohibitions of religious authority are repeatedly violated by those who profess to acknowledge their formal authority.

These observations do not mean that all citizens are lawless and defy authority; nor that all Christians are godless or their conduct unaffected by the tenets of their faith. It is obvious that to a large extent citizens are governed; and that the conduct of Christians is substantially qualified by the prescriptions of their churches. What is implied is merely that which specific laws will be obeyed or disobeyed by the individual citizen are decided by him under the specific conditions pertinent. This is what we mean when we refer to individual responsibility. It implies that which prescriptions of the church will be disobeyed by the individual are determined by him at a given time and place. This is what we mean by moral responsibility.

It may be thought that ineffectiveness of authority in specific cases is chiefly exemplified in matters of state and church, but not in those of smaller organizations which are more closely knit or more concretely managed. But this is not true. It is surprising how much that in theory is authoritative, in the best of organizations, in practice lacks authority—or, in plain language, how generally orders are disobeyed. For many years the writer has been interested to observe this fact, not only in organizations with which he was directly connected, but in many others. In all of them, armies, navies, universities, penal institutions, hospitals, relief organizations, corporations, the same conditions prevail—dead laws, regulations, rules, which no one dares bury but which are not obeyed; obvious disobedience carefully disregarded; vital practices and major institutions for which there is no authority, like the Democratic and Republican parties, not known to the Constitution.

We may leave the secondary stages of this analysis for later consideration. What we derive from it is an approximate definition of authority for our purpose: Authority is the character of a communication (order) in a formal organization by virtue of which it is accepted by a contributor to or "member" of the organization as governing the action he contributes; that is, as governing or determining what he does or is not to do so far as the organization is concerned. According to this definition, authority involves two aspects: first, the subjective, the personal, the *accepting* of a communication as authoritative, the aspects which I shall present in this section; and, second, the objective aspect—the character in the communication by virtue of which it is accepted—which I present in the second section, "The System of Coördination."

If a directive communication is accepted by one to whom it is addressed, its authority for him is confirmed or established. It is admitted as the basis of action. Disobedience of such a communication is a denial of its authority for him. Therefore, under this definition the decision as to whether an order has authority or not lies with the persons to whom it is addressed, and does not reside in "persons of authority" or those who issue these orders.

This is so contrary to the view widely held by informed persons of many ranks and professions, and so contradictory to legalistic conceptions, and will seem to many so opposed to common experience, that it will be well at the outset to quote two opinions of persons in a position to merit respectful attention. It is not the intention to "argue from authorities"; but before attacking the subject it is desirable at least to recognize that prevalent notions are not universally held. Says Roberto Michels in the monograph "Authority" in the

Encyclopaedia of the Social Sciences,[1] "Whether authority is of personal or institutional origin it is created and maintained by public opinion, which in its turn is conditioned by sentiment, affection, reverence or fatalism. Even when authority rests on mere physical coercion it is *accepted* [2] by those ruled, although the acceptance may be due to a fear of force."

Again, Major-General James G. Harbord, of long and distinguished military experience, and since his retirement from the Army a notable business executive, says on page 259 of his *The American Army in France*: [3]

> A democratic President had forgotten that the greatest of all democracies is an Army. Discipline and morale influence the inarticulate vote that is instantly taken by masses of men when the order comes to move forward—a variant of the crowd psychology that inclines it to follow a leader, but the Army does not move forward until the motion has "carried." "Unanimous consent" only follows cooperation between the *individual* men in the ranks.

These opinions are to the effect that even though physical force is involved, and even under the extreme condition of battle, when the regime is nearly absolute, authority nevertheless rests upon the acceptance or consent of individuals. Evidently such conceptions, if justified, deeply affect an appropriate understanding of organization and especially of the character of the executive functions

Our definition of authority, like General Harbord's democracy in an army, no doubt will appear to many whose eyes are fixed only on enduring organizations to be a platform of chaos. And so it is— exactly so in the preponderance of attempted organizations. They fail because they can maintain no authority, that is, they cannot secure sufficient contributions of personal efforts to be effective or cannot induce them on terms that are efficient. In the last analysis the authority fails because the individuals in sufficient numbers re-

[1] New York: Macmillan.
[2] Italics mine.
[3] Boston: Little, Brown and Co., 1936.

gard the burden involved in accepting necessary orders as changing the balance of advantage against their interest, and they withdraw or withhold the indispensable contributions.

We must not rest our definition, however, on general opinion. The necessity of the assent of the individual to establish authority *for him* is inescapable. A person can and will accept a communication as authoritative only when four conditions simultaneously obtain: (*a*) he can and does understand the communication; (*b*) *at the time of his decision* he believes that it is not inconsistent with the purpose of the organization; (*c*) *at the time of his decision,* he believes it to be compatible with his personal interest as a whole; and (*d*) he is able mentally and physically to comply with it.

(*a*) A communication that cannot be understood *can* have no authority. An order issued, for example, in a language not intelligible to the recipient is no order at all—no one would so regard it. Now, many orders are exceedingly difficult to understand. They are often necessarily stated in general terms, and the persons who issued them could not themselves apply them under many conditions. Until interpreted they have no meaning. The recipient either must disregard them or merely do anything in the hope that that is compliance.

Hence, a considerable part of administrative work consists in the interpretation and reinterpretation of orders in their application to concrete circumstances that were not or could not be taken into account initially.

(*b*) A communication believed by the recipient to be incompatible with the purpose of the organization, as he understands it, could not be accepted. Action would be frustrated by cross purposes. The most common practical example is that involved in conflicts of orders. They are not rare. An intelligent person will deny the authority of that one which contradicts the purpose of the effort as *he* understands it. In extreme cases many individuals would be virtually paralyzed by conflicting orders. They would be literally unable to comply—for example, an employee of a water system ordered to blow up an essential pump, or soldiers ordered to shoot their own comrades. I suppose all experienced executives know that when it is necessary to issue orders that will appear to the recipients to be contrary to the main purpose, especially as exemplified in prior habitual practice, it is usually necessary and always advisable, if practicable, to explain or demonstrate why the appearance of conflict is an illusion. Otherwise the orders are likely not to be executed, or to be executed inadequately.

(*c*) If a communication is believed to involve a burden that destroys the net advantage of connection with the organization, there no longer would remain a net inducement to the individual to contribute to it. The existence of a net inducement is the only reason for accepting *any* order as having authority. Hence, if such an order is received it must be disobeyed (evaded in the more usual cases) as utterly inconsistent with personal motives that are the basis of accepting any orders at all. Cases of voluntary resignation from all sorts of organizations are common for this sole reason. Malingering and intentional lack of dependability are the more usual methods.

(*d*) If a person is unable to comply with an order, obviously it must be disobeyed, or, better, disregarded. To order a man who cannot swim to swim a river is a sufficient case. Such extreme cases are not frequent; but they occur. The more usual case is to order a man to do things only a little beyond his capacity; but a little impossible is still impossible.

Naturally the reader will ask: How is it possible to secure such important and enduring coöperation as we observe if in principle and in fact the determination of authority lies with the subordinate individual? It is possible because the decisions of individuals occur under the following conditions: (*a*) orders that are deliberately issued in enduring organizations usually comply with the four conditions mentioned above; (*b*) there exists a "zone of indifference" in each individual within which orders are acceptable without conscious questioning of their authority; (*c*) the interests of the persons who contribute to an organization as a group result in the exercise of an influence on the subject, or on the attitude of the individual, that maintains a certain stability of this zone of indifference.

(*a*) There is no principle of executive conduct better established in good organizations than that orders will not be issued that cannot

or will not be obeyed. Executives and most persons of experience
who have thought about it know that to do so destroys authority,
discipline, and morale.[4] For reasons to be stated shortly, this principle cannot ordinarily be formally admitted, or at least cannot be
professed. When it appears necessary to issue orders which are initially or apparently unacceptable, either careful preliminary education, or persuasive efforts, or the prior offering of effective inducements will be made, so that the issue will not be raised, the denial of
authority will not occur, and orders will be obeyed. It is generally
recognized that those who least understand this fact—newly appointed minor or "first line" executives—are often guilty of "disor-
ganizing" their groups for this reason, as do experienced executives
who lose self-control or become unbalanced by a delusion of power
or for some other reason. Inexperienced persons take literally the
current notions of authority and are then said "not to know how to

[4] Barring relatively few individual cases, when the attitude of the individual indicates in advance likelihood of disobedience (either before or after connection with
the organization), the connection is terminated or refused before the formal question
arises.

It seems advisable to add a caution here against interpreting the exposition in terms
of "democracy," whether in governmental, religious, or industrial organizations. The
dogmatic assertion that "democracy" or "democratic methods" are (or are not) in
accordance with the principles here discussed is not tenable. As will be more evident
after the consideration of objective authority, the issues involved are much too complex and subtle to be taken into account in *any* formal scheme. Under many conditions
in the political, religious, and industrial fields democratic processes create artificial
questions of more or less logical character, in place of the real questions, which are
matters of feeling and appropriateness and of informal organization. By oversimplifi-
cation of issues this may destroy objective authority. No doubt in many situations
formal democratic processes may be an important element in the maintenance of
authority, i.e., of organization cohesion, but may in other situations be disruptive, and
probably never could be, in themselves, sufficient. On the other hand the solidarity
of some coöperative systems (General Harbord's army, for example) under many conditions may be unexcelled, though requiring formally autocratic processes.

Moreover, it should never be forgotten that authority in the aggregate arises from
all the contributors to a coöperative system, and that the weighting to be attributed
to the attitude of individuals varies. It is often forgotten that in industrial (or political)
organizations measures which are acceptable at the bottom may be quite unacceptable to the substantial proportion of contributors who are executives, and who will
no more perform their essential functions than will others, if the conditions are, to
them, impossible. The point to be emphasized is that the maintenance of the contributions necessary to the endurance of an organization requires the authority of *all*
essential contributors.

use authority" or "to abuse authority." Their superiors often profess the same beliefs about authority in the abstract, but their successful practice is easily observed to be inconsistent with their professions.

(*b*) The phrase "zone of indifference" may be explained as follows: If all the orders for actions reasonably practicable be arranged in the order of their acceptability to the person affected, it may be conceived that there are a number which are clearly unacceptable, that is, which certainly will not be obeyed; there is another group somewhat more or less on the neutral line, that is, either barely acceptable or barely unacceptable; and a third group unquestionably acceptable. This last group lies within the "zone of indifference." The person affected will accept orders lying within this zone and is relatively indifferent as to what the order is so far as the question of authority is concerned. Such an order lies within the range that in a general way was anticipated at time of undertaking the connection with the organization. For example, if a soldier enlists, whether voluntarily or not, in an army in which the men are ordinarily moved about within a certain broad region, it is a matter of indifference whether the order be to go to A or B, C or D, and so on; and goings to A, B, C, D, etc., are in the zone of indifference.

The zone of indifference will be wider or narrower depending upon the degree to which the inducements exceed the burdens and sacrifices which determine the individual's adhesion to the organization. It follows that the range of orders that will be accepted will be very limited among those who are barely induced to contribute to the system.

(*c*) Since the efficiency of organization is affected by the degree to which individuals assent to orders, denying the authority of an organization communication is a threat to the interests of all individuals who derive a net advantage from their connection with the organization, unless the orders are unacceptable to them also. Accordingly, at any given time there is among most of the contributors an active personal interest in the maintenance of the authority of all orders which to them are within the zone of indifference. The maintenance of this interest is largely a function of informal organization. Its expression goes under the names of "public opinion," "organization opinion," "feeling in the ranks," "group attitude," etc. Thus the common sense of the community informally arrived at affects the attitude of individuals, and makes them, as individuals, loath to question authority that is within or near the zone of indifference. The formal statement of this common sense is the fiction that authority comes down from above, from the general to the particular. This fiction merely establishes a presumption among individuals in favor of the acceptability of orders from superiors, enabling them to avoid making issues of such orders without incurring a sense of personal subserviency or a loss of personal or individual status with their fellows.

Thus the contributors are willing to maintain the authority of communications because, where care is taken to see that only acceptable communications in general are issued, most of them fall within the zone of personal indifference; and because communal sense influences the motives of most contributors most of the time. The practical instrument of this sense is the fiction of superior authority, which makes it possible normally to treat a personal question impersonally.

The fiction [5] of superior authority is necessary for two main reasons:

(1) It is the process by which the individual delegates upward, or to the organization, responsibility for what is an organization decision—an action which is depersonalized by the fact of its coördinate character. This means that if an instruction is disregarded, an executive's risk of being wrong must be accepted, a risk that the individual cannot and usually will not take unless in fact his position is at least as good as that of another with respect to correct appraisal of the relevant situation. Most persons are disposed to grant authority because they dislike the personal responsibility which they otherwise accept, especially when they are not in a good position to accept it. The practical difficulties in the operation of organization seldom lie in the excessive desire of individuals to assume responsibility for the organization action of themselves or others, but rather

---

[5] The word "fiction" is used because from the standpoint of logical construction it merely explains overt acts. Either as a superior officer or as a subordinate, however, I know nothing that I actually regard as more "real" than "authority."

lie in the reluctance to take responsibility for their own actions in organization.

(2) The fiction gives impersonal notice that what is at stake is the good of the organization. If objective authority is flouted for arbitrary or merely temperamental reasons, if, in other words, there is deliberate attempt to twist an organization requirement to personal advantage, rather than properly to safeguard a substantial personal interest, then there is a deliberate attack on the organization itself. To remain outside an organization is not necessarily to be more than not friendly or not interested. To fail in an obligation intentionally is an act of hostility. This no organization can permit; and it must respond with punitive action if it can, even to the point of incarcerating or executing the culprit. This is rather generally the case where a person has agreed in advance in general what he will do. Leaving an organization in the lurch is not often tolerable.

The correctness of what has been said above will perhaps appear most probable from a consideration of the difference between executive action in emergency and that under "normal" conditions. In times of war the disciplinary atmosphere of an army is intensified— it is rather obvious to all that its success and the safety of its members are dependent upon it. In other organizations, abruptness of command is not only tolerated in times of emergency, but expected, and the lack of it often would actually be demoralizing. It is the sense of the justification which lies in the obvious situation which regulates the exercise of the veto by the final authority which lies at the bottom. This is a commonplace of executive experience, though it is not a commonplace of conversation about it.[6]

[6] It will be of interest to quote a statement which has appeared since these lines were written, in a pamphlet entitled "Business—Well on the Firing Line" (No. 9 in the series "What Helps Business Helps You," in *Nation's Business*). It reads in part: "Laws don't create Teamplay. It is not called into play by law. For every written rule there are a thousand unwritten rules by which the course of business is guided, which govern the millions of daily transactions of which business consists. These rules are not applied from the top down, by arbitrary authority. They grow out of actual practice—from the bottom up. They are based upon mutual understanding and compromise, the desire to achieve common ends and further the common good. They are observed *voluntarily*, because they have the backing of experience and common sense."

II. The System of Coördination

Up to this point we have devoted our attention to the subjective aspect of authority. The executive, however, is predominantly occupied not with this subjective aspect, which is fundamental, but with the objective character of a communication which induces acceptance.

Authority has been defined in part as a "character of a communication in a formal organization." A "superior" is not in our view an authority nor does he have authority strictly speaking; nor is a communication authoritative except when it is an effort or action of organization. This is what we mean when we say that individuals are able to exercise authority only when they are acting "officially," a principle well established in law, and generally in secular and religious practice. Hence the importance ascribed to time, place, dress, ceremony, and authentication of a communication to establish its official character. These practices confirm the statement that authority relates to a communication "in a formal organization." There often occur occasions of compulsive power of individuals and of hostile groups; but authority is always concerned with something *within* a definitely organized system. Current usage conforms to the definition in this respect. The word "authority" is seldom employed except where formal organization connection is stated or implied (unless, of course, the reference is obviously figurative).

These circumstances arise from the fact that the character of authority in organization communications lies in the *potentiality of assent* of those to whom they are sent. Hence, they are only sent to contributors or "members" of the organization. Since all authoritative communications are official and relate only to organization action, they have no meaning to those whose actions are not included within the coöperative system. This is clearly in accord with the common understanding. The laws of one country have no authority for citizens of another, except under special circumstances. Employers do not issue directions to employees of other organizations. Officials would appear incompetent who issued orders to those outside their jurisdiction.

A communication has the presumption of authority when it originates at sources of organization information—a communications center—better than individual sources. It loses this presumption, however, if not within the scope or field of this center. The presumption is also lost if the communication shows an absence of adjustment to the actual situation which confronts the recipient of it.

Thus men impute authority to communications from superior positions, provided they are reasonably consistent with advantages of scope and perspective that are credited to those positions. This authority is to a considerable extent independent of the personal ability of the incumbent of the position. It is often recognized that though the incumbent may be of limited personal ability his advice may be superior solely by reason of the advantage of position. This is the *authority of position.*

But it is obvious that some men have superior ability. Their knowledge and understanding regardless of position command respect. Men impute authority to what they say in an organization for this reason only. This is the *authority of leadership.* When the authority of leadership is combined with the authority of position, men who have an established connection with an organization generally will grant authority, accepting orders far outside the zone of indifference. The confidence engendered may even make compliance an inducement in itself.

Nevertheless, the determination of authority remains with the individual. Let these "positions" of authority in fact show ineptness, ignorance of conditions, failure to communicate what ought to be said, or let leadership fail (chiefly by its concrete action) to recognize implicitly its dependence upon the essential character of the relationship of the individual to the organization, and the authority if tested disappears.

This objective authority is only maintained if the positions or leaders continue to be adequately informed. In very rare cases persons possessing great knowledge, insight, or skill have this adequate information without occupying executive position. What they say ought to be done or ought not to be done will be accepted. But this is usually personal advice at the risk of the taker. Such persons have influence rather than authority. In most cases genuine leaders who give advice concerning organized efforts are required to accept positions of responsibility; for knowledge of the applicability of their special knowledge or judgment to concrete *organization* action, not to abstract problems, is essential to the worth of what they say as a basis of organization authority. In other words, they have an organization personality, as distinguished from their individual personality, commensurate with the influence of their leadership. The common way to state this is that there cannot be authority without corresponding responsibility. A more exact expression would be that objective authority cannot be imputed to persons in organization positions unless subjectively they are dominated by the organization as respects their decisions.

It may be said, then, that the maintenance of objective authority adequate to support the fiction of superior authority and able to make the zone of indifference an actuality depends upon the operation of the system of communication in the organization. The function of this system is to supply adequate information to the positions of authority and adequate facilities for the issuance of orders. To do so it requires commensurate capacities in those able to be leaders. High positions that are not so supported have weak authority, as do strong men in minor positions.

Thus authority depends upon a coöperative personal attitude of individuals on the one hand; and the system of communication in the organization on the other. Without the latter, the former cannot be maintained. The most devoted adherents of an organization will quit it, if its system results in inadequate, contradictory, inept orders, so that they cannot know who is who, what is what, or have the sense of effective coördination.

This system of communication, or its maintenance, is a primary or essential continuing problem of a formal organization. Every other practical question of effectiveness or efficiency—that is, of the factors of survival—depends upon it. In technical language the system of communication of which we are now speaking is often known as the "lines of authority."

It has already been shown that the requirements of communication determine the size of unit organizations, the grouping of units, the grouping of groups of unit organizations. We may now consider the controlling factors in the character of the communication system as a system of objective authority.

(*a*) The first is that *channels of communication should be definitely known*. The language in which this principle is ordinarily stated is, "The lines of authority must be definitely established." The method of doing so is by making official appointments known; by assigning each individual to his position; by general announcements; by organization charts; by educational effort; and most of all by habituation, that is, by securing as much permanence of system as is practicable. Emphasis is laid either upon the position, or upon the persons; but usually the fixing of authority is made both to positions and, less emphatically, to persons.

(*b*) Next, we may say that *objective authority requires a definite formal channel of communication to every member of an organization*. In ordinary language this means "everyone must report to someone" (communication in one direction) and "everyone must be subordinate to someone" (communication in the other direction). In other words, in formal organizations everyone must have definite formal relationship to the organization.[7]

(*c*) Another factor is that *the line of communication must be as direct or short as possible*. This may be explained as follows: Substantially all formal communication is verbal (written or oral). Language as a vehicle of communication is limited and susceptible of misunderstanding. Much communication is necessarily without preparation. Even communications that are carefully prepared require interpretation. Moreover, communications are likely to be in more general terms the more general—that is, the higher—the position. It follows that something may be lost or added by transmission at each stage of the process, especially when communication is oral, or when at each stage there is combination of several communications. Moreover, when communications go from high positions down they often must be made more specific as they proceed; and when in the reverse di-

---

[7] In some types of organizations it is not unusual, however, for one person to report to and to be subordinate to two or three "superiors," in which case the functions of the superiors are defined and are mutually exclusive in principle.

rection, usually more general. In addition, the speed of communication, other things equal, will be less the greater the number of centers through which it passes. Accordingly, the shorter the line the greater the speed and the less the error.

How important this factor is may be indicated by the remarkable fact that in great complex organizations the number of levels of communication is not much larger than in smaller organizations. In most organizations consisting of the services of one or two hundred men the levels of communication will be from three to five. In the Army the levels are: President (Secretary of War), General, Major-General, Brigadier-General, Colonel, Major, Captain, Lieutenant, Sergeant, men—that is, nine or ten. In the Bell Telephone System, with over 300,000 working members, the number is eight to ten.[8] A similar shortness of the line of communication is noteworthy in the Catholic Church viewed from the administrative standpoint.

Many organization practices or inventions are used to accomplish this end, depending upon the purpose and technical conditions. Briefly, these methods are: The use of expanded executive organizations at each stage; the use of the staff department (technical, expert, advisory); the division of executive work into functional bureaus; and processes of delegating responsibility with automatic coördination through regular conference procedures, committees for special temporary functions, etc.

(*d*) Another factor is that, in principle, *the complete line of communication should usually be used.* By this is meant that a communication from the head of an organization to the bottom should pass through every stage of the line of authority. This is due to the necessity of avoiding conflicting communications (in either direction) which might (and would) occur if there were any "jumping of the line" of organization. It is also necessary because of the need of interpretation, and to maintain responsibility.[9]

---

[8] Disregarding the corporate aspects of the organization, and not including board of directors.

[9] These by no means exhaust the considerations. The necessity of maintaining personal prestige of executives as an *inducement to them* to function is on the whole an important additional reason.

(e) Again, the *competence of the persons serving as communication centers, that is, officers, supervisory heads, must be adequate.* The competence required is that of more and more *general* ability with reference to the work of the entire organization the more central the office of commmunication and the larger the organization. For the function of the center of communication in an organization is to translate incoming communications concerning external conditions, the progress of activity, successes, failures, difficulties, dangers, into outgoing communications in terms of new activities, preparatory steps, etc., all shaped according to the ultimate as well as the immediate purposes to be served. There is accordingly required more or less mastery of the technologies involved, of the capabilities of the personnel, of the informal organization situation, of the character and status of the subsidiary organizations, of the principles of action relative to purpose, of the interpretation of environmental factors, and a power of discrimination between communications that can possess authority because they are recognizably compatible with *all* the pertinent conditions and those which will not possess authority because they will not or cannot be accepted.

It is a fact, I think, that we hardly nowadays expect individual personal ability adequate to positional requirements of communication in modern large-scale organization. The limitations of individuals as respects time and energy alone preclude such personal ability, and the complexity of the technologies or other special knowledge involved make it impossible. For these reasons each major center of communication is itself organized, sometimes quite elaborately. The immediate staff of the executive (commanding officer), consisting of deputies, or chief clerks, or adjutants, or auxiliaries with their assistants, constitute an executive unit of organization only one member of which is perhaps an "executive," that is, occupies the *position* of authority; and the technical matters are assigned to staff departments or organizations of experts. Such staff departments often are partly "field" departments in the sense that they directly investigate or secure information on facts or conditions external to the organizations; but in major part in most cases they digest and translate information from the field, and prepare the plans, orders, etc., for transmission. In this capacity they are advisory or adjutant to the executives. In practice, however, these assistants have the function of semi-formal advice under regulated conditions to the organizations as a whole. In this way, both the formal channels and the informal organizations are supplemented by intermediate processes.

In some cases the executive (either chief or some subordinate executive) may be not a person but a board, a legislature, a committee. I know of no important organizations, except some churches and some absolute governments, in which the highest objective authority is not lodged in an *organized* executive group, that is, a "highest" unit of organization.

(f) Again, *the line of communication should not be interrupted during the time when the organization is to function.* Many organizations (factories, stores) function intermittently, being closed or substantially so during the night, Sundays, etc. Others, such as army, police, railroad systems, telephone systems, never cease to operate. During the times when organizations are at work, in principle the line of authority must never be broken; and practically this is almost, if not quite, literally true in many cases. This is one of the reasons which may be given for the great importance attached to hereditary succession in states, and for the elaborate provision that is made in most organizations (except possibly small "personal" organizations) for the temporary filling of offices automatically during incapacity or absence of incumbents. These provisions emphasize the non-personal and communication character of organization authority, as does the persistent emphasis upon the *office* rather than the *man* that is a matter of indoctrination of many organizations, especially those in which "discipline" is an important feature.

The necessity for this is not merely that specific communications cannot otherwise be attended to. It is at least equally that the *informal* organization disintegrates very quickly if the formal "line of authority" is broken. In organization parlance, "politics" runs riot. Thus, if an office were vacant, but the fact were not known, an organization might function for a considerable time without serious disturbance, except in emergency. But if known, it would quickly become disorganized.

(g) The final factor I shall mention is that *every communication should be authenticated*. This means that the person communicating must be known actually to occupy the "position of authority" concerned; that the position includes the type of communication concerned—that is, it is "within its authority"; and that it actually is an authorized communication from this office. The process of authentication in all three respects varies in different organizations under different conditions and for different positions. The practice is undergoing rapid changes in the modern technique, but the principles remain the same. Ceremonials of investiture, inaugurations, swearing-in, general orders of appointment, induction, and introduction are all essentially appropriate methods of making known who actually fills a position and what the position includes as authority. In order that these *positions* may function it is often necessary that the filling of them should be dramatized, an essential process to the creation of authority *at the bottom*, where only it can be fundamentally—that is, it is essential to inculcate the "sense of organization." This is merely stating that it is essential to "organization loyalty and solidarity" as it may be otherwise expressed. Dignifying the superior position is an important method of dignifying *all* connection with organization, a fact which has been well learned in both religious and political organizations where great attention to the subjective aspects of the "membership" is the rule.

This statement of the principles of communication systems of organizations from the viewpoint of the maintenance of objective authority has necessarily been in terms of complex organizations, since in a simple unit organization the concrete applications of these principles are fused. The principles are with difficulty isolated under simple conditions. Thus, as a matter of course, in unit organizations the channels of communication are known, indeed usually obvious; they are definite; they are the shortest possible; the only lines of authority are complete lines; there is little question of authentication. The doubtful points in unit organization are the competence of the leader, never to be taken for granted even in simple organizations; and whether he is functioning when the organization is in operation. Yet as a whole the adequately balanced maintenance of these aspects of simple leadership is the basis of objective authority in the unit organization, as the maintenance of the more formal and observable manifestations of the same aspects is the basis of authority in the complex organizations.

III. *Reconciliation with Legalistic Conceptions*

Legalistic conceptions of authority, at least somewhat different from those we have presented, seem to have support in the relations between superior and subsidiary organizations. A corporate organization, for example, is subject to the law of the state. Is not this a case where authority actually does come down from the top, from the superior organizations? Only in exactly the same sense that individuals accept objective authority, as we have described it. A subsidiary or dependent organization must accept law to give law its authority. Units of organization, integrated complexes of organization, and dependent organizations make and must make the subjective decision of authority just as individuals do. A corporation may and often does quit if it cannot obey the law and still have a net reason for existence. It is no more able to carry out an unintelligible law than an individual, it can no more do the impossible than an individual, it will show the same inability to conform to conflicting laws as the individual. The only difference between subsidiary, or dependent, unit and group organizations and individuals is that the denial of authority can be made directly by the individual, and either directly or indirectly by the unit, group, or dependent or subsidiary complex. When it is direct, the effect of the law or order upon the organization as a whole is in point; when it is indirect the effect is on the individuals of whose efforts the whole is made up. Thus no complex can carry out a superior order if its members (either unit organizations or individuals) will not enable it to do so. For example, to order by law working conditions which will not be accepted by individual employees, even though the employer is willing, is futile; its authority is in fact denied. The employees quit, then the organization ends.

But in the final analysis the differences are not important, except occasionally in the concrete case. The subsidiary organization in point of fact derives most of its authority for most of its action from its own "members" individually. They may quit if they do not accept the orders, no matter what the "ultimate" authority; and no absolute or external authority can compel the necessary effort beyond a minimum insufficient to maintain efficient or effective organization performance. An important effect of the ascription of legalistic origin of a part of the formal authority of subsidiary and independent organizations has been its obscuring of the nature of the real authority that governs the greater part of the coöperative effort of such organizations.

There is, however, a considerable quantitative difference in the factor of informal organization, that is, the factor of public opinion, general sentiment. This is not a difference of principle, but merely one of the relationship of the size of the informal organization relative to the individual or formal group. A strong individual can resist the domination of opinion if it is confined to a small number; but rarely if there is in question the opinion of an overwhelming number, actively and hostilely expressed. Now the size of any subsidiary organization is small compared with the informal organization that permeates the State; and this wide informal organization will usually support "law and order" regardless of merits if the question at issue is minor from its point of view. The pressure on the subjective attitude of individuals or on that of subsidiary or dependent organizations is strong ordinarily to induce acceptance of law in an "orderly" society.

But this informal support of objective authority of the State depends upon essentially the same principles as in the case of ordinary organizations. Inappropriateness of law and of government administration, lack of understanding of the ultimate basis of authority, indifference to the motives governing individual support, untimely or impossible legislation as is well known destroy "respect for law and order," that is, destroy objective political authority. In democracies the normal reaction is to change law and administration through political action. But when majorities are unable to understand that authority rests fundamentally upon the consent of minorities as well as of majorities, or when the system is autocratic or absolute, the liquidation of attempted tyranny is through revolution or civil war. Authority lies always with him to whom it applies. Coercion creates a contrary illusion; but the use of force *ipso facto* destroys the authority postulated. It creates a new authority, a new situation, a new objective, which is granted when the force is accepted. Many men have destroyed all authority as to themselves by dying rather than yield.

At first thought it may seem that the element of communication in organization is only in part related to authority; but more thorough consideration leads to the understanding that communication, authority, specialization, and purpose are all aspects comprehended in coördination. All communication relates to the formulation of purpose and the transmission of coördinating prescriptions for action and so rests upon the ability to communicate with those willing to coöperate.

Authority is another name for the willingness and capacity of individuals to submit to the necessities of coöperative systems. Authority arises from the technological and social limitations of coöperative systems on the one hand, and of individuals on the other. Hence the status of authority in a society is the measure both of the development of individuals and of the technological and social conditions of the society.

THE NATURE OF LEADERSHIP

BY CHESTER I. BARNARD

L EADERSHIP has been the subject of an extraordinary amount of dogmatically stated nonsense. Some, it is true, has been enunciated by observers who have had no experience themselves in coordinating and directing the activities of others; but much of it has come from men of ample experience, often of established reputations as leaders. As to the latter, we may assume that they know how to do well what they do not know how to describe or explain. At any rate, I have found it difficult not to magnify superficial aspects and catch-phrases of the subject to the status of fundamental propositions, generalized beyond all possibility of useful application, and fostering misunderstanding.

Seeking to avoid such errors, I shall not tell you what leadership is or even how to determine when it is present; for I do not know how to do so. Indeed, I shall venture to assert that probably no one else knows. These statements may seem strange and extreme, but I hope to convince you that they are not expressions of false modesty or of ill-considered judgment. At any rate, what I intend to discuss is *the problem of understanding the nature of leadership.*

The need for wide consideration of this subject was most forcibly impressed upon me by two observations, made on a single occasion, which revealed the extent of public misunderstanding of it. Some time ago I attended a large joint conference of laymen and members

Reprinted by permission of the publishers from *Organization and Management*, by Chester I. Barnard, Chapter IV, pages 80–110. Published by Harvard University Press, Cambridge. Copyright © 1948 by the President and Fellows of Harvard College.

of the faculty of an important university to consider the subject of educational preparation for leadership. At this meeting my first observation was that *leadership* was confused with *preeminence* or *extraordinary usefulness* both by speakers and by audience. In their view a leading writer, artist, pianist, mathematician, or scientist exemplifies leadership substantially as does an executive or leader of an organization. No one appeared to be aware of the double meaning of "leadership" and its implications for the discussion of the subject of preparing "leaders." Among the meanings of the verb "to lead" we may say that one is: "to excel, to be in advance, to be preeminent"; and another is "to guide others, to govern their activities, to be head of an organization or some part of it, to hold command." I think the distinction between these meanings is rather easy to see. Most individuals matured in a well-organized effort recognize it as a matter of course, so that it may be difficult for many who from long experience thoroughly understand the distinction to believe such a confusion common. I fear that it is common, however, and is making cooperation and adequate organization increasingly difficult.

My second observation at this meeting, further evidence of the same fact, was this: During the period of open discussion, a well-known engineer protested the subjection of engineers to supervision or management by those not engineers. The superiority of engineers in nearly all respects, especially in intellect, training, and science, was implied. Though the audience was not one of engineers, it expressed derision generally at the absurd state of affairs portrayed. Could there have been a more striking proof of the misconception of the subject these several hundred earnest, intelligent, educated people were discussing—how better to prepare people to be leaders?

These observations show the importance of public discussion of the problem. Mere knowledge of how to solve it would not be sufficient. Often, in similar matters, when a solution is available it will not be accepted unless the problem itself is either acknowledged as such by reliance upon a responsible authority or is recognized and accepted by agreement and understanding. Otherwise a correct solution is merely "one man's idea, a little queer"; and a "solution" is something that cannot be made effective because it *will* not be used.

This seems often not to be adequately taken into account in the discussion of social and organization "remedies."

Now it seems to me evident that the problem of leadership, like some others which now obsess us, is not yet suitably formulated. For this reason, if for no other, it is not generally understood. This needs emphasis because within our own organizations we usually do not experience much difficulty on this account; for we already have an approximately common understanding or sense, coming from long interconnected experience, which is workably adequate. Such an understanding is a substitute, and a superior one, for abstract knowledge of the matter—at least for any I imagine being available for a long time. But outside these circles of intimate experiential knowledge, understanding fails, even among leaders.

Not only misunderstanding but positive need for leaders warrants our attention to this subject. The large scale integrations of our present societies—the great nations, the immense organizations of war and peace, of culture and religion—make the needs of leadership relatively greater and its functions more complex than heretofore, so that the necessary proportion of leaders to the population has greatly increased. In other words, the "overhead" of any organization or society clearly tends to expand more rapidly than its size. Moreover, technology and specialization make the arts of leadership even more complex than consideration of size alone would indicate. These facts suggest that scarcity of leaders of requisite quality may already limit the possibility of stable cooperation in our societies.

I think we may agree, then, that public misunderstanding and misinformation, and the need for provision of more adequate leadership, both urge our effort to understand the nature of leadership. My present attempt to contribute to this end ought chiefly, I think, to make evident the present obscurity of the subject and the complexity of the functions and conditions involved in it. This method of approach will surely try our patience and may be discouraging to some; but we shall be wise in this matter not to give answers before we have found out what are the questions. The attitude that I think we may best have has been admirably stated by T. S. Eliot:

The fact that a problem will certainly take a long time to solve, and that it will demand the attention of many minds for several generations, is no justification for postponing the study. And, in times of emergency, it may prove in the long run that the problems we have postponed or ignored, rather than those we have failed to attack successfully, will return to plague us. Our difficulties of the moment must always be dealt with somehow; but our permanent difficulties are difficulties of every moment.[1]

In the light of these preliminary remarks it may be well for me to state the meaning of the word "leadership." As I use it herein it refers to the quality of the behavior of individuals whereby they guide people or their activities in organized effort. This is its primary significance. Organized effort takes place, however, in systems of cooperation which often include property or plants. When this is so, the activities coordinated relate to, or are connected with, the property or plant, and the two are not separate. Hence, the management or administration of such properties, as distinguished from the command or supervision of personnel, is also included as a secondary aspect of leadership.

Whatever leadership is, I shall now make the much oversimplified statement that it depends upon three things—(1) the individual, (2) the followers, and (3) the conditions. We shall agree at once, no doubt; but unless we are careful, I suspect that within an hour we shall be talking of the qualities, capacities, talents, and personalities of leaders as if the individual were the exclusive component of leadership. Therefore, let me emphasize the interdependence by restating it in quasi-mathematical language, thus: Leadership appears to be a function of at least three complex variables—the individual, the group of followers, the conditions.

Now the points to note here are two. First, these are variables obviously within wide limits, so that leadership may in practice mean an almost infinite number of possible combinations. Second, if we are to have a good understanding of leadership we shall need a good under-

[1] T. S. Eliot: *The Idea of a Christian Society*, Harcourt, Brace & Co., New York, 1940.

standing of individuals, of organizations, and of conditions, and of their interrelationships so far as relevant to our topic. Do we have that now? I am sure we do not. Yet I fear this may be thought an extreme theoretical view unless I give some demonstration of its correctness, and at the same time give some idea of how we might at least approach some better practical understanding.

In undertaking this, I shall depart from the scheme of the three variables and proceed along more everyday lines. To present my suggestions of possibilities as to the nature of leadership, I shall give the following: (i) A general description of what leaders have to do in four sectors of leadership behavior; (ii) Thoughts concerning certain differences of conditions of leadership; (iii) Some remarks about the active personal qualities of leaders; (iv) A few notes on the problem of the development of leaders; and (v) Observations about the selection of leaders.

I. Four Sectors of Leadership Behavior

Leaders lead. This implies activity, and suggests the obvious question "What is it that they have to do?" Now, I must confess that heretofore on the few occasions when I have been asked: "What do you *do?*" I have been unable to reply intelligibly. Yet I shall attempt here to say generally what leaders do, dividing their work under four topics, which for present purposes will be sufficient. The topics I shall use are: The Determination of Objectives; The Manipulation of Means; The Control of the Instrumentality of Action; and The Stimulation of Coordinated Action.

Unfortunately it is necessary to discuss these topics separately. This is misleading unless it is remembered that, except in special cases or when specially organized, these kinds of action are not separate but closely interrelated, interdependent, and often overlapping or simultaneous. Therein lies one reason why it is so difficult for a leader to say what he does or to avoid misrepresenting himself. He does not know how to untangle his acts in a way suitable for verbal expression. His business is leading, not explaining his own behavior, at which, though sometimes voluble, he is usually rather inept, as we doubtless all are. Indeed, as I shall show later, it is *impossible* for him to be aware of this behavior in the sense necessary to explain it except very generally on the basis of his observations of others as well as of himself.

The Determination of Objectives

Let us consider the first sector of behavior.

An obvious function of a leader is to know and say what to do, what not to do, where to go, and when to stop, with reference to the general purpose or objective of the undertaking in which he is engaged. Such a statement appears to exhaust the ideas of many individuals as to a leader's *raison d'être*. But if they are able to observe the operations closely, it often disconcerts them to note that many things a leader tells others to do were suggested to him by the very people he leads. Unless he is very dynamic—too dynamic, full of his own ideas—or pompous or Napoleonic, this sometimes gives the impression that he is a rather stupid fellow, an arbitrary functionary, a mere channel of communication, and a filcher of ideas. In a measure this is correct. He has to be stupid enough to listen a great deal, he certainly must arbitrate to maintain order, and he has to be at times a mere center of communication. If he used only his own ideas he would be somewhat like a one-man orchestra, rather than a good conductor, who is a very high type of leader.

However, one thing should make us cautious about drawing false conclusions from this description. It is that experience has shown it to be difficult to secure leaders who are able to be properly stupid, to function arbitrarily, to be effective channels of communication, and to steal the right ideas, in such ways that they still retain followers. I do not pretend to be able to explain this very well. It seems to be connected with knowing whom to believe, with accepting the right suggestions, with selecting appropriate occasions and times. It also seems to be so related to conditions that a good leader in one field is not necessarily good in others, and not equally good under all circumstances. But at any rate, to say what to do and when, requires an understanding of a great many things "on the whole," "taking everything into account," in their relations to some purpose or intention or result—an understanding that leads to distinguishing effectively between the important and the unimportant *in the particular concrete situation,* between what can and what cannot be done, between what will probably succeed and what will probably not, between what will weaken cooperation and what will increase it.

The Second Sector—The Manipulation of Means

There is undoubtedly an important difference between the kind of effort we have just considered and the direction of detailed activities that are parts of technical procedures and technological [2] operations as the subsidiary means and instruments of accomplishing specific objectives already determined. Sometimes an exceptional leader can effectively guide technical operations in which he has no special competence, whereas those of high competence are often not successful leaders. I shall not attempt a general explanation of these facts; but on the whole we may regard leadership without technical competence as increasingly exceptional, unless for the most general work. Usually leaders, even though not extraordinarily expert, appear to have an understanding of the technological or technical work which they guide, particularly in its relation to the activities and situations with which they deal. In fact, we usually assume that a leader will have considerable knowledge and experience in the specifically technical aspects of the work he directs. I need not say much about this, for it seems to me that at present we overestimate the importance of technical skill and competence and undervalue, or even exclude, the less tangible and less obvious factors in leadership.

Nevertheless, the technical and technological factors in leadership not only constitute a variable of great importance, but they introduce serious difficulties, which should be mentioned, especially in respect to (1) the development of types of leaders, and to (2) the limitations these technical factors place upon the "mobility" of the leaders in an organization or society, and also (3) because of the restrictive effect of

[2] Throughout I use "technological" exclusively to refer to conditions of physical technology—plants, machines, chemical processes; and "technical" to refer either to systems of procedure in accounting, management, etc., or in a more general sense to cover both ideas.

technical study and experience on the *general* or "social" development of individuals.

(1) It is almost a matter of course that leadership "material" will be inducted into organization through some particular technical channel. Such channels are now highly specialized. When the course has been run, the man has been trained for leadership only with respect to a narrow range of activities. Otherwise he is untrained, and hence (2) the mobility of leadership resources may be seriously reduced because it is difficult to use a good leader of one narrow field in another field or in more general work—a fact which I suppose is now well recognized at least in all large organizations of industry and government and education. This difficulty, which is real, has become exaggerated in our minds, so that in my opinion we all—leaders and followers—tend to overlook superior leaders who at the moment may be lacking particular technical qualifications.

(3) Concerning the third difficulty—the effect of specialization upon the individual—it is only necessary to note that while men are concentrating upon techniques, machines, processes, and abstract knowledge, *they are necessarily diverted to a considerable extent from experience with men, organizations, and the social situations, the distinctive fields of application of leadership ability.* Thus at the most impressionable period they become so well grounded in "mechanical" attitudes toward non-human resources and processes that they transfer these attitudes, then and later, toward men also.

The technical sector of leadership behavior is not a new thing in the world, but its importance has greatly increased. By technology and specialization we have accomplished much; but the resulting complexity of leadership functions and the restriction of the development and supply of general leaders seems to me one of the important problems of our times.

The Third Sector—The Instrument of Action

Leadership obviously relates to the coordination of certain efforts of people. There is little coordination or cooperation without leadership, and leadership implies cooperation. Coordinated efforts constitute organization. *An organization is the instrumentality of action so far as leaders are concerned, and it is the indispensable instrumentality.* Many promising men never comprehend this because of early emphasis upon plants, structures, techniques, and abstract institutions, especially legal institutions such as the law of corporations.

The primary efforts of leaders need to be directed to the maintenance and guidance of organizations as whole systems of activities. I believe this to be the most distinctive and characteristic sector of leadership behavior, but it is the least obvious and least understood. Since most of the acts which constitute organization have a specific function which superficially is independent of the maintenance of organization—for example, the accomplishment of specific tasks of the organization—it may not be observed that such acts at the same time also constitute organization and that this, not the technical and instrumental, is the primary aspect of such acts from the viewpoint of leadership. Probably most leaders are not ordinarily conscious of this, though intuitively they are governed by it. For any act done in such a way as to disrupt cooperation destroys the capacity of organization. Thus the leader has to guide all in such a way as to preserve organization as the instrumentality of action.[3]

Up to the present time, leaders have understood organization chiefly in an intuitive and experiential way. The properties, limitations, and processes of organization as systems of coordinated action have been little known in abstraction from concrete activities and situations; but the persistence and effectiveness of many organizations are evidence that leaders know how to behave with respect to them. On the other hand, we know that many very able, intelligent, and learned persons have neither understanding nor correct intuitions about concrete organizations.

The Fourth Sector—The Stimulation of Coordinated Action

To repeat a commonplace, it is one thing to say what should be done, and quite another to get it done. A potential act lies outside or-

[3] The conception of the nature of organization—as a system of coordinated *activities*—involved in this paragraph is carefully developed and defended in *The Functions,* chapter vii, "The Theory of Formal Organization," and is made more explicit in the article "Comments on the Job of an Executive." See the preliminary note of the title page.

ganization, and it is one task of leaders to change potentiality into the stuff of action. In other words, one important kind of thing that leaders do is to induce people to convert abilities into coordinated effort, thereby maintaining an organization while simultaneously getting its work done. I need hardly say that this kind of activity of leaders is sometimes the most striking aspect of what they do. In a broad sense this is the business of persuasion. Nor need I say that the sorts of acts or behavior by which executives "persuade" to coordinated action are innumerable. They vary from providing the example in "going over the top," or calm poise inspiring confidence, or quiet commands in tense moments, to fervid oratory, or flattery, or promises to reward in money, prestige, position, glory, or to threats and coercion. Why do they vary? Some obvious differences of combination in leaders, in followers, in organizations, in technology, in objectives, in conditions, will occur to you. But the effective combinations are often so subtle and so involved in the personalities of both leaders and followers that to be self-conscious about them, or for others to examine them when in process, would disrupt them.

* * *

My chief purpose in this brief account of four sectors of leadership behavior has been to indicate how interconnected and interdependent they are and to suggest how great is the variation in what "leadership" means specifically, depending upon the relative importance of the kinds of behavior required.

II. *The Conditions of Leadership*

Already it has been necessary to allude at least by implication to differences in conditions of leadership, such for example as are involved in the degrees and kinds of technological operations. I shall now confine the discussion to differences of conditions of another sort, relating to the degree of tension of the action of leaders, followers, or both. It will be sufficient to consider only the two extremes.

The first is that which we may call stable conditions. These may be complex and of very large scale; but they are comparatively free from violent changes or extreme uncertainties of *unusual* character or implying important hazards. The behavior of leaders under such conditions may be calm, deliberate, reflective, and anticipatory of future contingencies. Leadership then is lacking in the dramatic characteristics often observed at the other extreme, and this is one of its difficulties; for its function of persuasion must be carried on without the aid of emotional drives and of obvious necessities and against the indifference often accompanying lack of danger, excitement, and sentiment. Stable conditions call for self-restraint, deliberation, and refinement of technique, qualities that some men who are good leaders under tense conditions are unable to develop.

The other extreme is that of great instability, uncertainty, speed, intense action, great risks, important stakes, life and death issues. Here leaders must have physical or moral courage, decisiveness, inventiveness, initiative, even audacity; but I believe we tend to overstate the qualities required for this extreme, due to its dramatic aspects and because the outcome of action is more easily judged.

This is enough to suggest that differences of conditions of this type, that is, differences in tension, are important factors in leadership behavior. It should be apparent that we could expect only rarely to find men equally adapted to both extremes, and that quite different types of leaders are to be expected for this reason. Yet it is obvious that emergencies may be encountered in any kind of cooperative effort, and that leaders have to be adapted to function under wide ranges of conditions. Indeed, intermittent periods of severe stress are the rule in navigation, in military organizations, in some kinds of public utility work, in political activity, to cite a few examples in which particular types of *flexibility* are necessary to continuous leadership. It may be apparent here, as perhaps it was in considering the sectors of leadership behavior, that the practical problem in selecting specific leaders would be to ascertain the *balance of qualities* most probably adapted to the conditions or to the variations of conditions.

III. The Active Qualities of Leaders

I have already stated why I do not think it useful to discuss leadership exclusively in personal terms. Leaders, I think, are made quite as much by conditions and by organizations and followers as by any qualities and propensities which they themselves have. Indeed, in this connection, I should put much more emphasis upon the character of organizations than upon individuals. But this is not the common opinion; and I certainly should not fail to discuss that quite variable component, the individual.

I shall list and discuss briefly five fundamental qualities or characteristics of those who are leaders, in their order of importance as regarded for very *general* purposes. Probably I shall not include qualities that some think essential. I would not quarrel about what may be only a difference in names or emphasis. Perhaps, also, there will be disagreement about the order I have chosen. This I shall mildly defend, my chief purpose being to correct for a current exaggerated and false emphasis. The list follows: (I) Vitality and Endurance; (II) Decisiveness; (III) Persuasiveness; (IV) Responsibility; and (V) Intellectual Capacity.

I. Vitality and Endurance

We should not confuse these qualities with good health. There are many people of good health who have little or moderate vitality— energy, alertness, spring, vigilance, dynamic qualities—or endurance. Conversely, there are some who have poor health and even suffer much who at least have great endurance. Generally, it seems to me, vitality and endurance are fundamental qualities of leadership, though they may wane before leadership capacity does.

Notwithstanding the exceptions, these qualities are important for several reasons. The first is that they both promote and permit the unremitting acquirement of exceptional experience and knowledge which in general underlies extraordinary personal capacity for leadership.

The second is that vitality is usually an element in personal attractiveness or force which is a great aid to persuasiveness. It is sometimes even a compelling characteristic. Thus few can be unaffected by the violent energy with which Mussolini throws his arms in the Fascist salute, or by the vehemence of Hitler's speech, or by the strenuous life of Theodore Roosevelt. Similarly, we are impressed by the endurance of Franklin D. Roosevelt in campaign.

The third reason for the importance of vitality and endurance is that leadership often involves prolonged periods of work and extreme tension without relief, when failure to endure may mean permanent inability to lead. To maintain confidence depends partly on uninterrupted leadership.

II. Decisiveness

I shall be unable to discuss here precisely what decision is or involves as a process, but I regard it as the element of critical importance in all leadership, and I believe that all formal organization depends upon it. Ability to make decisions is the characteristic of leaders I think most to be noted. It depends upon a propensity or willingness to decide and a capacity to do so. I neglect almost entirely the appearance or mannerism of being decisive, which seems often to be a harmful characteristic, at least frequently misleading, usually implying an improper understanding and use of authority, and undermining confidence. Leadership requires making actual appropriate decisions and only such as are warranted.

For present purposes decisiveness needs to be considered in both its positive and negative aspects. Positively, decision is necessary to get the right things done at the right time and to prevent erroneous action. Negatively, failure to decide undoubtedly creates an exeedingly destructive condition in organized effort. For delay either to direct or to approve or disapprove, that is, mere suspense, checks the decisiveness of others, introduces indecisiveness or lethargy throughout the whole process of cooperation, and thus restricts experience, experiment, and adaptation to changing conditions.

III. Persuasiveness

The fundamental importance of persuasiveness I have already mentioned. Here I refer to the ability in the individual to persuade, and the propensity to do so. Just what these qualities are defies description; but without them all other qualities may become ineffective. These other qualities seem to be involved, yet not to be equivalent. In addition, persuasiveness appears often to involve or utilize talents, such as that of effective public speaking or of exposition or special physical skills or even extraordinary physique, and many others. The relation of specific talents to leadership we cannot usefully consider further here. But at least we may say that persuasiveness involves a *sense* or understanding of the point of view, the interests, and the conditions of those to be persuaded.

IV. Responsibility

I shall define responsibility as an emotional condition that gives an individual a sense of acute dissatisfaction because of failure to do what he feels he is morally bound to do or because of doing what he thinks he is morally bound not to do, in particular concrete situations.[4] Such dissatisfaction he will avoid; and therefore his behavior, if he is "responsible" and if his beliefs or sense of what is right are known, can be approximately relied upon. That this stability of behavior is important to leadership from several points of view will be recognized without difficulty; but it is especially so from that of those who follow. Capricious and irresponsible leadership is rarely successful.

V. Intellectual Capacity

I have intentionally relegated "brains" to the fifth place. I thereby still make it important, but nevertheless subsidiary to physical capacity, decisiveness, persuasiveness, and responsibility. Many find this hard to believe, for leaders especially seem to me frequently to be inordinately proud of their intellectual abilities, whatever they may be, rather than of their more important or effective qualities.

A Digression on the Importance of the Non-Intellectual Abilities

This attitude may be partly due to a confusion between preeminence and leadership—an instance of which I gave in my introduction—and partly to the high social status now given to intellect, to which I shall refer later. Disagreement as to the subordinate place

---

[4] An extended exposition and illustration of this definition are given in *The Functions* in Chapter xvii, "The Nature of Executive Responsibility."

to which I here assign intellect may also be partly due to a matter of definition; for I think we usually confuse *acquirement* by intellectual processes with responsive, habitual, intuitive *expression* or *application* of what has been acquired, which I take to involve processes largely non-intellectual.

However, I believe sensitiveness about our intellects is often due especially to the fact that the part of behavior *of which we are most conscious* is at least largely intellectual, whereas much of our most effective behavior, such as reflects vitality, decisiveness, and responsibility, is largely matter-of-course, unconscious, responsive, and on the whole has to be so to be effective. Self-consciousness in these respects would at least often check their force, speed, or accuracy. Moreover, leaders, like others, are for the most part unaware of their most effective faculties in actual behavior, for they cannot see themselves as others do.

This last point is so important both in theory and in practical administration that I think it worth further consideration here. The point is easy to prove, but its implications are difficult to explain. For the proof we may take, as an example, speaking and its accompanying gestures. It is well known that no one hears his own voice as it sounds to others chiefly because much of the vibrations of the speaker's voice are conducted within the structure of passages of the head. I believe that an individual without previous experience rarely recognizes his own voice from a good reproduction. Some are greatly surprised and often displeased at hearing such a reproduction for the first time. Obviously, too, an individual cannot see his own demeanor or many of his movements. Yet in all our relations to others the use of voice and gestures is of first importance and both are effectively controlled to a considerable extent so as to accomplish specific reactions in listeners. If we cannot hear and see ourselves as others do, how can we accomplish such control of our behavior?

I think the explanation may be as follows: We learn to correlate our own speech and action, as we hear and feel them, with certain effects upon others. We are only approximately successful, and some are much more so than others. Listeners and observers, on the other hand, learn to correlate the entirely different thing, our observable behavior, with our meanings and intentions. This is also only approximate, and is done more successfully by some than by others. Since leadership primarily involves the guidance of the conduct of others, in general, leaders need to be more effective than others both in conveying meanings and intentions and in receiving them.

These fundamental processes are certainly not to any great extent intellectual. We all know the capacity to understand the logical significance of sentences, even when written or printed, is limited, and that repeatedly we understand by the manner of speaking. We can with some success teach by logical processes what to do in the operation of a machine or process, though even here we know that often to state a direction correctly in language is to mislead, whereas an incorrect statement especially with appropriate gesture or facial expression may well convey the precise meaning. But to teach by logical exposition how to behave with other people is a slow process of limited effectiveness at best. This is why I think it will be widely observed that good leaders seldom undertake to tell followers *how* to behave, though they tell what should be done, and will properly criticize the manner of its doing *afterward*. Whereas inferior leaders often fail by trying, as it were, to tell others how to live their lives.

The Limitations of Intellectuals

Whatever may be the explanation of our strong predilection for our intellectual attainments, it is difficult to evade the emphasis I have placed on other qualities in leadership. We all know persons in and out of practical affairs of superior intellects and intellectual accomplishments who do not work well as leaders. In matters of *leadership*, for example, they prove to be irresponsible (absent-minded, non-punctual), non-decisive (ultra-judicial, see so many sides they can never make up their minds), non-persuasive (a little "queer," not interested in people). Moreover, we can observe that intellectual capacity rarely rises above physiological disabilities in active life, that the utmost perspicacity is useless for leadership if it does not decide issues, that persuasive processes must take full account of the irrational by which all are largely governed, that responsibility is a moral or emotional condition.

The Importance of Intellectual Capacities

Intellectual abilities of high order may achieve preeminent usefulness. They are sometimes an important element in leadership but not sufficient to maintain it. However, as a differential factor—that is, other qualities being granted and adequate—intellectual capacity is of unquestioned importance, and especially so in the age in which complex techniques and elaborate technologies are among the conditions of leadership. Leaders of the future, in my opinion, will generally need to be intellectually competent. However, the main point, which I wish greatly to emphasize, is that intellectual competency is *not* a substitute, at least in an important degree, for the other essential qualities of leadership.

Some Effects of Exaggerated Intellectualism

Though it may be unpleasant to some, I have laid stress upon my opinion in this matter for two principal reasons. The first is that under present trends an excessive emphasis is placed upon intellectual (and pseudo-intellectual) qualifications by responsible "selecting" authorities, which artificially limits the supply of leaders. The same excessive emphasis upon the intellectual is made by followers who are intellectuals. Thus it is often difficult for them (experts and professionals of many kinds) who have no administrative capacity (or interest) to follow even extraordinary leaders. This is a form of conceit frequently accompanied by exhibitions of temperament and disruptiveness, and by false, ruthless, and irresponsible professions of individualism and freedom, especially professional and academic freedom. All of this tends to a limitation of the supply of competent leaders, because it discourages men from undertaking the work of leadership, and it restricts their effectiveness.

My second reason is that a general condition amounting to intellectual snobbishness, it seems to me, has a great deal to do with industrial unrest. I see this in the propensity of educated people, whatever their economic status or social position, to underestimate the intelligence and other important personal qualities of workmen; in the tendency of some supervisors, quite honestly and sincerely, to blame failure to lack of brains in subordinates instead of to the stupidity of instructions; in the assumption of some men that "pure bunk" dressed up in "high brow" jargon is effective in dealing with people; in the excessive popularity of white-collar occupations; in the desire of so many intellectuals to tell others how to eat, save money, dress, marry, raise families, take care of their own interests. These are symptoms of attitudes and it is the latter, not the symptoms, which are important. They cause division of interest and lack of sympathetic understanding that are destructive of cooperation and cannot be corrected by mere "measures of good will."

I am well aware that there are differences in the intellectual capacities of men and know that such differences are important, especially as respects the ability to acquire knowledge and understanding by study in those matters which can only be learned in this way. Nevertheless, after a fairly long experience in dealing with many classes of men and women individually and collectively, the destructive attitudes I am attacking seem to me to be unwarranted by anything I know about intellect, education or leadership. Intellectual superiority is an obtrusive thing which even intellectuals dislike in others except as they *voluntarily* give it their respect.

Our Ignorance of the Qualities of Leadership

After this long digression it may have been forgotten, though observed, that in this discussion of personal qualifications I have failed, with one exception, to define my terms. Though in a general way I am confident that my meaning is understood, greater precision of meaning seems quite impossible, at least without extended space, and is not needed here. Indeed, a significant fact to emphasize is that neither in science nor in practical affairs has there yet been attained a degree of understanding of these qualities now vaguely described which permits much clear definition even for special purposes.

It is worthwhile to illustrate this with reference to "decisiveness." The making of decisions is one of the most common of the events of which we are conscious both in ourselves and others. We believe that many decisions are momentous either to ourselves, to our enterprises, or to our society. We may agree that those incapable of making *any* decisions are at least morons if not insane. We are aware that to make decisions is a leading function of executives. We also know that decisions are made collectively, as in committees, boards, legislatures, juries, and that such work is one of the most characteristic features of our social life. Yet decisive behavior, as contrasted with responsive behavior, seems to have received little attention in the psychologies,[5] in the literature of logical operations, in sociology, and seldom in economics. Moreover, in business I rarely hear appraisals of men in terms of their capacity for decisions, except when they fail apparently for lack of ability to decide. It seems clear that we know so little of this quality or process that we do not discuss it as such, though "decision," "decisive," and "decisiveness" are words frequently on our lips.

I am aware, as I said earlier, that I have omitted several qualifications of leadership which are commonly stated. In my intention, they are all comprehended in the five I have named or in some combination or derivation of them. Three omitted qualifications are great favorites: "honesty" ("character"), "courage," and "initiative." They may be added; but for myself I find them words which depend for their meaning in the specific case upon the *situation*, not merely the individual, either as interpreted by the actor or leader or others, and that his interpretation will often differ from the interpretations made by different observers.

[5] While writing this sentence I have taken off the shelf at random more than a dozen books on psychology and social psychology. In only two is "decision" indexed (Lewin: *Principles of Topological Psychology* and Guthrie: *The Psychology of Human Conflict*) and in both cases the citations are few and quite secondary. Of course, perhaps all of the elements of the decisive processes may be covered in all these books, though from my recollection of them I doubt it. The fact is that one of the most conspicuous factors in common current observable behavior simply has not been recognized as such, notwithstanding that decision is the culmination of whatever we mean by "free will," "will," "voluntary," "determined" (in some meanings). The situation recalls what one psychologist has said of others, though in another connection: "All such explanations fail to explain why we think that A is A. For, even when the psychologists told us that A really was B, we stubbornly persisted in calling it A and not as B . . . For in the long run it has proved to be more profitable to accept an A as an A and explain it as such . . ." (K. Koffka, *Gestalt Psychology*, Harcourt, Brace and Co., Inc., 1935, p. 179.)

In any case, the important point is that the qualifications of leadership, however discriminated and however named, are interacting and interdependent. We do not assemble them as we would the ingredients of a compound, yet we may suppose that different combinations of qualities produce quite different kinds of leaders, and that the qualities and their combinations change with experience and with conditions.

IV. The Development of Leaders

I think I have now shown that my profession of ignorance of this subject and my doubts with respect to the knowledge of others concerning it were both justified. Yet I recognize that however lacking in knowledge we may be, we nevertheless endeavor in our educational systems and at least in the larger organizations to increase the number of available leaders and their competence. It might be suggested that I should say something on this aspect of the subject in the light of my earlier remarks. I shall confine myself briefly to development methods and, in the next section, to the processes of selection.

Concerning the development of leaders, I shall in this section discuss the following topics: (I) Training; (II) Balance and Perspective; and (III) Experience.

I. Training

As I understand it, the only qualification for leadership that is subject to specific preparatory training by formal processes is the intellectual, including therein the inculcation of general and special knowledge. My opinion as to the relative importance and status of intellectual qualities has already been stated to the effect that such qualities are increasingly necessary to effective leadership in technical and technological fields and also in large-scale organizations where complexity and the remoteness of concrete activities call for capacity in the handling of abstract material. The latter are the conditions in which leadership also usually involves management of extensive cooperative systems as well as of organizations.

Nevertheless, I believe it should be recognized that intellectual preparation by itself tends to check propensities indispensable to leadership. For example, study and reflection on abstract facts do not promote decisiveness and often seem to have the opposite effect. Analysis, which broadly is characteristic of intellectual processes especially in the early stages of education and experience, is the reverse of the process of combining elements, of the treatment of them as whole systems involved in concrete decisive action, for instance in persuasion. As a result of intellectual training many prefer to recognize only what has been stated or is susceptible of statement and to disregard what has not been stated or is not susceptible of statement. The emphasis upon abstract facts characteristic now of the "more intelligent" and dominant classes of our population has its results, in innumerable instances, in the "fallacy of misplaced concreteness," the confusion of the fact with the thing and of *an aspect* with an indescribable whole, in the disregard of the interdependence of the known and the unknown.

An example of this or of its general effects may be found in the excessive emphasis upon knowledge as against skill in nearly all fields except sports and individual artistic performance. Yet but a moment's reflection is needed to acknowledge that many of the noteworthy efforts of scientist, teacher, lawyer, physician, architect, engineer, clergyman—to take professions in which intellectual discipline and experience are indispensable—are expressions not of intellect but of skills, the effective behavior by which the appropriate adjustment to the infinite complexity of the concrete is accomplished. Indeed, we repeatedly confess the point in our practical emphasis upon experience, if not upon intuition, in every profession.

Nowhere is the emphasis upon fact to the exclusion of the thing to which it relates more harmful, it seems to me, than in the human side of industrial relations. We may think of employees as mechanics, clerks, laborers, or as members of an organization, but to lead requires to *feel* them as embodying a thousand emotions and relationships with others and with the physical environment, of which for the most part we can have no knowledge.

The dilemma which this state of affairs presents is, I think, concealed by the increasing extent to which prestige and status based on education are the basis of general social and industrial discrimination. I mean by this that a certain intellectual and educational status has become important, to the relative disregard of other qualifications, in getting a job, or at least a job generally regarded as desirable or distinctive. We can hardly help believing that an attitude is useful to society as a whole if we find that same attitude socially imposed upon us as individuals.[6]

II. Balance and Perspective

It may be thought that changes in curricula might be sufficient to correct for the tendency toward distortion of judgment which I have described. This may be possible in the future but not yet. So far as I know there is not developed the basic material for such changes, and it is unlikely that there will be unless my view of this problem, assuming it to be correct, should be accepted widely. But at best I should expect such studies only to offset the prejudices inculcated, possibly excepting the humanities, by higher education.

Hence, for the present, it seems to me that balance, perspective, and proportion in the senses relevant to leadership are to be acquired almost exclusively from responsible experience in leading.

III. Experience

In speaking of experience, it will be well to avoid the common error of regarding it as primarily a matter of repetition through a period of time. When experience is merely repetition of action, it is better called practice to acquire patterns of behavior. It is often convenient as a rough approximation to speak of hours, days, months, or years of experience, but we know that some men learn slowly, others quickly. Moreover, the possibility of learning depends upon activity. If nothing happens, little can be learned. Significant experience is secured largely by adapting one's self to varieties of conditions and by acquiring the sense of the appropriate in variations of action.

---

[6] An analogous problem is presented in "oversaving" theories of depressions, in which it is asserted that it is possible for a society as a whole to oversave, whereas the desire to save is commendable as to individuals.

The acquirement of experience under modern conditions presents us with another dilemma; for the refined specialization and the technical complexity through which men are now introduced into the world of affairs give limited opportunity for general experience in leadership. The most "natural" opportunities at present formally available seem to me to be the small *general* business, political party work in communities, and perhaps to a less extent, labor union leadership. These are insufficient sources for the supply of general leaders. Hence, we need to develop the artificial methods of giving wide experience which are now attempted to some extent in large organizations.

The effect of technical work is so strongly opposed to the acquirement of experience in the arts of leadership that I cannot forbear to add a suggestion that encouragement should be given in gaining experience informally in "extracurricular" activities. In fact, though we can as yet apparently do little in a formal way to develop leaders, we can encourage potential leaders to develop themselves, to seek for themselves the occasions and opportunities when leadership is needed, to learn the ways of making themselves sought as leaders, to acquire experience in leading by doing it. I have myself been so encouraged and inspired in my youth and since then, as no doubt we all have, so that to give such encouragement seems to me an important private and social duty; but I believe whatever we do in this respect will be harmful if not done in full realization that *there is no substitute for the experience of recognizing and seizing opportunities, or for making one's own place unaided and against interference and obstacles*; for these kinds of ability are precisely those that followers expect in leaders.

V. Selection

Thus we have to recognize that leaders, almost blindly created by physiology, physical environments, social conditions, and experience, are now secured chiefly by selection, not by formal preparation. Our success is relative in the sense that we select as best we may of the quality that is presented but are little able to affect favorably that quality as a whole except as to the intellectual element. If this is a fact, it is admittedly difficult to observe, because to do so requires comparison of what we have with what we think we might have. Yet if we believe it to be a fact, it implies a precarious position; for the most perfect selection would not suffice to give adequate leadership if the supply of the "raw material" were of inferior quality, any more, for example, than the best selection among untutored electricians would be likely to afford an adequate supply of superior electrical engineers.

The test of adequacy of leadership is the extent of cooperation, or lack of it, in relation to our ideals; and this is largely a matter of the disposition of followers. Even in this brief discussion it should be stated that in all formal organizations selection is made simultaneously by two authorities, the formal and the informal. That which is made by formal authority we may call appointment (or dismissal), that by the informal authority we may call acceptance [7] (or rejection). *Of the two, the informal authority is fundamental and controlling.* It lies in or consists of the willingness and ability of followers to follow.

To many who have struggled and worried regarding appointment or dismissal of leaders, and to whom the maintenance of formal authority is the very keystone of cooperation, order, and efficiency, what I say may seem absurd or even subversive. But we have all many times proved it correct. For has not our first question always been in effect "Can he lead and will they follow?" If our answer were "No!" would we not appoint at the peril of our own leadership? And when there has been failure of followers to follow, writhe as we would, were not our only recourses to change the leader or possibly to change the followers?

If it is thought that this doctrine is subversive, this may be because it is thought to be what uninformed preachers of the vague thing called "industrial democracy" want, and we suppose they know less

---

[7] Under some, usually small or local, situations leaders are acclaimed spontaneously and are induced or forced to lead by pressure of social opinion. There is often some element of this even in large and institutionalized organizations, chiefly expressed on the negative side, i.e., it is socially or organizationally not countenanced to quit leading or to refuse promotion, and loss of "caste" would be involved.

of leadership and organization than even we do. But what they advocate and what we fear is the transfer of *formal* authority from leaders to voters, forgetting that the informal authority must finally determine, whatever be the nature of the formal authority. Indeed, this latter fact is the chief reason for our fear; for we recall the men who have been enthusiastically elected but never followed. As to most (but not all) leadership, *appointment* by responsible leaders has proved, and I believe will continue to prove, more effective and more satisfactory to followers than any other formal process.[8] And the followers make the leader, though the latter also may affect and must guide the followers.

I turn now to the process of selection, by formal authority of appointment or dismissal. In the selective process we eliminate for positive disqualifications—bad health, lack of ability to decide, irresponsibility, lack of adequate intellectual or technical ability. Frequently this is all disregarded most conveniently by saying "lack of experience" when what we mean is "lack of successful experience." For although a few eliminations are made for positive disqualifications, the really important basis of selection is that of prior achievement. Since we know so little about the qualifications for leadership, this often proves a fallacious method, sometimes resulting in tragic errors and often in a great deal of foolish rationalization. Nevertheless, we must confess that the past record is the best basis of selection we have. Thirty years ago Mr. Theodore N. Vail, a great leader and organizer in his day, and then President of the American Telephone and Telegraph Company, said to me: "You never can tell what a man will do by what he has done; but it is the best guide you have." I believe this still to be true; but I do not think it is an adequate basis for selection of leaders for our society of the future.

If leadership depends, as I have said, upon the individual, the followers, and the conditions, there must be many failures that are not the result of original errors of selection. For men, followers, and con-

---

[8] My reasons are developed at length in the lecture, "The Dilemmas of Leadership in the Democratic Process," cited in the preliminary note. [This lecture appears on page 24 of *Organization and Management*; see reference to this book in the credit on page 432.—Editor]

ditions all change. We are prone to forget this and to condemn, perhaps because it imposes upon us one of the most serious problems in the selective process. Failure of leadership if not corrected by replacement means the checking of the experience and development of potential leaders. Hence the elimination of super-annuated, obsolete, and incompetent leaders is recognized as extremely important in most organizations, perhaps most systematically in the Army and Navy. But this process is extremely delicate; for though followers cannot follow those who cannot lead, those who have been superior leaders embody or personify the spirit of an organization and represent the aspirations of their followers. Crude dismissal at any level of organization destroys morale and ambition and thus does violence to organization itself. In all types of organizations I believe this often means retaining a leader in the interest of everyone concerned after he has passed the peak of his capabilities and sometimes even when the latter have become inadequate. When this is a matter of favoritism there can be no good defense of it; but when it is a part of the process of *organizing leadership* involving the supplementing of incapacities by auxiliary leaders, it must be defended.

Here we are confronted with another problem of balance—another of the dilemmas of our subject. Who will say that we now know enough about it or are sufficiently successful with respect to it?

Conclusion

In this short study of one aspect of life, I have tried to emphasize the extent of our limitations and the importance of overcoming them, both from the standpoint of the effect of public blindness to the nature of the problem—which results so often in obstruction and in destructive criticism—and also from the standpoint of preparation to meet the future needs for leaders. These are ever increasing as the integrations of our societies grow larger, and as specialization and technological progress continue. Whether such an account is depressing, perhaps appalling, or is challenging and inspiring, will depend, I suppose, upon one's philosophy, outlook, or temperament.

It is in the nature of a leader's work that he should be a realist and should recognize the need for action, even when the outcome cannot be foreseen, but also that he should be idealist and in the broadest sense pursue goals some of which can only be attained in a succeeding generation of leaders. Many leaders when they reach the apex of their powers have not long to go, and they press onward by paths the ends of which they will not themselves reach. In business, in education, in government, in religion, again and again, I see men who, I am sure, are dominated by this motive, though unexpressed, and by some queer twist of our present attitudes often disavowed.

Yet, "Old men plant trees." To neglect today for tomorrow surely reflects a treacherous sentimentalism; but to shape the present for the future by the surplus of thought and purpose which we now can muster seems the very expression of the idealism which underlies such social coherence as we presently achieve, and without this idealism we see no worthy meaning in our lives, our institutions, or our culture.

DOUGLAS MURRAY McGREGOR

(1906–1964)

DOUGLAS McGREGOR, like Elton Mayo, stands for the behavioral scientist's growing role in developing approaches to effective management. His great contribution was his brilliant articulation and advocacy, in the Theory X / Theory Y proposition, of the management philosophy he believed necessary to meet today's and tomorrow's needs, in contrast with what he called conventional methods.

An iconoclast in management thinking, McGregor was at the same time a knowledgeable one whose straightforward way of expressing himself is reminiscent of Mary Parker Follett. He was trained as an educator and a psychologist, and initially he taught psychology at Harvard and the Massachusetts Institute of Technology. But from 1954 until his death he was professor of industrial management at M.I.T.; and his experience in management practice was extensive, principally as president of Antioch College and consultant to Standard Oil Company (New Jersey), Union Carbide Corporation, and other important companies.

"The Human Side of Enterprise," which follows, was the first published statement of his Theory X / Theory Y thesis. It has gained increasing acceptance as more managers have adopted the methods of management by objectives in an effort to win the commitment of their groups. "New Concepts of Management" extends Theory Y into the future. The paper has special reference to that proliferating member of the organization, the professional employee, whose importance to managers grows by leaps and bounds as emphasis increases on research and technology.

———————————

THE HUMAN SIDE OF ENTERPRISE

BY DOUGLAS M. McGREGOR

I T has become trite to say that the most significant developments of the next quarter century will take place not in the physical but in the social sciences, that industry—the economic organ of society—has the fundamental know-how to utilize physical science and technology for the material benefit of mankind, and that we must now learn how to utilize the social sciences to make our human organizations truly effective.

Many people agree in principle with such statements; but so far they represent a pious hope—and little else. Consider with me, if you will, something of what may be involved when we attempt to transform the hope into reality.

Let me begin with an analogy. A quarter century ago basic conceptions of the nature of matter and energy had changed profoundly from what they had been since Newton's time. The physical scientists were persuaded that under proper conditions new and hitherto unimagined sources of energy could be made available to mankind.

We know what has happened since then. First came the bomb. Then, during the past decade, have come many other attempts to exploit these scientific discoveries—some successful, some not.

The point of my analogy, however, is that the application of theory

Reprinted by permission of the publisher from *Leadership and Motivation: Essays of Douglas McGregor,* Chapter I, pages 3–20. Edited by Warren G. Bennis and Edgar H. Schein, with the collaboration of Caroline McGregor. The M.I.T. Press, Cambridge. Copyright © 1966 The Massachusetts Institute of Technology.

in this field is a slow and costly matter. We expect it always to be thus. No one is impatient with the scientist because he cannot tell industry how to build a simple, cheap, all-purpose source of atomic energy today. That it will take at least another decade and the investment of billions of dollars to achieve results which are economically competitive with present sources of power is understood and accepted.

It is transparently pretentious to suggest any *direct* similarity between the developments in the physical sciences leading to the harnessing of atomic energy and potential developments in the social sciences. Nevertheless, the analogy is not as absurd as it might appear to be at first glance.

To a lesser degree, and in a much more tentative fashion, we are in a position in the social sciences today like that of the physical sciences with respect to atomic energy in the thirties. We know that past conceptions of the nature of man are inadequate and in many ways incorrect. We are becoming quite certain that, under proper conditions, unimagined resources of creative human energy could become available within the organizational setting.

We cannot tell industrial management how to apply this new knowledge in simple, economic ways. We know it will require years of exploration, much costly development research, and a substantial amount of creative imagination on the part of management to discover how to apply this growing knowledge to the organization of human effort in industry.

May I ask that you keep this analogy in mind—overdrawn and pretentious though it may be—as a framework for what I have to say this morning.

Management's Task: Conventional View

The conventional conception of management's task in harnessing human energy to organizational requirements can be stated broadly in terms of three propositions. In order to avoid the complications introduced by a label, I shall call this set of propositions "Theory X":

1. Management is responsible for organizing the elements of pro-

ductive enterprise—money, materials, equipment, people—in the interest of economic ends.

2. With respect to people, this is a process of directing their efforts, motivating them, controlling their actions, modifying their behavior to fit the needs of the organization.

3. Without this active intervention by management, people would be passive—even resistant—to organizational needs. They must therefore be persuaded, rewarded, punished, controlled—their activities must be directed. This is management's task—in managing subordinate managers or workers. We often sum it up by saying that management consists of getting things done through other people.

Behind this conventional theory there are several additional beliefs—less explicit, but widespread:

4. The average man is by nature indolent—he works as little as possible.

5. He lacks ambition, dislikes responsibility, prefers to be led.

6. He is inherently self-centered, indifferent to organizational needs.

7. He is by nature resistant to change.

8. He is gullible, not very bright, the ready dupe of the charlatan and the demagogue.

The human side of economic enterprise today is fashioned from propositions and beliefs such as these. Conventional organization structures, managerial policies, practices, and programs reflect these assumptions.

In accomplishing its task—with these assumptions as guides— management has conceived of a range of possibilities between two extremes.

The Hard or the Soft Approach?

At one extreme, management can be "hard" or "strong." The methods for directing behavior involve coercion and threat (usually disguised), close supervision, tight controls over behavior. At the other extreme, management can be "soft" or "weak." The methods for directing behavior involve being permissive, satisfying people's demands, achieving harmony. Then they will be tractable, accept direction.

This range has been fairly completely explored during the past half century, and management has learned some things from the exploration. There are difficulties in the "hard" approach. Force breeds counter-forces: restriction of output, antagonism, militant unionism, subtle but effective sabotage of management objectives. This approach is especially difficult during times of full employment.

There are also difficulties in the "soft" approach. It leads frequently to the abdication of management—to harmony, perhaps, but to indifferent performance. People take advantage of the soft approach. They continually expect more, but they give less and less.

Currently, the popular theme is "firm but fair." This is an attempt to gain the advantages of both the hard and the soft approaches. It is reminiscent of Teddy Roosevelt's "speak softly and carry a big stick."

Is the Conventional View Correct?

The findings which are beginning to emerge from the social sciences challenge this whole set of beliefs about man and human nature and about the task of management. The evidence is far from conclusive, certainly, but it is suggestive. It comes from the laboratory, the clinic, the schoolroom, the home, and even to a limited extent from industry itself.

The social scientist does not deny that human behavior in industrial organization today is approximately what management perceives it to be. He has, in fact, observed it and studied it fairly extensively. But he is pretty sure that this behavior is *not* a consequence of man's inherent nature. It is a consequence rather of the nature of industrial organizations, of management philosophy, policy, and practice. The conventional approach of Theory X is based on mistaken notions of what is cause and what is effect.

"Well," you ask, "what then is the *true* nature of man? What evidence leads the social scientist to deny what is obvious?" And, if I am not mistaken, you are also thinking, "Tell me—simply, and without a lot of scientific verbiage—what you think you know that is so unusual. Give me—without a lot of intellectual claptrap and theoretical nonsense—some practical ideas which will enable me to improve the situation in my organization. And remember, I'm faced with increasing costs and narrowing profit margins. I want proof that such ideas won't result simply in new and costly human relations frills. I want practical results, and I want them now."

If these are your wishes, you are going to be disappointed. Such requests can no more be met by the social scientist today than could comparable ones with respect to atomic energy be met by the physicist fifteen years ago. I can, however, indicate a few of the reasons for asserting that conventional assumptions about the human side of enterprise are inadequate. And I can suggest—tentatively—some of the propositions that will comprise a more adequate theory of the management of people. The magnitude of the task that confronts us will then, I think, be apparent.

Perhaps the best way to indicate why the conventional approach of management is inadequate is to consider the subject of motivation. In discussing this subject I will draw heavily on the work of my colleague, Abraham Maslow of Brandeis University. His is the most fruitful approach I know. Naturally, what I have to say will be overgeneralized and will ignore important qualifications. In the time at our disposal, this is inevitable.

Physiological and Safety Needs

Man is a wanting animal—as soon as one of his needs is satisfied, another appears in its place. This process is unending. It continues from birth to death.

Man's needs are organized in a series of levels—a hierarchy of importance. At the lowest level; but preeminent in importance when they are thwarted, are his physiological needs. Man lives by bread alone, when there is no bread. Unless the circumstances are unusual, his needs for love, for status, for recognition are inoperative when his stomach has been empty for a while. But when he eats regularly and adequately, hunger ceases to be an important need. The sated man has hunger only in the sense that a full bottle has emptiness. The same is true of the other physiological needs of man—for rest, exercise, shelter, protection from the elements.

A satisfied need is not a motivator of behavior! This is a fact of profound significance. It is a fact which is regularly ignored in the conventional approach to the management of people. I shall return to it later. For the moment, one example will make my point. Consider your own need for air. Except as you are deprived of it, it has no appreciable motivating effect upon your behavior.

When the physiological needs are reasonably satisfied, needs at the next higher level begin to dominate man's behavior—to motivate him. These are called safety needs. They are needs for protection against danger, threat, deprivation. Some people mistakenly refer to these as needs for security. However, unless man is in a dependent relationship where he fears arbitrary deprivation, he does not demand security. The need is for the "fairest possible break." When he is confident of this, he is more than willing to take risks. But when he feels threatened or dependent, his greatest need is for guarantees, for protection, for security.

The fact needs little emphasis that since every industrial employee is in a dependent relationship, safety needs may assume considerable importance. Arbitrary management actions, behavior which arouses uncertainty with respect to continued employment or which reflects favoritism or discrimination, unpredictable administration of policy—these can be powerful motivators of the safety needs in the employment relationship *at every level* from worker to vice president.

Social Needs

When man's physiological needs are satisfied and he is no longer fearful about his physical welfare, his social needs become important motivators of his behavior—for belonging, for association, for acceptance by his fellows, for giving and receiving friendship and love.

Management knows today of the existence of these needs, but it often assumes quite wrongly that they represent a threat to the organization. Many studies have demonstrated that the tightly knit, cohesive work group may, under proper conditions, be far more effective than an equal number of separate individuals in achieving organizational goals.

Yet management, fearing group hostility to its own objectives, often goes to considerable lengths to control and direct human efforts in ways that are inimical to the natural "groupiness" of human beings. When man's social needs—and perhaps his safety needs, too—are thus thwarted, he behaves in ways which tend to defeat organizational objectives. He becomes resistant, antagonistic, uncooperative. But this behavior is a consequence, not a cause.

Ego Needs

Above the social needs—in the sense that they do not become motivators until lower needs are reasonably satisfied—are the needs of greatest significance to management and to man himself. They are the egoistic needs, and they are of two kinds:

1. Those needs that relate to one's self-esteem—needs for self-confidence, for independence, for achievement, for competence, for knowledge.

2. Those needs that relate to one's reputation—needs for status, for recognition, for appreciation, for the deserved respect of one's fellows.

Unlike the lower needs, these are rarely satisfied; man seeks indefinitely for more satisfaction of these needs once they have become important to him. But they do not appear in any significant way until physiological, safety, and social needs are all reasonably satisfied.

The typical industrial organization offers few opportunities for the satisfaction of these egoistic needs to people at lower levels in the hierarchy. The conventional methods of organizing work, particularly in mass production industries, give little heed to these aspects of human motivation. If the practices of scientific management were deliberately calculated to thwart these needs—which, of course, they are not—they could hardly accomplish this purpose better than they do.

Self-Fulfillment Needs

Finally—a capstone, as it were, on the hierarchy of man's needs— there are what we may call the needs for self-fulfillment. These are the needs for realizing one's own potentialities, for continued self-development, for being creative in the broadest sense of that term.

It is clear that the conditions of modern life give only limited opportunity for these relatively weak needs to obtain expression. The deprivation most people experience with respect to other lower-level needs diverts their energies into the struggle to satisfy *those* needs, and the needs for self-fulfillment remain dormant.

Now, briefly, a few general comments about motivation:

We recognize readily enough that a man suffering from a severe dietary deficiency is sick. The deprivation of physiological needs has behavioral consequences. The same is true—although less well recognized—of deprivation of higher-level needs. The man whose needs for safety, association, independence, or status are thwarted is sick just as surely as is he who has rickets. And his sickness will have behavioral consequences. We will be mistaken if we attribute his resultant passivity, his hostility, his refusal to accept responsibility to his inherent "human nature." These forms of behavior are *symptoms* of illness—of deprivation of his social and egoistic needs.

The man whose lower-level needs are satisfied is not motivated to satisfy those needs any longer. For practical purposes they exist no longer. (Remember my point about your need for air.) Management often asks, "Why aren't people more productive? We pay good wages, provide good working conditions, have excellent fringe benefits and steady employment. Yet people do not seem to be willing to put forth more than minimum effort."

The fact that management has provided for these physiological and safety needs has shifted the motivational emphasis to the social and perhaps to the egoistic needs. Unless there are opportunities *at work* to satisfy these higher-level needs, people will be deprived; and their behavior will reflect this deprivation. Under such conditions, if management continues to focus its attention on physiological needs, its efforts are bound to be ineffective.

People *will* make insistent demands for more money under these conditions. It becomes more important than ever to buy the material goods and services which can provide limited satisfaction of the thwarted needs. Although money has only limited value in satisfying many higher-level needs, it can become the focus of interest if it is the *only* means available.

The Carrot and Stick Approach

The carrot and stick theory of motivation (like Newtonian physical theory) works reasonably well under certain circumstances. The *means* for satisfying man's physiological and (within limits) his safety needs can be provided or withheld by management. Employment itself is such a means, and so are wages, working conditions, and benefits. By these means the individual can be controlled so long as he is struggling for subsistence. Man lives for bread alone when there is no bread.

But the carrot and stick theory does not work at all once man has reached an adequate subsistence level and is motivated primarily by higher needs. Management cannot provide a man with self-respect, or with the respect of his fellows, or with the satisfaction of needs for self-fulfillment. It can create conditions such that he is encouraged and enabled to seek such satisfactions *for himself*, or it can thwart him by failing to create those conditions.

But this creation of conditions is not "control." It is not a good device for directing behavior. And so management finds itself in an odd position. The high standard of living created by our modern technological know-how provides quite adequately for the satisfaction of physiological and safety needs. The only significant exception is where management practices have not created confidence in a "fair break"—and thus where safety needs are thwarted. But by making possible the satisfaction of low-level needs, management has deprived itself of the ability to use as motivators the devices on which conventional theory has taught it to rely—rewards, promises, incentives, or threats and other coercive devices.

Neither Hard nor Soft

The philosophy of management by direction and control—*regardless of whether it is hard or soft*—is inadequate to motivate because the human needs on which this approach relies are today unimportant motivators of behavior. Direction and control are essentially useless in motivating people whose important needs are social and egoistic. Both the hard and the soft approach fail today because they are simply irrelevant to the situation.

People, deprived of opportunities to satisfy at work the needs which are now important to them, behave exactly as we might predict—with indolence, passivity, resistance to change, lack of responsibility, willingness to follow the demagogue, unreasonable demands for economic benefits. It would seem that we are caught in a web of our own weaving.

In summary, then, of these comments about motivation:

Management by direction and control—whether implemented with the hard, the soft, or the firm but fair approach—fails under today's conditions to provide effective motivation of human effort toward organizational objectives. It fails because direction and control are useless methods of motivating people whose physiological and safety needs are reasonably satisfied and whose social, egoistic, and self-fulfillment needs are predominant.

For these and many other reasons, we require a different theory of the task of managing people based on more adequate assumptions about human nature and human motivation. I am going to be so bold as to suggest the broad dimensions of such a theory. Call it "Theory Y," if you will.

1. Management is responsible for organizing the elements of productive enterprise—money, materials, equipment, people—in
   the interest of economic ends.
2. People are *not* by nature passive or resistant to organizational
   needs. They have become so as a result of experience in organizations.
3. The motivation, the potential for development, the capacity for
   assuming responsibility, the readiness to direct behavior toward organizational goals are all present in people. Management does not put them there. It is a responsibility of management to make it possible for people to recognize and develop
   these human characteristics for themselves.
4. The essential task of management is to arrange organizational
   conditions and methods of operation so that people can achieve
   their own goals *best* by directing *their own* efforts toward organizational objectives

This is a process primarily of creating opportunities, releasing potential, removing obstacles, encouraging growth, providing guidance. It is what Peter Drucker has called "management by objectives" in contrast to "management by control."

And I hasten to add that it does *not* involve the abdication of management, the absence of leadership, the lowering of standards, or the
other characteristics usually associated with the "soft" approach
under Theory X. Much on the contrary. It is no more possible to
create an organization today which will be a fully effective application of this theory than it was to build an atomic power plant in
1945. There are many formidable obstacles to overcome.

Some Difficulties

The conditions imposed by conventional organization theory and
by the approach of scientific management for the past half century
have tied men to limited jobs which do not utilize their capabilities,
have discouraged the acceptance of responsibility, have encouraged
passivity, have eliminated meaning from work. Man's habits, at-

titudes, expectations—his whole conception of membership in an industrial organization—have been conditioned by his experience under these circumstances. Change in the direction of Theory Y will be slow, and it will require extensive modification of the attitudes of management and workers alike.

People today are accustomed to being directed, manipulated, controlled in industrial organizations and to finding satisfaction for their social, egoistic, and self-fulfillment needs away from the job. This is true of much of management as well as of workers. Genuine "industrial citizenship"—to borrow again a term from Drucker—is a remote and unrealistic idea, the meaning of which has not even been considered by most members of industrial organizations.

Another way of saying this is that Theory X places exclusive reliance upon external control of human behavior, while Theory Y relies heavily on self-control and self-direction. It is worth noting that this difference is the difference between treating people as children and treating them as mature adults. After generations of the former, we cannot expect to shift to the latter overnight.

Before we are overwhelmed by the obstacles, let us remember that the application of theory is always slow. Progress is usually achieved in small steps.

Consider with me a few innovative ideas which are entirely consistent with Theory Y and which are today being applied with some success:

Decentralization and Delegation

These are ways of freeing people from the too-close control of conventional organization, giving them a degree of freedom to direct their own activities, to assume responsibilities, and, importantly, to satisfy their egoistic needs. In this connection, the flat organization of Sears, Roebuck and Company provides an interesting example. It forces "management by objectives" since it enlarges the number of people reporting to a manager until he cannot direct and control them in the conventional manner.

Job Enlargement

This concept, pioneered by I.B.M. and Detroit Edison, is quite consistent with Theory Y. It encourages the acceptance of responsibility at the bottom of the organization; it provides opportunities for satisfying social and egoistic needs. In fact, the reorganization of work at the factory level offers one of the more challenging opportunities for innovation consistent with Theory Y. The studies by A. T. M. Wilson and his associates of British coal mining and Indian textile manufacture have added appreciably to our understanding of work organization. Moreover, the economic and psychological results achieved by this work have been substantial.

Participation and Consultative Management

Under proper conditions these results provide encouragement to people to direct their creative energies toward organizational objectives, give them some voice in decisions that affect them, provide significant opportunities for the satisfaction of social and egoistic needs. I need only mention the Scanlon Plan * as the outstanding embodiment of these ideas in practice.

The not infrequent failure of such ideas as these to work as well as expected is often attributable to the fact that a management has "bought the idea" but applied it within the framework of Theory X and its assumptions.

Delegation is not an effective way of exercising management by control. Participation becomes a farce when it is applied as a sales gimmick or a device for kidding people into thinking they are important. Only the management that has confidence in human capacities and is itself directed toward organizational objectives rather than toward the preservation of personal power can grasp the implications of this emerging theory. Such management will find and apply successfully other innovative ideas as we move slowly toward the full implementation of a theory like Y.

---

* A philosophy and method of industrial organization developed by Joseph Scanlon, onetime steelworker who became a lecturer at Massachusetts Institute of Technology.—EDITOR

Performance Appraisal

Before I stop, let me mention one other practical application of Theory Y which—while still highly tentative—may well have important consequences. This has to do with performance appraisal within the ranks of management. Even a cursory examination of conventional programs of performance appraisal will reveal how completely consistent they are with Theory X. In fact, most such programs tend to treat the individual as though he were a product under inspection on the assembly line.

Take the typical plan: substitute "product" for "subordinate being appraised," substitute "inspector" for "superior making the appraisal," substitute "rework" for "training or development," and, except for the attributes being judged, the human appraisal process will be virtually indistinguishable from the product inspection process.

A few companies—among them General Mills, Ansul Chemical, and General Electric—have been experimenting with approaches which involve the individual in setting "targets" or objectives *for himself* and in a *self*-evaluation of performance semi-annually or annually. Of course, the superior plays an important leadership role in this process—one, in fact, which demands substantially more competence than the conventional approach. The role is, however, considerably more congenial to many managers than the role of "judge" or "inspector" which is forced upon them by conventional performance. Above all, the individual is encouraged to take a greater responsibility for planning and appraising his own contribution to organizational objectives; and the accompanying effects on egoistic and self-fulfillment needs are substantial. This approach to performance appraisal represents one more innovative idea being explored by a few managements who are moving toward the implementation of Theory Y.

And now I am back where I began. I share the belief that we could realize substantial improvements in the effectiveness of industrial organizations during the next decade or two. Moreover, I believe the social sciences can contribute much to such developments. We are only beginning to grasp the implications of the growing body of knowledge in these fields. But if this conviction is to become a reality instead of a pious hope, we will need to view the process much as we view the process of releasing the energy of the atom for constructive human ends—as a slow, costly, sometimes discouraging approach toward a goal which would seem to many to be quite unrealistic.

The ingenuity and the perseverance of industrial management in the pursuit of economic ends have changed many scientific and technological dreams into commonplace realities. It is now becoming clear that the application of these same talents to the human side of enterprise will not only enhance substantially these materialistic achievements but will bring us one step closer to "the good society." Shall we get on with the job?

NEW CONCEPTS OF MANAGEMENT

BY DOUGLAS M. McGREGOR

I SHARE with a number of colleagues in the field of management, and with a few managers, the conviction that we will witness during the next couple of decades some profound, far-reaching changes in the strategy utilized to manage the human resources of enterprise. These changes will not be superficial modifications in current practice, but basic revisions of certain concepts that have dominated management thinking during the past half century or more.

The circumstances that will ultimately force these changes are already developing, but their significance is not yet widely recognized. They can be summed up in terms of four trends that are clearly apparent in our society today:

1. *The explosive growth of science* (both behavioral and physical), which is yielding knowledge relevant to every function of enterprise—finance, sales, advertising, public relations, personnel, purchasing, manufacturing—as well as research and engineering.
2. *The rapidly increasing complexity of technology* in both office and factory—and in related aspects of everyday life such as transportation and communication.

Reprinted by permission of the publisher from *Leadership and Motivation: Essays of Douglas McGregor,* Chapter II, pages 21–29. Edited by Warren G. Bennis and Edgar H. Schein, with the collaboration of Caroline McGregor. The M.I.T. Press, Cambridge. Copyright © 1966 The Massachusetts Institute of Technology.

3. *The growing complexity of industry-society relationships* with government, consumers, suppliers, unions, stockholders, and the public generally. As a result of world-wide economic development, relations with other cultures will add substantially to these complexities.

4. *The changing composition of the industrial work force.* Today more than half the employees of industry in the United States are white-collar. Within the white-collar group, we are witnessing a rapid growth of "exempt" salaried personnel, which includes managers and professionally trained people of all kinds. In one large company, the exempt salaried group has grown from 19 per cent to 35 per cent of total employment in the last decade. The curve is accelerating in line with Parkinson's law, but for reasons other than his witty analysis would suggest.

One major consequence of these trends is that in a few years the single largest and most influential class of employees in most industrial organizations will be professional managers and specialists of many kinds, populating every department and every function. Their utilization of various branches of scientific knowledge to solve practical problems will be the primary basis for planning, decision making, and policy formulation from top to bottom of the organization. As a result of the first three trends I have mentioned, they will be both indispensable and powerful, and the necessity to make full use of their competence and training will force a revolution in managerial strategy.

The conventional strategy of management—and the policies and practices as well as organization structures that have developed to serve it—was evolved with the blue-collar wage earner as its primary object. Even he is changing substantially in his education, economic status, attitudes, and competence. But the primary problems of the next several decades will center around the professional specialist. Our present strategy, policies, and practices are quite inappropriate to the task of directing and controlling his efforts. Briefly, let us see why.

Intellectual Creativity

The first and most important reason is the nature of the professional's contribution to the success of the enterprise. His work consists essentially of creative intellectual effort to aid management in its policy making, problem solving, planning, decision making, and administrative activities.

Such professional work cannot be "programmed" and directed the way we program and direct an assembly line or an accounting department. The methods of the industrial engineer are simply irrelevant to it. The management of such work consists chiefly in establishing objectives—the hoped-for results—and in obtaining the professional's commitment to them. It is part of the professional's unique value that he is capable of determining the steps necessary to achieve the desired objectives. Often he knows more about this than his boss does.

This kind of intellectual contribution to the enterprise cannot be obtained by giving orders, by traditional supervisory practices, or by close systems of control, such as we now apply to blue-collar and clerical workers. Even conventional notions of productivity—based as they are on concepts of effort per small unit of time such as the hour or day—are meaningless with reference to the creative intellectual effort of the professional specialist.

In addition, the complexity of the problems to be solved, the nature of the decisions to be made, frequently will demand collaborative effort by many professional specialists from *different* fields ranging clear across the behavioral, biological, and physical sciences. As yet, management has acquired but little knowledge or skill with respect to the management of such collaborative teams, or in developing organizational structures that will provide for their effective utilization.

There has been considerable interest in recent years in "creativity," but this interest has centered on identifying people with creative potential and on such gimmicks as brainstorming. Management has not yet considered in any depth what is involved in *managing* an organization heavily populated with people whose prime contribution consists of creative intellectual effort.

Professional specialists are human beings, of course, but their values, their expectations, and their needs are substantially different from those of the blue-collar worker on whom we have lavished our attention in the past.

What Professionals Want

Economic rewards are certainly important to the professional, but there is ample research to demonstrate that they do not provide the *primary* incentive to peak performance. Management's real task with respect to economic rewards is to administer them in ways that professional employees accept as *equitable*, in order to avoid dissatisfactions and preoccupations that interfere with performance. If they are poorly administered, economic rewards can *lower* productivity below a modest, satisfactory level; they do not appear to be particularly potent in raising it above that level.

Much more crucial to the professional—*provided economic rewards are equitable*—are such things as:

> *Full utilization of his talent and training,* which means critical attention to the nature of his work, the organization of the functions in which he participates, the challenge built into his job, and his freedom from close and detailed supervision.
>
> *His status,* not only within the organization but externally with respect to his profession. Our tendency to regard staff functions, where most professionals reside, as "burdens" on production is but one way in which we prevent him from achieving status.

In addition, despite some rather paternalistic concessions such as permission to attend professional society meetings, management tends to bind the professional to the enterprise in a fashion that minimizes his opportunity to achieve status and recognition among his colleagues in his field. Publication, and participation in the affairs of professional societies, are far more important sources of status than mere attendance at meetings. Yet, even where competitive secrets are not involved, such activities often are regarded as undesirable distractions from the professional's primary responsibilities to his company. In fact, they contribute to his value, as well as to his status and satisfaction.

His opportunities for development within his professional career. Our elaborate programs for *management* development provide few opportunities today for the *career* development of professional specialists.

Conventional policies and practices with respect to promotion penalize the man who does not aspire to a managerial job, by requiring him to change his function and assume different responsibilities. Promotion, for the professional, means receiving rewards and recognition for doing better exactly what he has been doing already. Management has given little heed to these values of the professional so far, or to their policy implications. The professional's long-term career expectations are of fundamental importance to him. In private practice or in academic institutions, he is accustomed to choosing among alternative opportunities in terms of these values. Industrial management, on the other hand, is accustomed to exercising a substantial amount of "career authority" over its managerial employees at all levels. The individual is evaluated, promoted, rotated, and transferred in terms of the needs of the organization almost irrespective of his personal career motivations. These incompatible points of view are certain to come into conflict as professional employees become more numerous and more indispensable to industry.

This inconsistency, it is worth noting, has political implications of more than minor significance. One of the distinguishing features of our Western democratic society, we proudly affirm, is that the individual is *not* the servant of the state. It is interesting that the largest and most powerful institution in this same Western society—industry—characteristically administers promotion policies (which profoundly affect the lifetime careers of its employees) with almost complete emphasis on "the needs of the organization." Only his freedom to quit—a freedom that is often too costly to exercise after he has built up a substantial equity in company benefit plans—protects the individual from being in fact "a servant of the corporation" in this rather basic way.

Two Qualifications

Among the qualifications that should be discussed, with respect to these generalizations, two must be mentioned to prevent misunderstanding.

First, I have talked about a class of people—professional specialists—as though they were all alike, all possessed of the same attitudes, expectations, values, and needs. Obviously, they are not; like any other class of human beings, they differ one from the other in every one of the respects I have mentioned.

Behavioral scientists have studied two groups of professionals lying at the extremes of a range. At one extreme are the "locals" who readily adjust their values and aspirations to the organization that employs them. At the other end are the "cosmopolitans" whose primary identification is with their professional field regardless of where they are employed. Note, however, that there is no evidence to indicate that competence, ability, or potential contribution to the organization are localized in any one part of this range. The comments I have made about professionals should be taken as applying broadly to the middle of the continuum.

Second, although I have directed your attention to a single class of employees, it is obvious that the trends in our society will affect other groups as well. Line managers, for example, will themselves inevitably become more professional, both in training and outlook. The work of wage earners and clerical personnel, as well as their attitudes and expectations, will be materially affected. The growth in numbers and influence of professional specialists in every function of the business will nevertheless be the most dramatic of these changes, and the one requiring the most drastic alterations in management strategy.

Self-Direction Is Essential

The four trends described earlier will necessitate many changes in traditional managerial policy and practice. None of them will come about easily, or by superficial modifications in conventional practice. Personnel "gadgetry" will not do the job.

Perhaps the primary change will be in a deep-seated and long-standing conception of managerial control. This conception concerns the necessity for imposing direction and limitations on the individual in order to get him to perform the work for which he is hired. It is, however, an observable characteristic of human beings that they will exercise *self*-direction and *self*-control in the service of objectives to which they are committed. These are matters of degree, of course, but I find few managements who are consciously moving in the direction of substituting self-control for externally imposed controls. The movement, if any, appears to be in the opposite direction, because this concept of self-control is erroneously associated with "soft" management.

In the recognition of this capacity of human beings to exercise self-control lies the only fruitful opportunity for industrial management to realize the full potential represented by professional resources. Creative intellectual effort of the kind upon which management will increasingly rely—in order to remain competitive—is a function of genuine commitment to objectives, under conditions that provide for a substantial degree of *self*-direction and *self*-control.

It is for this reason above all that I believe we are going to see a basic, almost revolutionary change in managerial strategy during the next two or three decades. It will not be possible in the future—because of the trends outlined earlier—for management to rely exclusively on intuition and past experience and "common sense," either in making or implementing its decisions. It will be no more possible tomorrow to manage an industrial enterprise than it is today to fly a jet aircraft "by the seat of the pants." Creative intellectual effort by a wide range of professional specialists will be as essential to tomorrow's manager as instruments and an elaborate air-traffic-control system are to today's jet pilot.

But traditional managerial strategy is primarily geared to the elaborately "programmed" and closely supervised activities of the blue-collar production worker and the clerical employee. As professional specialists become the single largest and most important class of employees in the enterprise, this traditional strategy will become hopelessly inadequate. Its greatest inadequacy will be with respect to its central concepts concerning the control of organized human effort. Management by objectives and self-control will inevitably replace management by authority and externally imposed control. In the long run this change in strategy will affect not only professional employees but all the human resources of enterprise.

Industrial management is not entirely unaware of the necessity for change in its strategy. There is already some genuine concern over the inadequacy of current methods of control. Symptoms of underlying difficulties have been apparent for some time in industrial research laboratories (where professionals are numerous) and in engineering functions (where they are becoming so). But there is as yet little recognition that these are symptoms that will soon spread to every phase of business activity. When this recognition does occur, we will have the impetus for the development of a new managerial strategy without which the enterprise of the future will be unable to prosper.

SELECTED BIBLIOGRAPHY

THIS BIBLIOGRAPHY constitutes a list of suggested reading for those who wish to explore further the writings of the management classicists whose work is included in this volume. The selections, except for recent classic writers, have been drawn largely from the more complete bibliographies in *The Golden Book of Management* (London: Newman Neame Limited, 1956), edited for the International Committee of Scientific Management (CIOS) by L. Urwick.

ROBERT OWEN (1771–1858)

Books and Papers:

1812 *A Statement Regarding the New Lanark Establishment*. Edinburgh.

1813– *A New View of Society*. London. American edition (from the
1814 third London edition), New York: E. Bliss & E. White, 1825.

1815 *Observations on the Effect of the Manufacturing System*. London: Hatchard.

1817 *Plan to Relieve the Country from Its Present Distress*.

1821 *Report to the County of Lanark*.

1927 *A New View of Society*. Edited by G. D. H. Cole. London: Everyman. A representative selection of Owen's writings.

CHARLES BABBAGE (1792–1871)

Books:

1826 *A Comparative View of the Various Institutions for the Assurance of Lives.* London: J. Maurman.
1830 *Reflections on the Decline of Science in England and on Some of Its Causes.* London: B. Fellowes.
1832 *On the Economy of Machinery and Manufacturers.* London: Charles Knight. American edition, Philadelphia: Carey & Lea, 1832.
1848 *Thoughts on the Principles of Taxation, with Reference to a Property Tax and Its Exceptions.* London: J. Murray.
1864 *Passages from the Life of a Philosopher.* London: Longmans, Green.

Papers:

1822 "The Application of Machinery to the Calculation of Mathematical Tables." *Mem. Astronomical Society*, Vol. I, p. 309.
1829 "Essay on the General Principles Which Regulate the Application of Machinery." *Metropolitan Encyclopaedia.*

CAPTAIN HENRY METCALFE (1847–1917)

Book:

1885 *The Cost of Manufactures and the Administration of Workshops, Public and Private.* New York: John Wiley & Sons.

Paper:

1886 "The Shop Order System of Accounts." *Trans. ASME*, Vol. 7, pp. 440–488.

HENRY ROBINSON TOWNE (1844–1924)

Papers:

1886 "The Engineer as an Economist." *Trans. ASME*, Vol. 7, pp. 428–432.

1889   "Gainsharing." *Trans. ASME*, Vol. 10, pp. 600–626.
1912   "Axioms Concerning Manufacturing Costs." *Trans. ASME*,
       Vol. 34, pp. 1111–1129.
       "General Principles of Organization Applied to an Individual
       Manufacturing Establishment." *Trans. Efficiency Society*,
       Vol. 1, pp. 77–83.

FREDERICK WINSLOW TAYLOR (1856–1915)

   Books:

1910   *Shop Management*. New York: Harper & Bros.
1911   *Principles and Methods of Scientific Management*. New York:
       Harper & Bros.
1912   *Concrete Costs* (with S. E. Thompson). New York: Harper &
       Bros.
       Scientific Management. Hanover, N. H.: Dartmouth College.

   Papers:

1895   "A Piece Rate System." *Trans. ASME*, Vol. 16, pp. 856–903.
1903   "Shop Management." *Trans. ASME*, Vol. 24, pp. 1337–1480.
1906   "On the Art of Cutting Metals." *Trans. ASME*, Vol. 28, pp.
       31–350.
1911   "The Gospel of Efficiency." Articles in *The American Maga-
       zine*, Vols. 71–72.

HENRY LAURENCE GANTT (1861–1919)

   Books:

1910   *Work, Wages and Profits*. New York: Engineering Magazine
       Co.
1916   *Industrial Leadership*. New Haven, Conn.: Yale University
       Press.
1919   *Organizing for Work*. New York: Harcourt, Brace and Howe.

Papers:

1902 "A Bonus System of Rewarding Labor." *Trans. ASME*, Vol. 23, pp. 341–372.

1903 "A Graphical Daily Balance in Manufacture." *Trans. ASME*, Vol. 24, pp. 1322–1336.

1908 "Training Workmen in Habits of Industry and Co-operation." *Trans. ASME*, Vol. 30, pp. 1037–1063.

1915 "The Relations Between Production and Costs." *Trans. ASME*, Vol. 37, pp. 109–128.

1918 "Efficiency and Democracy." *Trans. ASME*, Vol. 40, pp. 799–808.

RUSSELL ROBB (1864–1927)

Book:

1910 *Lectures on Organization.* Series of talks at the Harvard Business School. Privately printed.

Paper:

1921 "Taking from the Few for the Many." *The Atlantic Monthly*, September, pp. 421–423.

HARRINGTON EMERSON (1853–1931)

Books:

1900 *Efficiency as a Basis for Operation and Wages.* New York: Engineering Magazine Co.

1912 *The Twelve Principles of Efficiency.* New York: Engineering Magazine Co.

1913 *The Scientific Selection of Employees.* New York: The Emerson Co.

Papers:

1904 "A Rational Basis for Wages." *Trans. ASME*, Vol. 25, pp. 868–883.

1905 "Shop Betterment and the Individual Effort Method of Profit-Sharing." *American Engineer & Railroad Journal*, Vol. 80, No. 2, pp. 61–64.
1908 "The Modern Theory of Cost Accounting." *Engineering Magazine*.
1911 "Standards of Efficiency in Shop Operation." *Iron Age*, Vol. 87, No. 3, p. 204.
1912 "Comparative Study of Wage and Bonus Systems." New York: The Emerson Co.
1915 "Personality in Organization." *Journ. Efficiency Society*, Vol. 4, No. 2, pp. 16–19.

ALEXANDER HAMILTON CHURCH (1866–1936)

Books:

1914 *The Science and Practice of Management.* New York: Engineering Magazine Co.
1916 *The Proper Distribution of Expense Burden.* New York: Engineering Magazine Co.
1923 *The Making of an Executive.* New York: D. Appleton & Co.
1930 *Overhead Expense in Relation to Costs, Sales and Profits.* New York: McGraw-Hill Publishing Co.

Papers:

1900 "The Meaning of Commercial Organization." *Engineering Magazine*, Vol. 20, No. 3, pp. 391–398.
1910 "Organization by Production Factors." *Engineering Magazine*, Vol. 38 (in 6 parts).
1911 "Intensive Production and the Foreman." *American Machinist*, Vol. 34, Pt. 2, pp. 830–831.
       "The Meaning of Scientific Management." *Engineering Magazine*, Vol. 41, pp. 97–101.
1912 "The Principles of Management" (with L. P. Alford). *American Machinist*, Vol. 36, pp. 857–861.
1913 "Practical Principles of Rational Management." *Engineering Magazine*, Vols. 44 and 45 (3 parts in each).

1914 "The Scientific Basis of Manufacturing Management." *Journ. Efficiency Society*, Vol. 3, pp. 8–15.
"What Are Principles of Management?" *Journ. Efficiency Society*, Vol. 3, pp. 16–18.

LEON PRATT ALFORD (1877–1942)

Books:

1924 *Management's Handbook* (editor). New York: Ronald Press Co.
1928 *The Laws of Management Applied to Manufacturing*. New York: Ronald Press Co.
1934 *Cost and Production Handbook* (editor). New York: Ronald Press Co.
Henry Laurence Gantt, Leader in Industry. New York: The American Society of Mechanical Engineers.
1940 *The Principles of Industrial Management for Engineers*. New York: Ronald Press Co.

Papers:

Dr. Alford's contributions to the transactions of The American Society of Mechanical Engineers are too many to be enumerated. The scope of his papers included high-speed drilling, industrial relations, preferred numbers, factory construction and arrangement, production control, and the evaluation of manufacturing operations. In addition, he wrote papers for the Society for the Promotion of Engineering Education, the American Management Association, and the American Engineering Council, as well as others which were given in England, Japan, and Germany.

HENRI FAYOL (1841–1925)

Books:

1921 *L'Incapacité Administrative de l'Etat—Les Postes et Télégraphes*. Paris: Dunod. Originally published in *Revue Politique et Parlementaire*, March 1921.

1925 *Administration Industrielle et Générale—Prévoyance, Organization, Commandement, Coordination, Contrôle.* Paris: Dunod. English translation, *General and Industrial Management,* by Constance Storrs, London: Pitman, 1949, with a foreword by L. Urwick. Originally published in 1916 in the *Bulletin de la Société de l'Industrie Minérale.*

1927 *L'Eveil de l'Esprit Public.* Paris: Dunod.

      Papers:

1900 Paper on "Administration" to Congrès des Mines et de la Métallurgie.

1908 Discourse on "General Principles of Administration" to Jubilee Congress of Société de l'Industrie Minérale.

1918 "Importance de la Fonction Administrative dans le Gouvernment des Affaires." *Bulletin de la Société d'Encouragement pour l'Industrie Nationale.*

1919 "L'Industrialisation de l'Etat." *Bulletin de la Société de l'Industrie Minérale.*

1023 "La Doctrine Administrative dans l'Etat." Second International Congress of Administrative Science, Brussels, 1923. English translation, "The Administrative Theory in the State," by Sarah Greer, in *Papers on the Science of Administration,* edited by Luther Gulick and L. Urwick. New York: Columbia University Press, 1937.

FRANK BUNKER GILBRETH (1868–1924)

      Books:

1909 *Bricklaying System.* New York and Chicago: The Myron C. Clark Publishing Co.

1911 *Motion Study.* New York: D. van Nostrand Co.

1912 *Primer of Scientific Management.* New York: D. van Nostrand Co.

1916 *Fatigue Study.* New York: Sturgis & Walton Co.

1917   *Applied Motion Study.* New York: Sturgis & Walton Co.
1953   *The Writings of the Gilbreths.* Edited by William R. Spriegel. Homewood, Ill.: Richard D. Irwin, Inc.

Papers:

1915   "What Scientific Management Means to America's Industrial Position" (with Lillian Gilbreth). *Ann. American Academy of Political and Social Science,* Vol. 61, p. 208.
1916   "Graphic Control of the Exception Principle for Executives." *Trans. ASME,* Vol. 38, p. 123.
1921   "Process Charts" (with Lillian Gilbreth). *Trans. ASME,* Vol. 43, p. 1029.
       "Symposium. Stop-Watch Time Study. An Indictment and a Defence" (with Lillian Gilbreth). *Bull. Taylor Society,* Vol. 6, p. 97.
1923   "Science in Management for the One Best Way to Do Work." Milan, Italy: Società Umanitaria.

OLIVER SHELDON (1894–1951)

Books:

1923   *The Philosophy of Management.* London: Pitman.
1928   *Factory Organization* (part-author with Northcott, Wardropper, and Urwick). London: Pitman.

Papers:

1923   "The Elimination of Waste in Industry" to 16th Rowntree Lecture Conference, Oxford.
1925   "Management as a Profession" to 21st Rowntree Lecture Conference, Oxford.
1928   "Function of Administration and Organization," "Industrial Organization," "Distribution of Responsibility." *Dictionary of Industrial Administration.* London: Pitman.

Mary Parker Follett (1868–1933)

Books and Papers:

1920 *The New State.* New York and London: Longmans, Green.
1924 *Creative Experience.* New York and London: Longmans, Green.
1927 *Business Management as a Profession.* Edited by Henry C. Metcalf. Chicago: A. W. Shaw Company.
1941 *Dynamic Administration: The Collected Papers of Mary Parker Follett.* Edited by H. C. Metcalf and L. Urwick. London: Pitman; New York: Harper & Bros.
1949 *Freedom and Co-ordination: Lectures in Business Organization by Mary Parker Follett.* Edited by L. Urwick. London: Pitman.

Harry Arthur Hopf (1882–1949)

Papers:

1931 "Whither Management?" *Proc. American Life Convention,* 26th Annual Meeting, Pittsburgh, Pa.
1932 "The Evolution of Organization." *Proc. National Association of Cost Accountants,* Annual Convention, Detroit, Mich.
1935 "Management and the Optimum." *Proc. Comité International de l'Organisation Scientifique,* 6th International Congress, London.
1943– "New Perspectives in Management." Series of 15 articles in
1945 *The Spectator.* Philadelphia: The Chilton Company.
1944 "Organization, Executive Capacity and Progress." *Proc. Life Office Management Association,* Annual Conference, Boston.
1945 "Executive Compensation and Accomplishment." Financial Management Series No. 78. New York: American Management Association.
1947 "Historical Perspectives in Management." Ossining, N.Y.: Hopf Institute of Management (Publication No. 7). Originally published under the title "Who Were the Pioneers of Management?" as a review of *The Makings of Scientific Manage-*

ment, by L. Urwick and E. F. L. Brech, in THE MANAGE-
MENT REVIEW (NewYork: American Management Association),
Vol. XXVI, pp. 59–64, 114–115, 167–175.

GEORGE ELTON MAYO (1880–1949)

Books:

1933 *The Human Problems of an Industrial Civilization*. Boston:
Division of Research, Harvard Business School.
1945 *The Social Problems of an Industrial Civilization*. Boston: Division of Research, Harvard Business School.

Papers:

1930 "Changing Methods in Industry." *The Personnel Journal*, Vol.
XX, No. 1.
1939 "Routine Interaction and the Problem of Collaboration."
American Sociological Review, Vol. IV.
1941 "The Descent into Chaos." Boston: Harvard Business School.
1945 "Supervision and What It Means." Lecture given at McGill
University, January 30th. *Studies in Supervision*. Montreal:
McGill University.

CHESTER IRVING BARNARD (1886–1961)

Books:

1938 *The Functions of the Executive*. Cambridge: Harvard University Press.
1948 *Organization and Management*. Cambridge: Harvard University Press.

DOUGLAS MURRAY McGREGOR (1906–1964)

Books:

1960 *The Human Side of Enterprise*. New York: McGraw-Hill
Book Co.

1966 *Leadership and Motivation: Essays of Douglas McGregor.*
      Edited by Warren G. Bennis and Edgar H. Schein, with the
      collaboration of Caroline McGregor. Cambridge: The M.I.T.
      Press.
1967 *The Professional Manager.* Edited by Warren G. Bennis and
      Caroline McGregor. New York: McGraw-Hill Book Co.

      Papers:

1944 "Getting Effective Leadership in the Industrial Organiza-
      tion." *Journal of Consulting Psychology,* Vol. VIII, No. 2.
1946 "Re-evaluation of Training for Management Skills." In *Train-
      ing for Management Skills.* Personnel Series No. 104. New
      York: American Management Association.
1953 "Line Management's Responsibility for Human Relations."
      In *Building Up the Supervisor's Job.* Manufacturing Series
      No. 213. New York: American Management Association.
1955 "The Changing Role of Management." *The Technology Re-
      view,* Vol. LVII, No. 6.
1964 "Can you Measure Executive Performance?" *International
      Management,* Vol. XIX, No. 6.
      "Behavioral Science—What's In It for Management?" *Busi-
      ness Management Record,* June, 1964.

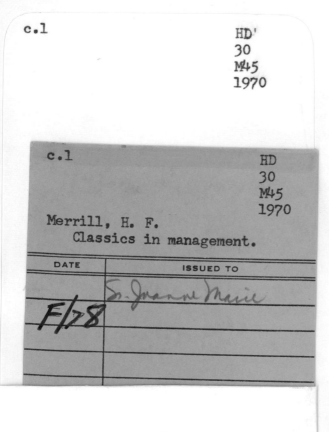

ABOUT THE EDITOR

HARWOOD F. MERRILL is a graduate of Cornell University and holds an MBA from the Harvard Business School. He spent more than two years on the HBS research staff and, under a Guggenheim Foundation fellowship, conducted the research and prepared the text for *Case Studies in Commercial Aviation*, published by the McGraw-Hill Book Company.

His experience includes positions as assistant director of advertising for Curtiss-Wright Corporation and as a reporter and managing editor, *Forbes Magazine*. Co-founder of Magazines of Industry, he was editor of its first publication, *Modern Industry*, and later was named editorial director of all company publications.

In 1949 Mr. Merrill joined the Eagle-Picher Company as general manager of its Paint and Varnish Division, and in 1953 he was appointed assistant to the president of the parent corporation, with responsibility for public and community relations and personnel policies.

In 1956 he joined the American Management Association as editor in chief. Later he became vice-president, editor, and a director, and he was vice-president for membership and publications when he retired in 1967. For several years he was also president of the American Foundation for Management Research, an AMA affiliate.

Since his retirement Mr. Merrill has served as a management consultant and has continued to write on management subjects. Among his other publications are *The Responsibilities of Business Leadership* (editor; Harvard University Press, 1949) and *Developing Executive Skills* (co-editor, with Elizabeth Marting; AMA, 1958).